Augsburg College
George Sverdrup Library
Minneapolis, Minnesota 5540⁴
WITHDRAWN

D0204602

Women in Changing Japan

WOMEN IN CHANGING JAPAN

Edited by   Joyce Lebra
Joy Paulson
Elizabeth Powers

WESTVIEW PRESS

WESTVIEW SPECIAL STUDIES ON CHINA AND EAST ASIA

All rights reserved. No part of this publication may be reproduced or transmitted in any form or by any means, electronic or mechanical, including photocopy, recording or any information storage and retrieval system, without permission in writing from the publisher.

Copyright 1976 by Westview Press, Inc.

Published 1976 in the United States of America by

Westview Press, Inc.
1898 Flatiron Court
Boulder, Colorado 80301
Frederick A. Praeger, Publisher & Editorial Director

Library of Congress Cataloging in Publication Data
Main entry under title:

Women in changing Japan.

   1. Women--Japan--Addresses, essays, lectures.
2. Women's rights--Japan--Addresses, essays, lectures.
I. Lebra, Joyce C. II. Paulson, Joy. III. Powers,
Elizabeth.
HQ1762.W65   301.41'2'0952   75-33663
ISBN 0-89158-019-0

Printed in the United States of America.

Photo credits. Schoolgirl, mother and child, elderly woman, women in kimono, woman in rice paddy by Gail Bernstein; woman in Western dress by Joyce Lebra; woman with motorbike by Kazuhiro Nakamichi.

HQ
1762
W65

Dedicated

*to all the women who shared
their lives with us.*

130499

PREFACE

It is a time when women in many parts of the world are questioning the roles, life styles, and values by which women have lived for centuries. As American women engaged in studying various aspects of the life patterns of Japanese women in many walks of life, several of us decided to join in publishing this volume. We come from a variety of backgrounds, experience, and perspectives. Sister Rose Marie Cecchini and Laura Jackson both did extensive research for M.A. theses under the direction of Professor Kazuko Tsurumi at Sophia University; the results of their studies are included here. Elizabeth Mouer's chapter is based in part on research she did for an M.A. thesis at Keiō University. Professor Gail Bernstein's research was conducted during 1974-75 in rural Shikoku. Sheila Matsumoto's work reflects her experience of several years' residence in Nagoya, plus interviewing and translation of diaries. Elizabeth Powers has done research and writing on her topic over a period of several months in Japan. The rest of the chapters are based not so much on extensive research as on conversations with women in specific occupational categories. The same questionnaire was used as a guideline for interviews with housewives, office ladies, factory workers, service industry workers, teachers, women in the professions, women in the media, and women in politics.

Our goal was to ascertain the degree to which women in Japan today are departing from the traditional feminine ideal—an ideal that prescribed a domestic, subordinate, and often subservient role for women. While women have been granted legal and political rights in the post-World War II period, it has not always been apparent that they have been able to exercise these rights fully. We have in these chapters explored this general question, using data based on our interviews and conversations. We have looked at life styles, work situations, goals and values of these women, in many cases letting the women speak for themselves. We have not attempted to say the last word on Japanese women, but rather to point the way toward further research.

We would like to express our gratitude to several individuals who have been especially helpful in facilitating research and contacts and appointments with individual women: Professor Teru Kachi, Professor and Mrs. Shirō Honma, Mrs. Kinko Satō, Miss Yukiko Sawabe, Mrs. Mitsuko Whitney, Mrs. Elizabeth Mouer, Mrs. Sheila Matsumoto, Mrs. Yoko Sugimoto and her mother, Miss Kazuko Ōta, Mr. Mikio Katō, Mrs. Takeko Sakakura, Mr. and Mrs. W. Nagai, Mrs. Keiko Beer, Ms. Yumiko Kinoshita of the Aichi Kinrō Kaikan, and the

Women's and Minors' Bureau of the Labor Ministry. For assistance with the manuscript thanks go to Ruth Major, Aladeen Smith, and Lindsay Murdock. For errors of fact, translation, and interpretation responsibility rests with the authors and editors.

Joyce Lebra — Boulder, Colorado
Joy Paulson — Boulder, Colorado
Elizabeth Powers — Tokyo, Japan

FOREWORD

by Kazuko Tsurumi

This excellent collection of essays written by twelve American women scholars on Japanese women may very well be a harbinger of the new trend of publication of the study of Japanese women by their foreign counterparts. Previously it was Japanese women who were one-sidedly interested in American women, studying them and imitating their life-styles. But the new trend reveals that our interest is mutual and that we might be able to compare notes for mutual benefit.

Mutual as our interest now is, however, there are some salient points of difference between the American and Japanese approaches to the study of women in their respective societies. The American women scholars and students, from what I know of them, are daring and courageous in making direct contact with Japanese women in various walks of life, not only through interviews but often through living and working with them, sharing joys and sorrows of their everyday lives. This contrasts with the Japanese approach to American women which has hitherto been based mainly on secondary information. The spirit of empiricism and participant observation is a strong point that pervades the entire work collected in this volume.

There is another characteristic of this work. All the authors in the present book are highly qualified career women in academic, religious, and business institutions. They all know from their own first-hand experience what it is like to be a woman working in a male-dominated world. Japanese society is also male-dominated; in that sense the American and Japanese working women share common problems. However, it is my contention that Japanese culture is woman-oriented. It is both an advantage and a disadvantage for Japanese women to live with a culture in which female components assert themselves, while in the social order male elements predominate. The American authors in this book seem to have dug deeply into this paradoxical structure of female existence in present-day Japan.

Professor Joyce Lebra is a well-known historian who has already made important and original contributions to the analysis of male organizations, political and military, in Japan. Now I trust Professor Lebra's judgment of Japanese society even more, since she proves in this present work that without a study of its women, one's knowledge of Japanese society would never be complete. And it is rightly so.

The images of Japanese women as they emerge in this volume will prove to be invaluable mirrors for both American and Japanese women, and, for that matter, also for the men of either society.

Sophia University
September 22, 1975

CONTENTS

ABOUT THE CONTRIBUTORS

Gail Lee Bernstein, associate professor of Oriental Studies at the University of Arizona, lived as a participant-observer in a farm village in Ehime Prefecture, where, supported by a Japan Foundation fellowship, she studied the lives of rural Japanese women. She is presently writing a book about contemporary Japanese village life. Professor Bernstein is the author of chapters on Kawakami Hajime in two separate collections.

Eileen Carlberg has a B.A. in economics from Oberlin College. She is currently working on a Ph.D. in political science at the University of Colorado. Her major areas of interest are Japan's political system and women's participation in government.

Rose Carter has a B.A. in Asian Studies from the University of California at Riverside. She spent her junior year abroad in Tokyo. She is presently studying Japanese and teaching English at a private girls' school near Tokyo.

Rose Marie Cecchini, a Maryknoll Sister, has lived in Japan for thirteen years. She holds an M.A. in sociology from Sophia University and is enrolled in a Ph.D. program at Sophia, where she taught sociology from 1971 to 1973. She is assistant director of the Year-in-Japan program at Sophia and participates in UNESCO-sponsored activities in Tokyo.

Lois Dilatush was born in Shanghai, China, and spent many childhood summers in Japan. She graduated from Ohio Wesleyan University, received her M.A. from Oberlin College and her Ph.D. from the University of Colorado. She is now associate professor of sociology at Metropolitan State College in Denver, Colorado, where she teaches courses in sociological theory and in the sociology of sex roles.

x

Laura Jackson received her B.A. in psychology and anthropology from the University of Kansas in 1971 and since then has been living in Japan. She became interested in bar hostesses while working in a bar in Sapporo. She later worked at a bar in Tokyo's Ginza area while working on an M.A. thesis on the subject of bar hostesses. She received her M.A. in Far Eastern Studies from Sophia University and is presently employed in Tokyo.

Joyce Lebra is professor of Japanese history at the University of Colorado. She holds a Ph.D. from Harvard/Radcliffe and has spent eight years in Japan doing research and writing. Among her books on Japan are *Jungle Alliance: Japan and the Indian National Army* (Singapore: Asia/Pacific Press, 1971); *Ōkuma Shigenobu, Statesman of Meiji Japan* (Canberra: Australian National University Press, 1973); and *Japan's Greater East Asia Co-Prosperity Sphere in World War II* (Kuala Lumpur: Oxford University Press, 1975).

Sheila Barton Matsumoto holds a B.A. in sociology from the University of Indiana and has done graduate work in education. She has taught in Michigan and in Nagoya, where she resides with her Japanese husband. She is fluent in Japanese and accomplished in the arts of the koto, tea ceremony, and flower arrangement.

Mary Lou Maxson holds a B.A. in East Asian Studies from the University of Colorado, where she has taught courses in Japanese aesthetics. She is particularly interested in the folk arts and conducts tours to Japan focusing on centers of folk art.

Elizabeth Knipe Mouer has lived in Tokyo for six years. She holds an M.A. from Keiō University, where she did her thesis on education for women during the Tokugawa and Meiji periods. She has written for *Agora*, a journal on women in Tokyo. She teaches English and does translating. She is accomplished in the arts of the koto, tea ceremony, and flower arrangement.

Joy Paulson is a graduate student in history at the University of Colorado. She has a B.A. in East Asian Studies and history from the University of Colorado and has taught courses on Japanese women in experimental studies there. She hopes to do her dissertation on Japanese women and the media.

Elizabeth Powers graduated from Indiana University and the University of Texas in Germanic languages. She studied for two years in Germany and was an editor at the University of Texas Press for two years. She also worked as editor of International Publications at the University of Tokyo Press.

CHAPTER 1
EVOLUTION OF THE FEMININE IDEAL

The traditional image of Japanese women has evolved, while the status of women has devolved, in response to the influences of Buddhism, Confucianism, and the Samurai ethic. Is it possible to see the Japanese woman as she was before these cultural determinants, stimulated by Chinese influence, produced the woman held to be ideal by Japanese society up to World War II? Have there been changes in that ideal since World War II?

The forest surrounding the shrine honoring Japan's supreme deity, the sun goddess Amaterasu, is pervaded by a sense of Japan's mythic feminine cosmogenesis and matriarchal antiquity. But there is no recorded history of matriarchy for women to point to. We can only consult the ancient myths to discover the indigenous Japanese woman.

The Japanese had no written language for recording history until the Chinese language was introduced. The *Kojiki* [Record of Ancient Things], compiled in 712, and the *Nihongi* [Chronicles of Japan], 720, are the chief Japanese sources of early Japanese history. As historical accounts, however, they are marred by several factors. Written with the political aim of strengthening the ruling dynasty, the contents are selective. Furthermore, not only were they written in Chinese, but Japanese scholars had for three centuries been influenced by Chinese literature, Chinese philosophy, and Chinese patriarchy. Nevertheless, as the earliest official written records they are extremely valuable guides to Japanese myth, legend, and history.

Reflecting the presence of both Japanese and Chinese thought, the *Kojiki* and the *Nihongi* contain strong-spirited female deities as well as repressed wives. This tension between Japanese and Chinese

1

culture affects the status of women up to the final codification of the female image during the Tokugawa period (1600-1867).

Japan's creator-goddess, Izanami, was strong and free spirited. In the *Nihongi*[1] version of the creation myth Izanami and her brother, Izanagi, have created the islands of Japan and are planning to populate the islands with gods and goddesses. They circle the heavenly pillar and Izanami, meeting Izanagi, exclaims spontaneously, "How delightful. I have met with a lovely male." Unfortunately, her exuberance is curbed by Izanagi, who insists she remain silent until he, the superior male, has spoken. The choice of human sexual reproduction as the means of heavenly creation indicates a positive attitude toward sex on the part of the ancient writers. The starring role played by the female probably parallels her actual role in Japan before Confucianism; but the injunction on the female to remain silent until the male has spoken implies Chinese patriarchal influence.

Izanami's spirit remains untrammeled to the end of her life. Giving birth to the fire god, Izanami is burned and dies. Weeping and lamenting his loss, Izanagi follows her to the Land of Darkness. She tells him she cannot return with him to heaven, and instructs him not to look at her. Izanagi secretly lights a torch and, seeing her putrefying body, realizes he has been polluted by the presence of death, and flees. Shamed and angered, Izanami pursues him. Blocking her path, he faces her and breaks their troth—pronounces the divorce formula. She threatens to strangle one thousand of his people each day if he divorces her. His response is a counter-threat to cause fifteen hundred people to be born each day. A remarkable end to a relationship which produced the beautiful islands and kindly deities of Japan, the story contains female sacrifice and divorce as well as a strong woman.

The brightest child produced by Izanami and Izanagi was Amaterasu, a beautiful girl who was promptly named for the sun and given the heavens to reign over. In her relations with her brother, the storm god Susano-o, who, because of his troublesome behavior, has been sent to rule the earth, Amaterasu displays her spirit and strength. When she hears that Susano-o has asked to visit her in heaven, she suspects his intention is to rob her of her queendom. She arms herself and, meeting him with a mighty cry of defiance, insists he demonstrate the purity of his intentions. Their quarrel is very likely "an echo of quarrels between a woman ruler in a matriarchal society and a vigorous brother or other male relative jealous of her power."[2]

Allowed to stay, Susano-o displays his troublesome character. Amaterasu tolerates his mischief to a point. When he destroys the banks of her paddy fields and lets horses in among the rice plants, she exercises forbearance. But when, by his crude behavior, he pollutes her palace she is outraged and withdraws to a cave, leaving the world in darkness.

The plaint of Queen Suseri-Bimi in the *Kojiki*[3] illustrates an oppressed wife. She complains to her husband, Opo-Kuni-Nusi, that while he has wives "like the young grass" on every island, she, "being a woman," has but one husband. Suseri-Bimi's predicament foreshadows that of the Heian women, confined within their homes while their men were free to wander.

Chinese records state that from A.D. 147 to 190 Japan was divided by civil war and anarchy until the rise of a woman ruler, Pimiku (sun princess). She was old and unmarried. By her skill in magic she gained favor with the people who made her their queen. When she died, a great tumulus was raised over her and more than a thousand attendants followed her in death. A king was raised to the throne and civil war again broke out. Order was not restored until a relative of Pimiku, a girl of thirteen, was made queen. Chinese travelers to Japan during China's Wei Dynasty (220-265), impressed by the frequency of female rule, refer to Japan as the "Queen Country." They also mention polygamy, writing that men of high rank had four or five wives. The women were faithful, they said, and not jealous.[4]

It is a mixture, then, of fact and myth, Japanese and Chinese thought, which is presented in the early Japanese chronicles. From about A.D. 600 written documents were available to *Nihongi* compilers, so a transition can be made from myth to history.

Six empresses ascended the throne during the two centuries following 592, ruling a total of 113 years. These two centuries were crucial to the development of the imperial institution. Written histories, the *Kojiki* and the *Nihongi*, established the Yamato clan as the legitimate imperial clan by "proving" its descent from the sun goddess. The Seventeen Article Constitution of 604, the Taikwa Reform Edict of 645, the Taihō Code of 702 and its revised version, the Yōrō Code, all served to strengthen imperial rule by introducing Chinese methods of government.

It appears that during this early foundation-laying phase of Japanese history female rulers functioned in an interim capacity, preventing succession disputes and providing a stabilizing effect. Accomplishments during their reigns have often been attributed to male regents. The larger-than-life reputation of Crown Prince Shotoku Taishi, reputed author of the Seventeen Article Constitution, completely overshadowed the reign of his aunt, the Empress Suiko, a skillful and functional ruler in her own right.

During the reign of Empress Gemmyō the first permanent capital was established at Nara, and the Taihō Code was carefully revised to make it more acceptable to indigenous Japanese custom.

Women were also used by politically ambitious families, notably the Soga and later the Fujiwara, to consolidate their relationship with the imperial family. Daughters and nieces from those families were married to all possible heirs to the throne.

Historians often say that this period is unusual for its large number of female rulers, intimating that there was an unexplained increase unique to the period. This statement ignores the evidence in mythology and the ancient Chinese records of earlier female rule. It also under-emphasizes the fact that women were suddenly and effectively prevented from ruling after the reign of Empress Kōken in the eighth century.

Buddhist influence was on the rise even before Kōken's reign. Her father, Emperor Shomu, had very nearly made Buddhism a state religion. As his successor, Empress Kōken received the brunt of the court's anti-Buddhist reaction. The Fujiwaras were also gaining ascendancy over the throne as they improved their political position by skillful exercise of marriage politics.

Kōken was an unmarried ruler, a feature which invites speculation. Her relationship with the Buddhist monk, Dōkyo, incensed the Fujiwaras—not because of her liaison as such but because of the possibility that a monk, over whom they had no control, might assume the throne. Between them, Kōken and Dōkyo commanded enough respect (for the throne and for Buddhism) to hold off opposition, but when Kōken died, Dōkyo was banished by the Fujiwaras. Kōken was succeeded by a male. When he died, the council of ministers, swayed by Fujiwara influence, refused to elevate a woman to the throne. This custom continues to the present time. Kōken remains discredited, a symbol of feminine frailty.

Just as women were kept from the throne by custom rather than law, so their status was defined by custom. From the descriptions of female deities in the myths and the numerous women rulers between the sixth and eighth centuries, it can be assumed that the status of women was similar to that of men. In the *Nihongi*, the childless Princess Kasuga, grieved that her name will become extinct, is granted a granary "to bear her name for ten thousand generations."[5] At some point, in the name of political stability, a choice must be made between matrilineal and patrilineal descent. No doubt the threat to Fujiwara power by Kōken precipitated the shift to male rule, but custom protected the status of women for several centuries.

The Taihō Code, 702, and its revised version, the Yōrō Code, 718, based as they were on Confucianism, abolished the matriarchal system inherent in Japan's clan organization. They established a patriarchal system, called for the subjection of women in the Confucian manner, and discriminated against women in matters of property, marriage, and divorce. But, as we have seen, the codes were unevenly and incompletely accepted by Japanese society. In the case of women especially, the code "remained in many respects little more than a legal fiction or a set of abstract ethical principles, and the actual conditions of women, particularly outside the capital, had never been brought down to the level it had set."[6] Yet, the groundwork was laid for the loss of female autonomy. A Japanese proverb, "The womb is a borrowed thing," reflects the growing view of women's adjunctive role as bearer of the male line.

The difference between law and custom can most clearly be seen in the marriage residence customs of the Heian period (794-1185). In 794 the capital was moved to Heian Kyō (Kyoto) to escape the "baleful influence of Buddhism" at Nara and to gain river access to the sea. Though temporarily escaping religious interference, the imperial court eventually became so entangled in ritual and ceremony it very nearly strangled to death. The first Heian emperor, Kammu, was also the strongest. His successors were unable to resist the influence of the nobles which replaced Buddhist influence. The Fujiwara family continued to strengthen its position by marrying its women to heirs to the throne. The success of this policy was due to the marriage residence customs. The Taihō and Yōrō codes had prescribed a Chinese patrilocal system in which the bride is brought to live in a subordinate position within the groom's family, but literature of the period describes a completely different system.[7]

Three main types of marital residence customs occur in society: patrilocal, in which husband and wife take up residence with the husband's parents; matrilocal, in which they reside with the wife's parents; and neolocal, the establishment of a separate independent household. Less common is a fourth type—duolocal, in which the husband and wife live separately; the husband visits the wife but does not move in with her. Marriage residence among aristocrats in the Heian period is described as matrilocal, duolocal, or neolocal. It was never patrilocal.[8]

It is easy to see the advantages of Heian residence customs for an ambitious family with a good supply of daughters and nieces. In a patrilocal system the daughter moved to her husband's family's home and her father lost contact, not only with her but with her husband and children as well. In a matrilocal arrangement, however, there was continuing contact with the son-in-law and an opportunity for the father to exert control on his grandchildren.

If matrilocal residence custom served Fujiwara political ambitions, it also provided some security for women with good connections. The Confucian *Shichikyo,* or seven reasons for divorcing a wife, had been part of Japanese law since the eighth century when they had been enunciated as part of the Taihō Code.[9] The seven reasons (failure to give birth to a son, gossiping, lewdness, jealousy, stealing from her husband, disobedience toward his parents, and disease) were a moot point because in fact it was possible for divorce to be effected in the Heian period by a husband simply ceasing to visit his wife. In actual practice, however, the social stability of the time prevented great frequency of divorce, especially when compared with the sixteenth century. A husband was not likely to offend a powerful father-in-law by casting off his wife any more than a father would permit his daughter to embarrass her influential husband by deserting him. The permanence of a political alliance of this sort in spite of the feelings of the couple involved is illustrated in *The Tale of Genji* by the marriage between Prince Genji and Lady Aoi, daughter of the Minister of the Left, a powerful man who maintains the respect of others even after his retirement. Genji and Aoi do not care for one another, but Genji, out of respect for the Minister of the Left, visits Aoi just enough to keep up appearances; Aoi's father is so pleased by and proud of Genji he treats him with unfailing cordiality.

The women whose fathers were dead or refused to acknowledge them were, of course, in a much less secure position. They were rarely the primary or political wife. If they found husbands it was usually in the more tenuous position of second wife. Least secure were those unprotected women who entered the third and most casual "mistress" relationship and who were frequently abandoned.

A paradox of the Heian period can be seen in the lives of aristocratic women. Limitations were placed on their physical activity by custom, which dictated they not be seen by men other than their husbands and fathers. Even in their own quarters they sat hidden by screens. Out of doors, they were transported in closed carriages. Their activity was further hampered by layers of voluminous robes and floor-length hair. Nevertheless they were allowed to inherit and retain property. It was possible for Heian women to be financially independent, but they were dependent on men to conduct their business affairs. In *The Tale of Genji,* the "Palace in the Tangled Woods" is literally falling apart because the owner has no male protector to take charge of its maintenance.

The education of women was limited to areas such as penmanship, music, and poetry, but these skills were highly developed. Heian women are responsible for many of Japan's greatest literary achievements, including the world's first novel, *The Tale of Genji.* Written by Lady Murasaki Shikibu, daughter of a minor official, it is considered an authoritative source of information on Heian court society.

Thus, while women had no rights by law, they still retained some status by custom. The aspects of Buddhism which define their character had begun to make inroads on society's attitude toward women. The form of Buddhism which reached Japan through China contained antifeminine elements not common to Buddhism generally.

Buddhism taught that woman's nature was inherently evil. "But what was the good of trying to please women?" Genji asks himself. "If they were not fundamentally evil they would not have been born as women at all."[10] Labeling her a temptress, Buddhism attacked female sexuality—"Woman is a creature with the look of an angel . . . but a diabolical spirit in its inmost heart" and "Woman is full of sin; nothing is to be dreaded so much as a woman." Even today, the proverb "Behind the crime is a woman" reflects the Buddhist image of women.

Until the end of the Heian period, women were defined mainly in terms of what they should not do. The growth of feudalism and the Samurai ethic beginning in the Kamakura period (1185-1333) developed expectations of what women should do.

In the latter part (1086-1185) of the Heian period the gradual erosion of centralized power and the decay within the Fujiwara family led to social, cultural, and military decline. The protracted civil wars, which culminated in the ascendancy of the Minamoto clan in 1185, also removed some of the culturally imposed limitations on the physical and mental activity of women. In this less structured society the freedom and strength of women grew, and the Kamakura period became a high point in the status of Japanese women.

This period, following the tradition of Yoritomo, was noted for the honesty and efficiency of its administration. It was also a hiatus in Japanese history. There was no large scheme, no single purpose to which the individual, especially the woman, was sacrificed. The Kamakura Hōjo Regency (1205-1333) was stable. The old codes of the central government which had been so repressive to women were again supplanted, this time by indigenous clan laws. The *Jōei Shikimoku,* drawn up in 1232 by the Minamoto and Hōjo families, was based on their own clan regulations.[11]

The Kamakura period, like the Heian, presents a paradox in the status of women, but the paradox is reversed. While still making a career of marriage, courtiers were encouraged by the fluid society to discard wives at will. As power changed hands, wives were also changed to permit a new, more potent, connection. On the other hand, the rights of women to inherit and own property were clearly defined in the *Jōei Shikimoku.*[12] More important, these rights were upheld in practice.

Many documents survive from the Kamakura period showing that women inherited estates and the control of peasants to run them; and showing that they were able to bequeath these to daughters. Women engaged in lawsuits over land and sometimes even won. Also, the documents indicate that many rich and independent women had considerable local authority.[13] The principal Kamakura chronicle, in 1200, records the confirmation of property ownership by a woman. This woman had faithfully served the wife of Kiyomori and as a reward had been given land in fief. With the defeat of Kiyomori, the execution of her husband, and the rise of Yoritomo to shōgun she was concerned that her fief might be confiscated. However, a judgment was given that she might retain her fief undisturbed, and she was confirmed in possession.[14] This right was lost with the rise of feudalism.

The conservative aspects of Buddhism had continued to hold women in disdain, and that the church also favored wifely submission is evident in the Buddhist moral tale, *The Captain of Naruto.* Written in the late thirteenth century, it describes the emperor's infatuation for a young woman, the wife of a captain, who has caught his attention. She manages to avoid being found for a time but at last the emperor tracks her down and sends for her. Greatly upset, she tells her husband, who urges her to go to the emperor. She weeps and protests but he says, "If you fail to go, out of pride, it is sure to look very bad, and who can say what will become of me?"[15] The lady goes to the emperor, the captain is promoted, and we have a fine example of submission—the wife to her husband and the captain to the emperor.

Any description of the possibilities for women during the Kamakura period must include some notice of Hōjō Masako. When Taira Kiyomori defeated Minamoto Yoshitomo he spared the lives of Yoshitomo's three sons including Yoritomo, who was reared in Eastern Japan by an influential chieftain of Taira stock, Hōjō Tokimasa. Masako, Tokimasa's daughter, eloped with Yoritomo rather than marry the high court official her father had chosen for her. Yoritomo eventually became shōgun but after his death Masako and her father set up a regency which became the real power behind the office of shōgun. When Masako's son rebelled, she had him murdered. When her father opposed her, he was exiled. When her younger son was assassinated, she replaced him as shōgun with a two-year-old great-grandnephew of Yoritomo, installed her brother as regent, and ruled through him. Masako, in effect, replaced the victorious Minamoto Clan with her own Taira Clan. Founder of the system of Regents, she might be considered the founder of feudalism as well—an ironic thought considering the effect on women of feudalism. In Ackroyd's words:

We can, then, sum up the position of women in the Kamakura period by noting that in an age when feudal institutions were in process of taking shape, the matriarchal principle retained its vigor but the bases for masculine domination had been laid down. When, after more than half a century of warfare, we enter the next period, the Muromachi (1392-1490), the picture has changed.[16]

While Buddhism had not generally held that women were excluded from salvation, the strict Tendai and Shingan sects taught that women suffered from original sin as well as *Goshō*, the Five Obstructions, which prevented them from attaining any of the five states of spiritual awareness which men were capable of attaining. A woman's only hope for salvation lay in the possibility of being reborn as a man. Women were warned in a fifteenth-century history that they were agents of the devil sent to prevent men from following the way of Buddha. "As regards her husband, it reminds her: Even if he seems more lowly than you are, man is the personification of the Buddha and has the sense of reward and punishment as well as that of mercy . . . you must bear in mind that you have married a Buddhist saint."[17] Thus the stage is set for the loss of women's rights and their complete subjugation in the tight grip of feudalism.

The samurai ethic, which served feudalism by its emphasis on courage, strength, and absolute loyalty to one's feudal lord, had seemed at first advantageous to women. Girls were trained in the spartan virtues and learned to use weapons. The samurai's wife went to live with her husband and helped him manage the property. If he died, she inherited the property and functioned, as her husband had, as vassal to the lord. As equal inheritance was abandoned, however, women's property rights and status declined. The shift to patrilocal residence can be seen here as well as the seeds of wifely submission.

One of the features of feudalism which worked against women was the need to keep holdings intact. Also, the Muromachi (1338-1500) administration was not as honest as the Kamakura administration had been and a woman could no longer appeal to the authorities for protection of her land. As a result, the whole system of inheritance underwent a radical change. While formerly the property had been divided up among all the children, now one son was chosen as the chief heir. The other children all received small shares but the end result was that the individuals were weak and of necessity dependent on the chief heir.

By 1500, the whole of Japan was at war, and the sixteenth-century woman was subject to political expediency. Given in marriage to lull a suspicious opponent, a woman often became a hostage when hostilities erupted. Mothers, daughters, sisters, and wives were married, divorced, and sometimes given as outright hostages. "In fact, despite all the pious theory about the immorality of remarriage by women, they were passed from hand to hand to suit the convenience of their male relatives."18 Hideyoshi divorced his sister from her husband (who killed himself in protest) and married her, at the age of forty-three, to Ieyasu to conclude a treaty; he also married the younger sister of his chief concubine to four successive husbands.19

Living in an age when only brute force was valued, women learned to accept themselves as less valuable than men. One woman, widowed and cast adrift with a son and a daughter, threw the girl in a pond to drown so she would be better able to help her son become a warrior.20

It was with the status of women at this low ebb that Japan entered the Tokugawa period (1600-1868), 250 years of feudalism during which the status of women was finally defined. With the country unified under the military shōgun Tokugawa Ieyasu, a system was needed to fix the social order so as to preserve the status quo. Japan's social order was comprised of four classes: the samurai ruling class; the peasant; the artisan; and the lowest class, the merchants, who were considered parasitic by Confucian concepts. Neo-Confucianism emphasized doing one's duty according to one's place and "the need to maintain proper human relationships in terms of the five basic relationships."21 The five basic relationships were lord/subject, father/son, husband/wife, elder brother/younger brother, and friend/friend. This concept was particularly useful to the Tokugawa rulers in their effort to establish a society based on the relationship between superior and inferior persons. Confucianism was officially adopted by Ieyasu.

Marriage remained primarily a political relationship. Feudal lords needed shōgunal approval before contracting marriages. The lord (*daimyo*) supervised in turn the marriages of his retainers and the peasants. This ultimate control assured loyalty and regulated the labor supply.22

The Neo-Confucian scholar most influential in defining the role of women was Kaibara Ekken, 1631-1714, a writer of moral tracts intended for dissemination among the common people. Kaibara was one of the few scholars who used the popular style of writing and his works were widely read, even by the poor. His *Onna Daigaku* [Great Learning for Women] became a part of nearly every Japanese household, and its "wisdom" became the primary text for women, since it reinforced the feudal aim of perfecting the family system. "For the tyranny of the family system, women had to be mentally killed—deprived of the strength with which to ward off the disgraces heaped upon them."23 Marriage was the only acceptable condition for a woman. Thus the sole purpose of her education should be learning to please her future husband and especially his parents, to whom she was to become virtually a slave. Instructing the young female regarding her parents-in-law, Kaibara says:

> While thou honorest thine own parents, think not lightly of thy father-in-law! Never should a woman fail, night and morning, to pay her respects to her father-in-law and mother-in-law. Never should she be remiss in performing any tasks they may require of her. With all reverence must she carry out, and never rebel against, her father-in-law's commands. On every point must she inquire of her father-in-law and mother-in-law, and abandon herself to their direction. Even if thy father-in-law and mother-in-law be pleased to hate and vilify thee be not angry with them, and murmur not.[24]

A wife's relationship to her husband was slightly different, similar to the lord/subject basic relationship:

> A woman has no particular lord. She must look to her husband as her lord, and must serve him with all worship and reverence, not despising or thinking lightly of him. The great lifelong duty of a woman is obedience. In her dealings with her husband, both the expression of her countenance and style of her address should be courteous, humble, and conciliatory, never peevish and intractable, never rude and arrogant—that should be a woman's first and chiefest care.[25]

The dependency of a woman on her husband's family gave rise to proverbs such as "The joys and sorrows of a lifetime depend on a stranger." Particularly cogent is the way women were taught to see themselves. According to Kaibara:

> The five worst infirmities that afflict the female are indocility, discontent, slander, jealousy, and silliness. Without any doubt, these five infirmities are found in seven or eight out of every ten women, and it is from these that arises the inferiority of women to men. A woman should cure them by self-inspection and self-reproach. The worst of them all and the parent of the other four is silliness. . . . Such is the stupidity of her character that it is incumbent on her, in every particular, to distrust herself and to obey her husband.[26]

Small wonder the Japanese still quote the proverb, "A woman's thinking is shallow." In spite of her extreme "stupidity," the wife is given the responsibility for the household. "In her capacity as wife, she must keep her husband's household in proper order. If the wife be evil and profligate, the house is ruined."[27] Women were encouraged to remain within the home, even to the extent of foregoing religious participation. "To temples (whether Shinto or Buddhist) and other like places where there is a great concourse of people, she should go but sparingly til she has reached the age of forty."[28] This device very effectively prevented women from any meaningful contact with other women.

Separation of the sexes was mandatory from about the age of seven, and even after marriage the young wife "must avoid the intimacy and familiarity of her husband's kinsmen, comrades, and retainers, ever strictly adhering to the rule of separation between the sexes."[29] While women were forbidden intimacy with the opposite sex, impoverished farmers sometimes had to sell daughters to houses of prostitution to pay their taxes.

The Confucian concept of the feminine role kept women out of school. The pronouncement by a Tokugawa official, "It is well that women should be unlettered. To cultivate women's skills would be harmful. They have no need of learning. It is enough if they can read books in *kana.* Let it be that way,"[30] sums up Tokugawa attitudes toward the education of women. An estimated 40 percent of boys and 10 percent of girls were being educated outside their homes—in clan schools, *terakoya* (temple schools), and a few Jesuit institutions—at the close of the Tokugawa period. Of the girls attending schools, the great majority were in the metropolitan areas. These girls were most likely daughters of merchants since shopkeepers' wives needed to read and write to help in the shop.[31] The majority of girls, especially in the small towns and countryside, were tutored at home using moral tracts such as the *Onna Daigaku* and the *Onna Chōbōki.* The *Onna Chōbōki,* in addition to explaining how women have declined, contains practical advice for women. How to detect pregnancy, charms for an easy delivery, and a warning not to eat crabs lest the child come out sideways were part of the housewife's education. There were also hints on etiquette and deportment and cosmetic suggestions for hairdressing, tooth-blackening, and the application of powder.[32]

Women's legal status during the Tokugawa period was completely dependent, first on her father, then on her husband, and eventually on her son. "A woman is thrice without a home." The *Onna Daigaku* reiterated the "Seven Reasons for Divorce," which contributed a great deal to a woman's insecurity and hence her willingness to please. There were no provisions for a woman to divorce without her husband's consent. In any case, a woman was unlikely to initiate a divorce since "A woman, once married, and then divorced, has wandered from the 'way,' and is covered with great shame, even if she should enter into a second union with a man of wealth and position."[33] In extreme cases, a woman's only alternatives were suicide or flight and, according to Joyce Ackroyd, there were several temples of divorce where a distressed wife might be given sanctuary and, after serving three years, restored to her parents. Since Japan had no official divorce law, and no divorce court, it was only necessary for the husband to write a short statement of his intention. These Letters of Divorce were known as "three lines and a half," indicating their brevity.

A married woman's existence was controlled by her husband's family. If her husband died, her father-in-law could "divorce" her by simply "sending the wife away." A woman was unable to become head of a household, to adopt or become guardian of her own child, own property, or make contracts in her own name. The family being all important, woman's function as "heir provider" in the context of Confucianism, feudalism, and ancestor worship had rendered her, on the eve of the Meiji Restoration, virtually devoid of legal rights.[34]

Unable to adapt to the growing merchant class or an economy based on money rather than rice, and harassed by Western intrusion, feudalism finally collapsed. The young lower-class samurai reform group who took power in the 1868 Restoration of the Imperial Rule were conservative men whose rallying cry was *Sonnō jōi*—revere the Emperor and repel the barbarians. More reactionary than revolutionary, they succeeded in establishing capitalism and restoring rule by emperor but lacked the ideals of individual rights and personal freedom. For the reformers, the family unit retained its prime importance.

In Meiji Japan, as during the Tokugawa period, the family (*ie*, or house) was considered the basic unit of a sound empire. The main function of the *ie* was to preserve the family from generation to generation. The household head was the link between generations. He was also the family's public and legal representative. According to Tokugawa feudalism, the male vassal was a juristic person with rights and privileges, while the female vassal had only duties and obligations. Women could not conduct ancestral rites nor were they permitted to play a public role in society. The headship, therefore, almost invariably succeeded to a male, usually the eldest son. If there were only daughters, a son was frequently adopted and married to the oldest daughter. The family head was the ultimate authority in all family decisions.

The position of head carried responsibilities as well as privileges. The *ie* provided security for the parents in their old age. Younger brothers could rely on the *ie* in time of need. The family head was expected to arrange good marriages for the daughters of the household. A widowed or divorced woman could return to the *ie*, but as her return reflected on the head's choice of husband, her position if she returned was often untenable. The head was expected to manage the business affairs of the house prudently. According to Chie Nakane, the *ie* is more than a residence system or authority structure. "Rather, the *ie* is a corporate residential group and . . . a managerial body."[35] The Meiji Civil Code (1898) was designed to protect this system.

When the first draft was criticized because it did not support Japanese custom regarding the *ie,* the sections on family and succession were rewritten. The revised version of the code, rather than improving the status of women, simply codified existing custom, providing additional sanctions to the family system.

There were some champions of women's rights who opposed continuance of the family system in the code. Arinori Mori, education minister in 1885, supported education for women, a single standard of morality, and criticized concubinage. Yukichi Fukuzawa, also an educator, championed equality of opportunity for women. He advocated equality in marriage, separate households for married couples, and the sanctioning of second marriages for women. He believed a change of attitude toward women should accompany their education so they might utilize what they learned. Fukuzawa wrote two critiques of the *Onna Daigaku.* One, in the manner of J. S. Mill's *The Subjection of Women*, he titled *Shin Onna Daigaku* [The New Greater Learning for Women]. The other was *Onna Daigaku Hyōron* [Greater Learning Critique]. The two books earned him many enemies.

The revised version of the Meiji Civil Code was approved despite opposition. The code upheld the family as the basis of the "Japanese morality of loyalty and filial piety and the national polity."36

Under Meiji law, marriage was still a transaction between two families rather than two individuals. Neither a man under thirty nor a woman under twenty-five could legally marry without the consent of the family head. The husband chose the place of residence, perpetuating patrilocal subjection of women. A marriage was not legally binding until it was registered. The groom's family usually did not register the marriage until the wife had proven she could adjust to the family or until she had borne an heir. The husband now had to get his wife's consent for divorce unless she was guilty of adultery, ill-treatment of lineal descendants, or other serious misconduct. The requirement for consent was moot in the case of nonregistration of the marriage. Also, it was easy for the husband's family to bring pressure on the wife to give her consent. A widow needed her in-laws' permission to remarry; it was seldom forthcoming.

The law discriminated against women in cases of adultery. For women, adultery was both a civil and a criminal offense. A wife could be divorced and imprisoned for two years. There was no penal sanction against adultery by the husband nor could he be divorced for adultery with an unmarried woman, since it did not affect the purity of the family line. If he were guilty of adultery with a married woman he could be divorced only if the husband of the woman involved brought suit against him.37 A proposal in 1931 to revise the criminal law to extend the penal sanction for adultery to men was opposed on the ground that "the courts would be swamped and the government would lose considerable revenue."[38]

Meiji civil law gave women the right to divorce, which they had not had prior to 1898, on the grounds of cruelty, desertion, or serious misconduct, but not for infidelity. Divorce was weighted heavily to the interests of the husband, however, because he kept the children, even if he were at fault. A divorced woman was subject to strong social disapproval. She was often reluctant to return to her former *ie* dependency. For these reasons, women seldom exercised their right to divorce.

Other rights given to women in the Civil Code include the rights to become the head of a household, to inherit, own, and manage property, and to act as guardian to children. These rights were, however, subject to major qualifications. A wife was not a juristic person in the same sense that her husband was; she had to have his consent to transact business. Without it, her contracts were voidable. Though she "owned" the property which was hers before marriage, he had the right to possession and management and could easily convert it by selling it and buying something else in his name. A woman could succeed to headship only if there were no lineal heir. In most cases, if a son was not born, one was adopted. A wife inherited after the lineal descendants. Succession to property and succession to headship were separated under Meiji law. A daughter could succeed to property but her claim to the family headship came after that of all male heirs including a recognized illegitimate son. Thus, though "owning" the property, she was subject to the family head, whose authority was recognized by Meiji law.

Realizing that education was essential to modernization, Meiji leaders gave it a high priority. The stated aim of the 1872 Education Ordinance was the education of all segments of society. By 1910, virtual literacy was achieved.[39] The quality of education of boys and girls, however, was unequal. The purpose of the girl's education was to produce the good wife and wise mother necessary for the maintenance of the family system. Elementary schools were coeducational. Separate tracks for boys and girls began at the secondary level. Boys went to middle school; the same level for girls was the girls' high school. The middle school had two courses for boys, one practical and the other preparatory for higher education. Girls' high schools placed "special emphasis upon the development of national morality and the cultivation of womanly virtues."[40] Graduates of the girls' high schools were eligible for women's normal schools for training teachers. National universities were only open to men.

Several forces were active in moderating these unequal conditions in social and political spheres and in the education system. Christian missions established many schools for girls in the 1870s and the 1880s. Curricula included algebra, geometry, history, and philosophy. The progressive education offered by Christian schools for girls earned attacks by the press during the nationalist reaction of the 1890s.

Government-sponsored normal schools for women produced mainly primary school teachers. The school founded by Umeko Tsuda in 1900 (now Tsuda College) offered a course for teachers of secondary schools. A private medical school for women was founded in 1900, and the following year the Japan Women's University was opened by Jinzō Naruse.[41] Curriculum for girls' schools stressed the social inferiority of women and perpetuated the feudal ideal of womanhood.[42] The education offered women at most colleges was equivalent to junior college. After 1913 a few women were admitted to the imperial universities at Sendai, Fukuoka, and Sapporo, but admission to the most prestigious imperial universities at Tokyo and Kyoto was denied. By World War II, forty women were in imperial universities compared with 29,600 men.[43] That Japanese women remained *hakoiri musume*—box-enclosed maidens—is illustrated by this description, written in 1935, by Shidzue Ishimoto of her mother:

> She is intelligent, modest, unselfish, and always thoughtful of the other members of the family. She is particular about her manners, and impresses everybody she meets with her graceful dignity. Strict with herself, and formal, she plays the part of a samurai's wife, majestically, as if in a dramatic performance. She rises earlier and retires later than anybody else in the family. She has never allowed herself to enjoy a lazy Sunday morning in bed, and the sickbed is the only place for her to rest. Nobody ever saw her sit in a relaxed manner: she is always erect, wearing her kimono tightly with her heavy sash folded on her back. . . . "Endurance" and "repression" are her greatest ideals. She says to me, "Endurance a woman should cultivate more than anything else. If you endure well in any circumstances, you will achieve happiness."
>
> . . . .
>
> My mother was especially assiduous in educating her children. She made every effort to further their development but her feudal concept of "man first, woman to follow" was clearly seen in her treatment of her sons and daughters. Of course the daughters took sex discrimination for granted, as they did not know anything else.[44]

Women today describe endurance as a negative strength, not manifested externally.

Writing about the same time as Ishimoto, Etsu Sugimoto describes the life of a young girl in *A Daughter of the Samurai.* Boys and girls did not play together and each had their own games. The studies of boys and girls were completely different; a girl's studies intended to make her a better wife. A samurai's daughter was imbued with the same strength of character as her brother, but the daughter's husband became her lord and her loyalty was to him. When she was married, she was brought by her family to the groom's house and thereafter she was lost to her own family, as if she had died. Even if she became a widow she deferred to the wishes of her husband's family.

A movement for social and political equality for women occurred as part of the general civil rights movement in the 1870s and 1880s. While the promulgation of the constitution in 1889 seemed to be a step toward parliamentary government and popular participation, it was offset by a nationalistic anti-individualistic reaction, expressed by the passage of the first Peace Preservation Law in the same year. Article Five of this law prohibited women from joining political associations and from sponsoring or attending political meetings. Because of this prohibition, women's organizations until before 1919 were literary or philanthropic in character.[45] The W.C.T.U., the Y.W.C.A., and the Women's Patriotic Society were all established during this period, the first two maintaining international connections.

The Seitōsha (Blue Stocking Society) was the first organization to express a feminist tone. Founded by Reicho Hiratsuka in 1911, its stated aim was to encourage unknown writers through its publication *Seitō*. The magazine reflected the influence on its members by feminist authors, notably Ibsen. *Hedda Gabler* and *A Doll's House* were discussed extensively—Nora became a focus of debate. "The women of the Seitōsha were worried over Nora's fate after leaving home, while the public was more concerned over the fact that she had left home."[46]

Seitō became the object of government censorship and was banned. Economic conditions ended its publication in 1916 but its membership carried over to the Association of New Women, begun in 1919.[47] The first women's organization with political objectives, its founders included Fusae Ichikawa as well as Hiratsuka. The immediate goal of the Association of New Women was the abrogation of Article Five of the Peace Preservation Law. Its objectives also included equal rights for both sexes, a clarification of the social significance of the home, safeguarding the rights of women—by eliminating factors injurious to them—and the establishment of a women's labor union.[48] Labor conditions were extremely poor at this time, especially for women and children, because of the push to industrialize. Socialist women did not function as a party because of the political restrictions on women, but they were an active element in the movements to improve labor conditions, to abolish restrictions on political participation by women, and to gain suffrage for women.[49]

After two years of struggle, the Association of New Women saw its Peace Preservation Reform Bill passed in 1921. Women could attend and hold political meetings but they could not, until the occupation, join or organize political parties. But public criticism and opposition had weakened the group. Hiratsuka resigned and the Association of New Women disbanded.

Two other developments added impetus to the women's movement. One, the birth control movement, was inspired by Margaret Sanger. Shidzue Ishimoto, after visiting Sanger in New York, returned to Japan to begin her career as a birth control feminist. Others took up the cause, several clinics were opened, and a liberal magazine, *Kaizō*, invited Sanger to Japan in 1922. The Tokyo Police Bureau, fearing Sanger might introduce "dangerous thoughts," refused to grant her a landing permit, an action which only served to arouse public interest. Eventually permitted to land but not to lecture, Sanger's visit set off a wave of publications and translations of her work.[50]

Labor unions, legalized in 1923, adopted birth control as an aim but dropped it because of ideological differences with the Marxist left wing, a problem which affected the whole birth-control movement and cost valuable left-wing support.[51] The birth-control movement, never supported by the government, was completely suppressed in 1937 when the Sino-Japanese war produced a need for workers, soldiers, and babies.[52]

Another occurrence to influence the women's movement was the 1923 earthquake in Tokyo. Women, forced to take initiative, organize, and cooperate in the days following the disaster, gained valuable experience. Many members of an organization formed to deal with problems related to the earthquake later participated actively in the suffrage movement.[53]

Ichikawa left Japan for the United States before the passage of the Peace Preservation Reform Bill. Her visit began in 1920, the year following the achievement of suffrage by American women. She was greatly influenced by the enthusiasm and optimism of the women she met. When she returned to Japan in 1924, the women's movement, despite strengthening factors, was at a low point. Women were leaderless and disappointed in politics. Nevertheless, Ichikawa, with Shigeri Yamataka, organized the Women's Suffrage Union in December 1924. "The fact that she was able to organize this group during a chaotic period in the women's movement and sustain it for sixteen years indicates her strong incentive and determination."[54] The group hoped to have women included in the pending Manhood Suffrage Law, but it was passed in 1924 without extending the franchise to women.

At every Diet session following the granting of manhood suffrage, bills were presented for women's suffrage, women's civil rights, and the privilege of joining political parties; but to no avail. It was 1930 before the feminine civil rights bill passed the House of Representatives. The government announced itself in favor of civil rights for women in cities, towns, and villages—a political training ground for women—but city mayors, backed by the House of Peers, opposed the granting of any such rights. In response to this reaction, a revised bill raised the age of women eligible for civil rights to twenty-five (it was twenty for men), but even this limited bill was rejected by the House of Peers in March 1931.

Even as women were reorganizing for the next session, the Manchurian Incident began, and increasing military ascendancy over the civil government altered the women's movement and nearly ended the suffrage issue. In the face of rising totalitarianism, the women's movement shifted its emphasis to issues affecting women's daily life.[55]

In the early 1930s women were encouraged to produce children, but by the early 1940s the need for laborers became more immediate and unmarried girls were drafted to work in factories. Many married women also worked in factories. "It was no longer patriotic to marry young and bear many children. The old slogans disappeared from sight, and women were exhorted now to produce 'more airplanes' . . . . The militarists, formerly the staunchest supporters of 'women in the house,' now became the strongest advocates of 'women in the factories.' "[56] In 1939 women over twenty-five were ordered to work in mines; only pregnant women were excused. The Japan Women's Alliance was organized in 1937 to deal with current problems. Though its purpose was to cooperate with the government, it did oppose the use of female labor in coal mines.[57] By 1942 women were part of the total resource and manpower mobilization, and their activities were under firm government control. The Women's Suffrage Alliance was no longer in existence.

Women had of necessity assumed full responsibility for maintaining life during the war. As the men returned from the war, they resumed their former jobs. Resentful at being forced to return to their old status, women again focused on their lack of civil rights. With every reason to expect suffrage would be granted to women in the new constitution, women were told that their enfranchisement "would retard the progress of Japanese politics."[58] Forty women formed the Women's Postwar Policy Committee. As head of the political branch, Ichikawa went to see the head of the newly formed Liberal Party, who promised to include women's suffrage in the party platform.[59] The question remains whether the Diet would have granted suffrage without being urged by the occupation authorities.

In December 1945, the government announced passage of the Revised Election Law, giving men and women equal voting rights and equal electoral eligibility. The Imperial House Law, however, still does not permit a female on the throne. Women went to the polls for the first time on April 10, 1946, and elected thirty-nine women to the House of Representatives. This is still a record.

The Revised Election Law was the first of a series of laws guaranteeing equality for women. Licensed prostitution was abolished. Women were allowed to become heads of local governments and members of local assemblies. Schooling was made compulsory for nine years for all children. The 1947 Labor Standards Law provides equal pay for equal work regardless of sex. It also limits overtime and night work and prohibits underground, dangerous, and harmful work for women. Most important, it requires employers to give a total of twelve weeks' maternity leave to women who request it. A Women's and Minors' Bureau was established in 1948 in the Labor Ministry to protect working women and children and to improve conditions for women in general. The Eugenics Protection Law provides advisory service on marriage, gives birth-control information, and permits abortion with a physician's approval.

The Revised Civil Code of 1947 changed the position of women within the family. The intention of the code, in fact, was the abolition of the concept of *ie* with its powerful head. Women are assured equal property rights, freedom of marriage, and equal grounds for divorce. Children are to succeed equally, and widows are guaranteed the right of guardianship. A husband no longer has the right to manage property belonging to his wife, nor is the choice of domicile his alone. A wife is now a juristic person and can transact business without her husband's consent.[60]

One of the earliest postwar changes for women was in education. The reforms of 1945 included equal admittance, comparable standards, and coeducation at all levels in tax-supported schools, including the former imperial universities.

Have the new constitution, codes, and laws destroyed the feminine ideal as conservatives warned? Have women chosen to exert the new ideal or do they still live according to the old tradition?

The percentage of women voting has gradually increased. For the past five years it has been slightly higher than for men. In each of the past ten years, about two million more women than men have voted. Yet in those same ten years less than 2 percent of the House of Representatives and about 6 percent of the House of Councillors have been women. There are more women in the Japanese Diet than there are in the United States Congress, but there are not nearly enough to be effective. In local assemblies, in 1974, women comprised 1.25 percent of the total at the prefectural (state) level, 1.6 percent at the municipal level, but only 0.4 percent at the village level, reflecting perhaps a more conservative outlook in the villages.[61]

Women are taking greater advantage of educational opportunity. More girls than boys entered high school in the past five years. High schools are coeducational and presumably offer equal education. Home economics was made an elective subject in 1949. In 1956 it was made compulsory for girls. The time spent on home economics is a disadvantage for women who want to compete for university entrance. The requirement also permits former boys' schools, lacking home economics equipment, to continue to exclude girls.[62] The "good wife and wise mother" role can easily be inculcated in home economics courses.

The percentage of women going on to higher education, half that of men in 1950, is now very nearly equal—30.8 percent of the women to 31.6 percent of the men high school graduates in 1974.[63] They follow different educational tracks, however. Women comprise nearly 90 percent of the junior college enrollment and less than 20 percent of the four-year university enrollment. Moreover, half of the junior college women are in home economics courses.[64]

Women's universities rank between junior colleges and coeducational universities. The policy of many women's universities is to educate women for their role as mothers. Graduate schools at government-supported women's universities are virtually nonexistent. Some subjects are still considered unsuitable for women, especially the hard sciences and social sciences such as economics. Accordingly, most women, even at four-year coeducational universities, specialize in the humanities. One explanation for government reluctance to upgrade educational facilities for women is society's attitude that women's education does not yield a return on the financial investment. This attitude will persist so long as the assumption that all women must sooner or later marry and become dependent persists.[65]

Women comprise 40 percent of Japan's labor force. Nearly half of all women over the age of fifteen work—73 percent as clerical, service, and factory workers.

There is still a clearly discernible division of male and female labor. Nurses, nursery school nurses, and household workers are virtually all women. Judges, scientists, and managerial workers are nearly all men. Pay for women is half that for men. This is partially accounted for by the shorter duration of employment of women—five years compared with ten years for men—and by the slightly younger average age of women workers—thirty-three years to thirty-six years for men. *The Status of Women in Japan* explains that these two characteristics also lead to limited chances of promotion for women and reflect less education and less skill.[66]

An overwhelming number of women in Japan still opt for marriage. The marriage rate increased by nearly a fifth from 1930 to 1972, while the birthrate went down. The average number of children per family has dropped from five to less than three. The divorce rate increased immediately following the war but has since returned to the 1930 level of one in every ten marriages.[67] Changes in family patterns affecting women are the increase in the number of married women employed outside the home and the increase in nuclear families.

Let us turn our attention now to women by occupational category to see how far they have departed from the traditional ideal to take advantage of new rights and opportunities.

NOTES

[1] W. G. Aston, tr. and ed., *Nihongi*, Book I, p. 13.
[2] G. B. Sansom, *A History of Japan to 1334*, p. 32.
[3] Donald L. Philippi, ed., *Kojiki*, p. 11.
[4] G. B. Sansom, *Japan: A Short Cultural History*, pp. 29-31.
[5] Aston, Book II, pp. 12-13.
[6] Joyce Ackroyd, "Women in Feudal Japan," p. 32.
[7] William H. McCullough, "Japanese Marriage Institutions in the Heian Period," p. 105.
[8] *Ibid.*
[9] Ackroyd, p. 32.
[10] Lady Murasaki, *The Tale of Genji*, p. 666.
[11] Ackroyd, p. 32.
[12] *Ibid.*, p. 38.
[13] *Ibid.*, pp. 38-39.
[14] *Ibid.*, p. 39.
[15] Donald Keene, ed., *Anthology of Japanese Literature*, pp. 224-228.
[16] Ackroyd, p. 43.
[17] *Ibid.*, pp. 54-55.
[18] *Ibid.*, pp. 51-52.
[19] *Ibid.*
[20] In *Shiseki Shūran*, Vol. 25, p. 655, cited in Ackroyd, p. 52.
[21] Mikiso Hane, *Japan: A Historical Survey*, p. 86.
[22] Ackroyd, p. 52.
[23] Shidzue Ishimoto, *Facing Two Ways*, p. 291.
[24] L. Cranmer-Byng and Dr. S. A. Kapadia, eds., *Women and Wisdom of Japan*, pp. 37-38.
[25] *Ibid.*, p. 38.
[26] *Ibid.*, pp. 44-45.
[27] *Ibid.*, p. 41.
[28] *Ibid.*, p. 40.
[29] *Ibid.*, p. 41.

[30]Matsudaira Sadanoba, cited in Herbert Passin, *Society and Education in Japan*, p. 461.

[31]R. P. Dore, *Education in Tokugawa Japan*, p. 254.

[32]*Ibid.*, pp. 289-290.

[33]Cranmer-Byng, p. 37.

[34]Joyce C. Lebra, "The Feminine Ideal: With Reference to Japanese Law," pp. 11-12.

[35]Chie Nakane, *Human Relations in Japan*, p. 10.

[36]Kurt Steiner, "The Revision of the Civil Code of Japan; Provisions Affecting the Family," p. 172. Cited in Lebra, p. 16.

[37]Emma Nyun-Han, "The Socio-Political Roles of Women in Japan and Burma," pp. 152-156.

[38]*Japan Weekly Chronicle*, February 5, 1931, cited by Lebra, p. 21.

[39]Nyun-Han, p. 234.

[40]K. Yoshida and T. Kaigo, *Japanese Education*, p. 55.

[41]Lebra, pp. 9-10.

[42]Robert King Hall, *Education for a New Japan*, p. 418.

[43]*Ibid.*

[44]Ishimoto, pp. 9-12.

[45]Lebra, pp. 29-30.

[46]Dee Ann Vavich, "The Japanese Woman's Movement: Ichikawa Fusae, A Pioneer in Woman's Suffrage," p. 409.

[47]*Ibid.*

[48]Lebra, p. 51.

[49]George O. Totten, *The Social Democratic Movement in Prewar Japan*, pp. 360-361.

[50]Margi Haas, "The First Birth Control Movement in Japan, 1902-1937," pp. 7-8.

[51]*Ibid.*, pp. 19-20.

[52]*Ibid.*, p. 43.

[53]Vavich, p. 413.

[54]*Ibid.*, pp. 414-415.

[55]*Ibid.*, pp. 415-420.

[56]Yoko Matsuoka, *Daughter of the Pacific*, pp. 178-179.

[57]Vavich, p. 422.

[58]Shio Sakahishi, "Women's Position and the Family System," p. 131, cited in Vavich, p. 425.

[59]Vavich, p. 425.

[60]Lebra, pp. 44-46.

[61]Women's and Minors' Bureau, *Status of Women in Japan*, 1974, pp. 2-4.

[62]Masu Okamura, *Women's Status—Changing Japan*, pp. 79-80.

[63]Women's and Minors' Bureau, 1974, p. 6.

[64]Okamura, p. 80.

[65]*Ibid.*, pp. 78-83.

[66]Women's and Minors' Bureau, 1974, pp. 9-18.

[67]*Ibid.*, p. 26.

CHAPTER
2
WOMEN IN RURAL JAPAN

Misao Sakai Kawabata, sixty-six years old, lives with her husband in a small fishing village on the western seacoast of the island of Shikoku, where she talked about her life in a series of interviews in April 1975. Misao Kawabata's life story may be considered representative of pre-World War II Japanese rural women married to first sons; that is, women who lived with their husbands' parents and under the rule of their mothers-in-law. In her detailed description of family life, of working conditions in a silk filature factory, and of the agony of wartime Japan, Mrs. Kawabata provides a vivid social history of twentieth-century Japan from the woman's point of view.[1]

THE AUTOBIOGRAPHY OF A FARM WOMAN

I was born on October 22, 1909, in Tawarazu, Akehama township [Ehime Prefecture], one of six children and the second daughter of the Sakai family. My father's family name was Tanaka, but because he was adopted upon marriage into my mother's family, his name became Sakai.

My father grew rice, wheat, and potatoes on the Sakai land. When I was about six years old, the farm failed, however, and we lost our land. From that time on our family suffered. Father bought a horse and worked as a driver, transporting luggage or hauling lumber from the mountains. I grew up during the lowest point in my family's fortunes.

We lived in an old house together with my mother's father and mother—my maternal grandparents. My brothers and sisters all slept together in one room with my mother and father. I slept under the same quilt with father until I was twelve years old, and one of my sisters slept with my mother.

I loved my father very much. As an adopted son-in-law, he had little power in the household. Also, he had no property. There's an old saying, "If you have three helpings of rice bran, don't become an adopted son-in-law." Father drank a lot and was often scolded by grandfather. But he did not return to his own family home, even though he had trouble with his in-laws. He had a great sense of responsibility for his children.

Because our family was poor, my next younger sister was given up for adoption to a childless aunt. My oldest brother got a job at the Town Hall (*Yakuba*), and my second oldest brother worked with father. From the age of ten, after returning home from school, I worked as a baby-sitter for a wealthy family, carrying their baby around on my back. In return, I received my evening meal and gifts, such as a kimono, on New Year's Day and *Obon*. When the baby grew older, I did odd jobs around their house, such as weeding. If I came home late from school, my mother would scold me, though father never did. I don't remember my grandfather working very much, and my mother, whose eyes were bad, hardly worked at all.

EDUCATION

My eldest sister and I were eager to continue our studies beyond the six years of compulsory education. Although my brothers graduated from higher elementary school,[2] my sister had to stop after one year and went to work in a nearby silk filature factory (*seishi kōba*). With my brothers' help, however, I was able to complete the two years of higher elementary school (*kōtō-shōgakkō*) and went to school until I was fifteen years old. Afterward, I attended a night course to learn how to use the abacus, just as a hobby, because I wanted to continue studying.

In primary school (*shōgakkō*) I learned reading, arithmetic, and ethics (*shūshin*). We were taught loyalty, filial piety, respect for elders, and the Five Relationships. In fact, the first item on our report cards was ethics. We also learned drawing and calligraphy.

Both primary school and higher elementary school were coeducational and located right next to each other in Tawarazu, so I did not have to board away from home. In higher elementary school we learned simple geography and history lessons, mainly about Japan, but also some world history, such as the names of Washington and Columbus, and the story of Japan's "closed door" policy. We also learned about the opening of Japan in the Bakumatsu [1853-1868] period. In addition, we learned some science (*rika*), some more ethics, and, for women, *sahō*, which consisted of lessons in sewing kimono, cooking, and etiquette—such as how to stand up [from kneeling position], and how to walk on tatami, and how to slide open a door.

My grandfather did not believe in educating women. If he saw me reading, he would scold me. Women should do housework; they shouldn't learn how to use the abacus; they should only learn how to sew. If I didn't do well at schoolwork, however, he would also scold me!

When we reached twelve years of age, we girls were told we could not talk to boys, even if we met them on the road—even if they were our own cousins. There was an old saying, "A male after seven years of age does not sit with a woman" (*Danjo nanasai ni shite seki o onnachū sezu*). You could, however, talk with boys in your own home. Rules about sex were very strict.

After the age of eighteen, it was again possible to get together with boys at officially sponsored clubs, such as the Maidens' Association (*Shojokai*) and the Young Men's Association (*Seinendai*), where you could play cards or go on picnics together in a group. That's how I met my husband, in fact; we were both active in youth groups.

My sister and I both worked in the nearby silk filature factory from around the age of fifteen on. When she was nineteen and I was seventeen, she caught a cold, but continued to work. The cold turned into tuberculosis and she died. Then, when I was nineteen, my father died. He was only fifty-six years old. I was married shortly afterward.

MARRIAGE

My husband, Kawabata Yosaku, entered the Army when he was twenty-one years old and served one year of compulsory military duty in Tokushima Prefecture. After he returned home, he became head of the Young Men's Association while I was vice-head of the Maidens' Associations. We worked together planning social events and grew fond of each other in this way. In a sense, our marriage was a "love marriage" (*ren-ai*). We had a go-between (*nakōdo-san*) present for the official marriage ceremony, however. I was twenty and he was twenty-four when we married, in January 1929.

My husband's family had a reputation for being "high class." His father, like mine, was an adopted son-in-law. His mother's father, a successful tailor, had made enough money sewing Japanese-style clothes to build a fine house and storage shed. The family paid for my husband's middle school education in Uwajima, where he boarded for five years. His mother too was educated. She could read and use an abacus. This was rare among women her age. She expected the family members to behave as though they were members of the samurai class: if you made a mistake, you had to bow and say "Forgive me."

Our wedding celebration lasted three days, as was the custom at that time.[3] My in-laws' house was full of food and guests—mainly men—while women relatives, neighbors, and friends helped prepare the feast of fish and rice. On the first day of the wedding celebration, after dressing in my wedding robe and arranging my hair properly as a bride (we did not wear wigs in those days), I prayed in front of our family's Buddhist altar. I said to my dead father, "Today I am to be married. I am no longer a Sakai. I am becoming a Kawabata." And I cried.

My mother did not accompany me to my husband's house for the wedding ceremony. I said goodbye to her in our own home instead, before leaving with my husband-to-be, a few relatives, and the go-between to walk to his house, a short distance away in the nearby hamlet. It was nighttime, and the members of the wedding party all carried lanterns. My dowry consisted of a trunk with several kimono for the different seasons of the year; a sewing box (*haribako*), with implements for sewing, such as scissors, needles, and thread; and a mirror. The mirror was considered a woman's soul (*onna no tamashii*).

My marriage day was like hard labor. I had to sit on my knees motionless for about ten hours, in a tight sash (*obi*), my eyes downcast, looking properly shy. Brides are supposed to look demure and embarrassed. Everyone around me was eating and drinking, but I could not.

In the days that followed, I was busy serving guests and pouring saké. The day after the wedding ceremony, I changed into a more comfortable kimono and arranged my hair style with combs to signify that I was married. Then my mother-in-law took me around to pay formal calls on all the households in the hamlet. A bride usually paid a ceremonial visit to her own parents' home on the third day of the wedding celebration; I was so busy, I could not go until the fifth day when, accompanied by my husband and mother-in-law, who carried ceremonial red rice (*sekihan*) to present to my parents, we returned to my family home.

MOTHER-IN-LAW

My mother-in-law was fifty-four years old when I was married. We lived with her for the next thirty-eight years, until she died at the age of ninety-two. She was very *erai*[4] and very strict.

As daughter-in-law, I was the last person to eat and the one who ate the least tasty food. My mother-in-law did all the cooking. She also served the food. She ordered me around like a maid: "Misao, bring me those plates." If I washed a plate, she'd say, "Wipe it this way." I could not choose one chopstick by myself to bring to the table. If I broke a dish, I really worried. The only thing I could freely use were the things I had brought with me in my trousseau.

In those days a woman learned that her virtue (*bidoku*) lay in her self-sacrifice. You learned to do what your parents said. My father always taught me through the example of his own life that if both sides assert themselves, you can't get along in the family. One side must yield—the one that comes in from outside.

CHILDBIRTH

I conceived my first child within one month after I was married. Several months after that, in July, my name was officially entered in the household register (*koseki*), and in November, my daughter was born. It was only many years later, when I needed a copy of the household register for my child's school admission forms, that I learned when my name had been entered.[5]

I had five more children in the next eleven and one-half years. There was no birth control in those days. In my mother's day, you received a prize from the government if you had twelve children. We then found out, in the 1930s, that Japan was overpopulated. In my grandmother's time, there were far fewer children in an average family, because women practiced infanticide and did abortions on themselves. My mother heard about a woman who killed her own infant and was later questioned by the police. For this reason, my mother decided not to kill her last-born, my youngest sister. When I was about fifteen or sixteen years old, I remember hearing from my eldest sister something about birth control and the name of Margaret Sanger. My sister liked to read and may have read a newspaper article about it. However, in my days, unlike couples today, nobody practiced family planning.

Women worked until the last possible hour before giving birth—until they felt labor contractions. You knew how to time the labor pains. After you had given birth to one or two children, you could tell if labor was still a day away and even if you felt some pain, you kept working.

All six of my children were easy deliveries that took only about two to four hours each. When you gave birth, your husband left the house. If it was at night, he went to sleep in another room. During the day, he was out working. A woman's ability to endure was considered a beautiful virtue: you were not supposed to cry out in pain—that would be shameful.

At the time of birth, I called the nearby midwife. She handled the birth, boiled the water, cut the umbilical cord, and washed the baby. I still have the dried-up umbilical cords, each in a separate envelope with the child's name and date of birth written on it. After the cord was cut, I nursed the baby and changed its diapers. The diapers were made of old *yukata* or kimono material. I always had plenty of breast milk. In the old days, every woman had milk; it was rare not to have enough milk. The baby was fed on milk alone.

My mother-in-law was good to me and did things for me only at the time of my children's birth. I suppose she wanted healthy children. And I was cheap labor power. She gave me white rice, instead of the usual wheat, for the first two weeks. Also, I received *misoshiru* (bean paste soup) for breakfast. Usually we didn't have that for breakfast. She even put an egg in it and some fish, which was a luxury. We ate eggs and fish only when we were sick or after giving birth. Otherwise, we ate only wheat and vegetables.

After thirty-three days of confinement, I would take the baby to the neighborhood shrine. The following day, I would return to my job at the factory. Most mothers took off forty-four days.

For the first eight years of my marriage, I continued to work at the factory. During those years, I really suffered. My mother-in-law interfered with the children's upbringing. I could not handle the children the way I wanted to. I could not feed them what I wanted to. Although my life was hard—we did not have enough to eat and I worked many hours a day in the factory—the hardest thing for me to endure was my mother-in-law's strictness with my own children. I wanted to indulge them, but if they were noisy, or broke something, or even if they fell, she would scold them and me, saying that the mother's discipline was poor. She would not let my daughter play in the house with her friends because she was afraid they would dirty the house. The way she treated the children always made me want to cry. Sometimes I would go to the toilet to cry there by myself.

Still, my mother-in-law adored my eldest daughter, Yukie.6 She slept with her and my father-in-law in the big, two-story house, while my husband and I and the rest of our children lived in the two-room house across the road. To this day my daughter remembers being raised by her grandmother and has no memories of her own mother in her early years. I am grateful that my mother-in-law was enthusiastic about education, for she sent my daughter to girls' school (*jogakkō*) in Uwajima when she reached twelve years of age.

My mother-in-law took great care of my husband. He was, after all, her eldest son and the family heir. She fed him before feeding the children. She treated him, and not her own husband, as the head of the household. My husband at the time worked in a bank. When he came home from work, she offered him the choicest food. He ate white rice; we ate wheat sprinkled with a little rice. She washed my husband's laundry and the children's by herself; I was expected to do my own. When my husband went to war, she tried to examine my letters before I mailed them to him, telling me, "You shouldn't write that," or "That's no good."

I did not spend much time with my husband. In the evenings, he went to visit friends. It was not that my husband oppressed or enslaved me; rather, like me, he was completely obedient to his mother. To make up an example, if my husband, in another part of the country, had said, "Come, join me here," and my mother-in-law had said, "Don't go," I would not have gone. If I complained to my husband about his mother, he would scold me, saying that the young should defer to the old.

THE TAWARAZU SILK FILATURE FACTORY

I worked in the factory for fourteen years, between the ages of fifteen and twenty-nine. We began work at 4:30 a.m. and ended at 5 p.m. We had a thirty-minute break for breakfast at 6 a.m.; a one-hour break for lunch at 11 a.m.; and a ten-minute rest break at 3 p.m. At mealtimes, my mother-in-law's mother brought my baby to me to be nursed in a special room set aside at the factory for nursing mothers.

The factory employed about 400 people, mostly women. About 250 women made the thread; 80 refined it; and 55 men reeled the silk off the cocoons. We worked side by side in rows of 20 across, in a long, single-story wooden building. The thread was all exported for sale abroad.

The factory was founded by Saburō Kantoku of Tawarazu. Later, it became a stock company managed by two directors named Nakamura and Takaoka. They had a lot of power, and they were the most frightening. An auditor came once each month at payroll time.

We worked every day of the month except for the first and the fifteenth. We also had holidays on the first three days of the New Year, *Obon* [August], and the Flower-Viewing Festival [two days in April]. In addition, we were allowed to observe local festival days. In May, the factory closed down for one month, as the new silk worms were not yet born. Only the men stayed on to clean up. We women used May to mend our clothes or to make new clothes for our children out of our old kimono.

Although our wages were figured on a daily basis, we were paid only twice a year, at New Year's time and *Obon*. After 1934, we were paid once a month and were given insurance and an allowance for the cost of the midwife when we gave birth. I brought home about 20 to 24 yen a month. In those days, rice cost about 8 yen 20 *sen* for 60 kilos. So my monthly income bought about 180 kilos of rice. Today, the same amount costs 1 *man* 2 *sen yen* [about $40]. Three times that amount would be 3 *man* 6 *sen yen.* My wage was therefore equal to about 36,000 yen [$120] for 11 hours a day, 28 days a month [less than 40 cents an hour]. And I handed all of it over to my mother-in-law.

One year I worked as the examiner. I had to examine the work done by my fellow employees, weigh the thread, and record the amount. Wages differed according to the quality and quantity of the work completed. It was my judgment that determined differences in employees' wages. Each worker received a number according to her seat and the work she did. After finishing her spool of thread, she would fix her number to it and bring it to me for inspection. I examined it, recorded the amount I thought she deserved, and, by evening, I had receipts to hand out to all 200 workers.

The directors were always at our backs. If the work didn't please them—let's say the thread was too thick or too thin—the worker was told to take off the next day. Since the number of workers exceeded the number of seats, the boss could easily hire another woman. Then, when the punished person returned, another person was kicked out. As the one who checked the work, I felt I had responsibility for other people being out of work. The girl who was forced to take a day or two off then had to face an angry mother-in-law. I was tense for twelve hours a day that year.

If somebody lost her seat, she received a new seat with a new number, until the end of the month, when she was allowed to return to her own seat. I had to remember who was sitting where and to tally up their wages for all their seat numbers that month.

In this way we sent good quality silk at cheap prices to the United States.

FARMING

In 1936, my fifth child, a second son, was born, and in 1937, after
the China Incident, the factory closed down. I began farming instead.
I grew wheat and potatoes. My father-in-law helped and the children
worked in the fields when they had time off from school.

At that time, my two brothers had become fishermen. The children
and I helped my brothers, for a wage, during our slack farm season.
The men went fishing for sea slug (*iriko*) at night, lowering lights into the water to attract the fish and catching them in a net. They
returned in the morning, when my sisters-in-law and I took the fish
and first boiled, then dried it on the beach, working from dawn until
we finished. Hours depended on the size of the catch.

I also worked on squid-fishing boats, helping to pull in the nets.[7]
My mother-in-law never "went to the mountains" [i.e., never farmed
on the terraced slopes of the mountains surrounding the hamlet].
She stayed at home, doing all the housework and cooking.

WAR

Shortly before the start of World War II, my husband was commis-
sioned to teach military drill to the students at the Uwajima Middle
School. On May 7, 1941, he was drafted into the Army.

Before leaving for the front, my husband was sent to Matsuyama
[the capital of Ehima Prefecture]. I joined him there and we lived
together with our youngest child for several months, while my
mother-in-law kept our four other children. Three months before
Pearl Harbor, I gave birth to our sixth child.

This was a happy time for me, because I was free, for the first time
since I was married, but of course we did not know when my husband would be called to war. We sensed war was coming, but we
had no idea where the battleground would be. Finally orders came,
after Pearl Harbor, for my husband to go to the Philippines.

We returned home, where I sewed a sash for my husband to wrap
around his waist. During the war, when a man left for the Army,
it was the custom for each woman in the village to sew one stitch
in the sash for good luck. This was called a thousand-stitch belt
(*sennin-bari*). You were expected to act happy when a man from
your household left for war. Everyone gave presents and went to a
big send-off for the draftee.

I accompanied my husband as far as Uwajima, my last-born still
suckling at my breast. The middle-school students gave my husband

a send-off party. Then I returned home to spend the war years in my husband's parents' house.

We received my husband's monthly salary, which my mother-in-law kept. There was little to buy with the money, however. We grew our own food—potatoes, vegetables, and rice. Potatoes were grown in the summer, on a steep slope in the mountains, and harvested in October. Wheat was planted in the late fall and harvested in the spring. At dinner time, we first ate potatoes, to fill up our stomachs, then ate wheat gruel. We had plenty of vegetables, though we ate only what was in season: eggplant in summer and turnip and onions in the winter. We bought a little bit of rice at the store. Everything was rationed—rice, salt, soy sauce. We picked *warabi* (a bracken or mountain grass) in the mountains.

Water was drawn every day from a well a short distance from our house. Every morning I slung a bamboo pole with one bucket on each end over my shoulder and brought the day's water to the house. For washing, we drew water from another well that was less pure. For my baby's clothes and diapers, I tore apart my own clothes and resewed them. After fuel became scarce, I dug up the roots of pine trees that had been cut down, and burned them for fuel.

Only old people, children, and women were left in the villages. All the able-bodied males were drafted. There were only a few mar-riages—of men with an eye missing or a crooked arm. Brides during the war were expected to wear *mompe* (traditional pantaloons) and aprons, and to hang a ribbon across their chests that read *Dai Nihon Kokubō Fujin Kai* (The Greater Japan National Defense Women's Association). Nobody dressed like a traditional Japanese bride.

Like every other woman in the village, I was a member of the Greater Japan National Defense Women's Association. We dug trenches or holes in the ground to shelter the children during air raids. I was told by the town leader that it was my responsibility to protect our family's house. During air raids, I had to shut off all the lights in the house and go outside to observe where bombs were dropping so I could help put out the fires.

At night we slept dressed in *mompe*. Next to our quilts we kept cotton-filled floor cushions (*zabuton*) to protect our heads. We could tie these on our heads with ribbons in case of emergency. We also wrapped up our valuables and the ancestral tablets. Think-ing I might be killed, because I was not allowed to flee with the others, I taught my children where I kept their dried umbilical cords. Also, I divided my husband's military clothes among my three sons, giving each one an item of military apparel. (At that time, my husband was the highest-ranking soldier in Akehama township—equal today to the rank of lieutenant.) When the planes came, my mother-in-law took the tablets; my father-in-law carried the baby, and they and my other children fled to the mountains.

Although our village was never bombed, Uwajima was burned to the ground, and you could see the smoke for miles around.

The authorities asked us to blacken any outside white walls and, shortly before the end of the war, to contribute all items made of gold, silver, and copper to the war effort. We gave up whatever jewelry we had—even the gold from our teeth. We were told we could not have any desires until the war was over and Japan had won.

We never doubted Japan would win the war. When I think of it now, it seems ridiculous, but even after the two atom bombs were dropped, and we knew about Nagasaki and Hiroshima, we continued to believe we would win. Women were trained to use bamboo spears on the enemy. We should have known that a country which had all its able-bodied men at the front, and its women defending themselves with bamboo spears, could not win.

But we thought we could win, because we had had victories in Manchuria and China, after the China Incident [1937], and before that, in the Sino-Japanese and Russo-Japanese Wars. Each night, representatives of every household in the village, including my husband's parents, gathered at the shrine and prayed for victory. I got up early every morning and went to the same shrine, and I also walked to a more distant one to pray for victory and for my husband.

After 1943, we lost all contact with my husband. The few, simply written, censored letters that had come from the Philippines at the beginning of the war no longer came, and we resigned ourselves to his death. A year later, my fourteen-year-old daughter's entire school class at Uwajima girls' school moved to Osaka to work in a munitions plant. A year after that, when the house in which the girls were living burned down during a bomb raid, she returned home.

Toward the end of the war, I began to break under the strain. I developed a severe headache that lasted for one month. Once I fainted. My mother-in-law would not let me take to bed. I do not know what was wrong with me. In those days, medicine was not advanced; we did not know about high blood pressure or anything like that. And we did not have much medicine. But a doctor gave me some medicine and an injection, and after a month, I got better.

AFTER THE WAR

One day in the summer of 1945, town leaders told us there would be an important radio announcement. We were told to gather in the homes of the few families who owned radios. Ours was one of them. Over the scratchy radio we heard the Emperor say we must surrender. Some people could not hear clearly what he was saying; others refused to believe they had heard correctly. If you said, "We've lost," they would get angry and shout, "What fool thing are you saying!"

But I still remember the last words of the Emperor's surrender announcement, when he said the suffering would be too great if we continued fighting. I understood we were defeated. The Emperor said we must unconditionally surrender.

We were probably all in shock. I had believed Japan would win. How could I survive without my husband, without an income, and with six children? We were told the American soldiers would rape all the women. I was distraught. I went to bed for two days. I did not eat. I lost the will to work. My spirit was broken. That was August 15, 1945.

Exactly two months later, on October 15, 1945, my husband walked into our house. He was dirty and emaciated, and his clothes were tattered. It was hard to believe this was the same dignifed officer who had left four years earlier. My mother-in-law and I burst out crying, but I do not remember if any words came from my mouth. Thirty minutes earlier, we had heard that two military men from Akehama were returning home. That is all the advance notice we had been given.

My husband had walked from Uwajima through the mountains to our home. On the way he had stopped at our family gravesite and crawled around in the dark, on his knees, brushing off the grave-markers to see if any members of the family had died in his absence. We later learned he had been on the Marshall Islands. I do not know too much about those two years. When he drinks saké, he talks a bit about the war years. And once or twice a year, he wakes up screaming from a nightmare.

He told me that, when the bombs fell, the Japanese soldiers would leap into fox-holes. If you happened to leap to your right instead of to your left, you might be killed, while those in the fox-holes next to yours survived. Every day he expected to die. They probably ate rats and crabs caught along the beach. Once after returning home, he saw his mother scattering grain feed to the chickens and he said, "If we had had that much food, we could have fed several more soldiers." So I understood how little he had had to eat.

In the days following his return, while I sat silent, my mother-in-law reported to my husband on all that had transpired in his absence. She gave him a complete account of the family's finances. I did not say much to my husband, except I told him about the air raids. Our youngest son, who was by then four years old, did not recognize his father and hid his face with his hands in shyness.

Two months after my husband returned home, he collapsed, spitting up blood. He had a stomach ulcer. He was sick for the next five years. He urgently needed good food, but we had none to eat. In desperation, I set out to buy rice, illegally, from farmers in Onoda. It was spring 1946, and wearing only *zori*, I walked alone for two hours along mountain trails to avoid police surveillance. I bought 35 pounds of rice and wrapped it in cloth in the shape of an infant. Then I carried it on my back, as I would a baby, and returned the same day.

When the rice was all used up, I walked to my younger sister's house in Nomura to get more rice, some noodles (*udon*), and an inferior grade saké. On my way back, I got a ride in a truck. This time the truck was stopped by police, who were very strict in those days. They saw me clutching a bundle, ordered me out of the truck, and let the driver go on.

I was so frightened I felt I would defecate in my pants.

"I'll give you these things I'm carrying—here, take it, take anything you want—but please let me go to the toilet," I said.

They allowed me to use the toilet, and when I returned they questioned me and contacted my sister. She and a friend came to vouch for me. I told the police the food was for my sick husband. They not only let me go, but they let me keep the food, too.

I RECEIVE THE RICE LADLE

One day in January 1947, when she was seventy-two years old, my mother-in-law announced to my husband that she was retiring. From that time on, I received money to spend on food and clothes and I was allowed to do the family cooking. My mother-in-law "passed the rice ladle" to me.

I said to my husband, "You used to get special food from mother. But from now on, if I cook wheat, we'll all eat it." He agreed. From that time on, we all ate the same food. I was thirty-eight years old and had been married for eighteen years.

My husband's parents moved out of the house to the smaller two-room house across the road where we had been living, allowing my family to live alone in the big house. We all ate together, however, until their last few years, when they preferred to cook and eat their own food by themselves. Father died at the age of eighty-nine and mother at the age of ninety-two.

In the last four or five years of her life, my mother-in-law's mind was deranged. She could only remember her children as they were when they were young. If she saw my husband, she would say, "No, that's not my son. That's grandfather." She became completely dependent upon me. If I left her to go on an errand, she would feel lonely. She didn't recognize me, either. She called me "Mother."

After the war, my two brothers began profiting from their lumber business, because wood was greatly in demand for reconstruction. My husband got a job in the Post Office and we were able to live on his salary. When tangerines were introduced to replace potatoes and wheat, I worked in the tangerine groves. During harvest time, men and women alike carried 110 pounds of tangerines on their backs three times a day down the narrow mountain trails. There was only room for you to put one foot in front of the other. We inched along, bent in half under the load. Having taken over the household, I was not able to work much outside the house, however.

We were able to send all our children to high school (*kōtō-gakkō*) in Uwa township. They walked from home to school through the mountains. If they walked fast, it took them an hour and one-half. They left the house at 6 a.m., carrying lunchboxes. School started at 8 a.m. My youngest child—my third son—graduated from Ehime University's School of Agriculture and now owns three vegetable stores in Nagoya. My other two sons are salaried workers in the city and my three daughters are all married.

After my husband began working in the Post Office, I began handling his salary and set aside money for the children's education, but I lacked confidence to make money decisions on my own. It seemed odd to say to my husband, "Here's your money," or "Here's your allowance, mother." Therefore, I had my husband keep his salary and take care of the family's finance. When I needed money to buy something, I would ask him for it. I still lack self-confidence in buying household goods or clothes. Although I know how to buy food—I can tell if fruit is too high because it's out of season, for example—I hesitate to buy myself anything else, even when my children give me money gifts.

OLD AGE

In Japan, one's youth is hard, but old age is pleasant. Japanese old folks, especially in the rural areas, are fortunate. I do not have to work. We live on my husband's army and Post Office pensions—about $1,833 per year—plus money gifts from our children. Next year I shall begin getting about $33 a month as Social Security benefits. I would like to have a job, but there is no work available here. Right now we are engaged in discussions with my eldest son in Matsuyama about whether he will return here to live with us in our old age. The problem is, there is no source of income for him here.

I have many friends in Tawarazu. I belong to the Mothers-in-Law Club. Two of my daughters live nearby and recently I visited my son in Nagoya. Neighbors are kind, too, in the countryside. If they cook something special, they give some to you. I spend peaceful days talking to my friends or watching television.

Only in the last few years have I become *erai*—that is, after my mother-in-law died in 1967 and all my children left the house. Then there were only two of us left, my husband and I. Now I cook what I want to cook and eat what I want to eat, when I want to eat it. I also buy what I want to buy. But my husband still has the last word.

Since the end of the war, young wives have become *erai*. Before the war, men would walk ahead swinging their arms or carrying a small satchel, while their wives staggered behind carrying one suitcase in each hand and a baby on their backs. If it rained, the husband walked ahead carrying the umbrella. This was considered the natural order of things (*atarimae*). One of my husband's most vivid impressions of the Philippines was the way women were exalted. They would sit at outdoor concerts or ballgames holding open parasols over their heads and nobody behind them could see what was going on. Yet nobody complained.

In Japan, a man was expected to act *erai*. It was wrong for him to help his wife in the kitchen, even if she was rushed. My mother-in-law taught my eldest son he must never enter the kitchen. I do not know what my son does now. Both he and his wife work full time. Maybe he helps her with the housework. I notice, however, that he's somewhat inflexible in his character, because my mother-in-law always taught him the "correct" way to do things.

Mothers-in-law, too, have lost their power. I do not always agree with the way my grandchildren are being raised, but I never say anything. I do not feel I have the right to speak out. For example, in the old days, you gave the first offering of food to the mother-in-law.

Now you give it to the children. I can appreciate the reason for this: children need the nutrition more, because they are physically active and still growing. Another example of changes since the end of the war is television. Children have their own programs they want to watch. Most homes in Akehama have two televisions.

I envy young couples today—or rather, I think they have a good lifestyle. But I must say I am grateful to my mother-in-law for helping to raise good children and for appreciating the value of education. I also must admit I feel a certain pride in my past suffering— in the fact that I endured, that I was strong, that I could take it. My friends feel the same way about their own lives. When my mother-in-law died, her brother said to me, "You were the *erai* one."

THE CHANGING LIVES OF WOMEN IN RURAL JAPAN

Unprecedented changes in the Japanese countryside over the past two decades have dramatically transformed the lives of rural women. Improved educational advantages for girls, legal reform of women's status, and labor-saving technology in the home, especially washing machines and indoor running water, have provided the present generation of young farm wives with far greater independence and physical wellbeing than women of Misao Kawabata's generation. In addition, such historical forces as the drastic decline in rural population and the penetration of a cash economy into the once self-sufficient rural areas have opened up new opportunities, while at the same time creating new problems for the three and one-half million Japanese women still actively engaged in farming.[8]

One of the most important changes affecting the lives of farm women lies in the nature of their work. In the space of ten or fifteen years, women who have always worked as supplementary farm laborers have replaced their husbands and sons as major workers and even managers for their families' farms. With an ever-increasing number of rural men engaged in non-farm work, some in cities hundreds of miles from home, Japanese farming, long characterized as "family farming," has become "female farming," and women, who comprise over 50 percent of the agrarian work force, have emerged as the mainstay of Japanese agriculture.[9] Reminiscent of wartime years, some villages, emptied entirely of their male population, are occupied solely by women, the very young, and the very old.

Middle-aged farm women themselves have gone to work at part-time or seasonal jobs in textile factories, on ditch-digging teams, or as orderlies in hospitals, domestic servants in private homes, and hired hands on nearby farms. Over 40 percent of the Japanese farm wives work at some kind of outside employment,[10] earning an average of $600 annually, roughly 12 percent of their family's total income.[11] Significantly, farm women now enjoy the right to keep the money they earn and to spend it as they see fit.

Meanwhile, remarkably new relations between generations have appeared. Teenagers in Western dress rebel sullenly against parental authority; kimono-clad grandmothers, equipped with their own television sets, quietly retire into the background of family life; and women in their forties, caught between two different lifestyles, attempt to carve out new definitions of their place in the emergent farm family. This interplay of clothing styles, tastes in music, food, and television programs, and attitudes toward rural living in general has injected both variety and conflict into the once homogeneous, harmonious Japanese countryside.

The face of the landscape itself has changed. Where once rural Japan was crisscrossed with tiny, fragmented parcels of land, now entire rice plains evoke the rectangular symmetry of the checkerboard; and the few farmers clearing paddies of rocks are dwarfed by the bright yellow mechanical ploughs and heavy dump trucks that are helping to mechanize agrarian production. During the day, in hamlets where women commute daily to seasonal jobs and children to school, a ghost-town atmosphere of silence prevails, broken only by the occasional barking of a neighbor's dog or the squeaking wheels of a rusty baby carriage pushed slowly down the path by an elderly grandmother. Traditional rural Japanese culture, which for the last hundred years seemed impervious to modernizing influences, has not merely changed; in many—though not all—ways it shows signs of disappearing.

This study of contemporary farm women surveys three aspects of their changing lives: their work and attitudes toward their work, their social life outside the home, and their family relationships. Material for the study was collected mainly in Higashiuwa County, Ehime Prefecture, on the island of Shikoku, where, while living with a farm family in the hamlet of Bessho, Uwa township, I conducted interviews and surveys among county farm women over a six-month period in 1974-1975. Women in three of the county's four townships—Uwa, Nomura, and Shirokawa—were engaged mainly in rice cultivation and subsidiary businesses, such as animal husbandry, while female farm workers in the fourth township, Akehama, worked in citriculture.

WOMEN'S WORK IN RURAL JAPAN

The contemporary Japanese farm wife wears three different hats: she is homemaker, farmer, and contributing breadwinner. Her household responsibilities are more extensive than ever before. She not only bears responsibility for cooking, cleaning, laundry, sewing, and childrearing, but she now also is in charge of shopping, budgeting, paying bills, and guiding her children's education. (School graduation ceremonies are attended almost entirely by mothers.) In addition, the Japanese rural wife has certain traditional community responsibilities which are impossible to shirk.

Custom demands that all women in the neighborhood help prepare food for receptions following the funeral or wedding of a member household. Furthermore, each household sends one woman—usually the middle-aged daughter-in-law—to attend regular meetings of the Women's Guild of the Farmers Cooperative Association (*Nōkyō Fujinbu*). Women in the hamlet take turns as vice-head and, the following year, head of the hamlet-based branches of this nationwide women's organization and serve on the executive committee at the township or county level. Bessho farm wives felt it was incumbent upon them to participate in meetings and cooking classes sponsored by the Guild as well as to attend P.T.A. meetings and interviews with their children's teachers, even if attendance meant missing a day's work.

The rural Japanese woman's second major function is farming. "Housewife farming" has been facilitated by revolutionary changes in the technology of Japanese agriculture. Four combines operated by several hired drivers, for example, recently replaced the labor of all the farmers in Bessho, freeing thirty-seven farm households from the arduous labor of harvesting rice.[12] Nevertheless, modern machinery has not liberated the farm woman altogether from a steady routine of farming tasks.

Even where rice farming has been mechanized, much manual labor remains to be done, and this work tends to be done by women. Rice reserved for home consumption, for instance, is dried by spreading it on straw mats in the sun for three consecutive days—a time-consuming process. Similarly, vegetables for the family's food are grown and harvested almost entirely by manual labor. Women may also transplant tobacco seedlings from nursery beds to the fields and help in animal husbandry.

Furthermore, the mechanization of rice cultivation is possible only in those parts of the countryside amenable to large-scale farming. Terraced paddies irrigated on the sides of mountains must still be farmed in age-old ways. The actual work of transplanting rice seedlings into flooded paddy fields and of weeding the paddies throughout the summer is considered women's work in Japan. Years of literally back-breaking labor have produced elderly women with spines so bent they cannot stand upright.

Over 30 percent of present-day Japanese farm women farm on their own, while another 30 percent farm in equal amounts with other

members of the family.[13]   Although children are no longer required
to help with family farming, the farm wife may be assisted in her
work by her husband's parents. The Japanese call this work pattern
"three *chan* farming" (*san-chan nōgyō*); that is, farming done by the
three "chan"—*ojīchan* (grandfather), *obāchan* (grandmother), and
okāchan (mother). Because middle-aged women as well as men in
the rural areas have become part of the industrial work force in recent years, however, farming (and babysitting) by the elderly alone
has emerged as another common pattern. One eighty-year-old woman in Bessho tends the vegetable fields and cares for her great-
granddaughter, while the child's mother, father, and grandmother
work at outside jobs. With less than 40 percent of the average
farm family's income derived from farming, and the rest dependent
on wages, agriculture in Japan has become a secondary occupation
for women, the elderly, or both.[14]

A third and increasingly more time-consuming aspect of the farm
woman's work routine is her outside job. Of the thirty-seven farm
households in Bessho, only a few contain women whose sole tasks
center around the home. The female members of the other households all work, mainly at part-time, unskilled jobs near their homes.
Average daily wages for women in the county—lower than men's
salaries for equivalent jobs—are approximately $6.60 for ditch diggers
and $5 for textile workers. Hours are 8 a.m. to 5 p.m., with an
hour break for lunch and two rest breaks during the day.

Women have begun to work for a number of reasons. The most important reason is the farm family's growing   dependence on the
cash economy. Caught between government-fixed rice prices on the
one hand, and an annual rate of inflation that runs between 20 and
30 percent on the other hand, only about 15 percent of the nation's
five million farm households can live by farming alone.[15] Women
as well as men are working to supplement farm incomes.

In addition, farm women everywhere in Japan, exposed to urban
goods and lifestyles on television screens, are asking for more out
of life than their parents' generation had: they want western ready-
made clothes for themselves, advanced education for their children,
and processed foods for their tables. Their children want bread for
breakfast instead of rice, and jeans (called g-pants) instead of *mompe*
or baggy pantaloons, the traditional work clothes of the Japanese
farm woman. Such demands can only be met with cash on hand.

Mechanization of agriculture at once aided and necessitated the
farm woman's search for outside employment. While labor-saving
machinery liberated women from the most demanding aspects of
farming, the purchase of such equipment placed an additional drain
on the family's resources. Female labor has been tapped to help

defray the cost of the new equipment. Commenting on this seeming irony, one woman wrote, "We have put in machines to do our work, and we must work to pay for the machines."[16]

ATTITUDES TOWARD WORK

Outside work, especially when combined with farming, imposes a great drain on the energies of the farm woman. Articles published in local women's magazines bear testimony to the psychological and physical strains experienced by working farm wives. "What is this thing called material happiness?" one woman wrote. "When I return home from the factory, farm work is waiting. I have no time to rest body or soul. If only I had at least some time on Sundays, to bring the family together and go out for a drive, with only house-work and the laundry to do. . . ."[17]

Women worry that their outside jobs, which may take them away from their homes for much of the day, will have an adverse effect on their children. "I've often heard my mother say that [women] used to work even at night. But our childhood memories are of playing with mother or of helping her. I wonder what sort of memo-ries will remain for today's children when they grow up. . . ."[18]

Women also express concern that their outside jobs will disrupt their relationships with their husbands. The following quote expresses the conflict between the housewife ideal and the reality of the work-ing farm woman's life:

> When a couple works together [in the fields], they can understand each other's hardships and pleasures, but it is difficult to understand another's feelings when you work in different places. . . . After you return home from work, you have housework to do. You should be womanly, but after working outside as hard as a man, it is not easy suddenly to be-come womanly. Many times when I return home tired, I forget to say even a word of comfort to my husband. When the woman, too, is busy, she often carelessly neglects even to straighten up the house. In this way, she hurts her husband's feelings. When he reproaches her, she flies into a rage. At such times, she should apologize, but neglect-ing the usual good manners [lit., deference] between husband and wife, she wants to reply, "I haven't been playing around all day, you know." This hurts his feelings.[19]

Financial insecurity is the constant enemy of women whose families rely mainly on farming for a living. The lack of fixed work hours or of weekends off are also complaints they frequently voice. ("The farmer rests only on rainy days.") Some women consider farming "dirty." Young women are reluctant to marry into farm families, not only because they lack experience in farming, but also because they do not want to become the wife of a *dekaseginin*—an absentee farmer, who may be away from home half the year working in a distant city.20 The "bride famine" in the poorer agrarian areas is so acute, young men in search of wives must rely on "bridal banks" run by officials of the local Farmers Cooperative Association.

Embracing as she has the housewife ideal, the farm woman wants what she feels she has been deprived of—the chance to stay at home. Farm wives would prefer doing only domestic chores, such as learning new recipes or knitting. For all the women I spoke to, the ideal husband was the white collar, "salary man." The farm wife's dream is to be "just a housewife."

SOCIAL LIFE

Customs guiding the social life of farming communities, in particular those relating to sexual segregation, seem more resistant to change than any other aspect of rural Japanese life. Although men and women work together in paddies and on ditch-digging teams, they remain separated on most other occasions. As in the past, women do not attend hamlet council meetings, they do not participate in harvest festival activities, and they do not go to the various parties and celebrations to which their husbands are invited.

Sexual segregation of Japanese farmers extends even to man and wife. A couple's three-day honeymoon trip usually represents the first and last time they will travel together as a couple. Vacation trips, limited to two or three days per year at most for busy, financially hard-pressed farm couples, are taken in groups of the same sex. Women travel with fellow factory workers on trips paid for by their employer, or they may join trips arranged by the local branch of the Farm Women's Guild. Men travel in groups of four or five friends.

Even "progressive" couples may have difficulty transcending the "embarrassment" they feel when they appear in public together. Thus, the forty-year-old wife of a socialist party politician drives her husband to his political meeting, but waits for him outside the meeting room while he confers with a male-only group of constituents inside. Couples in their twenties who are experimenting with sexual desegregation of their social life appear uncomfortable at parties, and the women usually remain silent. The only occasions when married couples may legitimately appear together are the weddings and funerals of relatives. On other formal occasions, such as hamlet funerals, women don white aprons over dark slacks and serve as caterers, while their husbands, dressed in Western suits, white shirts, and ties, attend as honored guests.

Sexual segregation is less rigid before marriage. Nevertheless, although young people have opportunities to socialize with members of the

opposite sex in school classrooms and hamlet-based youth organizations, modified versions of the arranged marriage are still popular
among parents as well as young people themselves, because it is commonly believed that marriage partners chosen by one's parents in
consultation with respected, experienced go-betweens, have greater
chance of success. Moreover, in remote farm regions, where unmarried men and women are scarce, young people have no choice but
to rely on marriage brokers.

Despite their continued exclusion from most social events outside
the home, farm women today have acquired greater exposure to
the world beyond their homes through television, outside jobs,
shopping in town, and, if they are older, visits to their children in
the cities. Women in Bessho have more opportunities than their
husbands to develop their talents or to educate themselves through
numerous women's groups. In addition to the Women's Guild,
which was established in 1947 for the express purpose of elevating
the position of farm women and which offers cooking and nutrition
classes and leadership experience, there are age-based social clubs
for young married women and mothers-in-law, as well as clubs
formed to study flower-arrangement or *haiku*. While some of these
groups, such as Bessho's song club, are open to men—providing an
exception to the rule about sexual segregation—women are more apt
to take advantage of them. These new experiences help to counter
the farm woman's traditional isolation.
Moreover, the exclusion of women from hamlet functions shows
some evidence of breaking down. For no other reason than demo-
graphic default, women have gained admission into the hamlet
councils to represent their households in place of absent men, and
recently young girls in a fishing village in Akehama were allowed to
carry one of the festival floats, because not enough young boys were
available.

FAMILY RELATIONSHIPS

It is in the area of daily, face-to-face relationships within the home,
rather than in social life outside the home, that we can detect real
evidence of change in the farm woman's status. The change that
most affects rural housewives on a day-to-day level is what they
call *hatsugen-ken*—the right to speak their minds, to express themselves, to have an opinion and, what is more, to have their opinion
followed. The term also suggests freedom to fight with husbands
and mothers-in-law. Young women feel freer, in essence, to complain or nag, often in a distinctive whining tone, until their husbands
agree—or hit them.

A deeply inculcated respect for parental authority in the past inhi-
bited wives from openly arguing with their husbands in the presence

of his parents. Moreover, economically dependent as she and her husband both were on his parents, the daughter-in-law had no choice but to suppress her own opinions and emotions.

In present-day Japan, by contrast, husband and wife may both have cash incomes independent of the older generation of parents. Women no longer turn over their wages to their mothers-in-law or depend on them for their spending money; rather, they retain their wages and some women also manage their husband's wages, doling out an allowance to him. Possession of her own money is an entirely new experience for the younger farm woman, who is called upon to make many more consumer decisions than were necessary in the poorer and economically more self-sufficient lives of older farm generations. For this reason, education of farm women in consumer spending, budgeting, and record-keeping has become a major goal of the Women's Guild.

Further evidence of the increased independence of young and middle-aged couples is the fact that older people in Bessho have begun dividing their rice land while they are still alive. An heir may receive legal title to the land even before the death of his father. Although the two generations continue to farm together, the son enjoys a farm income separate from his parents, and this economic benefit, however small, accrues to his wife as well.[21]

Farm residence patterns, too, reflect younger couples' desire for greater independence. Instead of living together with their parents for the first ten or fifteen years of their married lives, young couples, whenever space and finances permit, occupy their own dwellings immediately upon marriage. The opportunity to "live apart" from the older generation—even though this means no more than sleeping in her own small one- or two-room house next door or across the road from her in-laws—can be a crucial factor affecting the wellbeing of a young wife.

At the same time, however, changes in the relative economic dependence of the young couple on their parents has also resulted in the decline in the status of women over fifty years of age, who recognize that they have lost their power to dominate their sons' wives, and who worry that they will not be cared for in their old age. As long as one son agrees to remain on the land, the parents have some security for their old age. The major problem confronting farmers of all ages, however, is the absence of heirs willing to remain on the farms, as long as the big cities promise higher incomes and greater financial security.

It is the generation of rural Japanese in their early forties for whom this problem is most pressing. They are the first members of their family to be educated in high school under the new democratic curriculum. Reluctant to impose strict discipline on their young-sters, eager to further their children's economic earning power through education, and inclined to encourage greater independence than they themselves had, middle-aged parents today sympathize with their off-springs' feelings of alienation from the land and their attraction to urban lifestyles. Witnesses to the declining rural population and sen-sitive to their children's aspirations, this transitional generation of Japanese in the countryside today views with a mixture of relief and regret the prospect of becoming their family's last generation of farmers.

NOTES

[1] Generous support from the Japan Foundation enabled the author to conduct research and field work for this study in 1974-1975.

[2] Under the pre-World War II educational system, all children attended six years of "com-pulsory education" (*gimu kyōiku*) between the ages of six and twelve. Afterward, children had a choice of attending school for two more years (*kōtō-shōgakkō*) or of enrolling in a five-year middle school course (*chūgakkō*) for boys or a four-year middle school course (*jogakkō*) for girls. Only the wealthy could afford these longer courses of study.

[3] The day before the ceremony, which was held at night, was spent on preparations, and the day afterward was reserved for a formal visit to the bride's family.

[4] Depending on the context, the word *erai* may mean powerful, superior, dominating, great (in a moral sense), strong, eminent, etc.

[5] A go-between, and the ceremony of *sansan kudo* (three rounds of toasts), made the mar-riage official, even without entering the name in the *koseki*. Families often waited until the daughter-in-law became pregnant before officially registering her name, however.

[6] Yukie Kawabata today is the wife of Tsunetoshi Tanaka, a Socialist Party politician and former Diet representative from Higashiuwa-*gun*, Ehime Prefecture. She and her family now live in the main house with her husband's mother, while Misao and her husband live in the detached house.

[7] Today five men work to pull in a catch of about 350 lbs., using an engine to drag the net.

[8] Women's and Minors' Bureau, *The Status of Women in Japan*, 1974, p. 10. The number is based on 1973 figures. Women employed in agriculture and forestry represent 17 per-cent of the total number of employed women. The total population engaged in agricul-ture is under ten million persons or approximately five million households, whereas until twenty years ago, there were fourteen million persons engaged in full-time farming. See *Nōkyō fujinbu techō* [Handbook of the Women's Guild of the Farmers Cooperative As-sociation, 1974], p. 121, and Akasaka Kazuo, "The Changing Farm Scene," p. 14.

[9] Women's and Minors' Bureau, 1974, p. 28.

[10] Fujin ni kansuru shomondai chōsa kaigi, ed., *Gendai Nihon josei no ishiki to kōdō* [Con-temporary Japanese Women's Attitudes and Behavior], p. 267. By contrast, a 1965 sur-vey showed 1,800,000 farm women, or 25 percent of all farm women, were employed in some kind of work outside the home. See Hashimoto Reiko, *Nōka fujin no mondaiten* [Some Questions Concerning Farm Women], in Matsushita Kei'ichi, ed., *Gendai fujin mondai nyūmon* [An Introduction to the Problems of Modern Women], p. 220.

[11] Fujin ni kansuru shomondai chōsa kaigi, p. 269, reports that 40 percent of employed farm women earned less than $330 and 60 percent earned less than $660 in 1972-1973. The farm household's total average annual income in 1971 was $5,043, with $3,490 de-rived from nonfarm sources. Thus, we can estimate that the farm woman's earnings con-stitute 12 percent of her family's total income and 16 percent of her family's income from nonfarm sources. For figures on farm income, see Akasaka Kazuo, p. 14.

[12]The author acquired much valuable information about farming in Japan from Mr. Shōichi Utsunomiya of Bessho, the leader of the Bessho machine cooperative.

[13]Fujin ni kansuru shomondai chōsa kaigi, p. 265. The smaller the landholding, the more likely that women will farm alone.

[14]Of the approximately 5 million households in 1970 engaged in farming, only about 830,000 specialized in farming, whereas 4.5 million farm households engaged in outside jobs as well as farming. In this latter category, 66 percent derived their income mainly from nonfarm sources. See Rōdōshō Fujin-shōnenkyoku, ed., Fujin no genjō [The Status of Women], p. 71. Since 1963, when the ratio of farm to nonfarm income was equal, nonfarm income steadily grew in importance, so that by 1971, it represented more than twice the amount of farm income. The author is grateful to Ms. Nagata Miho of the Uwa branch of the Farmers Extension Bureau (Nokyō Kairyō Fukyūshō) for providing these figures.

[15]Akasaka Kazuo, p. 15; Ehime-ken nen sekai nōringyō sensasu [Ehime Prefecture Annual World Farm and Forestry Census], 1971, p. 4. Sixty percent of farm women surveyed nationwide in 1972-1973 said they worked in order to pay for the basic necessities of life, while only 8.5 percent worked because they had more free time. Eighty percent of the farm women interviewed expressed the desire to continue working. Asked what they were living for (ikigai), women overwhelmingly answered "my children." See Fujin ni kansuru shomondai chōsa kaigi, p. 271.

[16]Minori (Harvest), no. 3 (1973), p. 20.

[17]Ibid., p. 22.

[18]Ibid., p. 43.

[19]Ibid., pp. 43-44.

[20]In Nomura township, one out of fifteen persons is a dekaseginin. In Tanisugi, one of the six villages comprising Nomura, 8 percent of the population of 1,500 is dekaseginin.

[21]One elderly couple in Bessho has turned over all their land to their son and receive an allowance from him. Another couple has given 60 percent of their holdings to their son, even though he is employed full time in his own business. Although their holdings are small, other families have split title to their land into two portions. By law, the land must be divided equally among a man's wife and all his children, regardless of sex. In practice, however, one son, usually but not necessarily the eldest, inherits all the land, after acquiring written releases from the other heirs in exchange for his verbal promise to care for the parents.

CHAPTER
3
WOMEN IN FACTORIES

In 1945, at the end of World War II, 44 percent of Japan's factories had been completely destroyed; the remaining were out-dated or near collapse.[1] At that time Japan lamented the scarcity of its natural resources. But today, it boasts that its major natural resource is a human one—the Japanese people. Indeed, Japan's industrial workers have constituted a formidable force in the country's rise as an economic power. Robert Cole, recognizing the importance of understanding this force, studied factory workers for four years in Japan. He published his results in 1971 but acknowledged:

> A major cleavage exists between male and female workers. The treatment of female workers and their work cycle is different enough from that of male workers to demand special attention, especially since discussions of blue-collar workers generally deal with male blue-collar workers.[2]

Today one-third of Japan's fourteen million factory workers are women. More than half are married, and many have children. Who are these five million women? What are their roles, attitudes, aspirations, problems?

HISTORICAL DEVELOPMENT

Japanese farm women, always contributing to the support of their families, traditionally worked in the fields along with the men. They also developed handicraft skills to supplement family incomes. Weaving, a skill especially developed by women, has often been romantically portrayed in the folklore of Japan. But a tragic tale began in

51

the 1870s when Japan industrialized this art. Young girls were forced to leave their families to work in factories from twelve to sixteen hours a day under stark conditions and to live in squalid over-crowded dormitories.

In the 1860s a silk blight swept Europe, increasing demand for oriental silk. The Japanese government readily responded to this opportunity to increase its foreign capital. Already there were small private silk factories in Japan, but in 1872, the government established the first large modern silk-reeling factory at Tomioka, in Gunma Prefecture. A French male supervisor and four French female technicians were brought from France to teach Japanese factory girls the operation of the French equipment. A month before the factory was to open, the government began recruiting Japanese girls, aged thirteen to twenty-five. But the recruiters were confronted by an unforeseen problem. It was rumored that anyone who would work at the Tomioka factory would have their blood sucked and body oils squeezed out by the foreigners.[3] This rumor was taken so seriously that the recruiters were unsuccessful in enlisting even one girl. Finally, the samurai and government officials dutifully sent their own daughters to the factory. One of the first to volunteer was Eio Wada, a daughter of a samurai from Shinshu, an area in mountainous Nagano Prefecture where cultivation of silk cocoons was widespread. She recorded her experience in a diary published in 1931, *Tomioka Nikki* [The Tomioka Diary]. Eiko related that she was able to endure the long hours, sweltering heat from the steam in the factory, and the humiliating treatment only because of her conviction that she must quickly learn the necessary skills in order to be of service to her country. While the French male supervisor was paid the equivalent of $600 a month and the French female technicians from $56 to $80 a month, the Japanese girls received from $1 to $1.75 for the same period.[4]

Because the government discontinued stipends to the samurai class in 1876, many samurai daughters supplemented family incomes by working in factories. In 1878, 40 percent of women in the Tomioka factory were daughters of the formerly prestigious samurai.[5] However, the majority of female workers in the many spinning and weaving factories that were rapidly being established in various parts of Japan were poorly educated farm girls. Thus, like the first weaving factory in Nagaoka in Niigata Prefecture, many factories began teaching the girls basic reading, writing, and arithmetic as well as the technical skills of mechanical weaving, sewing, and dyeing. A missionary in Japan, Sidney L. Gulick, reported in 1915:

> As to the education of factory girls, it is stated that out of 1,000, the number that had completed the required number of years of schooling (six) was 450, while 385 were entirely without education. Out of 1,000 girls, 453 were orphans . . . 611 came from farmers' homes,

166 from those of fishermen, and 55 from merchant homes, the remaining 168 being scattered. Factory girls earn and can save more than almost any other class. The average earnings per month are stated to be $4.67. The girl pays $1.20 for food, which is less than the actual cost, the factory providing the balance, namely $1.30. The average girl sends home fifty cents per month.[6]

Many of the factories did not purchase expensive foreign equipment, but relied on the dexterity and patience of the hard-working farm girls. *Jokō Aishi* [The Pathetic History of Female Factory Workers] by Wakizō Hosoi, himself a textile worker for fifteen years, was published in 1925. This book was significant in exposing to the general public the squalid conditions in the factories and dormitories, the cruel treatment suffered by factory girls, and the high rate of disease and suicide.

Masano Hayashi, now in her eighties, worked in a factory in Kurashiki, Okayama Prefecture, during her girlhood. She revealed her life and attitudes in an interview to Kōichi Ōtani, a Japanese journalist. Born in 1890 to a poor merchant family, Masano was the first of three daughters and was sent to work in a textile factory at the age of twelve, after completing four years of elementary school. Although her parents could not read, they signed a contract and a company recruiter advanced them money. Masano was eager to help her impoverished family. There were two working shifts of twelve hours each, from 6 to 6, with two fifteen-minute breaks and thirty minutes for lunch.[7] Once every ten days she had a day off. She learned to sew kimono during her time off. The inspectors were very strict, the food poor, and the rate of tuberculosis and other diseases high. For twelve hours' labor, she earned only enough to buy one cup of rice. But she didn't mind working; in fact, she didn't think the circumstances were difficult. She simply accepted the situation as the standard for the times. After all, women on the farms had to work much harder. Moreover, she enjoyed working. What Masano resented, however, was the name-calling by the townspeople who were financially better off than she was. It hurt Masano deeply to be called "dirty factory flea" or "textile snake." Like many factory girls, she gave all her earnings to her parents.

When Masano was eighteen, her parents "adopted" a young man to become her husband and carry on the name of their ancestors. Because he would come to live with their family as an "adopted son," she did not have to quit work and move away. She stressed during the interview that it was natural for women from poor families to continue working after marriage.

She quit the factory at twenty-four to take care of her growing family, but continued working by selling potatoes and beans. At the age of thirty (1920), she put her children in a nursery and returned to the textile factory.[8] After working an additional three years in the factory, her thrifty habits enabled her to open a bean curd shop in her home. Although she rose at 1 a.m. every morning, she found the work lighter than that in the factory. Masano gave birth to eleven children, but less than half of them survived.

Even now, as an octogenarian, Masano has not lost her zest for work. She is supporting herself by selling magazines, sweets, and bus tickets.[9]

As Masano's father was a vegetable-oil merchant, they lived in the town. But the majority of girls working in the factories were from farms. Shigemi Yamamoto interviewed many of these women and vividly described their lives in *A, A, Nomugi Tōge* [Nomugi Mountain Pass], published in 1969:

> For the boys the military; for the girls the factory;
> We reel the threads for our country.
>
> I began learning to reel the thread at twelve years old.
> I was thin as the thread itself.
>
> Trying not to tangle or break the thread,
> I worked until late at night.
>
> When we finish reeling the thread, we shall climb the mountain pass.
> It will be like a dream when we come to the first village.

This song was one that hundreds if not thousands of young mountain girls hummed when they became too exhausted to sing as they crossed snow-covered mountain paths in late autumn and early spring. After the autumn harvest, they would start for the silk-reeling factory in groups of fifty to a hundred. Their hair was arranged in the neat *momoware* traditionally worn by girls in their teens. On their feet they wore straw sandals and wrapped their legs with a red cotton cloth that gave support and protection to their legs for the three-day to one-week hike. The occasion was somber. The trip along the narrow mountain path through the Japan Alps is dangerous indeed. They tied themselves together so that none would slip off the narrow icy path down the side of the mountain. Also, in an icy blizzard, being tied together would prevent anyone from getting lost.

Why did they submit to low pay, long hours in the factory,[10] poor food, and unsanitary, overcrowded dormitories? First of all, contracts had been signed and money advanced to their parents by company representatives. But there were other reasons for working. Yamamoto, who interviewed many of these women in 1968, discovered that most of them found their work in the factories "more enjoyable than the work on the farm." It gave them an opportunity to know something of the world outside their isolated, impoverished farming villages. Moreover, for many of these women the most memorable and satisfying moment was returning home and giving

their poverty-stricken parents their earnings. This money would ensure their parents being able to survive the next winter should the
harvest be poor. The girls also often received some silk material to
make a kimono for their fathers or future husbands.

How important were the labor and sacrifices of these women to the
economic growth of their nation? In 1930, Japan had surpassed
Italy and China to become the world's leader in silk production, accounting for 34 percent of the world's silk. Silk also represented
one-third of all Japanese exports, thereby providing necessary foreign
currency to a country which was spending vast amounts building a
modern military machine, developing industries, importing expensive
equipment, and paying substantial sums to foreign advisors.

In the late 1930s and early 1940s, as the Manchurian invasion and
the Pacific War developed, more and more male workers were enlisted in the military, and industry came to rely on the women's
patriotic corps to provide replacements in the factories. From 1930
to 1940 the number of women employed in manufacturing grew
from 3,315 to 96,339. The number of women manufacturing weapons
grew from 888 in 1930 to 52,018 in 1940.11 The labor of these
girls was encouraged by such mottoes as "When you feel exhausted
from your work, think of the labor of the Imperial Army," "We
will work till we win for the emperor and our country," and "Cultivate womanly virtue." Also many high school students had to
leave their studies and work in the factories.

It was at this time, 1943, that Yoshiko Takagi, at the age of thirteen, began her thirty-seven-year career in the factory. Yoshiko described her career in a recent interview.

Yoshiko was eager to learn and had hoped to continue to high school.
But she was compelled to relinquish her dream and face the realities
and agonies of war. Yoshiko was the second oldest of seven brothers
and sisters. Soon after her father died of an illness, her older brother
was killed in the Philippines. Then her youngest brother died of disease. At thirteen, in order to support her mother and remaining
brothers and sisters, she began working at a flour mill. During the
war the factory was converted into a manufacturing plant for air-
plane parts. Yoshiko recalls high school students taking the places
of men sent to the war.

Yoshiko remained single, dedicating her life to her work and eventually becoming the only forewoman in one of the largest food industry companies in Japan. In spite of her dedication and profes-
sionalism, she suffered sex discrimination. As a woman, she was
made to retire at forty-seven, ten years earlier than men. For a
woman who found freedom, achievement, and pride in her work,
this was cruel. Much more readily she accepted the difference in

salary, which grew proportionally greater the longer she worked.

Both males and females received equal pay in the early stages of their development. But women's wages increased only minimally, so that by the age of thirty, a man's salary was double that of a woman's.[12] In prewar Japan the justification for this discrimination was that if women were paid the same as men, not only would they be more highly motivated to work, but also the power and prestige of the "head of the family" would be endangered. By association, this situation would weaken the traditional position of the emperor as head of the nation.

In December of 1945 the minister of welfare issued the following statement: "There are about 13,240,000 demobilized soldiers, and every effort must be made to return them to their previous jobs and at the same time to have women with jobs go back to their homes and be replaced by men. . . ."[13]

Thus, happiness for the Japanese woman was traditionally equated with home and family. More specifically, a woman was expected to be a good, obedient wife and a devoted mother. She would work until marriage but was encouraged to marry early and give birth to many children who would add to the human resources of the country. During the Pacific War there was a well-known slogan, "Give birth, increase the population, five children to a family." But when cheap labor was needed, married women were brought back into the labor market. They sacrificed personal desires and endured great difficulties, humbly submitting to serving their family, superiors, and country.[14]

On August 14, 1945, the emperor announced the surrender of Japan. Soon after, the seven-year American occupation began. On October 2, 1945, MacArthur recommended that the new constitution guarantee women the right to vote and run for public office, and that it ensure laborers the right to organize. (Promptly the first postwar women's labor union was formed.) On December 3, 1946, the new constitution also recognized new equalities for women, including equal rights in marital decisions and the right to inherit. Equal wages for equal work for men and women were written into the Labor Standards Law (art. 4), promulgated in 1947. This law also limited working hours and set minimum rest days (art. 61); prohibited work late at night (art. 62); restricted the employment of women in dangerous occupations (art. 63); banned work in mines by women (art. 64); ensured maternity leave (arts. 19 and 65); allowed provisions for a woman to request time to nurse her baby twice a day (art. 66); and recognized the right for a monthly menstruation leave (art. 67). Japan was the first country to grant a menstrual leave.

Thus, in a very short time, liberties which women in Japan had been advocating for decades were legally sanctioned. But rising postwar inflation and unemployment relegated this new freedom to paper. In 1947, fewer women were employed in factories (1,459,326) than were in 1920 (1,569,451). The number of women employed in the manufacturing of machinery in 1950 was only one-sixth of those employed three years earlier.[15] More women were being employed as maids. Prostitution was also rapidly increasing.[16] Thus more women were forced to return to the home, often to subservient positions in the traditional family system.

Postwar Japan was suffering not only the depression of defeat, but also spiraling inflation and general unemployment. In February 1949, Joseph Dodge, the president of the Bank of Detroit and an economic expert, proposed a new economic recovery plan to combat inflation. The plan temporarily deepened the recession, but two months later the foreign exchange rate of $1=¥360 was established. In June 1950 the Korean War began, and by March 1952 Japan was permitted by the Allied Occupation authority to manufacture military weapons. This stimulated the economy, and from 1950 to 1955 the number of women engaged in the following industries doubled: fabricated metal products (27,025 to 52,111); apparel and other finished textile products (84,613 to 171,352); furniture and fixtures (8,712 to 19,520); paper products (21,508 to 42,726); leather and leather goods (6,470 to 15,596); electrical machinery, equipment, and supplies (37,564 to 76,987).[17]

In recent years, since 1960, while the number of women engaged in textiles has remained stable, the number of women employed in assembling machines, especially electrical machines, has greatly increased (Table I).

Table I

Women Employed in Assembling Machines

	1955	1960	1965	1970	1974[18]
General machinery	43,804	92,330	138,597	199,125	214,000
Electrical machinery	76,987	253,330	353,248	662,895	640,000
Machinery for transportation	29,672	61,440	87,712	138,460	156,000
Precision machinery (cameras, watches, etc.)	27,142	54,580	85,761	114,600	123,000

An important postwar development was the legislative change of the family system, creating legal equality among the members.[19] However, this democratic change was not readily accepted by all Japanese. Efforts by conservatives in 1954 to revise the constitution stimulated protests from educators, social critics, and various women's groups who feared that such a revision would destroy the rights and freedom of women. Yet, a 1957 public opinion poll conducted by the prime minister's office indicated that many people did want to reestablish the traditional family system. They thought the father should be the powerful head of the house and his authority should pass on to the eldest son. The eldest son should be responsible for taking care of and providing for his parents, and continue as the head of the house. This opinion was especially prevalent among the less educated and those in rural areas.[20]

Although many factory workers were reluctant to accept the democratic family system, some women factory workers were beginning to envision what the constitution could mean for them. In the summer of 1954 women workers in a textile plant began to protest job injustices that they had taken for granted for years. They struck in pursuit of human dignity. Akiko Miyamoto participated in this first protest in the name of human rights.

Akiko came to the factory after completing middle school in 1952. Her father was a farmer. She was quick and efficient in learning her skills. She had been raised to accept whatever she was given, so she didn't object to being crowded with fourteen other girls in a fifteen-tatami-mat room, or to poor food, or to the over-strictness of inspectors. She was content with a monthly salary of ¥4,000, although half of it was retained for food. She managed to send ¥500 home each month. She wished that the quality of education offered by the company were better, but she had been taught that a woman shouldn't be ambitious.

Two years later she saw her first movie, a story about how women college students had protested feudalistic school rules which infringed on their human rights. The movie made Akiko think about her situation, about letters that had been opened and read before the inspector had passed them on to her, about the weekly obligatory recitation of Buddhist sutras, about the formal greetings she had to give to her senior colaborers, about the ridicule by the inspector if she chose to enjoy her free time with a boy. Akiko had taken these practices for granted, but she began to question them as violations of the rights and freedom of the worker. So she, too, participated in the dangerous and violent strike that declared the worker was not the property of the company.

Girls from neighboring textile factories immediately joined the fight, which soon attracted international attention. These young women were able to withstand humiliation and physical violence to win recognition of their rights. Within six months, the company agreed to respect the freedom of its female workers.

Akiko continued working actively in the union. In 1960 she married another factory worker, but continued working three additional years until the birth of their first son. To Akiko, realizing and fighting for her rights had had a profound affect on her life.[21]

In the last fifteen years, there has been a great increase in the number of women working in factories—from 3,125,419 in 1960 to 4,737,000 in 1974 [22]—while the number of women working in fishing or agriculture has decreased. In 1947, 8,609,003 women were engaged in farming and fishing; today, only 3,478,000.

Past president of Tokyo University and authority on labor, Professor Kazuo Ōkōchi speaks of the importance of the change to the family structure in *Reimeiki no Nihon Rōdō Undō* [Dawn of the Labor Movement in Japan]. In the fishing and agricultural areas, the woman helps the husband or father directly with the work. She is under his supervision. This situation provides the basis for a feudal relationship, the traditional family system where the male is the head of the household. When the father died, the oldest son inherited his authority and property. With women decreasing in these work categories but increasing in factories, they can be expected to become more independent, thus causing erosion in the traditional family system.

Another recent but important development in Japan is the use of women labor as part-time workers. The word "part-timer" first appeared in an advertisement recruiting salesgirls for a department store in 1954. The term applies to anyone who works less than eight hours a day. Part-timers are often relieved an hour earlier so that they can return home, welcome the children from school, and begin preparing dinner. Usually part-time workers do not enjoy benefits or promotion, and their hourly wage is less than that of full-time employees.[23] But such work provides women with families a way to help with family expenses without having the work interfere with their responsibilities as mothers and wives.

In summary, girls employed in the early textile industry were usually from poor farming regions. Girls were sent not only to contribute to the nation and the family finances, but also so they could learn basic skills and have contact with the new society. Their parents had signed contracts and received advance pay from recruiters who visited their homes. The factories were located in areas where the climate or geographical features were agreeable to the product. For example, silk cocoons needed a dry, cool climate and a source of mulberry leaves. The factories needed a source of water for the steam used in reeling the silk.

The girls lived in dormitories, working long hours with low wages, which they sent to their parents. When they married, they moved to the homes of their husbands and helped with the work on the farm. The status of a young wife in the family was the lowest position: she had no part in family decisions and her main role was to serve the members of the family.

During the war years many high school girls worked in the factories; perhaps only an hour or two was devoted to school instruction. During the war, most girls working in factories were young and un-married whereas more middle-aged, married women are engaged as full-time and part-time workers in modern Japan.

CONTEMPORARY TRENDS

The change in the life style of the average Japanese woman within the last twenty-five years has resulted in an increase in her leisure time. For example, although she stays in school longer and marries later, she has fewer children—two—so she is younger when the last child enters school. As the retirement age is extended, she is likely to be older when her husband retires. Her life span has increased to seventy-six years, the longest in the world. She has more mechan-ical conveniences and thus needs to spend less time doing household chores.

How do women utilize this new free time? Many women spend a regrettable amount of it lost in indecision. More and more women, however, are taking jobs. Because most of these women have not been prepared to work and have no marketable skills, they often take a job in a nearby factory or workshop.

Like male industrial workers, female factory workers have usually completed only middle school (nine years of education). Lately there has been a growing demand for high school graduates. Today 90 percent of Japanese girls graduate from high school, but they can easily find a job working in an office or elsewhere. They pre-fer these jobs to factory work, for which the pay is low and the work generally not appealing. Therefore, although factories, too, prefer younger girls, they are forced to hire older women with less education who tend to continue working longer, increasing the num-ber of middle-aged women working full-or part-time in factories.

To enable the reader to gain a clear impression of the types of in-dustries in which women are primarily employed, their salaries, and length of service, Table II is provided.

Many women are also finding part-time positions. This represents one of the most rapid and spectacular changes affecting women in factories. In 1972, there were some 383,000 part-time female in-dustrial workers. A year later their number had increased 77.8 per-cent to 681,000.[24] The average part-time worker is thirty-nine years old, works seven hours a day, twenty-two days a month, and

Table II

Salary and Length of Service of Female Operatives[25]

Industry	Sex Ratio	No. Employees (thousands)	Average Age	Length of Service	Monthly Salary
Textile	F	1,385	29.9	5.8	52,500¥
	M	766	35.3	9.0	96,200¥
Food and tobacco	F	518	39.4	5.6	45,300¥
	M	611	35.3	7.9	86,400¥
Electrical machinery	F	640	29.9	4.1	52,300¥
	M	915	30.8	7.3	91,900¥
Transport equipment	F	156	43.3	4.4	61,500¥
	M	934	37.1	9.3	111,300¥
Precision machinery	F	123	30.5	4.5	53,200¥
	M	197	32.0	7.8	87,500¥

earns ¥224 an hour.[26]   Job insecurity, lack of benefits, conflict with full-time workers, and job dissatisfaction are among the problems she encounters.

Another trend affecting women is the relocation of factories from the cities to the country. The price of land and availability of cheap labor are among factors encouraging industries to make this change. As a result, more farm women are finding employment in factories. During March and October, they are allowed time off for planting and harvesting.[27] The number of farm women employed in occupations other than farming, to the extent that farming is considered their secondary occupation, has tripled to 1,534,950 since 1965. (For the same period, rural male employees increased less dramatically from 2,513,221 to 3,388,480.)[28]

Only one-fifth of factory women are unionized. Half of these women are disproportionally employed in the textile industry. The leadership of the textile unions is dominated by men, however. While young workers feel the unions are not functioning effectively, union activists are frustrated by female factory workers' poor awareness of their rights.[29]

Throughout the nation, there are sixty-eight centers that have living facilities especially for working women. Many of these centers offer lectures on women's rights and problems, trying to awaken, enrich, and help working women. But the promoters find that factory women, who really need to be made aware, do not attend. Most factory workers are married with children. They are busy working and caring for a family and home. They will, however, dutifully attend a P.T.A. meeting or a class on child care, but feel they cannot justify taking time from their families to attend a class to broaden themselves as individuals.

THE CONTEMPORARY FEMALE FACTORY WORKER

Yasuko began working in a textile mill in Ichinomiya, a suburb of industrial Nagoya, three years ago. At first she was filled with excitement and eager to encounter the world outside her home town of Nagasaki in Kyūshū. When her father took her to the train station, he cautioned her to preserve her femininity. Upon completing middle school at the age of fifteen, she had expressed interest in working in a textile factory near Nagoya as many of her upperclassmen had done. She thought it would be exciting to live in a dormitory with other girls her age, earning a salary, and also be able to send money home occasionally. She wanted to find her own place in the world and was eager to see another part of Japan.

Her father, like his father before him, is a fisherman. Her two older brothers joined their father upon completing their compulsory education. Yasuko has never been on her father's fishing boat, although she has always wanted to. One day she announced at the dinner table that, like her brothers, she, too, wanted to join her father on the fishing boat. Surprised and amused, her father and brother laughed and repeated a saying among fishermen in Nagasaki, "The boat will sink if a woman comes aboard." Yasuko's older sister married at eighteen but has continued working as a coffee shop waitress in Nagasaki. Her younger sister, aged sixteen, was the first member of the family to continue to high school, and there is a younger brother, aged nine.

With the burden of raising a large family on a fisherman's wages, Yasuko's parents were not hesitant in signing the necessary papers and accepting the ¥25,000 ($83) preparation and transportation money from the company representative. Also, the company had assured the parents that Yasuko would be encouraged to continue her education. The factory's two eight-hour shifts would enable Yasuko to work one shift and to study the other. The company provides transportation to the nearby school and also has a high school on the factory grounds to enable students to attend in the evening. Thus workers on the early shift, from 5 a.m. to 1:30 p.m. (breakfast from 7:25 to 8), can attend afternoon and evening classes. Those on the afternoon shift, from 1:30 p.m. to 11 p.m.[30] (dinner from 6 to 6:45—plus two five-minute rest breaks), can attend classes in the morning at a nearby school. In this way they can complete high school in four years and even junior college in an additional three years.

Yasuko has been living in a company dormitory where four girls share each room. She works eight hours a day, standing and inspecting six large weaving machines to ensure that the warp threads do not break in the process of automatic weaving. If she notices that one of the threads has broken, she stops the machine immediately to repair it. While fixing the thread, she must keep an eye on the other five weaving machines as well. This causes her great tension. There is no point from which she can stand and inspect all of the machines at once, because three of them face each other.

Miyo, age thirty-six, began working full time three years ago. She is married and has one son (thirteen) and two daughters (ten and seven). She quit high school after a year and a half, and she worked as a nurses' aid in a nearby hospital for four years before marriage.

Like her husband, Miyo was born in mountainous Nagano Prefecture, where their families are farmers. They met through relatives, and were married when she was twenty-three and he twenty-six. After marriage, they moved to Nagoya, where Miyo's husband found work at an automobile assembly plant. His present salary is ¥200,000 a month.

By their first wedding anniversary, their son had been born. Miyo did piecework (*naishoku*) in her home at times for extra income while the children were small. When the younger daughter was four, Miyo heard from neighborhood friends that a small company manufacturing automobile accessories was recruiting women, so she applied.

Miyo's weekday schedule is fairly regular. She rises at 6 a.m., dresses, bows to the family shrine, prepares a simple breakfast of rice, bean paste soup, smoked fish, and tea, packs her husband's lunch, and awakens the family at 7. They eat their breakfast together while watching the news on television, but Miyo isn't able to concentrate on the news because she must think of all the minute details to be attended to before she leaves for work. While her husband dresses, she washes the breakfast dishes, puts away the bedding, and hangs the wash outdoors. Her husband waters his plants. It takes him forty-five minutes to get to work by car, so he leaves the house by 7:40. The two older children put away their own bedding and help clear the dishes from the table. The younger daughter feeds the pet bird.

School doesn't start until 9 a.m., but the children leave the house by 8. Miyo is the last to leave their small rented house after checking that everything is in order. When she first began working, she would take Eri-chan, the youngest, to a public child-care center before going to the factory. Now it takes her only twenty minutes by bus.

Miyo enjoys greeting the other workers while donning her gray cotton overblouse and tucking her short hair under a gray kerchief. By 8:30 a.m., she is sitting at her work bench and has put on a pair of glasses with very thick lenses. She feels embarrassed about having to wear them—a fact she has concealed from her husband—but they are necessary because her eyes have become terribly strained from binding the black seatbelts eight hours a day. During the forty-five minute lunch period, Miyo eats in the cafeteria with the women in her section. They talk and laugh about their families or about something at work, or complain how expensive things are. She used to like to knit, but now realizes that she should rest her eyes. At 4:45 p.m. she finishes work, doffs her uniform, politely excuses herself, and hurries home, picking up something for supper on the way. She places confidence in her son to take charge until her return and she feels relieved when she returns home to find that everything is all right. Miyo starts supper immediately. She asks the older daughter to take the clothes from the line and run the electric sweeper. The son prepares the family bath.

A little after 6, her husband arrives home, bathes, and passes the time before dinner reading the evening newspaper and playing with the younger daughter. The family eats together quickly while watching television. The children help clear the dishes, and Miyo serves tea. During these few moments before homework, the family has a chance to talk about school, work, or family. Miyo finds this the happiest time of her day.

After dinner, Miyo's husband likes to watch baseball or other programs on television. Miyo helps the children with their homework. The elder daughter is independent and helpful, but the younger still demands a great deal of attention and affection. She often asks her mother to quit work and stay at home doing piecework as she did before. This used to make Miyo feel she may be neglecting Eri, but she now explains that it's better that she work. She knows that although they can make ends meet on her husband's salary, money will be needed for the children's education, and she wants a home of their own. Then later she will have to save for their retirement. So she tells Eri-chan that she can buy her a new dress if she continues working.

At about 9:30, after helping the children with their homework, doing some ironing, washing the rice for the next day, laying out the children's clothes, and preparing the bedding, Miyo finishes reading a short story to Eri-chan and puts the children to bed. Miyo makes a few notes in the family budget book. As she eases herself into the bath, she allows herself utter relaxation.

Yasuko has twisted her long black hair on top of her head. She's working the late shift today and knows that her uniform will be drenched with perspiration by 3 p.m. Because of working a different shift each week, her sleeping habits are irregular. Today she was up by 8 a.m., even though she didn't have anything planned. She has quit her ambitious schedule of work and school. She realized within a few months that it was extremely difficult for a fifteen-year-old girl to do, at the same time, two difficult and demanding programs. Her job inspecting the looms demanded all her concentration. If she neglected spotting a snagged thread, she would be scolded by her section head. This would embarrass her in the eyes of her fellow workers and dormitory roommates. Her greatest fear was that her family and friends at home might hear of her carelessness from one of the other girls from Nagasaki.

This morning after tidying her corner of the room, she reread a letter from her younger sister. Her sister had written how happy their parents were to receive the summer bonus that Yasuko had sent home and what a help it was in coping with the rising cost of living. She wrote that they were looking forward to having Yasuko home for the August *Obon* vacation. Yasuko had been thinking of her family a lot lately, and often reread her sister's letter.

Yasuko joined some friends watching television to pass the time. Many of the other girls had quit studying, too, because they found working and attending classes exhausting and also because they couldn't understand how complicated English grammar, geometry, and ancient Japanese literature could be of use to them in their eventual vocation as housewives and mothers. Watching dramas and music shows on television appealed more to their romantic inclinations. They also were addicted to comic books (*manga*) for teenagers. Yasuko, too, now spends about three hours a day in front of the television and at least ¥1,000 a month on comics. She also likes to crochet.

She finished early today because she remembered it was her room's turn to clean the toilets. This had to be done before the afternoon shift began. Some of the girls thought a cleaning woman should be hired for this, or that the girls should at least be paid. When they protested, the wife of the company's president responded that cleaning up after someone is good practice in preparing to be a wife.

Yasuko's monthly salary is ¥55,000, plus ¥3,000 for changing shifts. Deductions are made for insurance (¥2,829) and for food (¥10,000). The company strongly urges their employees to save at least ¥1,600. This amount is automatically deducted, leaving Yasuko ¥29,171. She sends half of this to her parents. She tries to save ¥5,000 for her marriage and spends the remaining ¥9,585 on amusements or things for herself.

Miyo receives ¥65,000 a month, one-third of her husband's salary. She uses her money to supplement the family budget, buys extras for the children, and saves for a home of their own and the children's education. Miyo treats herself to a new dress each season from her earnings.

Yasuko and Miyo receive a bonus (usually two months' salary) twice a year, in June and in December. Yasuko sends the bonus home to her parents, while Miyo puts most of hers in savings. Yasuko and Miyo both have found that earning money and being able to make life "sweeter" for their families gives them a satisfying feeling of usefulness.

In Japan the starting salary for young men is usually not significantly higher than for young women. But a man's salary increases rapidly, so that by thirty-five, it will be 50 percent greater than a woman's, although they entered the company at the same time with the same educational background.[31] This condition persists in spite of article 4 of the Labor Standards Law of 1947, which provides that "the employer shall not discriminate women against men concerning wages by reason of the worker being a woman."

Yasuko is aware that there is a significant difference in wages of men and women but rationalizes that, after all, men have to support a family. Miyo is acquainted with some of the 10 percent of women workers who are widowed or divorced, and she understands their problems in supporting themselves and dependent children or parents on insufficient wages. Miyo thinks the gap should be lessened but not be made absolutely equal. With the same salary women should have to accept the problems and responsibilities of equality. She concludes that there would be no reason to get married if you couldn't depend on someone stronger and more powerful.

Miyo isn't sure how long she will continue working, but she wants to earn enough to help send her son to college and her older daughter to nursing school. She hopes to build a prefabricated house in the near future, and, if so, Miyo would like to stay home. But she also realizes that society is changing, and they may not be able to depend on their son to care for her and her husband in their old age. They will try not to have to depend on their son. They would also like to leave some money to their children to help them when they marry. They regret they have no business or skills to pass on to their children for making a living.

Yasuko has already decided she will quit the factory this year and return to Nagasaki. She misses her home and parents, and dislikes the drudgery of her work. She prefers a job with public contact and is thinking of becoming a clerk in a small shop or a coffee shop waitress. She is self-confident, gets along well with people, and believes she will be successful. She hopes eventually to meet and marry a kind, gentle young man. If she likes her job, she will continue working until the first baby is born. But if her husband were to object, she would quit.

Yasuko wants to depend on her husband. He will make the important decisions; she will execute them. She will devote herself to making her home a bright, comfortable place. She doesn't expect her husband to help with the housework, but won't object if he does. She believes she could also manage her household and hold a job. She would like to work to buy extras but believes her first duty would be as a wife whose place is in her home. She is convinced a man's happiness is in his work, and a woman's in her home.

When Yasuko began working three years ago, she was able to learn her job within a few days, but she was not taught the mechanics of the machines she operates. If one breaks down, she calls a boy who joined the company when she did but was trained to repair the machines. Yasuko admires him for his knowledge and is envious, but she doesn't think girls should know how machines function. Yasuko was, however, trained in safety.

Miyo received instruction in how her machine functions as well as in safety. But neither Miyo nor Yasuko received additional technical training which would enable them to advance. They realize they have no hope of promotion. Miyo would like to be promoted or, at least, placed in a position more appropriate to her physical ability. She fears that as she gets older her eyesight will become too weak for her to continue the work she is presently doing. She knows and accepts the fact that women are usually not promoted. She accepts this because she believes that to be in a position with more responsibility would demand a dedication which would conflict with the dedication she gives to her family.

For both Miyo and Yasuko an important motivation for working is the desire to contribute. Yasuko glows with pride and satisfaction when she gives her bonus to her parents. Her motive for contributing may change once she is married. Young brides have to prove themselves. They usually contribute the furniture, appliances, bedding, etc., when they marry. A Japanese bride is also expected to include with her dowry enough kimono, dresses, and personal belongings so she won't need to use "his" money for these items.

There is another factor motivating Miyo to work. She enjoys belonging. She looks forward to meeting her fellow workers each morning. When she came to Nagoya, she greatly missed her parents, brothers and sisters, and the friends she had known all her life. She didn't want to spend her husband's salary frivolously by joining a hobby group. There was no group she felt a part of. Working has given her a peer group she can relax with. She enjoys the company-sponsored outings twice a year. She is also fond of the end-of-the-year parties when groups of women get together at a Japanese-style restaurant to say farewell to the old year.

Her expectations are simple. She would like more money but also a more cheerful working environment, free from the distress of personality conflicts. Main problems stem from the situation of having a male boss over female workers. Favoritism or flirtation disrupts group unity and humiliates those involved. When the male supervisor scolds or corrects a female worker in front of her coworkers, working becomes unpleasant. Miyo also feels the tension to keep up in her work. If she gets behind, it could cause harassment. But generally Miyo enjoys the people she works with.

Yasuko is also dissatisfied with the low salary, environment, and tense human relationships, but her dissatisfaction is more intense. Like many young workers, she is not so likely to accept unfavorable conditions passively; she is more likely to complain. Yasuko's youthful expectations in leaving home and living with a group of girls her own age were naive. In the dormitory she was confronted with a very complicated but delicate and difficult code of human relationships. Each room of four girls composed a closed group. If one of the roommates seemed to be enjoying herself with someone from another group, she was considered disloyal. Forming cliques is common among teenagers in general, but in Japan, where belonging to a group is very important, these relationships can become excessively involved and constrictive. Yasuko feels compelled to do a good job at work in order not to disgrace her roommates.

Although the Labor Standards Law ensures that women may take a monthly menstrual leave, neither Yasuko nor Miyo take advantage of this law. Miyo sits at her binding machine and is not bothered much by menstrual discomfort. Yasuko stands at her work, and she suffers the first two days of each period. In the past she occasionally took the second day off, but she found it embarrassing to explain her absence to her male supervisor. Also she tends to be irregular. This caused her supervisor to suspect her of lying, and he subjected her to humiliating questions, such as why she took a day's leave the middle of last month but at the end of this month. Also, Yasuko has been taught she should be strong-willed and not let menstrual pains bother her. She doesn't want to give the impression of being a lazy worker and has found it simpler to go to work in spite of her discomfort.

Miyo and Yasuko agree women's abilities are not sufficiently utilized in industry. They feel the welfare laws are inadequate in helping working women.[32] They also think that women are limited in working opportunities because they are physically weaker. They tend to accept work limitations, but Yasuko remembers hearing one

of her coworkers once say if women received more technical training, they, too, could do the same work as men.

The majority of men (75 percent) believe that women are better
suited and happier doing simple repetitive tasks.[33] Yasuko thinks
they may be right, but Miyo disagrees. She believes that women
must be trained to perform more complicated technical work with
increased responsibility. In the future she expects women will find
a greater role as technical specialists in industry, but she does not
think they will be able to hold supervisory positions because of the
additional responsibility and dedication required. She feels women
shun responsibility at work because they are afraid it will conflict
with their obligations at home. Miyo thinks that society and government should continue efforts to enable women to work and
take care of their homes more easily. She wants more and better
child-care centers and more services to help prepare and place women in suitable jobs, especially for those women who return to
work in middle age. She hopes a system will be developed allowing
women to take time off for raising their children without having to
look for another job when they are ready to go back to work. She
also thinks that more fields should be open to women.

Concerning the women's and minors' protection laws, Miyo and Yasuko believe these to be necessary and favor their being strengthened.

Neither is absolutely convinced that it is good for women to work
after marriage. They agree that the main contribution a woman
makes to society is by marrying and raising children. She must
run her household efficiently, and her duties include managing the
household finances. On the twenty-fifth of each month, Miyo's
husband hands her an unopened envelope containing his monthly
salary. She keeps a meticulous accounting record, in which she records in detail all expenditures, even the price of a single egg. Failure to manage on her husband's salary would be considered not an
indication of his poor earning ability, but rather of her inefficiency
in budgeting. Nevertheless, nowadays she finds herself contributing
as much as 20 percent of the household budget from her pay.

Miyo disciplines her children but does not yell or slap the children
or send them to bed without supper. She corrects them by looking
stern and giving commands in a lowered voice with staccato rhythm.
The children say they are more afraid of her than of their father.

She makes all minor decisions by herself but discusses major ones
with her husband, who ostensibly makes the final decision. Miyo
admits that sometimes he just thinks he made the decision; actually she decides before broaching the subject, and she has become
skillful in presenting a problem in such a manner as to get her own
way. One of the decisions she makes is how the family will spend

Sundays and vacations. Sometimes on Sunday, Miyo will make a
rice-ball and barley-tea picnic for a day at the park. In spring the
family likes to hunt bracken (*warabi*) in the mountains or horse-
tails (*tsukushi*) along the river bank. During the short *Obon* vacation in August, they often return to Nagano Prefecture to visit
their parents and friends and participate in the festivals. She and
her husband feel the mountains are a part of themselves. They
miss the mountains and would like to return—perhaps in retirement.

Miyo's role as a mother is more important to her than her role as a
wife. She does try to serve her husband and take care of him, buy
his clothes, and clean up after him, but motherhood she feels is her
primary function, and running the house comes next. Miyo believes
that her marriage relationship with her husband is more modern than
that of her parents. She feels her husband respects her more and is
more eager to cooperate now that she is working.

Miyo often takes the children to a department store on Sundays.
She likes to window shop, and the children enjoy playing in the
rooftop playground or with the mechanical games in the game
room. Miyo is concerned about her children's incessant demands to
have things bought for them. She reprimands herself later for wasting her money, but she loves to see their delighted faces when she
can buy them something they want. Not having been able to have
these extras herself when she was a child, Miyo cannot resist giving
them to her children. More than anything, she wants her children
to have a better life than she did.

Her husband wants their son to receive more education than he did
so that he can become a white collar worker. White collar workers
are more respected and secure, he reasons. Miyo wants her daughters
to prepare themselves for the future by qualifying themselves to be
self-supporting. She is pleased that her older daughter wants to become a nurse. Miyo will encourage her to get a certificate. She also
thinks teaching is a suitable profession for a woman, and teachers
have traditionally been respected in Japan. For herself she does
not dream of pursuing a course to qualify her for a better job.
She regrets having quit high school but laughs at a suggestion that
she could learn some skill. "At my age!!!"

Yasuko, too, feels this age limitation, even at eighteen. She knows
girls who worked at the factory while continuing their studies.[34]
Some even became qualified nursery school teachers. She admires
these girls because they have been able to persevere in spite of many
obstacles, and now they can make a better life for themselves. Yasuko faults herself for not having done the same. She began regret-
ting she had quit classes a year later but was convinced that, since
she would be a year older than the other students, it was too late
to return.

Yasuko hopes for two sons and a daughter after she marries. She does not want her daughter to work in a factory. Like Miyo, she stresses that it's better for her daughter to learn a skill. School teaching would be ideal. For herself she will be satisfied taking some classes—cooking and advanced crocheting—to prepare her to be a good housewife.

Besides television and comics, for recreation Yasuko likes to shop. She also enjoys reading. Favorites are the biographies of Helen Keller and Kenji Miyazawa.[35] She sometimes looks at the newspaper but is only interested in the more sensational news (*sammen kiji*). Miyo doesn't have much time to read, and she regrets this because she liked reading novels as a girl. But now, with the five-day week taking effect, maybe she'll read more. On Sundays she does read the newspaper and enjoys a section in which readers tell of their own experiences and problems and how they overcome them.

One Sunday a month, a group of young people from Nagasaki who work in Nagoya-area factories meets. Yasuko usually attends. The organizers and leaders are boys. If the girls show leadership ability, they are thought unfeminine. Quiet but cheerful, submissive, obedient girls make better wives and mothers, it is thought. Since becoming wives and mothers is their goal, the girls take care to create a favorable impression.

Yasuko has little confidence in politicians. She probably will not vote when she reaches the voting age of twenty. Miyo, however, is acutely aware of social problems, and she is especially concerned about pollution, transportation, welfare, and inflation. She listens to the opinions of others, but decides by herself. She trusts that the candidate she votes for will do his best to solve the community's problems. She is fairly conscientious about voting.

One of the greatest problems women factory workers face is their dispensability. They are the cheap marginal labor—the last to be hired and the first to be laid off. Their destiny depends on the unpredictible world economy.[36]

Miyo suffers from weakened eyesight. Her neck and lower spine are also stiff from bending over a sewing machine eight hours a day. She feels isolated at her workbench and is under constant pressure to keep up the work pace. She feels that if she does not concentrate, her fingers may get in the way of the needle. She knows anyone could replace her: her abilities, personality, and experience have little effect on her job. She feels like a cog in the machinery, but she cannot understand why she finds herself easily irritated or nervous at work. Nevertheless, she prefers working to staying home and is happy to greet her coworkers.

Yasuko is more outspoken and less tolerant of hardships than is Miyo. Besides the physical strain on her legs and nerves, she wishes she did not have to work the second shift every other week. If her schedule were regular, she could take the cooking and crocheting lessons she is interested in. She also wishes she had more time for sports.

Miyo and Yasuko feel men are generally superior to women and prefer a man for a supervisor. They fear women are too emotional and will not perform well under pressure. Asked whether they would prefer to be male or female, Yasuko and Miyo readily respond, "Why a man, of course!" Yasuko explains that men do not bicker among themselves and they aren't upset by trifles. Miyo answers simply, "Men are free."

To Miyo femininity is gentleness; to Yasuko it is a neatly groomed girl with long hair dressed in kimono. Miyo and Yasuko are very conscious of the necessity to appear "feminine." They are not convinced that women should work and suspect it may be unfeminine.

They do enjoy a new confidence in themselves because they are able to work and, in Miyo's case, continue maintaining a home. Miyo feels her husband respects her more because of her capability, and he will do more around the house than he did before she started working. "Maybe he's just mellowing with age," she laughs. But she feels herself more worthwhile, and she proudly recalls overhearing her son brag on the telephone to a friend, "My Mom works!"

CONCLUSION

A recent survey reveals the following attitudes toward the abilities of men and women. Women factory workers believe they are equal to men in the following areas: cooperativeness, accuracy, responsibleness, ambition, creativity, and perseverance, while they believe men are superior in managing, judging, executing, problem solving, studying, enterprising, and positively asserting oneself. Japanese male industrial workers feel, however, that they are superior in all of these areas except two: they can't decide who is more cooperative and accurate. Women have poor concepts of themselves, but the view men have of their abilities is even more detrimental. When asked if they notice a tendency on the part of men to look down on women, male workers tend to respond negatively, while women workers answer that they do feel discrimination.[37]

The majority of factory women in Japan have been raised in the rural mentality. To be feminine is to be passive, submissive, accepting, and self-sacrificing. They are not women with vision or personal ambition. For many of these women, equal rights guaranteed in the constitution and labor laws are not personally meaningful.

They feel the constitution was written by "outsiders" (foreigners). Tradition is what they have been taught, and it determines their way of life. They want to lead peaceful, happy lives, enjoying the prosperity they have helped the nation earn. They do not want revolution; in fact, they really do not want to question the validity of their role. They seem to sense the pain and frustration that accompanies questioning.

NOTES

[1]Pru Dempster, *Japan Advances, a Geographical Study*, p. 174.

[2]Robert E. Cole, *Japanese Blue Collar: The Changing Tradition*, p. 147.

[3]The government issued a formal statement in May 1872 forcefully denying the truth of this rumor.

[4]Eiko Wada, *Tomioka Nikki, Tomioka Goki* [The Tomioka Diary and Postscript], p. 30.

[5]Reiko Mitsui, ed., *Gendai Fujin Undō Shinenpyō* [A Chronology of the Women's Movement], p. 9.

[6]Sidney L. Gulick, *Working Women of Japan*, p. 75.

[7]In 1883 a cotton-spinning mill in Osaka installed electric lights and started two shifts of twelve hours each. Soon it became a general practice for girls to work at night in factories.

[8]In 1920 the demand for refined Japanese silk soared to the highest in history. Also in this year, a survey of 317 factories in Tokyo showed that 37 percent of women in these factories were married and providing 32 percent of the family income. Many women were suffering from long hours, poor nutrition, insufficient sleep, and restrictions of freedom.

[9]Kōichi Ōtani, *Onna no Kindaishi* [Modern History of Japanese Women], pp. 47-51.

[10]In 1912 factory women in a spinning mill related their hardships of an eighteen-hour day in the factory to the newspaper.

[11]Office of the Prime Minister, Bureau of Statistics, *Shōwa 45nen Kokusei Chōsa* [The 1970 National Census], Table 1, pp. 22-23.

[12]Women's and Minors' Bureau, *Fujin Rōdō no Jitsujō—1953* [The Condition of Women Laborers—1952], Chart 19, p. 29.

[13]Aiko Iijima, *Japanese Women Speak Out*.

[14]This does not mean that Japanese factory girls were always submissive and cooperative. There have been a significant number of protests and strikes by Japanese women factory workers. The first occurred in 1886 in a silk-reeling factory in Yamanashi Prefecture. Women protested lengthening of working hours and lowering of pay. There are several accounts of girls being locked in the dormitories at night to prevent them from escaping. Fires had sometimes broken out, and many of the girls tragically lost their lives because they were unable to flee from the dormitories.

[15]*Shōwa 45nen Kokusei Chōsa*.

[16]On August 18, 1945, the Home Ministry circulated bulletins to various police chiefs telling them that facilities for prostitution should be established immediately for the occupation forces. A billboard reading "Office Girls Wanted: age from eighteen to twenty-five, housing, clothing, and food to be provided" was used to recruit the girls. More than half of the girls interviewed were accepted. These girls were referred to as "war consolers." Their purpose was to protect the chastity of Japanese women by providing an outlet for the appetites of the soldiers and officers of the occupation army. (Yasuko Itō, *Sengo Nihon Josei Shi* [The Postwar History of Japanese Women], p. 45.)

[17]*Shōwa 45nen Kokusei Chōsa*.

[18]1955 to 1970: *Shōwa 45nen Kokusei Chōsa*. 1974: Office of the Prime Minister, Bureau of Statistics, *Shugyō Kōzō Kihon Chōsa Hōkoku* [1974 Employment Status Survey—All Japan], pp. 50-51.

[19]Article 24 of the Constitution of Japan: Marriage shall be based on the mutual consent of both sexes and it shall be maintained through mutual cooperation with the equal rights of husband and wife as a basis. With regard to choice of spouse, property rights, inheritance, choice of domicile, divorce, and other matters pertaining to marriage and the family, laws shall be enacted from the standpoint of individual dignity and the essential equality of the sexes.

[20]Reiko Mitsui, pp. 230-233.

[21]Kōichi Ōtani, pp. 259-263.

[22]See fn. 19.

[23]Aichi-ken Rōdō Keizai Chōsashitsu, *Fujin Shūgyō no Jittai* [Women and Employment].

[24]Ministry of Labor, *Fujin Rōdō no Jitsujō* [The Condition of Women Laborers, 1973], Chart 16, p. 17.

[25]Ministry of Labor, *Chingin Kōzō Kihontōkei Chōsahōkoku* [Survey of Wage Structure], 1973.

[26]Ministry of Labor, *Funin Rōdō no Jitsujō*, Chart 40, p. 38.

[27]Toshio Sakayori and Yoshio Takagi, eds., *Gendai Nihon no Rōdōsha* [The Contemporary Japanese Worker], pp. 114-146.

[28]Ministry of Agriculture, *Nōson Chōsa Kekka Hōkokusho* [The Results of an Agricultural Investigation], Chart 8, pp. 16-17.

[29]Miyoko Shiosawa, *Kekkon Taishokugo Watakushitachi* [After Retiring for Marriage].

[30]Violation of Art. 62 of the Labor Standards Law: "The employer must not employ women during the hours 10 p.m. and 5 a.m."

[31]Women's and Minors' Bureau, *Fujin Rōdō no Jitsujō—1974* [The Condition of Women Workers—1974], Chart 38, p. 66.

[32]The Working Women's Welfare Law was established July 1972 to enable working women to "reconcile their dual responsibilities of work and home." It is interesting to note that men tend to feel that these laws are adequately helping women, while women feel they are not. (Refer: Aichi-ken Kinrō Kaikan,"Fujin Rōdōshitsu,"*Fujin Rōdō nikansuru Ishiki Chōsa* [Survey of Attitudes Concerning Working Women], 1973.

[33]*Ibid.*

[34]One-fifth of girls, aged fifteen through nineteen, working full time in the textile and food industries, are attending high school or junior college. (*Shūgyū Kōzō Kihon Chōsa Hōkoku*, Table 10, pp. 72-79.)

[35]Kenji Miyazawa (1896-1933) was a Japanese poet, writer, teacher, and researcher who dedicated himself to helping the farming community in Iwate Prefecture.

[36]Ministry of Labor, Minister's Secretarial, Statistics and Information Department, *Rōdō Tōkei Chōsa Ge* [Monthly Labor Statistics and Research Bulletin], Vol. 27, no. 3, March 1975, Graph 1, p. 3.

[37]Aichi-ken Kinrō Kaikan,"Fujin Rōdōshitsu."

CHAPTER
4
"OFFICE LADIES"

A young woman graduates from junior college in Tokyo and gets a job as a clerical worker. She lives at home and is able to contribute small amounts of money from her salary to her parents. She and her parents are pleased that she has been able to find this job; it gives her some freedom to buy the things she wants and enjoy occasional evenings in a coffeehouse with women coworkers and also to help with family expenses. They feel, too, that she will someday be a better and more understanding wife because of this experience. She is probably typical of a growing number of young Japanese women who achieve some education beyond high school. According to the latest figures, more than 32 percent of Japanese women continue on to junior colleges or universities.[1] She is also like many of her contemporaries in that she majored in the humanities in junior college,[2] and in that she does not plan to work more than three or four years before marriage.[3]

Another young woman finishes high school in a small town, moves to a nearby city, works in the office of a large company, and lives in the company dormitory.[4] Her costs are low in company housing, so she, too, can help her parents with small amounts of money out of her meager paychecks. Both she and the junior college graduate will work for three or four years, hoping perhaps to meet a middle-class *salariman* (one of the growing number of middle-class male office workers and junior executives) in her company, get married, stop work, and begin the "important" role of raising children and caring for a household. Or, either may marry someone arranged through an *omiai* by her parents. Such a pattern is today acceptable and even appropriate for many young women in Japan. They

75

are "OL's," "office ladies," temporary members of a growing work force of women who contribute to the Japanese economy in large numbers, whose work allows them to continue to be "ladies" and dutiful daughters and suitable wives, and whose cost to the businesses that hire them is very low.

Other women in this group called "office ladies" are married women in one of two categories. Some have remained at work after the birth of children (after an unpaid maternity leave) or have returned to work when children are in school or otherwise cared for. For most of them, working is a financial necessity, to supplement family income. They may be married to *salarimen,* but inflation in Japan has meant that even many "successful" marriages cannot survive without a second income. Some married women have returned to work after the childbearing years and after children are grown, apparently searching for something to keep them occupied after household duties have become minimal.[5]

A third, and still much smaller, number of "office ladies" are older single, widowed, or divorced women. For those in this category who do not live with or receive help from their parents, their often meager earnings must somehow support them and their children.

All of these "office ladies" have several things in common. First, they receive extremely low pay in comparison to male office workers and do not have access to the higher positions open to men. Second, they are expected as part of their work to serve tea and perform other "womanly" duties that make working conditions pleasant for their male coworkers. Third, they are contributing an important cheap labor supply in an economy that has been booming, until recently, since the end of World War II. Finally, they are told, both directly and indirectly, that while their work is necessary in modern Japan, their primary and most important role is still, as it always has been, to care for children, households, and husbands. Most of them, it appears, accept this last "condition of work" as a fact of life and "the way it should be."

Japanese women have not always been welcome, or needed, in the world of business. After the Meiji Restoration of 1868, when industrialization began in Japan and women were increasingly needed as part of the work force, women slowly entered the textile industry and developing heavy industries to do unskilled labor. As late as 1920, however, of the four million women who were engaged in gainful employment, only 500,000 (12.5 percent) were employed in offices.[6] The wages were low and the hours were long, but these women were able to contribute to their households' incomes. Women's wages were at that time only approximately one-third that of men's.[7] Following the end of World War II, and particularly since 1955, the number of women employed as office workers has skyrocketed. According to a recent survey, the highest percentage of working women in Japan today is involved in clerical and related jobs. In 1974, the percentage had reached 31.7, followed by women production process workers (assembly line workers), with 26.7 percent.[8]

There appear to be several reasons why women have been employed in increasing numbers in offices over the past twenty years. As Etsuko Kaji points out in a recent article:

> . . . almost 1,000 businesses opened jobs to women which had previously been reserved for males in the period 1966 to 1970. The 49 job categories in which women have joined or replaced men include programming, various types of clerical work, lathe operation, and drafting. Women have been introduced into these jobs as automation has simplified and rationalized labor processes and lowered job qualifications. Or, in some cases there simply aren't enough male workers to fill the positions, or women's wages are cheaper than men's. Not long ago, a manager at a major bank stated, "Recently it has been difficult to save on labor costs except by hiring women, and we plan to replace male workers with female to reduce the cost. Most women workers get married in about four years. This is the most important point in hiring them."[9]

In addition to pointing up the sheer economic motivation for encouraging more women into the labor force during Japan's boom years, the above quotation illustrates the important fact that women workers can be and are treated differently than are men. The general cultural concept of "appropriate" limits for women is continued by employers once women enter the labor market. Most companies still regard the woman's main roles in life as wife and mother and not as company employee. Once she reaches the age considered appropriate for marriage it is assumed that she will leave the company. Even if she does return following the childbearing years, her chances of attaining an important position or good salary are severely limited. Her responsibilities at home should outweigh those at the company, it is thought, and her salary is seen as merely supplementary to her husband's or father's, the main source of income for the family. Using these beliefs, companies are able to discriminate against women by avoiding various laws which establish equal treatment for men and women.

More and more women, however, are continuing to work in recent years, whether single or married, for economic reasons. Their positions are still low and their salaries are not even half (48.5 percent) that of men.[10] This discrimination exists despite the 1947 Labor Standards Law, which incorporates the principle of equal pay for men and women (Art. 4), and the Employment Security Law (1947), which provides all people with the opportunity to get jobs suitable to their abilities. Employers are able to find a means to avoid obeying these statutes by classifying women and men according to different scales. A man's position is permanent and important, while a woman's is only temporary and of marginal importance. Employers seldom place their female employees in positions of responsibility; this results in a lower salary scale and few company benefits. Few women qualify for old-age pensions according to the requirements of the Welfare Pension Scheme (1942), because one condition is that contributions must be paid for more than twenty years.[11] As a final example of many forms of discrimination, in spite of legislation to the contrary, many companies still require women to retire at marriage or at childbirth. According to a recent survey of 2,500 businesses (each employing more than thirty people), 11 percent require women to retire before thirty-five, and more than 33 percent deny women the opportunity of advancement to management positions.[12] In short, Japanese women are being allowed and encouraged to work, but the terms of their employment are different than those for men. Whereas men most usually enter business as a lifetime career, receiving promises of increasing benefits over the years and continuing protections, the large majority of women have no such protections coming out of the traditional system. Tradition for them, instead, seems to say only that they really should remain at home.

A specific example to illustrate the continuing discrimination against women in the job market is the case of C. Itoh and Company, Ltd., the largest trading company in Japan, with branches and subsidiaries around the world.[13] Forty percent of its 2,300 (1974) employees are women; women are primarily engaged in office work. A very large number of these women are junior college graduates; the company does not hire women graduates of four-year colleges. The average age of female employees is twenty-three, and the average length of their continuous employment is three to four years. Only women living at home with their parents are employed. When they attend employment interviews, they are required to be accompanied by their mothers, with whom company interviewers spend more time than they do talking with the applicants. Male employees are given two months of intensive training in every aspect of the company's activities. Women receive training only in specific job skills like telephone operator duties and things related to their hostessing-type work. Women are not considered employees but "female employees," a category which excludes women from the five ranks of male employees. Finally, women are virtually excluded from various systems of company benefits. For example, women from the age of twenty-eight until they reach retirement receive a ¥1,000 (slightly over $3) housing allowance per month. Men aged twenty-six (fifth rank employees) receive ¥6,000 per month, those aged twenty-seven (fourth rank employees) receive ¥9,000, and so on.

A few of the women suffering from this kind of discrimination in Japan today are beginning to question their secondary status and to fight for the equal rights which the law presumes to be theirs. Some of the women at C. Itoh and Co. have voiced their concerns, but without much support from fellow workers—men or women, union members or not. And occasionally there is a case like that of the woman from Iwate Prefecture (northern Honshu), who was dismissed at age thirty-one when she reached the "appropriate" age limit for females and would not retire. She filed suit in district court, and the judge ruled that the company had violated article 90 of the Civil Code by imposing an age limit. She was awarded a settlement of ¥333,000 in back pay and ¥32,900 in monthly salary until a final settlement was reached.[14]

This particular woman was employed on an *arubaito* (part-time) basis, a position which is especially low in terms of status, salary, and benefits, and which illustrates another kind of problem encountered by many Japanese women workers. A recent study showed that 20 percent of part-timers work the same number of hours as regular workers, and other figures indicate that in 33 percent of part-time jobs, working time is only one hour less than for full-time. Yet part-time workers are hired on a completely different wage system, as their work status is "temporary," and they are often not allowed to join unions.[15] Thus women employed as part-timers provide their employers with a cheap source of labor, and the employers incur none of the usual obligations Japanese companies have toward lifetime employees. One of the reasons, of course, that so many women take part-time jobs is that the jobs are available. Another important reason is that a real part-time schedule may be flexible, an important factor for working mothers to consider. Faced with combining their responsibilities in the roles of wife, mother, and employee, they may be forced to accept almost any working conditions, providing the schedule is flexible.

There are many other examples that could be given to emphasize the plight of the "office lady" in today's Japan. Perhaps a better way to provide more information about some of the women who fit in this category, however, is to present specific details from our study of a small number of "office ladies" whom we met and interviewed. Included among our respondents were women who work in banks and in small and large companies; women who are married, single, and divorced, and young women just out of school as well as a few who are older. We talked with all of them about their work experiences, future plans, problems, and opinions and attitudes on a number of questions related to the role of women. Beginning with brief biographies of two of them, we will let them tell their own stories and present their own ideas.[16]

KEIKO YAMAMURA

Although many young women these days are going on to college, some are satisfied with completing high school and finding jobs. This is Keiko Yamamura's case, a nineteen-year-old from Hokkaido in northern Japan who would probably suit better her black high school uniform than the Mitsubishi Bank uniform she wears. She came to Tokyo only last year after graduation, leaving her younger sister and elder brother to help her parents on the family farm. She entered the bank on the advice of her parents. Both of them had completed only elementary school, so they considered her high school education more than adequate. They, like the parents of many young farm and small-town girls, felt that it would be wise for Keiko to work a few years, to earn a little money and get some experience "in the world," before coming home to marry. The work experience might, indeed, help Keiko to make a better marriage match.

Keiko herself plans to work only a few years before returning home to join her family. She does not seem especially happy with her job, but she enjoys the friends she is able to make in the company dormitory. Because room and food are provided at extremely low rates, she is able to save money to take home to her family. She sees friends and being able to help her family as the main advantages to her working, not the job itself. To her, conditions of work, the very simple living accommodations she now has, the possibility for advancement or the lack of it, are all irrelevant. She, like many other young, temporary "office ladies," sees this period in her life as one of waiting, of preparation for the "real life" to come after marriage.

Keiko was one of the most traditional young women interviewed. When she was asked what the most important obligation of a woman is, what her most important contribution to society is, and what the ideal life is for a woman, she responded repeatedly, with a somewhat puzzled expression: "to be a good wife and mother and take care of the home." Working as a bank clerk is a temporary activity, she said. "Later I will be a wife and mother." With her parents' help she hopes to find a suitable husband through *omiai* (arranged marriage) and enter a good family, her goal in life. She certainly does not want to continue working, and it appears that she would have a considerable adjustment to make were she to find, after marriage, that her income was still necessary to her new family's welfare.

KAZUKO TANAKA

Kazuko is a twenty-seven-year-old woman, married to a fairly successful *salariman* whom she met two years ago while she was working as an "office lady" in the large manufacturing company where he still works. She was not asked to quit her job when she married her husband—there are several couples working there—but she wanted a job closer to the three-room apartment they had found, so she resigned. She found a job in a small, two-man office, where she now does general office work.[17] She feels that there is no opportunity for advancement in her present job, nor was there with her former employer. This is partly, she feels, because she lacks special training but also because, to a greater degree, she thinks, the higher-level jobs are held by men and reserved for them.

Kazuko's father was a government employee, but he died when she was just fourteen, leaving Kazuko and her two older brothers and one younger sister in their mother's care. Her mother then went to work as a clerk at a teacher's college. "She likes working," said Kazuko, with a smile. Perhaps the fact that her mother had been a housewife for many years and then was forced to go to work and found herself liking it is one of the reasons for some of Kazuko's expressed interest in continuing to work.

Although all of Kazuko's siblings achieved a college education (one brother is now working on a doctorate), she did not want to go to college when she finished high school in Tokyo. She feels that college education has real advantages for a woman, in terms of increasing her job skills and giving her "time to do things for herself," but she still is not sure that she will ever want to go to college. She does, however, want to "master English," which she now reads well and speaks haltingly, so that she can perhaps get a better job. Her present job is all right, she says, and she is satisfied with her present life style with her husband in their small Tokyo apartment. But she expresses in various ways her rather mild desire to go on working at least for a while, perhaps in a more challenging job.

Where Kazuko works now, she has no regular vacations or holidays, although she did say that her boss gave her a month off recently after her oldest brother was killed in an automobile accident. "He was very considerate." She does general office chores, acts as a "hostess," and of course serves tea to the men and their guests. When asked how she felt about serving tea and doing other "womanly" chores, she responded that she really did not like it too much, but it was expected of her. This is similar to the reaction of other respondents. Most of them said that they did not like to serve tea or clean off the desks of the men, but they added that this was expected of them and they therefore had no choice. One woman working in a larger office also commented that at least these chores gave her a chance to meet with other women in the kitchenette to chat. An older woman whom we interviewed said that she had served tea in her younger days, but that now the younger "girls" in the office had taken over that chore. She seemed to feel that this was "as it should be."

Unlike Keiko, Kazuko was quite articulate in her responses to many of the interview questions. Although she was raised quite traditionally, learning to sew, cook, and wash and studying *chanoyū* and calligraphy, she said that she felt perhaps the fact that her mother had worked made her realize that women are as good as men, and made her feel that perhaps children's training when they are growing up is too separated. "They should at least learn more about each other's roles." Her own brothers had more free time than she did when she was growing up, since she was required to do washing and cleaning for herself *and* for her brothers. They were responsible for preparing the bath. Although she did not directly question the fairness of this, she did feel strongly that girls should be given experiences and opportunities that would allow them to develop as persons. She also emphasized, however, that while she felt married women should definitely have their own interests, she also thought that the scope of that interest should be limited by a wife's primary duties as a wife and mother.

Kazuko hopes to have children "some day," and when she does she thinks perhaps she will go on working or go to college or learn more English, depending on her husband's plans and on whether or not he and she can arrange to move in with her mother-in-law. She believes women should be encouraged to do whatever they have the desire and talent to do, but always "if she wants to," a long way from what is *expected* of men—probably because she feels the most important obligation of a woman is to make the next generation "a good one." A woman's most important contribution to society is making men happy—"our goal is a man who can learn to be happy." "But," she adds, "that is also a man's most important contribution— we are all here to make each other happy!"

In Kazuko's case, married to a husband whose company is now planning to send him abroad for special study and training, a reasonable prediction might be that she will reach the point when she will not have to work and will still have the choice, given a possibly available mother-in-law, of continuing work or study or staying home to raise a family. She has some ideas that might allow her to continue "enjoying her freedom"—and some options in realistic terms. She said that when she married her husband she felt she had made the most important decision of her life, to "give up my freedom—but I had turned down several earlier offers." However, thus far, she seems to be able to exercise that freedom, and chances are that she will continue to have some options. Keiko's future is not that clear. She may be able to return to her home town, marry, and settle down to what for her is the primary goal: raising a family. Or, she may never marry, or she may marry a man who is unable to support a growing family. For Keiko, and many others like her, the future is uncertain. They may join the ranks of married women who are working as "office ladies" out of sheer financial necessity, still holding to very traditional views about the appropriate role for women in Japan, accepting whatever working conditions are offered to them out of need and notions of "what should be." For Kazuko, and perhaps a growing number of women like her who have some ideas about self-fulfillment as persons, the future is also uncertain. Their options now may appear to be broad. But if they "choose" to join or stay in the category of "office lady," they will encounter all the barriers, "special treatment," and traditional views that seem to be the pattern in today's Japan.

One problem that was not stressed by Kazuko, and that did not even occur to Keiko, is the question of what to do with children if a mother has to or chooses to continue working. Most of the married respondents we talked with said that they would like to continue working after having children but realized how difficult it would be to fulfill all three roles of wife, mother, and company worker. One young woman in particular said she hoped that by the time she had children the system of daycare centers would be developed more extensively than it is today.

There is a definite need for the expansion of the daycare system, a need which most of our respondents recognized. Those who were working with small children in the home were particularly concerned. With an increasing number of mothers working in recent years and with the trend toward the nuclear family (well over 50 percent by 1970), proper child-care facilities have become an increasing necessity. It is no longer common for grandparents to live in the same household with their married children, yet many couples living alone with their children need or desire to have both parents working. To help fill this need, a system of public and private nurseries has been initiated. Unfortunately, it is still far from adequate.

Private nurseries are functioning on a limited scale and are expensive, perhaps ¥25,000 per month, a fee which only higher-class families can afford. Public-nursery fees are less expensive, as the fee depends on the family's income, but their availability is very limited.[18]

According to a recent survey by the Ministry of Health and Welfare, the number of nurseries has not increased significantly from 1960 to 1974, but the demand for them has grown considerably.[19] Unless more facilities are provided, it is questionable at best what type of care is provided under the crowded conditions that now prevail. The media, especially in the last few years, frequently report cases of children being injured or even killed at nurseries, often implying that this would not have happened if the child had been at home being properly cared for by its mother. This situation certainly puts the working mother in a conflict. She is told, at times, that the economy really needs her contribution, or she works out of financial necessity. Then, in the absence of adequate daycare facilities, she is told that her place is really at home with her children. Only the creation of more daycare facilities would seem to offer a solution to this particular dilemma.

Another area of work-related concerns that was brought up by a number of our respondents, particularly those who were older and working to help out with family finances or because of personal choice, was the more general one of not being treated fairly at work. Keiko did not even seem conscious of such things, perhaps because of her clearly temporary orientation toward her work, and Kazuko, while expressing the desire to gain facility in English so that she could get a "better job," did not clearly articulate feelings of being treated unfairly. She was, for example, grateful for having been given time off on the occasion of her brother's death. Other respondents, however, did express direct resentment at what they termed unfair treatment. One older woman, married and a mother, did say, for example, that she felt men at work had not treated her fairly in her twenty years on the job. When pressed to describe what she meant by this statement, she did not give specific examples and, indeed, hastened to say that she has been able to endure, as she believes that men, after all, are better than women. Another respondent told us of a "minor" example of unfairness. In her company, most of the men in the office smoke cigarettes while working, yet women employees never do. Although there is no official company rule forbidding women to smoke, it is understood that it is more "appropriate" for women not to smoke while at their desks, in case visitors come by. Seeing women smoke at their desks would create a poor image of the company.

In general, such references to "minor" problems and vague expressions of feelings about unfair treatment, along with the rather universal complaints of our respondents about being expected to serve tea and clean the men's desks, represented these women's level of awareness of their realistic situation in the work force. Only one respondent, a young woman who was recently divorced and living alone, gave any direct criticism of the prevailing low salaries for women working in offices. Although she has considerable facility in

English and is expected to use it in her work, her salary is so low that without the help of her professional parents, who pay her entire housing cost, she would never be able to afford to live alone in her small but modern one-bedroom Tokyo apartment. Even she, however, echoed the thoughts of many other respondents when she pointed out that the men in her company have to work long hours and are expected to spend many evenings out eating and drinking with clients and colleagues if they hope to get ahead. Perhaps this kind of understanding of the pressures suffered by *salarimen,* along with the beliefs expressed by most of the respondents that men are really better than women and that woman's primary obligation is to home and family, account for the absence of much articulated resentment at the secondary status of "office ladies."

ATTITUDES AND OPINIONS

Most of the women with whom we talked expressed relatively traditional attitudes and opinions on most of the topics discussed. All were strongly of the opinion, for example, that the most important obligation and contribution of a woman in society are to be a good wife and raise good children. Most also felt that men were probably better than women, and more important to society. When talking about child-raising practices, most felt that boys and girls should be trained in the home differently, although several did express resentment at the way they had been raised to help with all the housework while their brothers sat idly by. It was particularly true for those who had been older sisters in their families that the responsibilities of helping to care for younger children and doing housework for themselves and their brothers were remembered as onerous. All of the respondents, when talking about their own families, also commented on how important their mothers had been in their growing up. When asked about this point, one of the women said that most Japanese children have little contact with their fathers as they are growing up. Typically, fathers are usually too busy with their jobs and leave child-raising, including help with schoolwork and discipline, almost totally to their wives.

One area in which there did seem to be significant difference between two types of respondents had to do with goals in life. The younger women who had come to the city from farm backgrounds expressed their goals only in terms of getting married and having children. The city-bred college or junior college graduates shared those goals, but they also expressed the desire more often to continue working, get a better job, save money for travel abroad, etc. Another area of difference between these two types was the question of what is meant by success for a woman. Women of the first group tended to be puzzled by the question, then answered it, if at all, in terms of the traditional feminine role. Women of the second group were more likely to say, as did one young woman: "To be successful is to have a purpose in life and to fulfill that purpose, regardless of what the purpose might be."

CONCLUSION

Within Japanese companies the position of "office lady" embodies to a very great degree the traditional feminine role. The situation may be changing somewhat with increased education of men and women and with new laws calling for job equality, but, until male employers and female employees come to think of female labor as permanent and important, women will continue to be placed in positions of low status, with accompanying low salaries and few benefits.

Although Japanese society has changed a great deal in recent years, educating its women more fully and encouraging them to enter the work force in ever greater numbers, there are at least two important barriers to the achievement of full equality for women workers. First, most women, even those who are working, accept the societal dictum that declares women to be basically and most importantly wives and mothers, subservient to men and not really capable of assuming male roles. They therefore join with men in accepting and maintaining their own exploitation in the work force. Second, companies that use "office ladies" to perform necessary though usually menial tasks and to add a "woman's touch" as hostesses are clearly reluctant to lose this large category of cheap, marginal workers. Were the "office ladies" to rise up and demand better pay and working conditions, the economic and social repercussions would be tremendous, affecting family life, traditional assumptions about men's and women's roles, and business practices alike.

At present, however, it appears that the women working as "office ladies" will go on being exploited and will suffer increasing conflicts as they attempt to adhere to traditional values and at the same time perform new roles. Perhaps in these conflicts lies the source of change in the attitudes and self-awareness of women as to what their role as women is. The continued expansion of the education of women, their continued use in the labor force, and the emphasis on maintaining their traditional place in a changing society create a mixture that seems bound to produce more contradictions and accompanying conflicts. The seeds of change are deep in Japanese society today, but it will be up to future generations of Japanese women to nourish them until they bear fruit.

NOTES

[1]Women's and Minors' Bureau, *Women Workers in Japan,* 1975, p. 24.

[2]Women's and Minors' Bureau, *The Status of Women in Japan,* 1974, p. 7.

[3]Several women's junior college faculty members with whom we talked agreed that most of their graduates work for a few years and then marry and stay home. The most popular jobs for these women are in offices, banks, or airlines.

[4]In 1974, 91.9 percent of all women in Japan had completed high school. Women's and Minors' Bureau, 1975.

[5]Within the last fifteen years, there has been a marked increase in working women between the ages of thirty-five to thirty-nine and fifty-five to sixty-four, with the largest increase among women aged forty to forty-four. Masu Okamura, *Women's Status,* p. 58.

[6]Takashi Koyama, *The Changing Social Position of Women in Japan.*

[7]Personal communication from Professor Hisako Hirota of the Economics Department at Japan Women's University.

[8]Women's and Minors' Bureau, 1975, p. 11.

[9]Etsuko Kaji, "The Invisible Proletariat: Working Women in Japan," in Task Force for the White Paper on Sexism—Japan, *Japanese Women Speak Out,* p. 31.

[10]Masu Okamura, p. 62.

[11]Women's and Minors' Bureau, 1974, p. 32.

[12]Kaji, p. 37.

[13]This example is taken in its entirety from "The 'Woman Power' Fraud. C. Itoh and Co.: A Case in Point," in Task Force for the White Paper on Sexism—Japan, pp. 11-13.

[14]*Asahi Evening News,* March 19, 1971, p. 3.

[15]Kaji, p. 34.

[16]The names and some of the details in the following two biographies have been changed to protect the anonymity of the respondents.

[17]It is important for non-Japanese readers to understand that office work in Japan generally does not include typing, because of the complexity of written Japanese. Few offices have the Japanese typewriter, which is more like a printing press, and only those that do business abroad are likely to have English alphabet typewriters. In the latter case, "office ladies" who operate them must either be bilingual or native English speakers; such jobs are among the higher paying jobs for women in offices.

[18]Personal communication from Professor Hisako Hirota of the Economics Department at Japan Women's University.

[19]Hisako Hirota, *Hataraku Haha-oya to Hoikujō Zukuri no Undō* [Working Mothers and the Nursery School Movement], Fujin Mondai Konwakai Kaiho Dai-ni juni-go, p. 3.

CHAPTER
5
WOMEN IN
FAMILY BUSINESSES

HISTORICAL BACKGROUND

Japanese architecture differs from that of the West in that the roof of a traditional Japanese building rests upon pillars rather than upon walls, creating a pavilion-like structure. The central pillar of the house is so symbolically important that a celebration is held to commemorate its erection at the time a building is started.

The central pillars of the Japanese family business world are its women. The stereotype of the Japanese woman is of the person in the background, never speaking unless spoken to, her husband's obedient servant, fulfilling his every wish, decorative and demure. One finds that quite the reverse is true in the homes and offices of the cottage industries and small and medium-sized businesses in Japan. Here one finds that behind the scenes—unsung and often unpaid—women are the centers around which these businesses operate. Society is slow to recognize overtly the influence of these women, but their "keystone" status in family businesses is an open secret.

Business in Japan takes a patriarchal attitude toward its employees. Large businesses provide housing and vacation facilities, maintain company stores where goods may be purchased at a discount, and hold classes for their employees in Japanese arts such as tea ceremony and flower arrangement. Some companies even provide schools where young employees can pursue their unfinished education. Small and medium-sized businesses cannot provide such facilities as schools and stores, but they often provide housing, food, and vacations for their employees. Because the number of employees is smaller, there is a closer family feeling in the smaller businesses. It has been said that the family customs of feudal Japan are preserved in this patriarchal method of conducting business.

Most of the larger businesses in Japan today had their origin in small family businesses during the Tokugawa period (1600-1868). This was the period when the merchants, although considered the lowest class under feudal law, were becoming powerful because of their control of the country's wealth.

During that part of the Tokugawa period called Genroku (1680-1730), most of the art and literature was produced for and about the merchant class. Chikamatsu Monzaemon (1653-1725), considered Japan's greatest playwright, wrote his *Love Suicides at Amijima* about a young paper merchant who left his wife for a prostitute. The long-suffering wife, true to her merchant-class upbringing, stayed faithfully at home to keep the business operating, even though she was fully aware of her husband's escapades.

Ihara Saikaku (1642-1693), Japan's first great novelist since the eleventh century, was sympathetic to the problems of the merchant class of the seventeenth century, especially to the women. This passage about Osan, the wife of an almanac maker, from his *Five Women Who Loved Love,* gives us an insight into the daily routine of a merchant's wife:

> Night and day for three years his wife diligently performed the many tasks which married life required of her, carefully spinning raw-silk thread by hand, supervising the weaving of cloth by her servant woman, looking after her husband's personal appearance, burning as little fuel as possible for economy's sake, and keeping her expense accounts accurate and up-to-date. In fact, she was just the sort of woman any townsman would want in his home.

> Their house was prospering and their companionship seemed to hold a store of endless bliss, when it became necessary for the almanac maker to travel to Edo for business reasons. . . . When he was ready to leave, he paid a visit to Osan's father in Muro-machi to tell him about the trip, and the old man was quite concerned about his daughter's welfare during the period of her husband's absence, when she would be left to manage all of his affairs. He wondered if there were not some capable person who could take over the master's business and also assist Osan in running the household.[1]

Whereas the Osan of the Genroku period still has her counterpart in the housewife-manager of the small and medium-sized family business of today, large businesses have outgrown the close family relationship, and women no longer have a place in their management.

Perhaps one of the reasons for this difference is that the woman in smaller business still thinks of herself as merely performing her role as wife of the family patriarch. There is no place for such a role in big business. Also, her modest evaluation of her position enables the woman in family business to perform her administrative functions without benefit of salary or overt recognition. The structure of big business is such that a woman in a high position would require both. At any rate, there are few, if any, women in administrative or managerial positions in the large businesses of today.

The Japanese family system that was carried over into the business world of today is called the *ie*. This was the patriarchal form of family structure that was codified in pre-World War II law. Under this system, headship of the *ie* or house (in the European sense, such as the "House of Usher") was passed from father to eldest son. If there were no son, often a daughter's husband was adopted into the family to assume its leadership. If there were no male relative capable of succession, a trusted manager might be adopted into the family as its successor. The blood line was not as important as the maintenance of the *ie* under the family name. It was not as important that the blood line continue as it was that the family structure continue, the new household head maintaining the paternalistic role.

The head of the house was not only the final authority in all family decisions, but was also responsible for the welfare of all members of the *ie*, who in turn owed him loyalty. He acted as a trustee for the House, its members, its belongings, its crest, and its name. The main family of the *ie, honke,* was headed by the eldest son and his lineal descendants. Branches, *bunke,* were sometimes established, headed by younger brothers. The *bunke,* even when located in another city, deferred to the decision of the *honke* head. Marriage, education, and finance were all matters affecting the *ie* as an entity and were, therefore, decided jointly by the *bunke* heads and the head of the *honke,* the final word resting with the *honke* head.

The wife of the head of the house held a position of responsibility for the household and its retainers next only to that of her husband and son. In the small and medium-sized businesses of today she still holds that position. It is she who meets and serves guests and business acquaintances. Like Saikaku's Osan she manages the budget, both of the household and that of the family business. Hers is the responsibility of dealing with tradesmen of the household, and, in the case of a business, she often controls the buying and the distribution of materials for subcontractors and checks any returned goods from them. She is, many times, the guide in policy matters both for her children and for the company employees. And, again like Osan, in her husband's absence she is "left to manage all of his affairs."

Like the feudal lord's lady and the merchant's wife, the woman in family business today cares for the needs, both physical and emotional, of the family retainers. All of her efforts are bent upon seeing that the members of the family and employees are working to preserve the *ie*, as represented by the family business. She is the central pillar around which the business structure is built.

A PROFILE

An example of the central role that a woman plays in the family business is shown by the life of Mrs. Namako Kobayashi, who is listed in the family corporation as its vice-president.

The neighborhood surrounding Mrs. Kobayashi's home is typical of those in the large cities of Japan. The streets are at odd angles to each other, and the map giving directions is a "crazy quilt" which must be followed carefully.

On first entering the neighborhood, you can see a row of unpainted wooden houses. These are joined together, and one can only glimpse inside. What is seen, however, reveals that some of them contain cottage industries, performing some small manufacturing or craft function. Interspersed with these small houses are walled homes of a more luxurious nature. Here and there are open shops: a small grocery store or a flower shop. One building of several stories is obviously an office building; through the glass windows workers can be seen seated at their desks. Occasionally a three- or four-storied apartment house, very narrow by Western standards, can be seen. There is also a luxurious condominium building with a black limousine waiting in the parking area under the raised first floor.

Mrs. Kobayashi's home is at the corner of two very narrow streets. There is a bell at the gate of the wall, which the maid answers and comes to greet the guests. Used more often than the gate is a side door around the corner, opening into the kitchen. After shedding shoes in the entryway, guests are led down a narrow hallway to a small room about eight by nine feet. An oriental rug of deep, rich tones covers the tatami mats on the floor. High on the wall of the room is a small Shinto shrine, and in the corner is a small *Butsudan*, a Buddhist shrine with pictures of departed members of the family. The television in the corner is turned on without the sound, with the time of day showing in the lower left-hand corner of the picture.

In the center of the room is a low square table covered with a hand-woven silk cloth. In the wintertime there would be heat in a pit under the table, and the table would be covered with a lightweight comforter that could be pulled around the sitter's waist for warmth. Now it is summer, and the maid brings refreshing small cold towels to the guests, who are seated on cushions on the floor by the table. Everything in the room reflects good taste, including the exquisite summer candies that the maid serves with iced sweet green tea.

Mrs. Kobayashi is seated at the table. She is not dressed in kimono, but in a Western-style dress of elegant material and design. She is petite and still shows signs of having been a beautiful young woman. While she is telling her story, several people come and go, and each is introduced to the guests and served in the same gracious manner. Some of the visitors are relatives, some are employees and business associates. There is always an air of relaxed good will. Everyone who enters seems to feel at ease with Mrs. Kobayashi, but at the same time they show great respect for her. The telephone is on a low stand by the table, and around the walls of the room are stacks of papers, probably invoices, bookkeeping books, newspapers, and magazines. It is obvious that the heart of the business is in this room.

Mrs. Kobayashi speaks of her life and her work in the Kanto Small Motor Company:

My name is Namako Kobayashi. I was born here in Tokyo in the house next door to where we are sitting right now. I am sixty-three years old. My father started manufacturing small motors only two years before I was born, and the family was living in very modest rooms adjoining the business. During my childhood we were relatively poor, because all of my father's income was being put back into his new venture.

Father was the seventh son of a family of nine children. He had only a fourth-grade education and then worked as an apprentice in machine work. At the age of sixteen he left his home, a small village near Hiroshima, vowing never to return until he had made his fortune. He traveled as far north as the island of Hokkaido learning his trade. Finally, at the age of twenty-one, he felt prosperous enough to return to his home village. He returned, but only long enough to take one of the local girls as his bride. The marriage had been arranged for him before his return.

My mother was only seventeen at the time. Although she had little education, she was a very intelligent woman. Often she was ashamed because she had not learned to read many of the *kanji*, the Chinese characters. She could read only the Japanese alphabet, the *kana*. However, Mother knew well how to make our modest home beautiful and our life comfortable.

My parents had four children, my older brother, me, and my younger brother and sister. My older brother died tragically when I was a child. After his death my parents poured all their affection onto me until my younger brother was born. Not that they were any less kind after that, but, because he would be my father's successor, my younger brother, Yoshihisa, was the hope and joy of the family. He was very interested in music. He could have had his own orchestra, he had so many instruments. Yoshi was very intelligent. However, when he was young he was more interested in his music and in having fun than in studying, so he didn't qualify for the best public school for boys. My father sent him, instead, to a very good private school. Later, at the university, he was a very good scholar.

My own education stopped after high school. Father believed in higher education only for men. This did not concern me at the time; I felt that this was only as things should be. However, I went to the best public high school in Tokyo. It was the first public school for women that stressed liberal education rather than domestic arts. I had to qualify by examination, and was very proud that I was accepted. During the time I attended school and for several years after that, I was given private lessons in calligraphy, flower arrangement, and tea ceremony. I have studied these three almost all of my life. One never really learns all there is to know about them, I think. At present, our business does not give me much extra time for study, but I am learning to play the *samisen* and to sing short songs of the *Noh* drama.

My brother was sent to the best university for which he could qualify. His training in mathematics and engineering would have further enriched our family business. However, while Yoshi was in college, World War II started. Caught up in the patriotism and emotion of the times, my brother enlisted as a *kamikaze* pilot. The family was devastated. We knew that the philosophy of the *kamikaze* pilots was to use themselves as human ammunition. It was suicidal, and the family had only faint hope that my brother would survive the war. Although we respected his wish to give his life for the emperor, we secretly felt that he had let the family down, because, as a college student, he was not required to join the military. Yoshi was killed three months before the war ended. It was a terrible blow for our family.

At that time I had been married for about seven years. The war years were bad, but fortunately my husband survived. Our separation during the war had given me some time to learn a little about household duties. We had always had maids, and I had always been busy with school work and other lessons, so I had not really given much thought to the running of a household. My sister was always the domestic one. I had always been more interested in studying and in the arts and had gone to a high school where these were stressed. My sister attended a domestic science high school. We have always had some problems in getting along, because we are so different, both in our tastes and emotionally. She is quick to show her anger or delight, whereas they say I am more reserved and am less inclined to show my emotions. She has always said that I was Father's favorite. Sister married one of our employees in spite of my father's disapproval. It was a love marriage, and she has been more or less in disgrace with the family ever since.

I married quite late in life for that period; I was twenty-five. I had had a number, quite a number—maybe twenty or more—of *omiai*, you know, the Japanese system of introducing prospective marriage partners. But I didn't find that any of the young men really appealed to me. My mother had said, "Marry a kind man, that is much more important than wealth," and she defended my right to marry someone acceptable to me. I must say that my parents were much more patient and lenient with me than most parents before the war. Through all these introductions, they never tried to force me into marriage, although I know they were concerned as to whether or not I would *ever* marry. My marriage prospects were the topic of numerous family discussions.

Then one day we heard a voice at the *genkan* (entry hall) calling, "*Gomen kudasai.*" Mother went to the entryway and found a nice-looking college graduate student there. He asked to see my father, and, much to my parents' surprise, asked if he could marry me. My parents refused at first; he was the second son of a widow, with very little family background. I admired his courage tremendously, however, and decided that this was the man with whom I would like to spend my life. I am not sure whether it was my "gentle persuasion" or the fact that my husband's study of mechanical engineering would benefit our business, but my father finally gave his consent.

After our marriage, my husband continued his graduate work, but also began to work in my father's business. Because my husband's family home was small, and his father's death had left his family poor, we lived with my parents in their large home in the Ueno district of Tokyo. My father's business had grown quite prosperous, and we were really quite wealthy before World War II. The war reversed our wealth, and we moved to this home where I am now living.

Even though we were no longer wealthy, we always had maids. For us they were and are a necessity. We maintain dormitories for our single employees, and the men eat at our home in the large dining room on the other side of the kitchen. I could not do all the cooking and serving by myself. The maids are paid by the company. Sometimes some of the factory workers help in the home; their work is all interchangeable. And, if we really need extra help for a special occasion, we can count on our employees' wives.

Fortunately, Mother trained the maids. As I said before, I am not too domestic. However, I do get up early in the morning and clean house while breakfast is being prepared. My conscience will not allow me to be idle while the housekeeper or maids are working.

Our housekeeper, Mrs. Tanaka, came to our family when I was a girl. She has trained most of the younger maids, but complains that they leave as soon as they are well trained. Girls are not so keen about domestic labor as they used to be.

During the war I had learned to keep the household accounts, and this was my main domestic duty—not such a heavy one. So, when my husband and I were reunited after the war, I had a very happy period when I could do just about as I wished. It is the only time in my life when I could read as much as I wanted. (I have always loved the classics—I have read the *Genji Monogatari* in its original ancient Japanese. I am also fond of the *Manyōshū*.) And I had time for more lessons in tea ceremony and flower arrangement. But my period of semileisure was not long-lasting. I was forced, without warning, to take over our family business. This is the way it happened:

As I said before, Yoshi was to have succeeded my father in the business, and his death left the business without an heir. Now, it is very important in Japan to have a successor prepared for the business. In Japanese business the employees are hired for their lifetime, and the business family has a strong obligation to its employees to keep the business operating efficiently in order to support them. So, soon after the war Father began to train my husband seriously to take over the business, and my husband was officially adopted into our family and took our family name.

My mother died about three years after the war, and I began to do as she had done and tried to help the employees with their families and with their personal problems. Even though I was trying to fill my mother's place, I was still not very busy. You see, unfortunately, we have never had any children, so my time was occupied only with what little I could do about people's personal problems.

My father died about a year after my mother's death, and my husband took over as president of the company. The business was running smoothly under his management, and I did not give much thought to it. Then, one day, my husband had his first severe attack of asthma. My period of semi-leisure came to an abrupt end. I not only had to care for my husband after his return from the hospital, but I had to learn everything about the business very quickly. During that period I averaged about four to five hours' sleep each night. My husband slowly recovered, but since that time I have continued to be very active in the business. There have been periods of recurrence of my husband's asthma when I had to take full responsibility, but most of the time we share the load. Most of his work is maintaining good relationships with people on the outside: customers, suppliers, people from government bureaus, and the like. I deal with people inside the business. I take care of the bookkeeping, see that the subcontractors have materials and check their work when it is done, and, still, I help the employees with their needs. Actually, there is not much to it. I just do what a woman can here at home to help her husband. It is not like going out to an office every day. My husband and I are in constant communication about the business; in fact, my sister and my niece say that is all we talk about.

I have no official office. All of my work is carried on right where we are sitting right now, at this table. As you can see, our little dining room is stacked high with papers, but it is very convenient here. People are coming and going here at all hours of the day and evening, and it is pleasant to stop and have some tea and cakes with them. Often at night now I stay up and drink saké with the business people—even after my husband has retired.

Things have really changed. My husband used to go out with the customers or some of the management, and then he'd bring everyone home, along with the geisha they had hired for the evening. Everyone would have a good time, joking and singing, and then we'd give the geisha a good tip and put her in a cab for her home. I was never jealous. This is a way of entertaining in Japan, and I am sure my husband was never involved emotionally other than with me. In fact, the geisha used to send me a gift at New Year's and Midsummer because we had given her such good business.

Yes, people—business people, relatives, employees—are always dropping in. Most of them are close acquaintances who never bother to use the front gate; they just come in through the kitchen to the dining room. Many times I listen to their problems or discuss marriage plans and so on with the employees or their families. Sometimes my husband and I are called on to act as go-betweens in a marriage. That happened just three months ago. A lifetime of working together makes people really close.

We vacation together, too. Every summer we rent part of an old inn on the seashore near the Izu Peninsula, and each week some of the employees come down, sometimes with their families, until all have had a visit. I generally stay all summer unless there is some special business here, such as taxes or government forms. Sometimes I come home so that my husband can stay past the weekend at the seashore. One of us tries to stay here at all times during the week to keep an eye on the business.

For that reason, too, my husband and I rarely travel together. When my husband travels, it is usually with some of our customers or employees. He often takes several of the employees or business acquaintances for a weekend trip. That way he can take his travel money out of the business. I am not so fortunate—I must pay for my travel out of my household allowance.

Last year I went to Europe with a group of my friends, all women who are employed in family businesses here in the neighborhood. We have a very loosely organized club and try do do something each month like attending a kimono show or a *kabuki* performance. Sometimes we go together to a hot-spring resort for a day or two. The time I spend with them is about the only time I am away from the neighborhood except for summer.

Our neighborhood is very close, made up mostly of related businesses. Most of the parts for our motors are subcontracted to small businesses in the neighborhood. We all know each other very well, and most of us have known each other since childhood, for these are all family businesses.

We have several relatives living nearby, most of them involved with us in the business. A number of years ago my husband's brother needed work, so we helped set him up in a small business making some of our parts. His wife helps him, but she is not as busy as I am, and often comes over here to talk (too much, sometimes).

My sister lives in another part of Tokyo. She had many children, and since we had none, one of her daughters came to live with us about fifteen years ago. At present my niece's fiancé is learning the business, and when they are married we will adopt both of them, since, as I said before, it is important that the business continue, and they will succeed us after we retire.

I am not exactly sure how my niece will do in the business, particularly if she has to take the full responsibility as I have had to do. She is a beautiful girl, a lovely dancer, Japanese style, and I am afraid I may have spoiled her just a bit. She seems more like she is my own daughter than my sister's—she is much more like me in temperament. I know she very much wanted to attend an art school, instead of the business college to which we sent her. Not that she protested; she went willingly and did very well. Perhaps she will be a better businesswoman than I—at least she has had the formal training in business that I never had.

I really feel that I have had a good life. My days are busy, and I enjoy them. I do not draw a salary from the business, but it takes care of my needs adequately. Sometimes my work has been difficult—I have had to learn what to do every step of the way. But truthfully, I have enjoyed the challenge.

WOMEN IN FAMILY BUSINESSES TODAY

It is characteristic of the Japanese as a nation that they are open to change and innovation, while, at the same time, very few of their traditional values are given up. The *ie* is part of the tradition that has been retained and has been carried into the business world. In fact, the family businesses worked so well under this traditional system, which has been tried and refined over the centuries, that they accounted for a major portion of the successful industrialization of Japan after the Meiji Restoration (1868).

Many remnants of tradition may be seen in Mrs. Kobayashi's story. Her comments on the necessity of an able successor because of the obligations to employees reflect the traditional idea of the household head as trustee and guardian of the House. She is a true descendant of Saikaku's Osan in that she has managed her household well, "keeping her expense accounts accurate and up-to-date," while at the same time proving her competence when, during her husband's illness, she was "left to manage all of his affairs."

In many ways Mrs. Kobayashi and her husband resemble the lady and lord of one of the great feudal houses of Japan. Just as, in the feudal period, the lord and lady cared for all the needs of the feudal retainers, so, today, the Kobayashis' span of responsibility covers the employee's entire life, his home, his leisure, and his family problems.

The lives of other women caught up in the orbit of the Kanto
Small Motor Company give further illustration of the Japanese
family system as revealed in business operations.

First, there is the housekeeper, Mrs. Ayako Tanaka, whom Mrs. Kobayashi mentioned. Mrs. Tanaka came to the Kobayashi home as a
young girl from the small village near Hiroshima where Mrs. Kobayashi's parents were born. She was a distant relative of the parents'
family. When Mrs. Tanaka reached a marriageable age, her marriage
to a Kanto Small Motor Company employee was arranged. Now
her husband is part of the company's top management. She, her
husband, and her children are treated as members of the Kobayashi
family. Her children were raised with Mrs. Kobayashi's niece. They
studied together and played together as children. Mrs. Kobayashi
helped them all with homework.

The relationship between the Tanaka family and the Kobayashis
is an example of the kinship feeling between employer and employee
in the family business. Mrs. Tanaka is trusted more as a family
member than as a servant. She waits on guests and sees that the
meals are cooked, but when only the family is present, her husband
may eat with Mr. Kobayashi at the small dining table, while Mrs.
Kobayashi helps Mrs. Tanaka with the serving, much as an ordinary
family would function. Her salary, and those of the other maids,
are paid by the company. Some of the younger maids work in the
factory when they are needed. The lines of distinction between
the household and the factory, between family and employee, are
much more blurred than they would be in a Western situation.

The arm of the company reaches out to touch the lives of the
wives of subcontractors. Mrs. Yukiko Wakamatsu's husband was
formerly an employee of Mr. Kobayashi. Now he has his own
small business in his home, which Mr. Kobayashi helped him establish. He and his wife stamp out labels as a subcontractor for
the motor company. Although Mrs. Wakamatsu and her husband
work together, he is often away and she is left alone with the
stamping machines. Mr. Wakamatsu's work is to take the finished
labels to the motor company and to procure needed materials. It
is he who deals with Mrs. Kobayashi. The time he spends away
from home is much more than can be accounted for by these duties,
but Mrs. Wakamatsu says little to her husband about this. She
feels that the business, after all, belongs to him.

A good part of the stamping is automatic, so Mrs. Wakamatsu fits
her housework and cooking into the time during which the machine
is running after she has set it up. She regrets, however, that she

has not much time for her children, and that her children's marks in school have not been very good. "I'm certainly no *kyōiku mama*," she said.[2]

Mrs. Kobayashi mentioned that she and her husband have acted as go-betweens in arranging marriages. The most recent wedding in which they took part was that of Takashi and Yukiko Okumura. Takashi is a distant relative of Mr. Kobayashi. He started working part-time for the company during high school. After his graduation, he moved into the company dormitory for single men. When Takashi reached a marriageable age, his parents asked the Kobayashis to look for a suitable wife. Mrs. Kobayashi made inquiries among several of her friends and acquaintances, and, upon their recommendation, introduced Takashi to three or four young women. In these cases, either Takashi or the young woman did not completely approve. Finally, Mrs. Kobayashi's *samisen* teacher recommended one of her students of good character. Mrs. Kobayashi, after determining that Yukiko was in good health and came from a good family background, arranged a meeting between the two. They liked each other at once. Yukiko says that Takashi had not been her ideal type of man, but that she felt he would be a good father and provider. Now she says she is very happy with her choice.

At the wedding ceremony, Mr. and Mrs. Kobayashi were the main participants other than the bride and groom, and they sat with them at the head table during the wedding banquet.

After the wedding, the Okumuras moved into a small company apartment two blocks from the Kobayashis. Last month, on the anniversary of Mrs. Kobayashi's father's death, Yukiko spent several days in the Kobayashi kitchen helping to prepare for the many expected guests. Having been the go-betweens at their wedding, the Kobayashis now feel doubly responsible for the welfare and guidance of the young Okumuras. In such a way the relationships between employer and employee are more and more interwoven.

There are many variations in the lives of women affected by the business *ie* of today. The wives of men in small and medium-sized businesses, as well as the wives of their employees, are often very much involved in the business. This is in contrast to the wives of men in large businesses, who sometimes see their husbands only very late at night or on Sunday. The small/medium business wives are generally part of a team. As one president of a medium-sized company said, "We share the load on a fifty-fifty basis." His wife, Mrs. Nakamura, has worked with him in his now very successful business since its inception thirty years ago. She goes to their office building and returns with her husband every day. She handles all the financial side of the business, as well as caring for the emotional needs of the company employees.

Sometimes women are directly in charge of businesses. In some very few cases they have started the company themselves; however, in most cases, the woman heading the business has been the daughter of the owner of a family business to which there is no male heir. Sometimes, even when a son-in-law has been adopted into a family without a male heir, control of the business may remain in the hands of the daughter.

Mrs. Kiyoko Fujimoto is representative of those women who are company presidents by inheritance, although she did not inherit her company directly. Her husband, who had been adopted into the family at the time of their marriage, was for a period president of the company after her father's death. However, he lived but a few years after the death of her father, and then the business fell on Mrs. Fujimoto's shoulders. In this case, the responsibility was a heavy one, because Mrs. Fujimoto had been busy with her home and children, and had not devoted a great deal of time to the company. Some relief came from the fact that several male relatives, whom she felt she could trust, were in charge of the technical and manufacturing areas of the business. This left her more freedom to learn to deal with customers and suppliers. In Japan, where people generally answer to titles rather than names, a male president would be addressed as *shachōsan* (Mr. President). She is still called *okusan* (Mrs. or Housewife), as one would address an ordinary housewife.

Unlike Mrs. Nakamura and Mrs. Kobayashi, who share in their husbands' earnings and do not have salaries of their own, Mrs. Fujimoto draws a salary from the business. Among the women mentioned so far, the only other receiving a direct salary is Mrs. Tanaka, the housekeeper. Many women in Japan today are working without pay in family businesses. Government labor-survey statistics show that in 1973 over five million women were listed as unpaid family workers (see Table I). Fifteen million women are listed as receiving some compensation, either as employees or as self-employed. This means that over one-fourth of the women working in 1973 received no salary. This condition shows some improvement since 1955, when *over half* of the women working were uncompensated (see Table II).

Table I

Number of Persons Employed by Status—1973

Status	Male	Female
Self-employed	6,570,000	3,090,000
Unpaid family workers	1,400,000	5,230,000
Employees	24,000,000	11,860,000
Total	32,110,000	20,210,000
Total persons employed	52,330,000	

Source: "Labor Force Survey," Bureau of Statistics, Office of the Prime Minister, as cited in *Status of Women in Modern Japan*, Ministry of Foreign Affairs, Japan, 1975.

Table II

Comparison of Total Female Unpaid Family Workers
with Total Female Workers and Total Persons Employed
1955-1973

Year	Female Unpaid Family Workers	Total Female Workers	Total Persons Employed
1955	9,020,000	17,000,000	40,900,000
1960	7,840,000	18,070,000	44,360,000
1965	6,920,000	18,780,000	47,300,000
1970	6,190,000	20,030,000	50,940,000
1973	5,230,000	20,210,000	52,330,000

Source: Bureau of Statistics, Office of the Prime Minister, as cited in *Status of Women in Modern Japan*, Ministry of Foreign Affairs, Japan, 1975; and *Statistical Handbook of Japan, 1972*, Bureau of Statistics, Office of the Prime Minister.

The statistics in Table III show that no unpaid women were listed as administrative and managerial workers. One wonders how women such as Mrs. Kobayashi, who are obviously handling managerial and administrative work for no salary, are listed. How realistic is the statistical picture? If, as in Table II, the statistics show over five million unpaid female family workers, how many more such workers are not even included in the statistics?

Table III

Unpaid Female Family Workers by Occupation—1973

Occupation	Female Unpaid Family Workers	Total Female Workers	Total Persons Employed
Professional and technical workers	40,000	1,370,000	3,320,000
Administrative and managerial workers	0	110,000	1,850,000
Clerical workers	320,000	3,990,000	8,100,000
Sales workers	1,030,000	2,830,000	7,030,000
Farmers, lumbermen and related	2,620,000	3,530,000	6,940,000
Workers in transport and communication	10,000	170,000	2,360,000
Craftsmen and production process	670,000	5,170,000	17,700,000
Laborers	80,000	560,000	1,580,000
Service workers	460,000	2,450,000	4,270,000
Miners, quarrymen and related workers	0	0	60,000

Source: Bureau of Statistics, Office of the Prime Minister, as cited in *Status of Women in Modern Japan,* Ministry of Foreign Affairs, Japan, 1975.

Whether they show the true picture or not, the statistics do indicate the trends in women's employment. The fact that unpaid workers are included at all in the statistics is indicative of their recognition.

Table IV shows that the industries employing the largest number of female workers were the wholesale and retail trade, manufacturing, and the services. It will be noted that about one-fourth of the women in the wholesale and retail trade were not paid, and that about one-tenth of the women in manufacturing and about one-tenth in the services are listed as unsalaried. It is the women in these industries who are discussed in this chapter, and in particular those who work in family businesses for no direct salary.

As to the other industries, the survey shows that the largest percentage of unpaid women were employed in agriculture and in fishing. It shows that over half of the work force on the farm in 1973 was composed of women, and of these, 73 percent were unsalaried. About one-fifth of the fishing industry was conducted by women,

Table IV

Unpaid Female Family Workers by Industry—1973

Industry	Female Unpaid Family Workers	Total Female Workers	Total Persons Employed
Agriculture and forestry	2,550,000	3,450,000	6,560,000
Wholesale and retail trade, finance, insurance, real estate	1,460,000	5,670,000	12,360,000
Manufacturing	600,000	5,420,000	14,360,000
Services	410,000	4,140,000	8,220,000
Construction	110,000	630,000	4,640,000
Fisheries and aquaculture	80,000	100,000	470,000
Transport, communication, electricity, gas, and water	20,000	450,000	3,690,000
Government	0	310,000	1,790,000
Mining	0	10,000	130,000

Source: Bureau of Statistics, Office of the Prime Minister, as cited in
Status of Women in Modern Japan, Ministry of Foreign Affairs,
Japan, 1975.

80 percent of whom received no direct pay. Traditionally, these two industries have occupied the whole family. Recently, however, in the rising economy, the farms and fishing boats are no longer able to support the families. The men are forced into industry, and the farming and fishing are mostly left up to the women.

It is also traditional for women to help in family businesses. Near the end of the Tokugawa era (1600-1868), the daughters of merchants were among the few women who were given an education. They were sent to school so that they could keep the accounts for the business. Today the family system is still affecting the lives of numerous Japanese women—wives, daughters, apprentices, employees—in the small and medium-sized businesses in Japan.

NOTES

[1] Ihara Saikaku, *Five Women Who Loved Love,* pp. 128-129.

[2] The trend in Japan today is for wives of salary men to spend much time encouraging their children to study—sitting by their sides while they do. These women have much more free time than formerly, and, since their husbands are occupied with business and often return late at night after spending the evening with a business associate, the wife's time is devoted almost entirely to the children—hence they are called "education mothers" (*kyōiku mama*).

CHAPTER 6
WOMEN IN
SERVICE INDUSTRIES

HISTORICAL BACKGROUND

The service industries conform in some ways to the traditional ideal
for women in Japan. We have seen that the status of women in
Japan devolved from an ancient age when woman was revered as
goddess, sun, or princess to a feudal period when woman was made
subservient and dependent on man. The ideology of a feudal military state defined woman as subordinate and dependent on man,
first as father, then as husband, and finally as son. Woman was thus
"thrice without a home." This ideological subordination of woman
was a Confucian and warrior elite ideal, but during the Tokugawa
period it became diffused throughout the lower classes. The samurai
value structure became also the value system for farmers, merchants,
and artisans. Kaibara Ekken's articulation of the subordination of
women in the *Onna Daigaku* left no doubt about the status of wom-
en. It was a prescription that was widely followed in practice.

Apart from the feudal ideology there were economic imperatives
which led to further debasement of the status of women, particularly
in the rural areas. Rural poverty in the Tokugawa period led to the
practice of "thinning" (*mabiki*) the population through female infanticide, a practice which is reflected in there being more boys
born than statistically probable. Farmers who allowed their
daughters to live often resorted to selling them into prostitution in
the cities as a way out of their own debts. Daughters thereby became indentured servants who assumed their fathers' debts and had
to work to repay the debts in turn to their employers. In a similar
way daughters were also indentured as geisha in Kyoto and Edo

107

where the geisha tradition grew. As future geisha the young apprentice *maiko* received training in playing musical instruments, particularly the *samisen* and *koto*, and in dance and the art of conversation. In education they were thus better off than their counterparts who were sold into prostitution, but in both cases they were indentured and worked many years to pay off debts of their parents.

The tradition of woman as the servant and subordinate of man has existed in many civilizations and in many ages in the history of the world. It is not unique to Japan, for most societies have been misogynous and have developed ways to ensure the subordination of woman to man. In Japan tradition has made the domestic role the feminine ideal. If a woman could not achieve this ideal because of economic or other circumstances then she worked in paid service to a man or to women of the aristocracy. The service industries thus developed as occupations sanctioned by the traditional ideology.

During the feudal period and the earlier Heian court era upper-class women were employed as court ladies either at the court of the emperor or shōgun or at lower levels within the feudal hierarchy. There were women who served as skilled hairdressers or seamstresses. Women of the lower classes worked as servant girls in the inns along the routes used by the daimyo trains, primarily the Tōkaidō, the great highway that connected Edo and the seat of shōgunal power with the port towns at the head of the Inland Sea. These inn girls were from poor families, but were probably better off than their counterparts who were indentured servants. They were local girls from farm families and were working before they reached the age of marriage. Artisans and merchants who provided goods and services to the daimyo and samurai were chiefly male. If girls were employed in the households of the feudal aristocracy, they worked as domestic servants.

Wives of merchants were an exception to this two-role pattern for women in the Tokugawa period. The wives of merchants were usually literate and were often account keepers. In the feudal economy their functions were only semi-legitimate, since Confucian ideology defined the merchants as parasitic and beyond the pale of orthodox economic activity. In this context women functioned in economic roles that were not open to women who remained within the feudal framework and class structure.

Farm women were another exception to the wife/servant role paradigm in Tokugawa Japan, for farm women did perform economically significant functions in rural families. Yet their lack of real power or status is reflected in the fact that their fathers, if they fell into penurious circumstances, could sell them into prostitution in the cities. Those who were sold to the cities were nonetheless more fortunate than the female infants who were "thinned."

The Meiji era, with its spectacular transformation and modernization in most areas, remained socially conservative and committed to the traditional family system. The Meiji Civil Code delineated women as basically "good wife and wise mother" and subordinated her legally to man. Women were not persons as defined in law. They were unable to own or to transmit property or to divorce. This ideology and legal disability remained in effect through World War II. Those women who before the war were forced to abandon the ideal and to find jobs remained largely in servant or at least subordinate capacities, whether in offices, factories, or in the service occupations.

Since the war more and more women have gone to the city from rural areas to find work for two or three years before finding husbands. Migrating to the city to work is today primarily a matter of choice rather than the coercion of earlier eras. In the city in recent times it is a common practice that when a middle-class girl has graduated from high school, junior college, or college, she may work for a year or two before marriage. When she reaches twenty-four or twenty-five she stops work and marries, according to prevailing custom and statistical evidence.

SERVICE INDUSTRY WORKERS TODAY

Today the employment patterns of women have not diverged markedly from before the war, despite great strides in legal status and education. One-third of all employed women are office workers, 28 percent are factory workers, and service industry workers are the third largest group, 14 percent. Women represent 50 percent of all those employed in service industries.[1] Except for agriculture, service industries have the highest ratio of female to male workers of any occupation. Women in the service industries also have the highest ratio of women's to men's wages of any occupation: 61.5 percent.[2]

There are nonetheless some significant changes in employment patterns of women workers in recent years. Two major changes in the female work force are the rise in absolute numbers of women workers and the rise in employment of mature and married women. While in 1953 the number of women working outside the home was 4.3 million, in 1973 it was 11.86 million.[3] Twenty years ago married women were half of all employed women; today they are two-thirds of the female work force.[4] Both the change in the over-all size of the work force and the change in the marital status of women workers have been reflected in the service industries. While many service industry workers are in their twenties or younger, there is another group of workers forty-five and older. Service industry girls in many areas have little opportunity for promotion, but the more mature women tend to work as owners, managers, or alone as self-employed workers. They therefore tend to fall into a higher salary bracket than the younger working girls. As with the female work force generally, there are relatively few women service workers in their thirties, when they tend to be at home raising children.

The employment of a dual-age-peak female work force is a matter of government policy as well as a socially sanctioned practice. The Economic Council of the Prime Minister's Office in 1963 proposed "extensive use of young, unmarried female workers in simple jobs," hiring "only a small number of educated women in supervisory positions," returning women to their families at "a suitable age for marriage," and rehiring "persons of middle age."[5] This policy ensures that women at both age levels will be hired at lower wages, without pensions, security, insurance, seniority bonuses, or other fringe benefits which male workers normally enjoy. Further, although the 1947 Labor Standards Law stipulates that wages are to be equal for women, in practice jobs are defined as different, whether or not they are in fact, so that discrimination in wages is possible and common.

The law, ostensibly designed among other things to protect the interests of women, has often been used in the opposite way. Employers are required by law to give maternity and menstruation leave. If employers are also required to pay equal wages, there are arguments against hiring women, in the view of many employers. Such leaves add pressure for employers to hire women at low-paying menial tasks, so that in fact their jobs often are different from those filled by men.

Enforcement of laws protecting equal rights for women is a mixed picture to date. One example is the practice of enforced retirement on marriage or when a child is born. A secretary sued in Tokyo District Court for violation of Article 14 of the Constitution when she was forced to retire at marriage. She won a judgment in 1966 in a ruling that "the system of retirement upon marriage is a breach of Article 90 of the Civil Code."[6] There are numerous other practices that are still common too, for example, earlier retirement for women. There are indications in judicial rulings that the Supreme Court is still supporting the traditional family structure, in disregard of the law. And in times of recession women workers are the first to be laid off.

Despite all the financial and traditional disadvantages confronting the working woman, there has always been a relatively large number of young women in the service industries. Apart from tradition there are other reasons for the high proportion of women in these occupations. While the educational level for women in general is rising, the majority of women still do not go beyond high school. Even women with college degrees cannot apply to take the entrance exams for most large firms. Women are therefore cut off from a major employment track followed by male college graduates: becoming a "salary man." Entrance into a large company insures a man a secure income for life. This comfortable route is not available to women. As one young woman said, "There is no way a girl with a B.A. can compete with a boy in Japan." For women, whether high school or college graduates, finding a job is a more difficult proposition. Many high school graduates, seeking a skill, attend vocational schools for six months or a year to learn to become beauticians or seamstresses. Thus equipped, girls are able to find positions in small establishments in the cities or regional towns. Most girls in their twenties or late teens working in service industries have followed this route to enter the work force.

Another track is also apparent, especially for women over forty in the service industries. These women must earn their own living. Typically they are divorced or widowed and enter the work force late in life, often with children to support. In some cases they own or manage establishments with their husbands. Today there are increasing numbers of mature women who are married but who still seek employment outside the home as a matter of choice rather than absolute necessity. In either case, these middle-aged women are often owners or managers of small establishments. They typically display considerable entrepreneurial skill and ingenuity, excelling in decision-making and initiative. They are excluded from employment within Japan's large business establishments, wherein a young "salary man's" future lies before him. This is a major difference between male and female employment patterns.

There is a thin but symbolically significant line separating women workers in the service industries from those in the *mizu shōbai* (see Chapter 7), the ladies of the night, not all of whom are prostitutes. Girls who go into the service industries want to and do acquire skills which enable them to enter "respectable" occupations such as beautician, seamstress, or airline stewardess. They attend a special or vocational school specifically designed to equip them for these jobs, and they thus avoid the pitfalls of menial office jobs. They regard themselves as part of the "legitimate" working force, and they recognize a distinction between themselves and bar hostesses or cabaret girls, who get jobs without particular qualifications in skill. Service industry girls realize that a bar hostess is not highly respected by society in general, and that she is hired on the basis of her face or her body. Recognition of this difference is part of the symbolic value of the service industry vocation. Waitresses, who are hired without special schooling and given minimal on-the-job training, mark the borderline between the service industries as a whole and the *mizu shōbai* workers. Service industry workers are technicians who take pride in their skills. Beauticians have since the war become licensed. Seamstresses are still often hired through the apprentice system, a practice which before the war was prevalent among beauticians as well. Though seamstresses are not licensed, their skills are highly developed and readily marketable.

The symbolic value of the skilled service industry worker is important, because she realizes that there may be more money in being a bar hostess, sometimes a lot more money. If she is not willing to sacrifice her respectability she remains in the service industries. If she is unable to resist the financial attractions of becoming a bar hostess she goes into the job with full recognition of the sacrifice she is making in social respectability. It is generally more difficult for a bar hostess than for a service industry girl to find a husband in middle-class society, but she has traded off this loss in return for what she hopes will be substantial financial gain.

One very articulate young woman described hostesses as the "drop-outs" of society who refuse to acquire a skill and have no other qualifications. "After becoming a hostess a girl generally deteriorates and is deprived of her intellectual ability," she continued. Yet many hostesses do have a sense of pride in their degree of financial success and the number of regular customers they are able to attract. This sense of pride enables them to deal personally with the opprobrium of society generally.

SERVICE INDUSTRY WORKERS SPEAK

The sample of workers interviewed here was small—sixteen women—and was not based on any statistical method of selection. With the exception of two in Nagoya the women were interviewed in Tokyo. The range of occupations included beauticians, seamstresses, restaurant and hotel managers and owners, waitresses, a room service girl, and an airline stewardess and clerk. Two bar hostesses were interviewed for comparative purposes, but a more complete treatment of this category may be found in Chapter 7. The selection of respondents primarily in Tokyo need not be viewed as a "biased sample," because women in Tokyo come from all parts of the country. For a specifically rural category see the chapter on farm women. In the chapter on factory workers a sample in Nagoya has been interviewed.

Service industry workers, especially those below the age of thirty, tend to come from the countryside to the city to find work. Their goal in some cases is to get away from the countryside, though they may return home for vacation or send money back to their parents occasionally. When they marry they choose boys in Tokyo, for most boys as well as girls have left the rural areas behind. Older women who manage or own small establishments were also often born in rural areas or towns rather than in Tokyo. In some cases they have come to Tokyo to go to school or marry. None of these women voices any intention of returning to the countryside even when she retires. This birthplace profile is usual for Tokyo residents, over half of whom were probably born elsewhere. Despite the congestion of the metropolis, no one seems to want to leave Tokyo. The capital is more than just a large governmental center, for in Tokyo are concentrated the intellectual and cultural life of Japan, the headquarters of most major enterprises, and the largest entertainment industry in the world. Few choose to leave a city which provides the finest cuisine of Paris or Peking, the best department stores in the world, art galleries and museums which attest to prodigious artistic creativity, and a pace and verve unmatched anywhere in Japan or perhaps in the world. Whatever one's level of education, high school graduate and Ph.D. alike add to and are nurtured by the vitality of Tokyo. Rural Japan, like rural America, has become the home of less than a fifth of the nation's population.

Respondents interviewed in the service industry category came from large families: the median family size was four children. Birth order apparently was not a critical factor in their leaving home to work or in working after marriage. Youngest as well as eldest children were represented among respondents. None of them had inherited businesses, though one beautician was taking over management of her mother-in-law's business and had been selected as the son's bride because of her profession and proficiency. She, like all other respondents, had selected her vocation herself.

Many of the respondents were daughters of "good families" whose fathers had attained high levels of education. Seven of the fathers were university graduates, and three were prewar graduates of technical or vocational schools. Six had gone only as far as primary or middle school. Most of them were not from impoverished backgrounds, though those girls from very large families left their families at a relatively early stage in life, i.e., when they graduated from high school. Fathers of older respondents in higher paying positions were not necessarily better educated than fathers of respondents under thirty. None of the respondents mentioned the influence of her father as a positive or negative factor in the choice of her vocation. In some cases, mothers influenced their daughters' choice of work.

Respondents' mothers were less well educated than fathers, though half the women over thirty had mothers who attended *jogakkō*. Younger respondents' mothers tended to be less well educated; only one had attended college and none had attended junior college. A few interviewees reported that their mothers worked in offices or shops, in some cases family enterprises together with their fathers. Most respondents reported their mothers taught them some knowledge of cooking, sewing, and other household arts. In those cases where mothers were working and were too busy to spend much time with their daughters, there were domestic servants who did housework and probably did not require the daughters to help. In any case, most girls studied some home economics in school.

Training in the home for one's role as a woman varied with age. Girls under thirty reported very little training to prepare for their roles as women or wives. The most conservative of the younger interviewees, Mrs. T., said her mother had taught her to respect men, that men are admirable, and that women must be strong inwardly but should not display their strength externally. Women should remain behind the scenes supporting their husbands. Several older respondents reported this kind of advice from their mothers also. This respondent concurred with her mother's advice and was acting it out in her own life. Older respondents reported receiving various kinds of advice from their mothers. One was told by her mother always to be bright, obedient, and *onnarashii*. The term *onnarashii*—womanly or ladylike—is always used with positive connotations. If a girl is *onnarashii* she will have an easier time finding a suitable husband. Gentleness and kindness were other virtues encouraged by mothers. Mrs. A. reported being taught to respect her mother-in-law and to preserve the family and *ie*, or house. Another woman from Kyushu noted that Kyushu is particularly strict in training girls for their roles as women, and that women in Kyushu are subordinated within the family more rigidly than women in other parts of Japan.

All public schools and colleges since the war are coeducational, and the general educational level of women is on the rise. Today, 82 percent of girls attend high school and 28 percent go on to college. What about the formal educational level of girls in the service industries? Of those interviewed, all had graduated at least from high school. Among those over thirty, there was a higher proportion who had attended higher schools, i.e., *jogakkō*. Among the younger girls only one was a university graduate, and she had graduated from Japan's most prestigious institution, Tokyo University. Her aspirations are significantly higher than those of any other respondent represented here. She hopes to study for a doctorate, preferably in the United States. She is the daughter of a junior college president and has obviously been exposed to a more academic family atmosphere than the other respondents. Many stated that they would like to go back to school, but when questioned about this response they had no specific plans, nor had they investigated the possibilities of attending night classes. One was taking classes in English at the Y.M.C.A. One respondent said her parents had wanted to send her to college, but she chose not to go, as she did not believe it would be of great help to her in her aspiration to be an airline stewardess. Instead, she had attended the Friends' High School because of its reputation as a good school for studying English. Several respondents had attended vocational school for one to three years beyond high school to study dressmaking or to learn the beautician's trade. One more mature woman graduated from junior college but was deterred by her mother from studying further.

Some women expressed frustration at not being able for financial or other reasons to study other subjects which would have prepared them for preferred vocations. Mrs. K. had an unfulfilled wish to study painting and to paint. Mrs. B. had wanted to go to college to study acting. Miss M., who had become a seamstress, said as a child she had always thought she would become a doctor or lawyer. Wartime conditions prevented her from obtaining the necessary education, but her life style still attracted the admiration of her friends. Miss T. said she had wanted to study Japanese history, but her mother had insisted that she attend sewing school for two years. She was in fact earning her living not in dressmaking but as a bar hostess. Miss N. as a child had wanted to be a journalist; instead she is a beautician.

Beyond their regular schooling, most interviewees have received some training in the polite feminine arts. A certificate from an ikebana school is today one of the requisites for finding a good husband, and the ikebana schools make huge profits on this universal market for refinement. A scandal a few years ago revealed that the male head of one of the largest ikebana establishments in Tokyo was guilty of tax evasion on a massive scale. Flower arrangement is the feminine art most commonly studied by women in the service industries. Nearly all respondents had spent some time studying *hana*. The tea ceremony is another popular study for girls in search of polish. Another art commonly studied is calligraphy, which is generally taught to both sexes in school. A few respondents said they preferred calligraphy to ikebana or *chanoyū*. Other arts studied by one or two respondents were *samisen, koto, nagauta* (old-style singing), dancing, and piano, which is a common skill of middle-class girls today, along with ballet. Only one respondent stated that she had never studied any of the polite feminine arts, no doubt reflecting her impoverished background.

The educational level of these women related to their reading habits and familiarity with the media. Most of these women had had no opportunity to develop their intellectual tastes to a high level of sophistication. They all nevertheless did read at least one daily newspaper regularly. Some reported reading two and even three papers daily, which would make them very well informed generally. A few admitted to reading weekly magazines, but several said they did not read or like weeklies. Weekly magazines have the reputation for stressing gossip and scandal, which is no doubt why some did not wish to admit they read them. Several regularly read one or more women's monthly magazines. Some reported their magazine reading is related to their work. Many stated they are fond of reading and

do read one or more books per month. One stated that she reads
twelve paperback novels a month. Another with highly developed
tastes in military history said that she buys about eight books a
month. Since she works at night and is in addition highly intelligent, her report is probably credible. Since these women all work
long hours, a few stated they had no time to read or watch television. Many watch news, movies, documentaries, and talk shows
on television. Only one admitted she watches women's programs
dealing with cooking or sewing. A few said they do not like wom-
en's programs. As women's programs are usually shown during the
morning hours and are directed to the tastes of housewives at home,
this response was understandable.

These respondents were selected on the basis of occupation, not of
marital status. The majority of them were married, however, and
they were therefore living a dual-role life style. The marital status
of service workers, as for women generally, depends partly on age.
Those over thirty were mostly married, divorced, or had lived as a
common law wife, with two exceptions in their thirties. One of
these was a top-ranking bar hostess who plans to retire in two years
at thirty-four and "find an American husband, because Japanese
husbands do not divorce their wives but American husbands do."
Several of the girls under thirty were also married. Those over forty
reported that they had arranged marriages, with two exceptions.
Two of the arranged meetings were through mothers-in-law, who had
selected the girls because of their ability and working skills. After
marriage both brides had lived for a time with their parents-in-law;
one continues to. Those under thirty who were married had met
not through arrangement but had married classmates or boys they
had met in connection with their work.

An *omiai* (arranged meeting) today in the city may mean simply a
formal or informal introduction, after which the couple will date and
get better acquainted. There is less family pressure to continue
through until marriage after an arranged meeting than there is in the
countryside, where an arranged meeting fifteen years ago might lead
to marriage when the couple did not know each other at all. It is
not uncommon for individuals today to have several arranged meetings. One young man known to this writer is said to have had fifty
omiai before he finally chose a wife. In the case of a semitraditional
omiai it is still usual for the *nakōdo* or go-between to perform the
introduction, after first informing both parties of the qualities and
virtues of the other. Pictures may be exchanged. If the *nakōdo* per-
forms this formal function he/she is paid at the wedding for services
rendered. The *nakōdo* may be consulted later if the couple have
marital problems.

All respondents, including those who had had arranged marriages,
stated they believed a woman should be able to choose her own

husband. Personal decision-making, however, like public decision-making in Japan, is a complex process. Even one woman who had lived with a married man for several years stated that she did not make the decision by herself, but had consulted her parents. Her father had given his sanction, saying that if she would have no regrets afterward he gave his approval.

While marriage was a nearly universal aspiration for these women as for most women in Japan, this did not preclude a desire to work. Though Miss T. intends to find a husband, she says, "There are two kinds of women: those who can remain at home and be good wives, and those who need to work outside. Those who can't stay home have the highest divorce rate. I would be in the second category." There is also the pride these women have in their ability to earn their own living. If suddenly widowed or divorced, the married women would still be able to make their own way financially. With the exception of waitresses and hostesses they are highly skilled workers who enjoy using their skills for the benefit of themselves and their clients.

Most women interviewed did their own housework, whether single or married. The exceptions were the more mature women in higher-paying positions, some of whom had maids or helpers at home. Some of these women articulated their disinterest in housework. Some of this domestic help was part-time, since a full-time maid is a phenomenon of the past except for the very wealthy. Even those husbands who supported the dual-role life styles of their wives did not actively help in domestic chores. Some women stated that their husbands did occasionally help, but when questioned about specific tasks it became apparent that the husbands did not participate. Since men in Japan tend to work very long hours and to return home late in the evening, it is obvious that, whatever their intentions, they simply do not have time to help their wives at home. There is very little evidence of any change in traditional patterns in this regard, according to a recent study of *tomobataraki* (working couple) families.[7] The percentage of time men spend helping their wives at home is still insignificant.

There are nevertheless indications among girls of marriage age that they are becoming more assertive in defining qualifications for husbands. In recent years the saying has been that a groom had to have "a house, a car, and no mother." Still more recently, there are three new conditions for a husband, the "three c's": a husband who shares the cleaning, cooking, and child care. Judging from Yamamoto's research findings, these conditions are more likely to be found in aspiration than in practice. Still, revolutions only occur in situations of rising expectations.

There is little time in the daily schedules of these women to spend with their husbands on leisure or recreation. Their husbands have even less time. Nor is this a traditional pattern in Japan. Husbands and wives do not typically spend an evening out together. If a husband is out in the evening he is probably out with colleagues from work, for business and for pleasure. This is a common means of maintaining good relations with work associates and a way in which important business is often conducted. One couple attending a mixed party recently admitted it was the first time in twenty-five years of marriage that they had been to a party together in the evening. Foreign couples were the catalyst in bringing them out together.

Most of the women questioned did not engage in any special recreational activity with their husbands on their day off, which has in some cases now become two days off per week. Even dinner is a meal which typically husband and wife eat separately more often than not. Companionship between husbands and wives is still unusual, if the daily schedule of these women is any indication. Some of the younger women reported that they spend their day off with their husbands.

Older respondents with children also stated they spent less time supervising their children's study than was usual with full-time housewives. The phenomenon of the over-protective *kyōiku mama* who watches over her son's every action and urges him on to pass exam after exam was criticized by most of these mature working women. *Kyōiku mama*s generally expend more energy on their sons' education than their daughters'.

Perhaps the working experience of these women influenced their relatively liberal attitudes and goals for their children. Most mothers of sons said they hoped their sons would be able to do what they hoped to do in life. For their daughters these mothers wished for a happy life and a happy home, and also the ability to work well, if they wished to work, and to be in good health. It was more common that marriage was mentioned as a life goal for daughters than for sons, though some mothers mentioned they hoped for a happy marriage for their sons. Some mothers expressed satisfaction with the activities of their daughters. Some stated, too, that childrearing today is less restrictive than it was twenty years ago, though several mentioned that mothers interfere too much in their children's lives.

Work was the common focal point in these women's lives, in actuality if not in ideal. They had in common the fact that they all work hard and they work long hours at a regular job. The working day of beauticians and seamstresses is particularly long, generally over eight hours. Many of the beauticians interviewed work nine hours a day six days a week. If they have a complaint regarding their work it is that the hours are so long. One owner-manager of a shop stated that she often is so busy that she cannot take time for lunch or even a shorter break during the day. Apart from these long working hours many service industry women, in addition, commute for as much as one or two hours daily. Owners and self-employed women in these occupations work particularly hard and expect their employees to work hard also. Miss M., who is self-employed, reported that for several years she did not get more than four hours' sleep a night. One does not get the impression that these women entrepreneurs have an exploitative attitude toward their employees. Their self-discipline and devotion to the work ethic is strong. Some reported working ten hours daily or even into the evening. The work schedules of airline stewardesses and room service girls vary from day to day, apparently because the work is so strenuous physically. Their work day is also more than eight hours, plus commuting time.

Though they worked strenuous hours and sometimes in difficult conditions, it was not only financial necessity which dictated the working life style of these women. In all cases they gained some satisfaction through their work. They expressed their satisfaction in various ways. Miss M. said she enjoyed being independent and able to earn her own living. Many in fact emphasized that they would be able to support themselves without their husbands, and some added that it was desirable for women to be able to earn their own living. Miss K. said what she liked most about her work is that "there are no limits. It has a very broad scope. I can do things for my clients which they can't do for themselves." Miss M. said she likes to "make lovely clothes for customers," and many expressed pleasure in being able to satisfy their customers. Others said they enjoyed the variety of activities and the opportunity to meet all kinds of people in their work. Mrs. B., a beautician-owner, said: "I enjoy my work. I am working for my own pleasure and health. I really feel that I am working for myself. There are no especially bad features of my work." Some said they had chosen their work—bar hostess, beautician, or waitress—because they thought it would be the easiest way to earn a living.

The work satisfaction of these women is reflected too in the length of time they aspire to work. Only two said they would stop working when they find a good husband. One of these is an extremely successful bar hostess who has no intention of continuing her occupation indefinitely. Several said they will continue to work so long as they are able and healthy, although in some cases their husbands are not enthusiastic about their working. Their sense of identity and worth is related to their being able to continue to work and to derive satisfaction therefrom.

One problem which sometimes dictates retirement on birth of a child is the general scarcity of child-care facilities in Japan. Unless a new mother has a mother or mother-in-law readily available, she is virtually forced to retire to care for her child herself, at least until the child reaches nursery school age. If she then returns to work the birth of a second child will simply create a repetition of the same pattern.

Two of these young women had recently quit jobs with a major airline, but for very different reasons. Mrs. Y. was extremely angry about discrimination against women in pay and promotion on the job, and had resigned to gain more education and a better job. The other, Mrs. T., had quit because she felt unable to function in her dual-role life style. Her highly idealistic expectations of herself as a wife did not allow her to continue to perform her job functions. She had no particular complaint about the job itself, though she worked for the same airline as did Mrs. Y., who also quit. Mrs. T. was the only one of those interviewed who abandoned a job because she believed work interfered with her role as wife. The traditional domestic ideal was exerting a powerful influence on her. As a kind of self-imposed penance for having failed to live up to her own rigid ideal of a wife—also the traditional ideal—she was divesting herself of a cherished job. She stated there were "other things" she wanted to do but could not do so long as she continued working. Among them she mentioned studying ikebana and the tea ceremony, the traditional feminine arts.

While work did not figure so prominently in the articulated life goals and aspirations of most of these women, it was clear that in terms of actual life style and self-image, work was of central importance to them. It was easier for these women to articulate their life goals in terms of the traditional domestic ideal, even though it appeared to be of more secondary importance to their real lives.

The service industry workers are not so highly organized as women in other occupations, for example, factory workers. If they work in a large firm they may belong to a company union, which is oriented to the interests of the employer as much as the employee. In part because of the strong paternalistic tradition, nevertheless, the hotel or other large employer gives some attention to the fringe benefits usual in a paternalistically structured economy. Company vacations and group travel are a feature of most employment situations, even smaller employers tending to provide for such vacations. In a smaller firm where relations between employer and employee are closer than in large firms, there is often a chance for recognition of ability and merit through functional and salary advancement. Larger firms such as airlines have more fixed policies regarding promotion and salary for women employees, as well as for men. Women are hired at lower-paying positions and are given lower salaries even if their qualifications are equal to male employees hired at the same time. Chance for advancement in a large firm is far greater for men, since companies in Japan uniformly anticipate that women will not work for more than two or three years before marriage. This policy has not changed despite the statistical evidence that more married women are entering the work force.

Mrs. O., who works as a room service girl in one of Tokyo's largest hotels, reports she belongs to a national hotel workers' union, but that she does not go to meetings except at bonus time or when there is a specific issue at stake. In cases of crisis she believes the union is helpful. There is no women's section in the union, but some of the women employees would like to organize one. One of the grievances of workers in this hotel is that there is no policy of promoting women after the age of twenty-nine, as the management feels that women over this age are no longer popular (i.e., attractive) with hotel guests. Despite this lack of opportunity for promotion and the fact that she is married, Mrs. O. intends to work until retirement age, fifty-five. It is apparent that Mrs. O. has been radicalized by her experience, for she reads *Akahata* (organ of the Communist Party) regularly and is considering joining the Communist Party, at the suggestion of a male friend. Mrs. Y., an airline employee, reported that the union was weak and in collusion with the company, which had created the union to compete with an earlier and stronger union. The company succeeded in undermining the first union and replacing it with a stronger company union. Nevertheless, the pilots and cabin crews have their own unions which continue to pose a problem for the company.

Pay with the airline is quite high by comparison with other service jobs. Stewardesses and desk employees start at a monthly base pay of ¥100,000 and get a twice-yearly bonus which nearly doubles the base pay, after the employee has been with the firm for two years. In addition there is a housing allowance. Yet there is no policy of promoting women to managerial positions, for again the company anticipates that women will retire within three years. Large firms are also still successful in discriminating in pay on the basis of sex. It is obvious that, as in other areas of work, employment with larger firms affords more fringe benefits than with smaller firms, and for this reason large firms can attract women despite discrimination. Smaller firms or shops in the service industries are not able to offer as broad a spectrum of fringe benefits to their employees. Instead they may provide smaller-scale, more direct, benefits such as meals, annual group vacations, uniforms, and functional recognition of special ability. Women in smaller organizations are less likely to be placed in positions where they simply serve tea or coffee to male fellow-employees, as is the case with workers in large offices. Their skills are functionally more important to the organizations which employ them.

Most of the unmarried women respondents are paid salaries which enable them to live apart from their families, in small apartments at a minimal level. They are able to provide their own food and housing and to dress in good taste. Beauticians and seamstresses appear to be particularly well groomed and to take pride in their appearance. Airline stewardesses and bar hostesses are sometimes able to dress according to high fashion. Service workers can generally put aside monthly savings and occasionally send money to their parents if they are not well off. This form of filial piety is especially evident if the daughter has left her parents behind in the countryside.

Service workers interviewed in this group responded in various ways to questions about their ideals, values, and attitudes. If their responses were not as sophisticated or complex as those of more highly educated women, they nevertheless held a diversity of views on issues of fundamental importance. Some of the differences may be attributed to generational factors. More mature women in higher paying jobs had developed philosophies which reflect longer experience, but also greater exposure to the traditional ideology. Younger women tend to have less to say on more philosophical issues than their middle-aged counterparts. Women from better economic backgrounds if anything adhere more closely to the traditional feminine ideal. At the same time the views of younger women are often less forceful.

Another question regarding the amount of freedom and independence a woman should have related to a woman's ability to earn her own living, a pattern deviant from the traditional ideal. Nearly all respondents feel that a woman should be able to support herself if she has the ability and wants to. Since these respondents are all working, this response is not necessarily surprising. Mrs. K., who began working later in life, felt more strongly about the advantages of the dual-role life style for women. "Usually I think it's better if they have some kind of work. Most women depend on men too much," she said. Only conservative Mrs. T. said, "No, women should not be able to earn their own living." She was projecting her own strong feelings that work interferes with a wife's obligations.

Other attitudes toward work were more diverse. All but one feel that if women have the ability to do the same work as men they should get equal pay. Yet the question of whether women should be able to do the same work elicited a number of qualifications. Mrs. M., who actually does work together with her husband in their bar, commented, "It's unreasonable to expect women to do the same kind of work. They must work at home as well, and men don't help with the housework, so they have a double burden, a very heavy burden." Miss A. feels, "Yes, but in some cases it's unreasonable. Men have more strength and it's necessary for some kinds of work to have more." Mrs. Y. added, "Well, it depends on the kind of

work. There are no mental limitations for women, though there may
be some physical ones."

The long working hours of service workers leave little time or energy
for social activities and contacts, especially for those who are married.
The pattern of social interaction for single working girls was very different from that for married women. Single girls eat out with friends
on the way home in the evening, anywhere from twelve to twenty
times a month. Or they sometimes stop for a drink or movies on
the way home. Middle-aged women and married women report going out a few times a month to a few times a year in the evening,
though they apparently enjoy such social activities. Some stated
they take brief vacations with friends rather than with their husbands. The manager-owners have little opportunity to go out with
friends, but state that their friends come to see them at work, or
that they consider their customers as friends and get satisfaction
from dealing with them in the work situation. Three of the more
financially successful women like to play golf on week-ends. Miss
T., the hostess, belongs to two country clubs, membership in which
would cost her several million yen; she plays with people she meets
at the clubs, mostly men. Mrs. Y., a young married woman who
apparently has an especially companionable relationship with her
husband, goes dancing with him in the evening occasionally. Several women mentioned they enjoy going shopping with their friends
on days off. Mrs. M., who is not especially affluent, swims or skis
regularly with her family, according to the season.

The political dimension was an area in which these women had not
developed strong opinions. There was unanimity, however, in the
belief that it was a good thing for women to be involved in politics.
Two mentioned that it was inadvisable to discuss politics with customers or guests, and Mrs. T. said airline stewardesses are forbidden
to talk politics while on duty. Some feel there should be no distinction between the sexes in political participation. Mrs. O., who
is considering joining the Communist Party, feels working women
should be more involved in politics, particularly where the interests
of older people and the status of women are concerned. Two of
the more sophisticated respondents had reservations about the wom-
en who are extremely visible politically. "Looking at it objectively,"
commented Mrs. I., "many women get into the House of Councillors
solely because of popularity in some other area. About half of them
are in politics because of their popularity." Miss T. tended to agree:
"It's a good thing for women to be in politics, but in Japan they are
superficial people. Anyone can get in. In the U.S. they have to go
to law school," she said.

These women were in unanimous agreement on the desirability of
the right to divorce for women. Only Mrs. T., who was obviously
working very hard at her marriage, said, "Yes, I approve of the

right, but I'll try as hard as possible to avoid divorce." There was far less agreement on the controversial issue of abortion and the pending revision of the abortion law to restrict the right of abortion. Several favored abortion, but others had reservations. Mrs. K. felt, "If the law is too strict people will find a way to get around the law, so it's better not to have too strict a law." Two of the more articulate women favored a stricter law because of the issue of personal responsibility. Miss M. stated, "People should think about the problem before it reaches the stage of abortion, and be responsible for the protection and preservation of life." The issue had a very real meaning for her, since she has raised a child outside marriage. Miss T., too, favored a stricter law, also mentioning the issue of personal responsibility. "Japanese women are too submissive," she said. "It's better to be stricter in sexual matters. In this business [hostessing] it's better not to have relations with customers, because if something happens they may not come back."

Because of heavy working schedules most of these women had no opportunity to participate in organizational activities. All of them who had raised children had belonged to P.T.A. while their children were in school, but several expressed doubt about the value of the organization. Mrs. Y., who had been active in P.T.A., said "everyone had to take turns at being an officer. I didn't like it." More middle-aged women than younger women belonged to professional organizations. Several belonged to owners' associations aimed at improving their tax positions. Mrs. Y. belonged to a consumer group connected with Shufuren. Its aim was to provide goods more cheaply, particularly milk, and to provide for distribution as well. She had also worked for the campaign of Fusae Ichikawa for election to the House of Councillors. Ms. Ichikawa has long been associated with consumer and women's issues, and she succeeded in a recent election despite her advanced age of over eighty.

Most respondents have some awareness of the disadvantages of being a woman in Japanese society, but many have definite notions about the worth of women generally and of themselves in particular. Over half admit to wishing at least as a child that they had been born a boy, but they divide equally on the question of whether men are superior to women. As Mrs. B. put it, "Women are stronger in endurance. This is the strong point of Japanese women. But the socialization of women in Japanese society is very strong, and there are still many things women can't do because of the influence of society, not because of lack of ability." Several others mentioned that the difference in role expectations and training accounts for differences in life patterns. Mrs. M. believes there is a generational difference. "Men in the Meiji period took things more in their stride," she said. "Today they throw a tantrum." She is an authority on male tantrums, for her husband beats her and has scarred her face. She has not divorced him because she has no confidence in her ability to support herself. Mrs. H., who owns and manages a chain of large restaurants with her husband, feels "Women are better in terms of getting things done." Mrs. Y. responded very spiritedly, "It's true that in contemporary Japanese society men occupy more important positions than women. But this is because they are maintained by the existence of the women who serve them. Their home life is managed by women, so they don't need to be concerned about it."

Those who feel most strongly that men are superior are the bar hostesses. Miss T. explained, "Yes, clearly men are better than women. The smartest woman is about on a par with the stupidest man. Girls don't have their own goals. My mother didn't teach me this; it's based on my own observation." Obviously a very able and intelligent girl, Miss T. belies her own protestations, which may in fact be the way she rationalizes the very subservient nature of her work. She appears to put herself down, or to put women down generally, in order to make her work psychologically acceptable to herself. It is interesting to note, at the same time, that she plans to retire from her occupation as soon as she is able financially, and that she has worked with great efficiency and determination toward this goal. She earns $80,000 a year.

Decision-making is a troublesome area for most respondents. Several women said they had never made an important decision alone, that they had always consulted with their families when making decisions. Others responded that the most important decisions they had made were related to marriage, i.e., to marry, not to marry, or to divorce. Work-related decisions were also important to these women. Mrs. B. and Mrs. K. said decisions relating to both marriage and to work and how to coordinate the two were the most important they had made.

Most women have a clear notion of the obligations and contributions of women in society. They feel that marriage and raising a family are primary obligations, but several mentioned that if a woman is working she has an obligation to utilize all her ability for her job. Mrs. I. summed up the attitudes of others: "A woman's obligations are to have a happy family, to alleviate the problems of others, and to have charm." Referring to contributions to society, many women mentioned promotion of the welfare of society generally, education of children, and the happiness of others. Mrs. Y. stated women have no special obligation "except the unavoidable experience of bearing a child," a duty to which she did not look forward. She added acerbically, "It is an irony and paradox that woman's duty is to make men prosper in their careers. Most women won't put it in this way." As if to prove her point, Mrs. Y. said woman's duty is "to make work easier for men."

What is success for a woman? This was a question which had never occurred to many of these women. A few had no idea of what constitutes success for a woman. Factors mentioned by some were a good marriage, giving men strength, social position and money, and being famous. Some thought maintaining a business and family as well would mean success. The most frequent response, however, was doing well at one's own objective. "There is no absolute standard," added Mrs. I., "it varies with the person."

A question was put to a male official high up in a government ministry: sociologists have often written about the "elite course" for men in Japan, leading to Tokyo University and a job in a large firm. Do you think there can be said to be an "elite course" for women? He replied, on the assumption that the question referred to the social elite, that most parents still prefer their daughters to graduate from college, to work for one or two years, and then to make a good marriage, i.e., to marry a man who has followed the "elite course." When it was suggested that the question referred perhaps to working women, he shifted the discussion to women in the professions, the small professional elite of doctors, lawyers, and professors. In this case he offered the opinion that there is no single track for women entering this highly selected elite. Chapter 9 speaks to this question in more detail. The term "elite," when applied to women, still conjures in many minds the image of a woman following the traditional domestic ideal—making a "good marriage," and achieving status vicariously through her husband.

If given the choice of anything in the next five years, what would you choose to do? This question also caused women to pause. Many things came to mind: meeting people, going to school, marriage, owning one's own shop, travel abroad. Two mentioned doing something in politics to improve the status of women, financially and otherwise. Several entrepreneurs said they would like to expand their businesses, but that this is a difficult time for business. Mrs. I. mentioned that she would like to "have the highest-class hairdressing establishment in Tokyo, and build a beautiful new building for it, but this is financially out of the question."

A final question, to define the ideal life for a woman, summed up the values, aspirations, and self-image for many of these women. Their own backgrounds were reflected in the variety of responses: to have enough money, not to go to an old people's home, to be healthy and happy, to be able to pursue one's own objectives, to have a happy family and prosperous business as well. Most common was the aspiration to have children and a happy home, to have someone to love.

A PROFILE

The service industry worker we meet here is a real woman, but her name and some of the minor factors have been changed. She shares with other women in the service occupations her values, her aspirations and her self-image. She is in the more mature, experienced age group. Her life style and words are her own. She speaks for herself.

My name is Yoshiko. I was born in the town of Maebashi in Gumma Prefecture forty-eight years ago. My father owned a saké manufacturing shop in town. He attended vocational school as a boy and never left Gumma Prefecture except when he went into the Army during the 1930s and served in China. My mother graduated from primary school. There were five of us in all, three girls and two boys. I was the youngest girl. Mother sometimes helped Father in the shop, but most of the time she was too busy cooking and washing. My parents' marriage was arranged. That was the usual way in those days. Mother worked very hard at home and in the shop. She always told us to be womanly and obedient. Sometimes she taught us songs, old-style songs. Sometimes there was a maid to help out at home when she was in the shop. She didn't have much time to teach us how to cook or sew, but we helped her with shopping and errands. Since I had two elder sisters I was usually excused from helping. When I was a child I can remember running into the shop when Father wasn't looking, because I liked the smell of the saké in the cypress wood barrels, and it was a good place to hide, too. Father had about seven employees in the shop.

When I was seventeen I graduated from women's higher school (*jogakkō*). My teacher recommended that I study further because I was a good student. I wanted to study to become a doctor or a lawyer, and my friends in school all thought I would become a doctor or a lawyer. But the war situation was very bad, food was scarce, and we had no luxuries. At the end of 1943 I had to work in a pharmaceutical factory for nine months. We lived in a factory dormitory, so I was away from home. In 1944 I studied for the entrance exams for college, but my parents couldn't afford to send me, so Mother advised me to go to vocational school to study sewing. I studied there for over a year.

While I was still in sewing school I fell in love. All young men were being sent to the war, and every time one left we thought we might not see him again. It happened so often with boys that we knew. He was older and very handsome and gentle, and I had never been in love before. We both thought we wouldn't survive the war. He was married, but we lived together for over a year. A son was born. My most important decision in life was to have this child. I wanted him and decided to live for my son. I didn't want to depend on any man. Finally I separated from my son's father and moved to Tokyo, but I didn't let him know my address. My son has never met his father. I don't know whether he is alive today. My mother had died near the end of the war, and my father disapproved of my living with a married man. Both my sisters got married and my brothers both went to college. But I couldn't live the way my father expected me to.

It isn't really so unusual for a single woman to have a child in Japan. There has always been the custom of men keeping mistresses, and often the mistress has a child or two. They are usually supported by the father even though they may be raised separately from his legal family. Sometimes men adopt the children they have by their mistresses. This is an old custom in Japan and no one is surprised if a man keeps a mistress. But I have never been supported by a man. I have been financially independent. This is why I am satisfied with my way of life.

I decided the only way to earn a living for myself and my son was to sew, and I have been sewing for nearly thirty years. I make a good living this way, and I have never had to depend on anyone. I own this house and have lived in it for the last fifteen years. I intend to work until I die. I like to be able to make attractive clothes for my clients. If I had a daughter I would teach her to be independent and to earn her own living. This is the most important thing in life. At first I thought only of how to exist. It was right after the war, I had lived alone, and I had a child. If it hadn't been for the war I might have married. My father often told me to get married, but I said this is the only way I can live, so please forgive me. Much later he came to understand me and was resigned to my life style. It was very hard at first. For several years I got only four hours' sleep a night.

Being a seamstress is a profession that is hundreds of years old in Japan. Did you know that Lady Ochikubo in the tenth century was a seamstress? Today the traditional seamstresses and even housewives take a kimono completely apart and then sew it back together again after it is laundered. I make Western clothes, not kimono. I read magazines that are useful in my work, like *Burda* and *Elle*. In Japan we follow European fashion magazines rather than American styles. Hairdressing is also a very old profession in Japan. The traditional woman's hair style took hours to arrange. Once it was arranged it had to be kept for several days, so women used to sleep with their necks propped up on porcelain pillows. They weren't very comfortable, but the hair was kept in place for the next day. The hairstyle and costume have to be coordinated, because you can't look at just one part of a woman's appearance. You have to look at the total woman. Of course today you can buy wigs in the old style. Kimono were very elaborate too, and sometimes a woman wore as many as a dozen layers. I'm glad clothes aren't that cumbersome today. Western clothes allow a woman to feel much freer as she walks. Wearing a kimono makes a woman feel completely different from wearing Western clothes. If I had been born in an earlier time I would have had to sew kimono.

My son leaves for work every morning at 8:30 and I start work at 9. I work all day, but I am beginning to slow my pace, because if I get too tired I get ill. I must take care of myself. I have several regular customers and I sew for them on order. I always have plenty of work. I work in the evenings as well as daytime, and on Sundays too. When I work in the evening I like to watch movies on TV. There is a good series of domestic drama on channel 6 at 10. I like to read for a couple of hours before I go to bed.

I have made a good living for myself and my son, though I have never travelled abroad. My son attended a private school. When he was in school I used to go to P.T.A. meetings, but I didn't really enjoy them. He wanted to become a doctor, and for five years I allowed him to be a *rōnin,* studying for university entrance exams. Finally I told him he had been a *rōnin* long enough and he should get a job. Now he works for a company, and he will be married in two months. My son's fiancee wants to live with me, though I would like to live alone. Now I make ¥120,000 a month, and I save half of it for life insurance. This is for my son's welfare. I have bought a condominium recently and I want to rent it.

When my son was a child I disciplined him myself, and he listened. He was not really much of a problem. I hoped for him that he would be able to do whatever he wanted in life. I think childrearing today is much freer than it was twenty years ago. My parents were stricter. Parents today don't say as much, and there are things they refrain from saying to their children. Of course some mothers are over-protective *kyōiku mamas.*

After I separated from my son's father I lived alone for several years. Then when I was thirty-five I met another man. He was much younger, a single student. By that time I had my own house and I wanted to keep it. But we lived together for several years, quite happily. He and my son were friends. I was not dependent on him financially. I didn't think it would be possible to marry because of our age difference, and anyway I didn't want legal ties. I wanted to separate whenever it ended, without saying anything but sayonara, with no recriminations and no regrets. I thought this was the best way, and this is the way it really happened. We never developed any hatred. Of course I suffered. But I was able to live as a woman for twelve years. If my son realized this it would lighten his burden of knowing that I have lived and worked for him for so many years. This was the only way I could live. I'm satisfied. I'm not lonely. I don't feel abandoned. I have my house with five rooms, and my son and his bride will be living with me, though I would enjoy living alone.

I think everyone is different and everyone has to live his or her own way. If a woman is satisfied with her life and believes she is doing well, then she is successful. Some women are dissatisfied with their lives, and if so they should change them. Women should assume responsibility for their own lives. If a woman lives with a family, then her obligation is to her husband and children. If she works she should use all her ability and do her best in the way she has chosen. I live as I want and I assume responsibility for my life. Some of my married friends envy me and say they would like to "try my life style just once," but I don't want to tell others to live as I do.

I am full of joy and full of grief. I feel I have lived really fully, more than others have. I have no envy of others and no regrets. I never have wanted to trouble anyone else. There were times of suffering, yes. . . . I am extremely happy my son is getting married. I want to die when I am full of happiness. Maybe happiness will have a different meaning for me in the future. I can laugh, but I have passed the feeling of being able to cry for myself. I have never had a bad image of myself as a single mother. A lot of people think I am married, and when clients come they always ask me where my husband is. Before my father died he wrote a last letter to me. He said he was grateful that I was able to make my own living and choose my own way. It made me extremely happy.

CONCLUSION

Women in the service industries pursue a variety of life styles. Some are married, some single, some have been common law wives. Some aspired to more education and a better job when they were younger, but circumstances did not allow them to continue in school. Nearly all are self-sufficient economically and would be able to support themselves if something happened to their husbands, though not all are confident that they could. They have in common that they work very long hours, six or sometimes even seven days a week, and that they derive considerable satisfaction from their work. Many are working in fields where they have no male competitors, in vocations traditionally filled by women. The service industries are in a sense particularly well attuned to the traditional feminine ideal of service to others. This is not to say that these women are not capable outside the traditional domestic role. Women who are themselves entrepreneurs—owners or sometimes managers of hotels, restaurants, and bars—have demonstrated that they are strong, skilled, creative and successful business women. They are closed off from employment in "Japan, Incorporated," the giant firms where salary men are secure in life-time positions. Yet even when they have become innovative and viable in their own establishments these women have not repudiated some of the more restricting aspects of the traditional feminine ideal or espoused a genuine dual-role ideology.

Society has not legitimated the economically independent role they know they are capable of playing. The pull of tradition on one of these women was so strong that she was turning her back on a cherished job so that she could better fill the single domestic role. In another case, a young woman who had graduated from a prestigious university found herself discriminated against and unable to compete with boys of the same qualifications. Women are still closed out of many fields by discrimination, often disqualified by their sex from taking entrance exams for positions in large companies.

The service industries are one alternative for young women attracted to skilled occupations for premarriage employment. Should they decide to remain in the work force or to return after raising children there are opportunities as owner/managers. Women are demonstrating in increasing numbers that in the semitraditional service industries they can, without abandoning their domestic role, become efficient, self-supporting entrepreneurs in middle age.

NOTES

[1]Women's and Minors' Bureau, *The Status of Women in Japan*, 1974, p. 10.

[2]Women's and Minors' Bureau, *The Status of Women in Japan*, 1973, p. 18.

[3]Social Education Bureau, *Women and Education in Japan*, p. 5.

[4]Masu Okamura, *Women's Status—Changing Japan*, p. 57.

[5]*Ibid.*, p. 58.

[6]*Ibid.*, p. 56.

[7]Cora Jean Emiko Yamamoto, "The Dual Work Families: The *Tomobataraki* Mother in Japan: An Emerging Pattern."

CHAPTER 7
BAR HOSTESSES

THE GEISHA

The role played by the hostess in Japanese society is not new, but rather is a more modern version of yesterday's geisha. Today hostesses occupy a low social position in a manner similar to that of previous geisha; however, differences exist in the types of women entering the professions and their social milieu, as well as their roles vis-à-vis their employers and customers.[1]

The existence of the geisha profession goes back much farther than Japan's recent past. Dancing girls called *shirabyōshi* appeared during the early part of the twelfth century;[2] at this time in Kyoto samurai and merchants both enjoyed the entertainment of these women, who were accomplished in singing and dancing. At Gion in Kyoto tea houses employed women to sing and dance for people going to the Gion Shrine to worship during the Tokugawa period. The antecedent of the true geisha in Edo was the *odoriko,* who was the first to handle the *shamisen* in that area and whose business prospered during the latter part of the seventeenth century.[3] Tokyo's Yoshiwara district was established during the early part of the seventeenth century, and the first geisha appeared there in 1762; twenty-five years later fifty geisha were entertaining there. Statistics in 1928 gave a rough estimate of seventy-nine thousand geisha throughout Japan, indicating the extent to which the profession prospered during the first sixty years following the Meiji Restoration.

The apprentices, or *shikomikko,* of geisha houses in the period following the Meiji Restoration were mostly young girls from poor

133

families. In a country where the average size of land farmed by a lower-class family provided barely enough food for all its members, the only means by which many of these families could feed a large number of children was to send some of them to work from an early age. Many geisha came from lower-class families in the Hoku-riku region and in the area surrounding Nagoya. In a manner similar to the custom practiced by upper-class families of sending their daughters to learn flute-playing, flower arrangement, and so forth, lower-class Nagoya families sent their daughters to become geisha; therein lay perhaps the only route by which the young women could receive an education, and the geisha house thus served the purpose of a finishing school.[4]

The futures of the majority of young women about to enter geisha houses were decided through no will of their own, but by their families. Confucian doctrines stressing the duty of the daughter to carry out her parents' wishes had already filtered down to the lower classes by the end of the nineteenth century, and in accordance with the traditional family system, subordinates were required to accede to the will of the household head for the sake of the entire family. Daughters thus accepted decisions made by the elders, no matter how repugnant their futures might appear to have been, for clearly there existed no other choice for them from either a moral or a financial standpoint.

The terms of the contract by which a young girl entered apprentice-ship to become a geisha specified the amount of money paid her parents or legal guardians as well as the length of time she was to remain in service to the geisha house. The amount of the girl's debt depended upon several factors—her length of service, her talents, her appearance, and the type of family from which she came—and the decision was reached upon agreement by the two parties signing the contract rather than in accordance with a fixed standard.

The apprenticeship period of the young girl, who usually entered the geisha house by the age of ten or twelve, required a great amount of physical labor, discipline, and patience: her duties included such tasks as scrubbing and cleaning, washing laundry, running errands for others, carrying the *shamisen* of older geisha, and helping the latter with dressing; in addition she attended dancing and *shamisen* lessons at the geisha school. Usually before her mid-teens she became a "half-geisha;" or *hangyoku*, after which time she entertained by pour-ing saké and dancing to the accompaniment of older geisha.

Having served as a *hangyoku* for a year or more, the young woman rose to the position of *ippon* (a full-fledged geisha), a level reached only after she had passed an examination attended by the madam of her house, authorities from the geisha headquarters office, and her *shamisen* and dancing teachers. The full-fledged geisha first worked for a period of time, perhaps two or three years, during which her status was called *marugakae;* the house received both her fees and her tips, and in exchange provided her with food and clothing in the same manner as when she had been a *shikomikko.* Following this period she began to receive tips from her customers while only her fees went to the house (*goshūgi-dori*); the tips were usually higher than the fees themselves, so attainment of this level would appear to represent a considerable advance for the woman. But actually the degree to which her financial condition improved at this level depended upon two factors—whether she was required to pay for the kimono necessary for *zashiki* parties, and, if so, whether she had the assistance of a generous patron (*danna*)[5] who would enable her to meet her expenses for work.

The term "skillful geisha" (*ude no aru geisha*)was never used in reference to the woman's entertainment abilities at parties, or to the amount of tips or fees she received; instead, it referred to her skill in managing and making use of her patron, or *danna.*[6] Usually the geisha acquired a *danna* at the time she became a *marugakae;* the prime motive was to enlist him for financial assistance so that she could leave the profession before her term of debt had expired.[7] Once the full-fledged geisha assumed responsibility for providing herself with *zashiki* party clothing, it became nearly impossible for her to meet her expenses, not to mention paying off her debt to the house. Hence, a patron was usually taken on by the geisha at an early stage, and many women were redeemed by their patrons before the age of twenty, escaping from their remaining periods of service in this manner.

The fate of the full-fledged geisha was thus determined largely by her success in acquiring a benevolent *danna.* Sheer talent in *shamisen* playing or dancing was a necessary, but not in itself sufficient, condition for her ability to pay off her debt. While the geisha who was popular with customers at parties might be given a larger percentage of her earnings, she still was unable to buy herself out of the profession at an early date except in rare cases. *Marugakae* who were unpopular with customers and thus were not often engaged for parties, or who had no patron to help them financially, could be resold by their employers to other houses.

Japan's prewar industrialization brought a variety of jobs for women that had not existed before; the numbers of young girls entering the geisha profession declined as families began to send their daughters to factories and textile industries to work. In addition, in 1944 the government forced the closing of first-class restaurants, bars, tea houses, and geisha houses, thereby putting thousands of geisha out of work. Many geisha fled the entertainment establishments completely and escaped to the country during the war; others, with no customers to pay for their skilled entertainment, were forced to prostitute themselves to earn a living.[8] A revival of the profession began by 1947, but only after a child welfare law had been passed forbidding the practice of taking in children under the age of eighteen to work as apprentices, thus preventing families from forcing young girls into the profession. This law also brought about lowered standards of training undertaken by the apprentices, whose period of training had to be greatly reduced if they were to attain the status of full-fledged geisha while still in their early twenties. As Japan became more Westernized and foreign forms of entertainment penetrated the masses, customers seeking geisha with highly developed skills declined in number, and many gave up this type of entertainment entirely in favor of other cheaper, more modern forms of entertaining guests. This trend, beginning as early as the latter days of the Meiji period, brought with it an increasing number of new positions for another profession—that of the *jokyū*. [9]

THE *JOKYŪ*

The "girl waiters" (*onna-boi*) of the new cafes and the "show girls" (*kamban-musume*) who catered to students in milk halls comprised the first members of the new profession known as *jokyū* during the 1910s.[10] The cafes originated in Tokyo, with only a few in other parts of the country at first. The young women who took up employment as *jokyū*, however, came largely from country areas; some had formerly worked as maids, others in restaurants, but the relatively attractive salaries offered by *jokyū* employers drew them to this occupation, especially if they had accumulated debts. Some had separated from their husbands or quit school prior to taking up the work. Fully half of the women of the profession in 1920 were between the ages of twenty and thirty, and a third were below the age of twenty.[11] Very few women chose to work as *jokyū* out of curiosity or a desire for excitement; instead, they realized that the work was more profitable, less tiring, and less time-consuming than other types of unskilled labor or apprenticeships. Unlike the geisha, the *jokyū* entered the profession without a debt to her employer, and she was free to quit her job at any time. Requirements for success involved only a good appearance, the ability to make conversation with customers, and the perseverance to withstand the teasing or rude behavior of drunks; training took the form of on-the-job imitation of other *jokyū*. While the salary itself was not impressively large, tips from customers made the work at some cafes highly profitable, especially in Tokyo's Ginza area.

The main drawback to the work appears to have been the damage it inflicted on the women's reputations. Many *jokyū*, having separated from their families in rural areas for financial reasons, lived alone in the cities. They were thus under fewer social controls from their relatives than were other women living with their families, a situation which to society suggested that they lacked virtue in their relations with men. Moreover, in contrast to geisha, most *jokyū* lived apart from their places of work, so employers usually had little power to control their sexual conduct. Some *jokyū* did form sexual relationships with their customers to escape the loneliness they felt in having to return to an empty, dreary apartment every night after work, or to earn money through privately practicing prostitution if their salaries and tips were not high enough to support them as well as perhaps their dependents. Employers in such areas as the old Yoshiwara sometimes used cafes as a front for prostitution, even after the end of the war, and women who came from the country to these establishments in search of work often were deceived by advertisements for *jokyū* positions until they had begun working there.

Earnings varied greatly among *jokyū*, depending upon the area in which they worked. For this reason *jokyū* tended to move from one establishment to another as often as every three or six months. The women themselves viewed the position as a temporary means of helping their families or themselves out of financial difficulties. Long-term employment was indeed impossible since one requirement for the work was youthfulness. Once past her twenties, the woman working in this occupation had little to attract customers; the money she earned from tips declined while she continued to pay expenses for clothing. Her employer lowered her salary as her ability to sell drinks declined, and employers of other establishments refused to hire her. High turnover rates brought customers to see fresh faces.

The postwar revival of the entertainment professions found the *jokyū* no longer wearing the distinguishing uniform of a white apron over a kimono, but instead dressing in the types of clothing that office women in daytime businesses wore. The term "cafe" disappeared from signs over establishments at which *jokyū* worked, and a greater variety of entertainment businesses appeared—cabarets, bars, tea shops not serving alcohol, night clubs, salons. With the prohibition of prostitution in 1956, the areas in which *jokyū* worked ceased to be legally sanctioned red-light districts. The name of the profession itself gradually changed—to that of hostess.

THE HOSTESS

The hostess profession today is only one of a variety of jobs open to women in Japan, and hence women who enter the profession have chosen it by measuring the working conditions of the hostess against those of other professions. Furthermore, women today have attained a much greater degree of freedom to choose their own work as compared with women before the war, and their reasons for seeking work depend less upon the financial conditions of their families and more upon their own preferences than ever before.

Today many of the exclusive Ginza bars employ women coming from families of middle-class backgrounds. Often these women do not support other members of their original families, nor have they taken up the work with the necessity for or the intention of doing so. Some even hide their work from their families, or incur the latter's disapproval when their occupation is discovered. This trend toward individual decisions among women concerning their work has not appeared only recently, but rather began even before the war among *jokyū*.

Hostess work is often chosen by the young woman because she wants a higher standard of living. Great numbers of women in Ginza bars held office jobs prior to their present work, while a smaller number have previously been engaged in blue-collar work. The one background factor that nearly all hostesses hold in common is their lack of a skill or specialized training which could enable them to get a more prestigious job with a high salary. In the words of a Ginza bar manager, "They wouldn't be here if they had such a skill."

The modestly skilled hostess of a Ginza bar can make two or three times as much money each month as her unskilled office counterpart, and if she has numerous regular customers who pay their bills, her earnings will be far greater. Moreover, these high profits can be obtained within a short period of time; unlike salaries for other jobs the hostess's earnings increase in direct proportion to her ability to sell drinks, rather than in proportion to the length of time she has worked at the job. Her experience only influences her profits initially, and after a very short period (six months to two years) she can reach the pinnacle of her earning power within the profession.

The hostess works approximately four to six hours each night, five or six nights per week. Full-time workers in other professions must be at the job at least forty hours per week. Also, the hostess can often choose the days she will be absent from work, and if she is not held by a contract to work a certain number of days per year, she can usually skip work as often as her finances allow her. Many hostesses take one- or two-week vacations several times a year, while others stay away from the bar one or two nights per week whenever they like; this type of irregular working schedule is not condoned by employers in other jobs.

Another factor draws some women to bars rather than to daytime work—their belief that night life is more suitable to their personalities. Some dislike getting up early in the morning to go to work, and say they prefer to be active at night. Others like alcohol, and find that bar life enables them to enjoy their work more because they can drink. Many women are probably attracted to the profession because they enjoy working with people in a social atmosphere. Perhaps others, out of a sense of vanity, wish to prove that they can attract men by their looks or personalities.[12] Many hostesses appear to be more extroverted than women in office positions, and the bar gives them more opportunities to express their opinions and assume leadership positions than does office work.

The woman choosing hostess work, then, has in most cases judged her personal abilities and character against the numerous job opportunities available to her. She has already attained some degree of financial independence, as evidenced by the fact that usually she has held another type of job previously. The much younger girl of prewar days who became a geisha was often completely inexperienced in any role other than that of daughter, and bears little resemblance to the adult woman who today enters hostess work after having attained considerable knowledge of society and experience in adjusting herself to social relationships with others.

The *jokyū*, on the other hand, often carried the greater financial burden of supporting her family living in the country and had fewer opportunities than the hostess for an education equivalent to that of other middle-class women. Her lower level of education, coupled with the smaller variety of white-collar jobs open to women at that time, limited the types of jobs available to her. Consequently, while many women had held blue-collar jobs prior to becoming *jokyū*, today's hostess more often tends to have worked in a white-collar office job. Like the geisha, the *jokyū* usually came from a lower-class economic background and entered her profession from financial necessity. The Ginza hostess today, however, has more extensive opportunities open to her because of her higher economic background, better education, and the greater supply of white-collar positions open to women.

The conditions under which hostesses are hired vary so greatly that it is meaningless to speak of an "average" hostess. Supper clubs, cabarets, night clubs, and bars all have different requirements for hostesses, and within these businesses the higher-ranking ones set standards quite dissimilar in many respects from those of lower rank. The scope of this study was limited only to hostesses working at first-class bars; their work generally does not include dancing, singing, or any other talent requiring a long period of training. Nor do they take on the work of carrying food and drinks to tables.

The hostesses in first-class Ginza bars form the top of the hostess hierarchy, with those in the Akasaka and Shinjuku areas ranking second and third. Bars in the outer areas of Tokyo as well as those in rural sections of the country employ hostesses under different systems whereby regulations concerning dress and appearance of hostesses are less strict and hostesses are not required to collect money from their customers.

A comparison of upper-class bars within the two areas of Shinjuku and Ginza shows that even here, employment conditions, the purposes for which customers patronize the bars, and the types of women working as hostesses vary considerably. Hostesses at first-class Ginza bars tend more often to have the responsibility of collecting money for bills, visiting the offices of their customers for this purpose in many cases. By adding a charge to the bill for this service, their nightly earnings become far greater. Entertainment at the Ginza bars is more expensive; men on company expense accounts, politicians, and the rich form a high percentage of the bars' customers, while in Shinjuku middle-class men spending their own money usually frequent the bars. Customers at Ginza's bars use bars to entertain business clients; those in Shinjuku bars are more likely to go for their own enjoyment. Again, following the ranking order, regulations concerning the dress and appearance of hostesses are stricter in Ginza bars, and contracts are more often signed between hostesses and employers prior to employment there.

The rank of a bar within a particular area depends upon the social and economic status of its customers, the atmosphere of the establishment (furnishings as well as whether live music is offered), the price of the drinks and snacks served, its reputation as a successful (or a declining) business, and of course the type of hostesses working there. In general, first-class Ginza and Shinjuku bars are not large; the management attempts to create a personal atmosphere and the number of hostesses employed varies from perhaps twenty to forty.[13] The furnishings are quiet and refined, and live music is offered by a pianist or small band. Customers rarely spend more than an hour or two at these bars, and often they bring business associates with them. Regular customers comprise the greatest number of men patronizing the establishments, and they request their favorite hostesses to sit with them instead of leaving the responsibility for hostess selection to the manager.

In lower-ranking Ginza bars as well as in those of other areas, the earnings may allow the hostess a high standard of living while she works, but it is primarily the hostesses of the first-class Ginza bars who can earn enough money to assure themselves a comfortable life after they have become too old to work as hostesses. For this reason hostesses, like the *jokyū,* move constantly from one bar to another, seeking better working conditions and hoping to move up in the ranks. Those at the top move because of the varying working conditions that also exist among the first-class bars.

Upper-class Ginza and Shinjuku bars actively recruit hostesses by utilizing bar scouts. In many cases these scouts are the men who work in the bars at night as managers or waiters (*boi*). Scouts recruit women by searching in the streets for hostesses on their way to work, by going to night clubs or cabarets, where hostesses are employed, or by following up rumors concerning successful hostesses at other places. The third method appears to be used extensively by Ginza scouts, who are well known for "stealing" successful hostesses working at other bars by offering exorbitant amounts of money as a type of "entrance allowance" (*shitakukin*). Men working at bars are generally acquainted with a number of hostesses working at other bars in the same area; hostesses and men employed at the bars tend to visit neighborhood coffee shops and restaurants before and after work, thereby acquiring frequent opportunities to meet each other. Moreover, the mobility of male employees at bars is undoubtedly as high as that of females there, so frequently the experienced male employee knows many hostesses at other bars with whom he has previously worked.

Hostesses themselves seek employment at other bars with the desire to find a place where they can increase their earnings. In considering the move to another bar, the experienced hostess may take into account the types of men who have been her regular customers at the bar where she previously worked. If she wishes to retain their patronage, she must make sure they will follow her to the new bar and will be able to pay a possibly higher fee for her services. The hostess whose profits come largely from her regular customers may continue working at a bar which pays her a lower basic salary rather than risk the loss of these customers by entering a more expensive bar offering a higher basic salary.

Contacts between hostesses at different bars may bring about a hostess's change to another bar, but even so the final decision for her employment usually rests with a male manager. These days the madam of the first-class bar is often only an employee herself (*yato-ware-mama*), having no real authority to hire hostesses. While it is important that the hostesses have good relations with the "hired mama" once she begins working there, the man whose job is to manage the establishment is usually the hostess's real employer. Some first-class bars do not even appoint a hostess to work as a "mama," but instead leave the leadership responsibilities to a number of hostesses who have worked there the longest and who have the most regular customers. Authority in these bars rests entirely with a male manager or bartender.

No fixed maximum age limit exists for hostesses, but rarely do bar managers hire women above the age of thirty-five or forty unless they bring a considerable number of regular customers with them to patronize the new bar. In many bars inexperienced women above the age of thirty will rarely be hired, unless they successfully deceive the employer about their ages.[14] The majority of hostesses are in their twenties, and usually by their late twenties they reach a peak of popularity with customers.

The employer judges the woman applying for hostess work primarily by her appearance—features, figure, clothing, carriage, etc.—if she is inexperienced. Only an employer who knows the reputation of an experienced hostess can decide whether her ability to entertain is sufficient. The applicant's degree of refinement, state of cleanliness, and ability to converse with ease are also taken into consideration, especially if many of the customers at the bar are older men. Managers of bars to which younger customers often come, however, as well as those of lower-class bars, do often consider the woman's "sex appeal" more than her refinement for employment.

The employer chooses hostesses not only on the basis of the types of customers patronizing the bar, but also with consideration to the types of hostesses already working there. If most hostesses at the bar are older and experienced, he will perhaps prefer a new face—a young woman with more sex appeal—to counterbalance the ages of the others and attract younger customers. Conversely, if many of the hostesses there are young, he will prefer a somewhat older woman who might appeal more to older customers.

Most bars maintain three types of hostesses: (1) those who are appointed by the manager (or "mama") to entertain customers and who are called "help"; (2) those who are appointed only by customers (*shimei*); and (3) those who are appointed both by customers and by the manager (or "mama") and who thus serve as both "help" and *shimei*. In some Ginza and Shinjuku first-class bars the desired ratio for the above types of hostesses is an equal number of each, while at many lower-ranking bars and at those in outlying areas, most or all of the hostesses are "help" only. In general, the *shimei* system has been adopted most prevalently by the expensive Ginza bars, where sometimes the majority of hostesses are working as *shimei*. The ratio of the particular bar reflects the type of customers patronizing the establishment, for men using their own money for personal entertainment tend to avoid bars employing *shimei,* since expenses are much greater there. Men on expense accounts who are entertaining business clients often prefer bars where they can appoint their favorite hostesses, with the security that they and their guests will be hospitably received.

The woman hired as "help" receives a basic nightly salary which may be as high as twenty thousand yen at some Ginza bars or as low as three thousand yen elsewhere. Unless the applicant receives *shitaku-kin* for buying clothes, she rarely signs a contract with the employer when she is hired as "help," nor does any fixed standard exist for determining her beginning salary. Employers hiring inexperienced women often pay different basic salaries, depending upon the impressions they receive of the women at their interviews. To prevent resentment toward the bar by other hostesses whose salaries may be lower, newly hired hostesses are sometimes advised to withhold information about their salaries from other hostesses.

The newly hired, inexperienced hostess receives most of her training while working. The manager, "mama," and other higher-ranking hostesses show her the tables at which to sit. Following the example of other hostesses, the inexperienced woman learns how to mix drinks at tables, light men's cigarettes, and serve food brought to the tables. The use of good manners with customers at all times is highly stressed at a first-class bar, and the employer or another hostess usually discusses methods of showing courtesy with the new hostess before she makes a mistake out of ignorance. Conversation is led mostly by more experienced hostesses at the table, and the new hostess rarely talks unless someone directly addresses her. Certain subjects may be considered taboo for hostesses to introduce into the conversation—personal questions about the customers, behind-the-scenes problems of the bar or its employees, or in some cases controversial subjects such as politics—so the new hostess wisely refrains from taking the lead in conversation-making until she has learned more about the subjects usually discussed and the personalities of the customers at whose tables she sits.

Introverted customers or those with emotional problems are frequently left to the "mama" or an older, experienced hostess to handle. Younger men sometimes feel shy around young hostesses, especially if they have never visited the bar before, so an older hostess may be called upon to provide a relaxing atmosphere before turning over the customer to a younger hostess. If a customer becomes drunk and acts rudely toward a younger hostess, the manager, the "mama," or a more experienced hostess will often intervene; in some cases the customer may be politely asked to leave. Older hostesses or the "mama" may try to convince the customer to refrain from drinking too much.

The bar's "mama" and other more experienced hostesses—who are often working as *shimei*—clearly have leadership in deciding which hostesses working as "help" are to sit with customers. The majority of customers at first-class Ginza bars charge their bills (*tsuke*) rather than pay cash, and are regular customers. Upon entering the bar this type of customer appoints a hostess to his table. That hostess then has charge of other hostesses sitting there, and may in fact appoint others to the table, especially if the customer asks that another hostess be called to sit with him. The "head hostess" who is first appointed by the customer receives, as a kind of service charge, a larger fee (e.g., ¥2,000) from the customer than does the secondarily appointed hostess (who may receive ¥1,000, for example). Such fees are automatically added to the customer's bill, and are thereby distinguishable from tips, which the customer may voluntarily pay in cash directly to the hostess sitting at his table at the time he departs. "Help" appointed by the manager or "mama" rather than by the customer generally do not receive a fee from the customer, although he may give such hostesses a tip later.

Whether by the preference of the hostess, who may wish to increase her earnings, or of the customer, who may prefer to charge his bills and pay later using his company's expense account, the decision that the hostess will collect for the customer's bills is usually reached through an agreement between the hostess and the customer with the consent of the manager. All three parties must agree to the decision: the manager must consent to letting the customer charge his bill and having the hostess collect for it, the hostess must agree to accept the responsibility for collecting the money, and the customer must consent to the added charge on his bill that will be given to the hostess.

Not all first-class bars require *shimei* to collect for their customers' bills; in some cases the manager assumes this responsibility or the customer pays at the bar. But the true *shimei* system at "clubs" includes this responsibility on the part of the hostess. Furthermore, if the customer later refuses or is unable to pay within a time limit,[15] the hostess herself must pay the amount of his bill to the bar. Many of the customers who do not pay their bills are owners of medium and small businesses, but even the customer using the large company's expense account may be unable to pay within the time limit if the budget for the company's expenses has been exceeded during that month. The number of customers not paying their bills has recently increased, which in turn has brought economic insecurity to many hostesses working as *shimei*. The great majority of bars employing the *shimei* system have at least a few hostesses working as *shimei* who are in debt to the bar for this reason.

Hostesses are generally willing to accept the financial risk involved in taking the responsibility for bill collecting. In the first place, the system "ties" the customer to the particular hostess who will collect for his bills; she will always be the first appointed by him to his table. Moreover, the customer who charges his bills will often tend to patronize the bar more frequently, as he does not need ready cash to pay his bills. The nightly salary of the *shimei* who has regular customers is also larger than the salaries of "help." But the primary financial gain for the hostess in becoming a bill-collector lies in her ability to take a percentage of the money she collects. The *tsuke* (or charge account) method of payment is more expensive for the customer than is cash payment for this reason. The amount of profit the hostess receives in collecting for the bills, however, depends upon the customer's willingness and ability to pay the extra charge she asks. If he does agree to pay her price (and the company's expense account budget allows him to do so), the hostess's profit will be considerable. If he refuses to accept the extra charge, the hostess will not receive a profit at all; while the bar recognizes the right of the hostess to take a percentage by adding her charge to the bill, management does not prosecute customers who fail to pay the amount. If the customer fails to pay even the amount which is demanded by the bar, the hostess herself must make up the difference. Even then, the bar generally refuses to prosecute as long as the hostess can pay out of her own pocket. The customer who continues to frequent the bar often but refuses to pay his bills may be discouraged from coming by both the bar management and the hostess. The manager may also personally attempt to collect the money owed by him; if he succeeds the customer's *shimei* forfeits all or most of her profit from the bill to the manager, and if he fails the financial responsibility remains with the *shimei.* But only in rare cases does the bar decide to take legal action against the customer. Legal prosecution involves expenses that would represent a financial loss to the bar. The hostess herself does not initiate legal action—she has no money to cover the expenses if she is far in debt, and she would lose all of her profit or more in expenses if she did bring suit against a customer.

The *shimei* whose regular customers usually do pay their bills can more than compensate for the losses incurred by an occasional customer who does not pay. But the accumulation of several non-paying customers, none of whom she can afford to prosecute individually, may quickly lead her far into debt with the bar. The bar, unable to collect money from the hostess, then asks that her debts be paid by her guarantor, or sponsor. Partly for this reason *shimei* at expensive Ginza bars are usually required to have a guarantor. If the debt accumulated by the hostess from several non-paying customers is quite large, and if her guarantor refuses to pay, the bar may then take legal action against her guarantor. This procedure is more profitable for the bar than taking legal action against any individual customer owing money to the hostess.

A second method by which the hostess may become indebted to the bar is when she accepts *shitakukin* at the time she is hired. This cash "gift" from the bar amounts to a debt: either the hostess must return the money by installment payments (if the amount is not large) or she must agree to make a certain amount of profit for the bar each month over a period of time.[16] Inexperienced women may accept this debt so that they can buy clothing for work; experienced women may desire other luxuries even if they already have a suitable wardrobe. A few may hope to receive the *shitakukin* and then escape the bar without returning the money.

The amount of the *shitakukin* is often quite large, and the employer therefore ensures that the hostess will be legally responsible for repaying the money by drawing up a contract. Conditions of the contract include the amount of the *shitakukin*, the amount of profit that the hostess must bring to the bar each month, and the number of months during which she must continue to bring this profit to the bar. If the hostess fails to meet the conditions of the contract, she is required to return at least part of the *shitakukin* amount.17

Even though she has signed a contract, however, the hostess can still disappear from the bar, move to another residence, and succeed in escaping without returning the money or fulfilling the contract. To prevent such occurrence the bar requires that she have a sponsor to guarantee payment of the debt if the hostess fails to do so.18 The sponsor signs a separate contract with the employer, assuming complete financial responsibility for the hostess. As mentioned before, he must also pay debts incurred by the hostess's failure to collect money from customers.

Such contracts are rarely for the benefit of the hostess or the sponsor. The employer does not guarantee to pay the hostess her basic nightly salary under the conditions of the contract, nor does he guarantee that her salary will be paid on time. Furthermore, the contract does not state that the management will take legal action against the hostess's customers if the latter refuse to pay their bills. Often the *shitakukin* is large enough, however, to persuade the hostess to agree to the terms of these one-sided contracts with conditions benefitting only the bar.

If the hostess owes money to her previous bar, the bar to which she moves pays her debt in the form of *shitakukin* under conditions of a contract. The hostess may also wish to borrow money from the bar to buy an apartment, an automobile, or another such personal luxury. While even first-class Ginza bars hesitate to lend the money to hostesses these days because of the economic slump, until recently such loans were often given hostesses who brought high profits to their bars. The hostess borrowing a large amount is usually asked to sign a contract under which she "works off" the debt over a period of time with profits from her customers, rather than returning the money in cash. This method of payment incurs no loss to the bar, for the contract's terms ensure that profits from her customers over the specified period of time will be greater than her debt. The bar thus serves the purpose of a bank for the hostess, and this method prevents her from moving so easily to another bar.

If the amount of the loan is small, the hostess may only be required to return the money in monthly installments. This method is often utilized when the bar gives the inexperienced hostess a small amount of *shitakukin* for clothing expenses. Such hostesses, because they are new, will not initially bring great profits to their bars, nor is their success as hostesses guaranteed by experience and a large number of regular customers, so the contract method of repayment may not be feasible. Under the monthly repayment system, a percentage of the hostess's salary is deducted by the bar over a period of time. A large loan would probably not be given the hostess unless she had a guarantor to ensure that she stayed at the bar until it was returned. The amount of money borrowed by a hostess and then returned through monthly deductions from her salary is called *bansu* (from the English "advance").

Monthly deductions may come about for a variety of other reasons if the hostess fails to observe the bar's requirements. These deductions are penalties, and the amount deducted from the hostess's salary is called *bakkin*. One regulation many first-class bars impose upon hostesses is that the latter bring a specified number of customers with them each month when they arrive for work at the bar. Hostesses therefore meet customers at a restaurant or coffee shop early in the evening, and then proceed from there to the bar together. The required number of times the hostess must bring a customer with her varies according to the bar and to the individual hostesses; *shimei* sometimes are required to bring as many as ten per month, although in other cases the bar only requires one per week. The hostess who brings a customer with her may arrive at the bar later than when she comes alone.

An alternate method of forcing hostesses to "drum up trade" is the requirement at some bars that they be appointed by customers a certain number of times per month. The hostess who comes with a customer can count his presence as one appointment. The majority of first-class Ginza bars have regulations concerning either the *dōhan* requirement (bringing a customer), or the *shimei* requirement (being appointed by a customer), or both. Thus, the hostess who is not popular with customers suffers having her basic salary reduced no matter how much time she works.

Coming late to work is also penalized: frequently the basic salary is reduced ¥1,000 if the hostess arrives thirty minutes late, ¥2,000 if she is one hour late, and so on. "Help" generally must arrive by the time the bar opens, while *shimei* with a few regular customers may come a half hour or an hour later. *Shimei* with many regular customers (or the "mama") are permitted to work the least amount of time. If the hostess fails to inform the management that she will not appear for work, she may also be penalized.

Deductions in the hostess's basic salary may occur if she fails to conform to the bar's requirements concerning her appearance. Most first-class bars have a "new dress day" (*oshare-no-hi*) at least once or twice a month, and if the hostess fails to provide a new dress for herself on that day, she will be penalized. Only expensive clothing (e.g., costing more than ¥50,000) can be worn in the bars. Thus, this regulation costs the hostess money whether she obeys it or not. Furthermore, many bars require that hostesses wearing kimono avoid exposure to the sun; kimono-clad women at these bars who have become suntanned after trips to Guam or Hawaii are penalized.

The hostess obeys regulations concerning her appearance not only to avoid penalties but also to compete successfully against others in winning the customers' favor. A *shimei* whose regular customer begins to appoint another hostess more frequently to his table loses face with all other employees of the bar. Conversely, if the hostess keeps up her appearance and works hard to please customers, she may successfully win more appointments from them, thus increasing her earnings.

All bar employees are required to attend regularly scheduled meetings, during which hostesses are encouraged to spend more money for their appearance, or chastised for having failed to do so. Sometimes the bar gives a monetary prize to the hostess who has brought in the largest number of customers with her to the bar (*dōhanshō*); in other cases a prize may be given to the hostess who has brought the greatest profit to the bar. Even if prizes are not given, a monthly chart showing the amount of profits made by *shimei,* the number of customers brought in by each hostess, or the number of appointments received by each hostess may be tacked up on the wall in a back room. The employer may also foster a sense of competition among hostesses by raising or lowering their basic salaries according to their popularity with customers.

The diverse ranking system thus forces hostesses to try harder to gain approval from customers. Hostesses working at bars where only "help" are employed do not have the same degree of motivation to compete with other hostesses; the number of customers who come to the bar makes no difference to the hostess's earnings if all hostesses are paid only the same basic nightly salary. However, when a true ranking system for hostesses is present within a bar, the hostess's popularity with customers greatly affects her monthly earnings, thereby increasing her incentive to compete with other hostesses. The ranking system is developed most highly within first-class Ginza bars, less so in Shinjuku bars, and reflects the highly competitive atmosphere present among hostesses at the top of the hierarchy.

To compete successfully against others, the hostess must spend a great part of her earnings in status maintenance. A conservative estimate of the percentage of her earnings allotted to necessary expenses for work would be 50 percent. Expenses include clothing, accessories, beauty parlor appointments (usually daily for Ginza hostesses), taxi fares (often necessary for the hostess wearing a kimono during bad weather), and gifts to customers. The bar provides no expense allowances for entertaining customers in restaurants, for commuting expenditures or for meals. Hostesses at first-class bars receive no insurance or housing benefits. Nurseries or child-care facilities are unavailable for those with small children. In short, all of the hostess's expenses, personal and work-related, must come from her own income.

The higher the hostess's rank, the greater her expenses become; to maintain her popularity with customers (and her status among other hostesses) she must continually refurbish her wardrobe. Not only are new clothes necessary, but she must constantly try for a fresh, new look to keep the interest of all her regular customers. The hostess who customarily dresses in kimono poses no exception to the necessity for spending money on a wardrobe, for while her kimono is not subject to changes in fashion, she still must spend a greater amount on a new kimono for each "new dress day" than do others buying Western clothing. Partly for this reason the hostess wearing a kimono is generally a higher-ranking woman; those working as "help" cannot afford to buy kimono so often, and prefer the less expensive Western clothing. The bar's manager (or "mama"), however, often advises older hostesses to wear kimono so as to please older customers with traditional tastes, and hence the choice in clothing does not always rest entirely with the hostess.

The highest-ranking hostesses have the most extensive wardrobes, for their incomes are the greatest. Those moving upward in rank increasingly spend a greater amount for appearance in proportion to their increasing incomes, while those moving downward in rank are forced to spend a smaller amount for their appearance. The hostess's popularity with customers determines her income, which in turn determines the amount of money spent on her appearance, reflecting her status. Rebellion against expenses for status maintenance results in disapproval by the management, loss of face in front of other hostesses, and loss of popularity with customers; consequently, her earnings decrease.

The necessity of large expenditures for expenses related to work forces the hostess to calculate carefully her earning ability. Hostesses working as "help" find it relatively simple to determine how much they can allot to expenses, for all or most of their earnings come from a basic salary. The *shimei,* however, cannot calculate her financial condition so easily because she may be forced at any time to reimburse the bar for debts incurred by unpaying customers. The *shimei* who calculates the amount allotted for expenses on the basis of the income she would receive if she could successfully collect from all customers will inevitably come out with less profit than she plans. A great number of hostesses run heavily into debt because they fail to recognize the extent to which their monthly incomes may fluctuate, depending upon factors beyond their control. The *shimei* can always calculate the highest possible profit she might make for a certain month, but she can rarely foresee the degree to which uncontrollable factors will decrease her earnings.

By adhering to conservative expenditures for status maintenance, the *shimei* whose customers pay their bills may reap great profits from her work within a few years. But too many expenditures on luxuries such as housing, travel, or clothing will result in small profit gains for even *shimei* whose customers do pay their bills; those with several nonpaying customers may soon find themselves so heavily in debt that they must rely on outside financial aid. The hostess whose expenditures exceed her bar earnings may resort to any of several methods to get herself out of debt to the bar—financial assistance from her sponsor, reliance upon a daytime job, prostitution. Changing bars for the sake of receiving *shitakukin* to pay off debts to the previous bar only brings a temporary solution to her financial problems unless her luck with customers is better at the new bar.

The Ginza bar offers an exclusive atmosphere by virtue of the exorbitant charges demanded for entertainment there. The price of drinks tends to increase in direct proportion to the percentage of regular customers. However, it caters best to customers wishing to bring guests for the purpose of establishing friendly relations with each other. Business transactions are feasible only when they involve relatively simple decisions without the need for secrecy, for even the expensive bar is too noisy, too open, and too distracting a place to facilitate prolonged discussions among customers. Moreover, the primary duty of hostesses—to entertain customers by talking with them—is much less suitable for private discussions between customers than were the duties of geisha, who often displayed their musical and dancing skills while customers talked. The "club," in evolving from the cafe through the status of bar and achieving its present function, clearly reflects the desire of its management to serve the needs of customers seeking an intimate atmosphere similar to that provided by geisha. But this need cannot be met when the establishment at the same time must offer entertainment to a variety of other customers. Furthermore, as long as hostesses exercise their ability to accept or refuse the best quality of service to customers, the latter can hardly rely upon the hostess's loyalty as customers formerly did with geisha. Because the geisha's earnings depended upon the length of time she was employed, she cared less about the number of customers who sought her services each night. But the hostess and the bar both profit more from a large number of customers buying only a few drinks than from a small number who remain for many hours.

The hostess, in contrast to the geisha of former days, sells her appearance rather than a talent or skill, and society for this reason often equates her profession with that of a prostitute. Moreover, the high standard of living that she may attain with her earnings invites criticism that she selfishly squanders money instead of saving it or using it to support her family. Criticism of her morality arises more from the fact that she lacks social restrictions than from actual proof that she behaves more "immorally" than other women. Hostesses at Ginza bars are rarely judged by their backgrounds, for their families' socioeconomic statuses are usually unknown even to those working at the same bar. Instead, they are judged by society's knowledge of hostesses in general, a stereotype which may be a somewhat true image of hostesses at some lower-class bars but not necessarily true of all hostesses at all bars.

Night life in bars is a temporary escape from the normal daytime activities, as seen through the eyes of society. Here hard reality can be forgotten as customers relax; even the dullest and most ignoble can receive the treatment of kings, if they pay for it. Those who work inside this world are "abnormal," for it represents not the reality of life but escape from it. The responsibility of hostess work is to perpetrate the dream upon customers, enabling them to forget their problems in the world outside; in so doing, the hostess is viewed as holding the power to lead customers astray from the "normal."

Thus, society in part disapproves of the hostess for the same reason that she can be called a member of the subculture: she works apart from the everyday humdrum of life. Inside her world the work has its own monotony; it loses the sparkle of excitement, the aura of the dream that outsiders attribute to it. But only those entirely within it know thoroughly that difference between others' perceptions and their reality, and to show society the bar's reality is to destroy its attractiveness.

Hostesses perceive themselves as little different from other women. If they do classify themselves in a separate category, they tend to see themselves as superior, reasoning that their work is more interesting and that it gives them greater financial power than other women attain. But their perceptions of others' opinions concerning hostesses are widely varied, indicating a contradiction between what they would like others to think and what the opinions of others actually are, as well as their belief that they are misunderstood by society.

The role that the hostess assumes is not autonomous from the society, but rather a negative one within it. Regardless of her opinion that society misjudges her, she fails to question the standards by which those judgments are made. Few hostesses wish to remain in their professions; their hope is to save money and get out as soon as possible—to reintegrate with society. As hostesses they may rationalize the status of their work in order to overcome feelings of self-degradation. Many believe the bar to be a necessity for society —perhaps as a place where informal psychotherapy heals the mental ills of the society's male population. Some believe that they actually promote family relations for their customers, who return home relaxed and rejuvenated after an evening at the bar. Hostesses make such rationalizations as a method of coping with their own contradictory opinions of their status, but they nevertheless see their work as temporary.

Hostess work gives women a temporary opportunity to earn money for other goals, but it can only be utilized as the means to an end rather than becoming the end in itself. Women usually become hostesses while still in their early twenties; once past their thirties, they are rarely hired. The work serves the purpose of filling in the time between childhood and the woman's entrance into marriage, but it cannot become a career within which the woman achieves a feeling of worthiness to society by her contribution to it.

TWO PROFILES

Mariko graduated from a two-year business school and began working at a company in Tokyo when she was twenty. Bored with her clerical job at the office, and dissatisfied with the low salary, she decided to study English at a night school. A language skill, she reasoned, might help her to get a better-paying job some day, so for a year she pursued language studies while working.

Her parents, however, felt that marriage would provide the best security for her future, and when Mariko was twenty-one they arranged for her to meet a man who they believed could at least give her economic security. Although he was considerably older than Mariko, she agreed to marry him, partly because she no longer felt sure that her English study would brighten her career prospects.

The marriage lasted a year. Often coming home from work drunk, the husband tended to take out his frustrations from his job on his wife, and Mariko, being so much younger than he, was unable to control him when he lost his temper. Finally she asked him to find another apartment and he moved out.

Fortunately Mariko had continued working at the office after she was married, so she did have her own income. But she had little hope that her salary would increase very much or that she would be promoted in her job, and the thought of continuing to work indefinitely was depressing. A friend at the office quit her job, and later confided that she had begun working as a hostess at a small bar in Ginza. When Mariko heard the amount of income her friend was making she applied at the bar which her friend had entered and, upon being assured of a job, she too left office work.

The bar that employed Mariko was not a top-ranking one, and competition among the nine hostesses there was virtually nonexistent since they were all hired as "help." The "mama," who owned the bar, strove for a friendly, cozy atmosphere and encouraged most of the hostesses to dress traditionally. Mariko enjoyed Japanese folk music, and customers often requested her to sing for them to the accompaniment of a guitarist. She was not insensitive to the derogatory remarks made occasionally by customers, but her sympathy and warmth made her popular with the older men.

Mariko had told her parents that she and her husband were separated, but she was afraid to confess that she had quit her office job to become a bar hostess. Her parents lived several hundred miles from Tokyo, and since Mariko's apartment had no telephone, their only communication with her was by letter except for Mariko's infrequent visits home. "I would quit working as a hostess if I knew that they suspected anything about it," she said.

Living apart from her husband and so far from her family, Mariko often feels lonely. She sometimes goes shopping during the afternoon with another hostess at her bar, but she rarely sees old school or office friends. "We no longer have much in common," she explains. "They are all either happily married or still working in offices, and most of them don't know that I am a hostess now." What Mariko hesitates to admit is that she fears her old friends will criticize her failure in marriage, as well as condemn her choice of work.

Mariko hopes to find a man who will marry her in spite of her first marriage. "If I found someone new I would have to tell him about my husband, of course," she says, adding that she would then ask her husband for a divorce. "But I wouldn't let him know about my bar job, and I would quit working before he learned about it." The disadvantage of being a hostess, however, is that it greatly limits her opportunities to meet a man who is not already aware of her job. Most of the customers at her bar are married, and she does not belong to an organization or associate with a group of singles who would introduce her to new men.

"My situation now is only temporary," she explains, referring to both her job and her marital situation. "Perhaps my husband and I can work out our problems after a year or two. Or perhaps I can marry someone else. But I can't continue working as a hostess. My parents would never accept it, and I'm not earning enough money to be really successful at it." She also worries that the "mama" may fire some of the hostesses, because not enough customers are patronizing the bar these days. "I am saving some money, but if I get fired, I'll have to look for another hostess job to support myself." She refuses to consider returning to office work.

Mariko believes that she was a victim of two practices which continue to be widespread in Japanese society. In the first place, she had been pessimistic about her chances of making a career of her office job because she knew that women in larger companies like hers could rarely hope to be promoted unless they had a specialized skill. She therefore believed that marriage would give her a better future. Secondly, because her career prospects seemed so limited, she had not resisted her parents when they persuaded her to undergo an arranged marriage with a man whose personality clashed with her own but which she did not discover until after the marriage.

Machiko is several years older than Mariko and has worked in a first-class bar in Akasaka. "I came to Tokyo when I was nineteen, looking for a job. Hostess work seemed to be the most profitable." Her outstanding good looks enabled her to get a job at a bar where she worked as a *shimei*. The competition was intense—in the beginning she was forced to spend more money on clothes than Mariko has. Within five years, though, she saved enough money to start her own bar in a suburb of Tokyo, with some financial assistance by her patron.

"At first the work was fun. I liked being able to buy expensive clothes, and I was happy that I didn't have to ask my parents for money. But I got tired of the types of people I had to work with. I never became good friends with the other hostesses. We sometimes went to the movies together in the afternoon, or to discotheques with customers after work, but my relationships with the other hostesses were too shallow."

Machiko's customers almost always paid their bills, and she budgeted her income very carefully. "After the first year I never spent any more money than I had to on clothes. I lived very cheaply because I wanted to get out of hostess work as soon as I could." One of her married customers offered to pay the rent for an apartment close to her bar if she would become his mistress. She accepted the proposition—"I liked him and it was a good way to cut down on my expenses." They continued the arrangement until a year after she had become the "mama" of her own bar.

When asked about her parents' opinion of her job as a hostess, Machiko says that at first they were displeased. "But later they began to respect me when they learned how much money I was saving."

Although the bar that she now owns is moderately successful, Machiko worries that she has not had enough experience to manage it well. She thinks that men know more about how to avoid paying high income taxes on the bar's profits. "In management, men are more naturally talented than women." It seems odd that such a statement should come from one of the few hostesses who have been successful enough to start their own business.

At present Machiko is living with a man two years younger than she, but she doubts that they will marry. "Even if I do marry, though, I will continue to manage the bar," she says.

Machiko believes that if women are willing to work as hard as men in her society, they will have the same opportunities to succeed. Unlike Mariko, however, her only employment experience has been in an exclusively female profession—that of hostess. While she does not regard marriage as the only possible future for her, she does think that men are inherently superior in the business world.

Mariko represents many hostesses in Tokyo today who drift into their profession because of their dissatisfaction with a low-salaried job they have previously held. Like others, she does not hope to make a career of hostess work, nor is she planning another career. The work provides a temporary income until she can find financial security in marriage. Machiko, on the other hand, was atypical in that she carefully planned for another career while she was working as a hostess. She disliked the superficiality of the bar world, and held herself apart from it as much as possible in her private life. Unlike many other hostesses, she used no money for travel abroad or for luxurious housing, and she spent only a minimum on her wardrobe.

Machiko's break with her family at an early age forced her to make decisions by herself, and she even ceased to care whether her parents approved of her work or not. Mariko, however, remains caught between shame for having entered a marriage that failed as well as for working as a hostess, and passivity regarding her present situation.

NOTES

[1] The field research for this study consisted of a set of written questionnaires distributed to one hundred and fifty hostesses and a series of oral interviews with hostesses, managers, bar-goers, bar madams, and bar waiters. The written questionnaires were distributed first in order to gain a knowledge of hostesses' backgrounds, living situations, and opinions concerning their work and the status and roles of women in Japan. The oral interviews served to provide the researcher with a limited number of in-depth character studies. Neither method of research can be satisfactorily analyzed; rather, both were undertaken as exploratory steps toward the goal of understanding the hostess's world.

[2] T. Fujimoto, *The Story of the Geisha Girl*, p. 4.

[3] *Ibid.*, pp. 10-18.

[4] Yasunosuke Gonda, *Goraku Gyōsha no Mure*, [A Group of the Entertainment Trade], p. 23.

[5] These terms as applied here refer to a man who contributes financial assistance to the woman in exchange for sexual favors.

[6] Gonda, p. 25.

[7] Saiyo Masuda, *Geisha Kutō no Hanseigai* [A Geisha's Half-Life of Struggles], p. 51.

[8] Yoshie Kishii, *Onna Geisha no Jidai* [The Age of Women Geisha], p. 133.

[9] *Ibid.*, p. 425.

[10]Kiyoko Nishi, *Shokugyō Fujin no Gojūnen* [Fifty Years' History of Working Women], pp. 174-175.

[11]Gonda, pp. 50-51.

[12]Such was the opinion of one bar's "mama."

[13]The term "club," which is generally used for first-class Ginza and Shinjuku bars, reflects this attempt by the establishments to convey an atmosphere of close interpersonal relationships.

[14]One manager stated that he fired hostesses at the age of thirty because in his opinion they became "neuter" by this age.

[15]The time limit varies from thirty to ninety days; however, many bars have been forced to extend their time limits as a result of the recent economic recession.

[16]This practice of offering *shitakukin* to hostesses upon their entrance into a club bears a semblance to the prewar geisha system whereby the young girl could only become an apprentice after indebting herself to the geisha house.

[17]If, for example, the hostess works only six months under a one-year contract, she must return half the amount of the *shitakukin*; if she makes only half the amount of profit specified in the contract, she likewise must return half of the *shitakukin* at the end of the year.

[18]Sometimes two sponsors are required. The hostess's sponsor in many cases is also her patron, or *danna*.

CHAPTER
8
WOMEN IN TEACHING

"Women Teachers Outnumber Men!" This is a headline seen in many Japanese newspapers a few years ago. Each spring since then, the new academic year has been accompanied by discussions centering upon the increasing number of women teachers, although a close look at the figures shows that even in 1974 women accounted for just barely over half (54 percent) of the faculty even at the elementary level. Although their numbers are increasing, in the same year women accounted for only 29 percent and 17 percent of the faculty at junior and senior high schools, respectively.[1] Accordingly, "Women Teachers" of the above headline can only refer to elementary school teachers.

There are several reasons for the considerable attention being given to women teachers in the primary schools. Women have been steadily entering the teaching profession in growing numbers in the postwar period. The fact that they have come to account for half the teachers on just one level is itself a symbol of the changes which have occurred in the teaching profession. As in many other countries, the pattern of entry for women into the professions begins at the lowest levels and then gradually spreads upward to the higher levels. In the case of the teaching profession this pattern is further strengthened by stereotypes and values concerning the "natural" role and the "true" abilities of women. Briefly stated, Japanese women have always been highly evaluated in terms of their ability to work well with children. The thought that women teachers would perhaps make good primary school teachers is perhaps a corollary which logically follows from the commonly accepted axiom that mothers are more naturally suited than fathers to rearing children. Following this line of reasoning, in prewar

Japan women teachers were most often seen in the primary schools, while teaching in the more intellectually demanding high schools and universities was reserved exclusively for men. Indeed, reflecting societal values in the educational system itself helped to perpetuate the notion that women were best suited for teaching the lower grades in elementary school. Above the elementary level, men and women were educated separately. Thereafter, men could enter a broad variety of schools which had been set up by the government in an effort to promote industrialization, while women from the upper middle class or above could at best attend a women's high school (jogakkō) at which they were taught primarily domestic sciences and literature. However, the vast majority of women received no more than six years of compulsory education.

With the new postwar constitution proclaiming sexual equality and the new educational system introduced by the American Occupation authorities, public secondary schools and universities became coeducational. Although the difference between the sexes in terms of enrollment in higher education is conspicuous, nearly the same percentage of men and women now graduate from high school (see Table I). At the university level, women account for 90 percent of

Table I

Percentage of Male and Female Graduates Continuing on for Further Education

Year	Junior High School Graduates		Senior High School Graduates	
	Males	Females	Males	Females
1951	51.4	39.6	30.1	12.9
1955	55.5	47.4	20.9	14.9
1960	59.6	55.9	19.7	14.2
1965	71.7	69.6	30.1	20.4
1970	81.6	82.7	25.0	23.0
1974	88.3	90.6	31.6	30.8

Source: Mombu-Shō [Ministry of Education], Gakkō Kihon Chōsa [Basic Survey of Schools] (Tokyo: Okura Shō Insatsu Kyoku, annual).

the student body at the two-year junior colleges which heavily emphasize the domestic sciences, but only 18 percent at four-year institutions. Although the number of women graduating from four-year colleges or universities is steadily increasing, the choice of curriculum and employment attitudes continue to be guided by traditional constraints. Progress is definitely occurring, but the awareness of, and interest in new opportunities in the professions tend to lag behind the high rate of economic growth. No doubt there is a percolation effect, and changes will occur at an accelerated rate in the future. At the present, however, the ideal for many, though by no means all women, continues to be the happily married housewife and homemaker.2 This orientation among women themselves, then, also explains at least partially the fact that nearly half the women in junior colleges major in home economics, while half the women at four-year institutions major in literature or language.3 Given this background, it is not surprising that 98 percent of all kindergarten and 54 percent of elementary school teachers were women in 1974, the majority of whom were junior college graduates. Reflecting the way in which women have come to play an increasingly important role, particularly in the education of younger students, teaching at this level has come to be known as a woman's "natural calling." Consequently, today nearly one-fifth of all graduates from two- and four-year institutions of higher education have majored in education.4

The rapid increase in the number of women teachers at all levels in Japan reflects broader changes occuring in society at large. First, of course, is the rising level of education among women as more continue on to college or the university. Second, perhaps reflecting the rapid growth of the Japanese economy and the growing number of opportunities in the world of business, fewer men have wanted to go into teaching.5 Third, women meet with much less discrimination and generally receive equal pay in the teaching profession. Therefore, teaching attracts a larger number of women applicants than most other careers.

In the first part of this paper, I will give a brief historical sketch of women as teachers in contemporary Japan, discuss some of the problems confronting women teachers, and then describe more fully the life of the average teacher. In the next section, I will present a historical picture of women teachers in Japan. Women teachers have not always enjoyed conditions as favorable as they do today. Moreover, while many of the more obvious sources of sex discrimination have been removed from the classroom, older attitudes toward women still remain below the surface, and some understanding of those attitudes as they relate to education is important if we are to appreciate fully the position of the woman teacher in present-day Japan. In the third part of this chapter, attention will be focused upon the many problems which continue to confront teaching women: salaries, child-care leave, promotion to administrative and other leadership positions, and the general social climate and intellectual environment in which they work. In the fourth section I will seek to illustrate some of the points made earlier by drawing upon the experiences of more than thirty teachers whom I interviewed during the summer of 1975. From these interviews it is hoped that some picture of the average teacher may be projected, while at the same time underlining the great variety of personalities and backgrounds which go into making up the female component

160

of the Japanese teaching profession at the elementary and secondary levels.

A CENTURY OF TEACHING

The notion that women should be "good wives and wise mothers" (*ryōsai kembō*) has been valued in both the West and Japan. The concept defined woman's role in society as that of wife and mother. Her upbringing, education and training were thus directed toward preparing her for this role. In order to perform that role, a formal education was not considered necessary until the late eighteenth century in the United States and perhaps not until toward the latter part of the nineteenth century in Japan. In the United States, the turning point can be said to have come in 1798 with Benjamin Rush's *Thoughts Upon Female Education.* Rush emphasized the important role which women fulfilled in educating children, and pointed out the inadequacies of schooling for women. Since the male heads of families were too preoccupied with their life outside the home, he wrote that

> ...a principal share of the instruction of children naturally devolves upon women. It becomes us therefore to prepare them by a suitable education for the discharge of this most important duty of mothers.[6]

The fact that by 1890 twice as many girls as boys graduated from American high schools attests to the importance which Americans attached to the education of women. On the other hand, the fact that women were to be found in almost none of the professions outside of secondary school teaching is indicative of one fact: education for women was designed primarily to produce "good wives and wise mothers."

The principles of America's own version of *ryōsai kembō* were brought to the attention of Japanese educators by Mori Arinori in the 1870s. As the first Minister of Education, he decided to set up educational institutions for women based upon the American concept. During the first decade of Meiji, educators (all men) were very receptive to Western ideas. But, like other ideas introduced from abroad, this concept too was eventually to be articulated with the Confucian vocabulary in order to suit the more conservative position of the Japanese government regarding women's proper role in Japanese society. Stated briefly, the government viewed women's education in terms of its practical value in preparing women for their unquestioned role as homemakers. It was thought that formal education should enhance their performance of that role. In other words, serious study for the sake of scholarship or personal growth was not accepted as necessary or really desirable.[7] Nevertheless, in 1872, less than twenty years after the arrival of Commodore Perry to Japan in 1853 and the subsequent opening up of the country after nearly four centuries of isolationism, the new Meiji government had established a national system of education. Elementary education became compulsory for all children. At the same time, moreover, there was a sudden increase in the demand for teachers. The government again followed the American example, and women were hired to teach in the new coeducational elementary schools. In addition to the belief that women were perfectly suited for teaching small children, there were two other more practical reasons for employing them. First, there was a shortage of qualified male teachers in a profession formerly considered respectable for men of the samurai ranks. Second, three women could be hired on the salary of two men, an economic consideration of considerable importance.[8]

In the beginning years there was much opposition among parents to sending their daughters to the elementary schools, for it was generally thought to be exceedingly unfeminine and altogether unnecessary for women to receive any scholarly training. School attendance rates during the beginning years of Meiji attest to this fact. As shown in Table II, in 1875 only 18 percent of all girls, in contrast to 50 percent of all boys, were enrolled in schools. Nonetheless, the gov-

Table II
Enrollment of Students in Elementary Schools (percentages): 1875-1930

Year	Total	Girls	Boys
1875	35.8	18.6	50.5
1880	41.1	21.9	58.7
1885	49.6	32.1	65.8
1890	48.9	31.1	65.1
1895	61.2	43.9	65.1
1900	81.5	71.7	90.6
1905	95.6	93.3	97.7
1910	98.1	97.4	98.3
1920	99.0	98.8	99.2
1930	99.5	99.5	99.5

Source: Kaigo Tokiomi, *Japanese Education: Its Past and Present* (Tokyo: Kokusai Bunka Shinkokai, 1968), p. 65.

ernment continued to encourage parents to send their children to school, and by 1910 nearly all school-age children were enrolled in elementary schools.

As for teachers, women accounted for only 1.2 percent of elementary teachers in 1871, the year compulsory education was instituted (see Table III). With the rapid increase in the number of school children, government normal schools were established throughout the prefectures to train teachers. And just as the number of girls

Table III
Percentage of Women Teachers in the Public Schools: 1873-1974

Year	Coeducational Elementary Schools	Girls' Schools (Jogakkō)	Middle Schools Grades 7-9
1873a	1.2		
1877	2.6	98.5	
1900	14.8	64.8	
1907b	25.9	59.4	
1927	33.0	42.2	
1940	39.9	42.8	
1945	54.2	NA	
1947c	49.1		22.7
1960	45.3		22.5
1970	51.2		27.3
1974	54.0		28.8

afirst year of elementary schools
belementary school increased to six years
cnew constitution promulgated

Source: Ichibangase Yasuko and Tsukamoto Shiuko, "Sankō Shiryō" [Reference Materials], in *Jokyōshi no Fujin Mondai* [Issues Concerning Women as Teachers], ed. by Ichibangase Yasuko, Kigawa Tatsuji and Miyata Takeo (Tokyo: Daiichi Hōki Shuppan Sha, 1974), pp. 188-192.

in the elementary school had been low in the beginning years because of lingering traditional values, the number of applicants to the Tokyo Women's Normal School (Tokyo Joshi Shihan Gakkō), which was established in 1874, was extremely low due to the same attitudes. These attitudes are also reflected in recorded instances of parents being opposed to sending their daughters off to such institutions. For example, one male parent wrote the following:

> I apologize from the bottom of my heart to all my esteemed ancestors for having raised a daughter who wanted to study at a women's normal school. Finding myself in such a dilemma, I consulted my wife, and found her also to be troubled by the fact that she gave birth to such a studious daughter. We held a family meeting to discuss the matter, and it was eventually decided by my father-in-law that it would be best to enroll her in the school rather than oppose a prefectural ordinance which had established the school for all qualified applicants. Thus, we let her go. However, so as not to bring shame to the honor of our family name, our daughter was enrolled under her mother's family name.[9]

Despite unfavorable public opinion, women managed to enter the teaching profession in growing numbers, and by 1900 they accounted for 15 percent of elementary school teachers and were steadily increasing (see Table III). The ideal of *ryōsai kembō* increasingly became the basic philosophy upon which school curricula were organized[10] and as the number of women teachers increased, many began to openly question whether women should be teaching at all. For example, in Tokushima Prefecture on the island of Shikoku (one of the four major islands of Japan), a great public debate took place over this matter. Those who favored having women teachers presented the following arguments:

(1) Women are very good with children. Furthermore, their gentle and patient dispositions make them perfectly suited for teaching.
(2) From an economic. standpoint, it is cheaper to employ women.
(3) As the national economy continues to expand, men will increasingly be needed for business and industry. Men will thus no longer have time to teach in the elementary schools.

Those opposing the employment of women teachers set forth the following items:

(1) Women are naturally weak, and as such should not be responsible for the education of young children who require an active and capable person.
(2) The supervision of an elementary school requires fortitude, perseverance and a number of other qualities which women do not possess.
(3) After women marry, they will bear children. As mothers, it is their duty to care for their children. However, should a woman enter the teaching profession, it would interfere with her responsibilities to her children, which are of foremost importance.[11]

While similar debates were held throughout the country on the "problem" of women teachers, more and more women entered the profession. Around the turn of the century the National Teachers Association (Zenkoku Rengō Kyōiku Kai) even asked that higher salaries be given to women teachers.

Coupled with the Russo-Japanese War (1904-1905), rapid industrialization resulted in an acute shortage of teachers in the early years of this decade. Moreover, school attendance was rapidly increasing (see Table II). Tetsu Ishidoya comments that "after the war, with the continued shortage of teachers (men), and also reflecting the fact that villages and towns throughout the nation were seeking ways to lighten the burden of rising educational costs, the number of women teachers gradually increased."[12] In 1908, the demand for elementary school teachers again jumped as compulsory education was increased from four to six years. By this time nearly all school-age children were enrolled in schools, and more than a quarter of all teachers were women. It was also about this time that government leaders and educators came to express serious concern about the rising number of women teachers. In 1918, at a time when women had come to account for 30.9 percent of all elementary school teachers, the government's Provisional Educational Council (*Rinji Kyōiku Kaigi*) wrote as follows:

> The number of female teachers has been increasing at a remarkable pace in recent years. How long will it be before their number overtakes the number of male teachers? ...When the responsibility for the education of the nation is put primarily in women's hands, we cannot cultivate vigor and virtuous simplicity in our citizens. . . . There should be a limit set on the number of female teachers.13

Undaunted by the lack of general public support, women continued to enter teaching. Though all were exceptional in that they held careers in what had formerly been exclusively a man's domain, few questioned the traditional belief that men are superior to women (*danson johi*). Indeed, most had been inculcated with the principles of *ryōsai kembō* and no doubt thought that the present division of labor which made good wives and wise mothers out of women was quite natural. Moreover, with the Russo-Japanese War, the nation was swept up by conservative nationalism. This resulted in increased growing support for the principles of *ryōsai kembō*, ensuring that the family system, and therefore the nation, would be strengthened.14 However, it should be noted that although many were servants to conservative government policy, some women teachers did participate in the social movements of the times. These movements focused upon various issues ranging from suffrage and women's rights to political ideology, and steadily gained momentum after World War I.15 Some activists like Itsue Takamure urged women teachers to act if any changes were to occur.16

That these women, many of whom were married, even had time for such "extra-curricular activities" is rather remarkable considering their teaching and family commitments.17 Indeed, the fact that they did participate at all suggests a very strong commitment to new ideas. Had it been physically possible, it is likely that more would have stepped forward in sympathy with these new movements.

Turning to a consideration of working conditions for women teachers in prewar Japan, one's remarks should be prefaced with the fact that teachers, like other women working outside the home, were burdened with the problem of having to fulfill two roles, one as teacher and one as housewife and mother. According to a report delivered by Tatsuo Morito to a meeting of the Social Policy Association (*Shakai Seisaku Gakkai*) in 1918, this is very clear:

> I'll tell you about a typical day in the life of a married teacher. She rises at 5:30 a.m.... Every morning she goes down to the stream to wash clothes and then tends to her children. At 7:20 a.m. she arrives at school. After classes are dismissed, she spends thirty minutes cleaning the classroom,

another twenty minutes grading papers, and from thirty minutes to an hour on lesson plans for the following day. Another thirty minutes is spent in additional miscellany, and by 5:00 p.m. she arrives home. Until dinner time she looks after her children. If there is time, she will do unfinished housecleaning. After dinner and the dishes, there is the bath. By eight or nine o'clock, she is ready to begin sewing and mending. There is no time even for reading the newspaper. In fact, the earlier she returns home from school, the more housework she finds herself doing. Since she gave birth to her children she has had scarcely any time for reading professional journals. The books she manages to check out from the library are more often than not returned unread.[18]

Women worked a full day to be sure. The load of some teachers was lightened by the fact that they had maids.[19] Others lived with relatives (most frequently their parents) and were able to utilize the extended family relationship to obtain care for their children and assistance in certain kinds of housework.

This provides a sharp contrast to the situation today where, with the labor shortage, housekeepers are rare, and certainly cannot be hired on the teacher's salary. Moreover, the nuclear family is becoming the norm and the built-in system of nursery care has disappeared. In addition, with urbanization and skyrocketing land prices, most middle-class families do not have the means to buy their own home. They must make do with very small, cramped apartments where it is usually not possible to have relatives come to live even temporarily. Accordingly, daycare centers, though still few in number, have been more than welcomed by women teachers in postwar Japan. With their dual roles, the working day of the female teacher *was* and still *is* long.

At work, women teachers faced blatant job and salary discrimination. One teacher described the situation in the early 'twenties as follows:

> Beginning salaries for men and women were fifty yen and forty-five yen, respectively, a 10 percent difference right from the start. Salary raises were left entirely to the discretion of the school principal, a man who would consistently give raises first to the male teachers and then, as funds permitted, to the women teachers he fancied. Were a teacher to become pregnant, she would be treated as though she had committed a grave crime, and would be excluded from any raise in salary. Moreover, the longer a woman taught, the greater the wage differential with her male counterparts.[20]

As shown in Table IV, according to the actual wage differentials in the Taishō period three women could be hired on the wages of two men.

In addition to the dual set of roles and lower wages, women had

Table IV
Pay for Men and Women Teachers in Taishō Japan

Year	First Four Grades of Elementary School			Upper Two Grades of Elementary School		
			Women / Men			Women / Men
	Men	Women	Men	Men	Women	Men
1915	19.75	14.83	.751	26.47	16.48	.623
1916	20.41	14.85	.728	26.47	16.41	.620
1917	20.80	15.20	.731	26.70	16.91	.633

Source: Mochitsuki Muneaki, *Nihon no Fujin Kyoshi: Sono Henkaku no Ayumi* (Women Teachers in Japan: An Historical Account of Change) (Tokyo: Rōdō Junpō Sha, 1968), pp. 45-46.

to face discrimination within their own profession. Reflecting the attitudes of the male educators of their times, they were allocated the lower grades and the easier, so-called "soft" subjects to teach. A survey taken in 1920 by the Imperial Teacher's Association (*Teikoku Kyōin Kai*), the largest and most influential professional organization for teachers at the time, clearly shows the attitudes of their male counterparts. The national survey of normal school superintendents (forty men) and elementary school principals (seventy-one men) was taken in order to determine various differences between male and female teachers. Asked to list personality traits of female teachers which make them suited for teaching, answers included the following: (1) care in faithfully following orders (superintendents, 67.5 percent; principals, 63.5 percent); (2) affability (57.5 and 45.0); (3) concern with detail (52.5 and 62.0); (4) skillfulness in subjects requiring manual dexterity (52.5 and 62.0); and (5) suitability for routine deskwork and officework (50.0 and 38.0). Asked then to list the *weak* points of women teachers, the following replies were given: (1) inability to do research (7.5 and 62.0); (2) inclination toward being too affectionate with children (60.0 and 41.0); (3) lack of practical knowledge or common sense (50.0 and 49.0); and (4) ineptitude at administrative work (35.0 and 27.0). In the same survey the respondents were asked about which grade levels were most suitable for women to teach. The vast majority answered that women were appropriate for the teaching of first (86 percent for superintendents and no figure for principals) and second (83 percent and 87.5 percent) grades. The figure dropped for third (48.0 percent and 75.0 percent) and fourth (22.5 percent and 37.5 percent) grades. None of the superintendents and less than 5 percent of the principals thought that women were suited to teach either fifth or sixth grades.[21]

Throughout the prewar period, popular and official opinion continued to deride and lament the steady increase of women teachers in the elementary schools, and the role of the woman teacher was limited primarily by the fact that the woman's place was thought to be in the home. It should be pointed out here that the belief that women belonged in the home was held not only by men, but by women as well. Even the most distinguished women educators advocated such views. The writings of two well-known women educators in prewar Japan have been selected to give some idea of the popular views regarding the role of women. Utako Shimoda was the founder of Jissen Jogakuen, a girls' school which emphasized the domestic arts. As a leader who defended the concept of *ryōsai kembō* in terms of its contribution to the achievement of nationalistic goals, in 1931 she argued as follows:

> A modern woman has a tendency to be rational and individualistic. Both tendencies came from abroad, and it is lamentable that the long-established, good, and beautiful customs of Japan have been corrupted by such influences. From childhood, the truly Japanese woman is trained in self-discipline. She will devote herself to "moral justice" and yet will control her feelings. She works hard to do her household chores without complaining, and never aspires to distinguish herself or to be rich. She supports her husband, and cares for her family. She is patient and devoted. Times have changed, and it is not the same now as it was in former days. But many educators still aim at educating women to be strong in heart and mind. To make wise mothers and good wives, that is the meaning of a real education, one which is able to develop completely the qualities of the "old-fashioned woman" first, before attempting to train one in modern ways.[22]

Kakei Atomi, founder of the Atomi Girls' School which catered to the daughters of the nobility, also advocated the importance of women serving the nation as good wives and wise mothers:

> Foreign-style education is important and indispensable at the present time, but it would be very dangerous to over-emphasize such education and thereby lose the spirit of the people as well as that of the country... A woman's virtue is found in the concept of self-sacrifice, which is usually described as work in the background, or as a thankless task. Women must not forget that they are the nameless heroines... Such women should be celebrated as good wives and wise mothers. This is the real meaning of life for women.[23]

During the first seventy years of public education, the number of women in the teaching profession steadily increased despite all the doubts and criticism expressed by educators, government leaders, and parents. All the while, they continued to accept low salaries and teaching assignments in the lower grades in the elementary schools. Moreover, throughout this prewar period, women teachers were plagued by reminders that a woman's place was in the home.

Although girls' high schools (*kōtō jogakkō*) were officially designated as schools for secondary education in 1890, and were staffed almost entirely by women teachers (see Table III), the curriculum was regulated by the Ministry of Education in keeping with the principles of *ryōsai kembō*. Government guidelines on curricula and controls on teachers were strengthened step by step over the years. Private schools for women, which were largely mission schools set up by the foreign missionaries in the early years of Meiji, provided more academic curricula which compared favorably with the boys' public middle schools. However, by 1900 their numbers had decreased sharply as the government prohibited religious instruction. Women were then left with the public girls' high schools, which were progressively oriented toward the domestic arts. The handful of women's colleges were all unaccredited. At the same time, as conservatism in the government kept in step with heightened nationalism, the number of women teachers in the women's secondary schools (there were no coeducational secondary schools and thus no other women teachers in secondary education) gradually decreased until they accounted for only 40 percent of the teaching staff by the end of World War II. Furthermore, regulations regarding curriculum became more numerous as the nation began to prepare for war. The fact that women had grown to account for 40 percent of all elementary school teachers also began to alarm educators and the government which they supported. In 1938 the Educational Inquiry Commission issued the following statement:

> Women teachers have increased to an extent found in the United States and Europe. This fact causes us great anxiety as to the future of our national system of education. Americans tend to base decisions on emotional considerations rather than upon fairness. This has resulted from the fact that 90 percent of all elementary school teachers are women. From the standpoint of both education and national needs...the number of normal school entrants should be set at a ratio of two men per woman.[24]

Nevertheless, as in the past, war again diminished the ranks of the male teachers, and women came to account for more than half of the elementary school teaching staff during World War II.

With the end of the war in 1945, the American Occupation forces organized a new government based upon American political ideology. Under the new Constitution (1947) and the School Education Law (1947), secondary education became coeducational and the universities were opened to women. No longer were women confined to teaching in elementary schools. The girls' high schools were abolished and in their place coeducational secondary schools were established. The same salaries were paid to all public secondary school teachers. Moreover, the Labor Standards Law provided women teachers with six weeks' maternity leave and an additional six weeks for child care. Teaching thus became one of the most attractive professions for women with a college degree. Despite various legal reforms, in other fields of work women have continued to face the same kinds of discrimination they had been accustomed to in the prewar period. That teachers succeeded in getting nearly equitable working conditions is in no small measure due to the untiring efforts of Nikkyōso (the Japan Teachers' Federation), a leftist union, which is the most powerful teachers' union in the country.

During the postwar years the representation of women teachers at the secondary level has gradually increased. Nevertheless, even today women account for only about 30 percent of all middle school teachers and less than 20 percent of all high school teachers. They rarely serve as school principals. The only exceptions are the kindergartens, which are usually independent schools. Women now head about 45 percent of all kindergartens.[25] There are indications, however, that the number of women teachers will continue to increase at all levels relative to the number of male teachers. According to one nationwide survey taken by Jiji Tsūshin Sha (Current Affairs Institute) on the numbers of new teachers in the public schools in 1973 (Table V), the percentage of women entering the teaching

Table V
Ratio of New Teachers in the Public Schools by Sex: 1973

	Women	Men
Elementary Schools	2.5	1
Middle Schools	1	1
High Schools	1	3

Source: Jiji Tsūshin Sha [Current Affairs Institute], "Jokyōshi Jidai o Irokoku Han'ei" [Clear Trend Shown Toward the Age of the Woman Teacher], *Naigai Kyōiku* (No. 2467: September 19, 1973), p. 2.

profession was high. Figures also indicate that women teachers account for as much as 80 percent of the new elementary school teachers in the metropolitan areas, while their numbers are comparatively low in the rural areas where industries are fewer and men still find teaching an attractive occupation.

In conclusion, one must say that women in the teaching profession have made great strides in the postwar period. At the same time, however, we must qualify that by saying that numerous "problems" remain with regard to salaries, child-care leave, promotion to administrative positions, and the lingering of traditional values. In the next section each of these will be taken up in detail. They are by no means "problems" unique either to Japan or to the teaching profession. They are for the most part the same problems women face everywhere.

PROBLEMS FACING WOMEN TEACHERS
IN CONTEMPORARY JAPAN

Women teachers are occasionally reminded by their male colleagues, by the parents of their students, and by the mass media that they are indeed a fortunate lot to be enjoying such optimal working conditions in an occupation which is free from discrimination. Yet, one survey taken in 1972 of 5,654 women who were primary and secondary school teachers found that more than half the respondents were dissatisfied with unfavorable working conditions, nearly four-fifths with their household set-up, and almost two-thirds with their present arrangement for childcare.[27]

Although the majority of the thirty women interviewed by this author expressed relative satisfaction with their treatment as teachers, when pressed to relate any awareness of unfair practices, it was found that serious problems do remain. In the following section, four "trouble areas" will be taken up: salary inequities, the early retirement system, the lack of women in administrative posts, and maternity and child-care leave.

INEQUITIES WITH REGARD TO SALARIES

In writing about salaries, one must first begin by stressing that blatant discrimination does not exist. As a general rule, the governments in most industrialized countries throughout the world have adopted an official policy of nondiscrimination between the sexes. While there is still a large list of unfinished business in this regard, and still a long way to go in the private sector, it can generally be said that the willingness of governments to move ahead in this area is reflected by the fact that male-female wage differentials are much narrower in the public sector. And nowhere is it easier to check for discrimination than in the paychecks of those having the same job title. Thus, teaching is one of the most advanced professions in this respect.

Nevertheless, less obvious kinds of discrimination remain. As mentioned above, the role of women as teachers has been circumscribed by the values of society as a whole. With regard to the payment of salaries, several practices continue to work to the disadvantage of women. The most important is the custom of designating a household head in all households for the purpose of employment. The extreme deprivation and the difficulties of making ends meet immediately after the war, coupled with the consequent demands of the labor unions for an age-based system of pay criteria tied to the life cycle of the household head in order to assure that each household would receive its minimum income requirements, resulted in various kinds of payments being made to the household head based upon his or her family responsibilities. In almost all cases, however, it is the husband who files as the household head at his place of work, with his wife being considered a secondary earner. Usually because of his greater earning capacity due to his favorable location in terms of occupation, firm size, industry, and educational background, it has been to the household's advantage to do so. At the same time, the systems of taxation, medical care and pension are based upon this distinction between the primary earner (the household head) and secondary earners (other household members). Family dependents are automatically declared on the return of the household head who, as stated above, is usually the husband.[28] Given the fact that taxes are deducted automatically at the source, even with a salary equal to her husband's, or that of her male counterpart, her take-home pay will be less due to lack of dependents.[29] Although a fixed percentage of each employee's salary is deducted for national health insurance and retirement pensions, those who have dependents again receive larger benefits. In the case of health insurance, benefits include all medical costs for oneself plus half for each dependent. Since the woman teacher technically has no dependents, she does not in reality receive that share which is paid to her male counterpart. Finally, in the case of retirement pensions, half of the pension will be paid to the dependent spouse or children of the household head should he die before his spouse. Women, who are not usually registered as household heads, do not leave their husbands or children any pension at all when they pass on.[30]

Finally, it should be added that while the number of women teachers has increased over the years, so too have the salary differences between college graduates in the teaching profession and those in other occupations in the private sector. The differential between men and women teachers grows larger as they age, but is not so great as in the private sector. The major reason for the difference between men and women in teaching is due in part to the receipt of certain benefits as the household head. However, more important is discrimination in promotion.[31]

Although the wage scale is based primarily upon seniority in the teaching profession in the postwar period, a promotion system based upon annual evaluations of teaching performance (*kimmu hyōka tokubetsu shōkyu*) has been instituted. In this regard, women teachers—who are allowed a three-day menstrual leave each month, between twelve and sixteen weeks' leave for maternity and child care, and an average of one hour per day child care leave during the first year after birth—are in a decidedly unfavorable position under this system of promotion. This is certainly one factor contributing to the higher incidence of promotions among men teachers.[32] In relation to this point, one should be aware of the fierce struggle which Nikkyōso has been waging against the Ministry of

Education's efforts to introduce an evaluation system which would place even more weight on subjective evaluations of teachers.[33] In addition, as mentioned above, very few women become school principals. Moreover, few are appointed as vice-principals or as head teachers (responsible for curriculum planning, textbook selection, teacher evaluation, and other specialized duties). All those titles bring with them extra pay.

Finally, in making salary comparisons, attention must be given to differences in retirement pay, a lump sum payment given upon retirement but based upon (1) one's length of employment (a rather geometrical relationship) and (2) one's final position. The problem of early retirement for women will be discussed below. Here I wish only to underline the fact that both criteria work to the disadvantage of women.

In closing, one should emphasize that the considerable amount of equality enjoyed by women teachers is for the most part limited to the public schools. The situation is quite different in the private schools (see Table VI). Although differences in the geographic

Table VI
Average Monthly Salaries at Private Schools: 1968
(1=¥1,000)

	Total	School Principal	Teacher	Assistant
Men	56.1	91.8	57.2	38.5
Women	36.1	42.7	39.4	30.2
Women/Men	.643	.465	.689	.784

Source: Ministry of Education, *Gakkō Kyōin Jukyu Chōsa* [Survey on the Supply and Demand of School Teachers] (1968).

location of male and female teachers, and particularly principals, also complicates comparisons, generally speaking the longer a woman teaches or occupies an administrative position, the greater the salary difference becomes.[34] At one private women's high school in Tokyo, I was told that women have resigned themselves to lower salaries. When I asked about union activity, the reply was that the school had no teacher's union. Furthermore, it was thought that the school would go bankrupt were a union to be established and women's wages made on par with those of men. Often these private schools are proud of their heritage as educators of future "good wives and wise mothers,"[35] and teachers who agree with this philosophy are hired. Compared with teachers at the public schools, these women tend to have a much lower level of awareness of sex discrimination, one factor no doubt accounting for their failure to organize for better wages.

RETIREMENT

A dual retirement system for men and women has always existed in Japan. In many private firms women are still pressured to "retire" upon marriage or the birth of the first child. Although teachers have not been subject to such pressures early in their careers, the retirement age for women teachers has always been lower than that for men. Besides affecting their life-time earnings, the practice also leaves women with a truncated career. In recent years, however, there has been much progress in this area in the private sector. Since 1966 when the Tokyo District Court first ruled that forced retirement of women upon marriage was unconstitutional, women have won a number of cases on this point each year. In 1975, the Tokyo High Court ruled that there is no good reason for setting an earlier retirement age for women.[36]

In the teaching profession the retirement age is set by the local prefectural authorities, and varies between fifty-two and sixty. Nikkyōso is working to make it a uniform sixty in all prefectures. Presently, differences exist not only among prefectures but also between men and women, for both teachers and principals. In twenty-six out of forty-seven prefectures, the retirement age for women is from one to nine years earlier than that for men. In nine of those prefectures, married women (whose husbands are gainfully employed) are forced to retire from one to seven years earlier than single women.[37] In 1975, the national newspapers reported a case involving a school board which refused to promote a teacher to principal until his wife resigned her teaching position.[38] In the past this kind of discriminatory policy was so prevalent and so commonly accepted that it did not generally receive news coverage. Indeed, we again come back to the traditional practice of thinking in terms of household heads.[39] In recent years, the Women's Bureau in the Japan Teacher's Union (Nikkyōso) and other teachers' unions have been working to end these kinds of unfair practices. However, even after the retirement age is formally made the same for both sexes, it is not uncommon for school principals (men) to begin asking teachers to resign after their fiftieth birthday.[40] The woman is approached informally by the principal in a paternalistic manner. It is suggested that she has been sacrificing her health with so much work, and that her face has been looking pallid recently. Or, the principal may even advise a young teacher with young children that it might be better for her to resign for the sake of her children. These attitudes remain prevalent, and are not altered so easily or quickly. It should be obvious that this kind of approach exerts a tremendous amount of psychological pressure on the teacher, creating anxieties in her as to her ability to teach or even to be adequate as a person. This in turn affects her work performance. Rather than competing openly for her attitudes or trying to convince her of a certain ideology, people taking this common approach are giving her wrong information which in turn confuses her as to her ability to judge reality.

Although there are very few surveys on retirees, one taken in 1972 of 2,792 retired women teachers (see Table VII) provides fairly recent information. Two-thirds had taught continuously until retirement. Of those whose careers were interrupted, two-thirds were for

Table VII
Length of Service of Retired Women Teachers: 1972

	Number of years				
	less than 10	11-20	21-30	31-40	over 40
Taught continuously (65.8%)	11.7%	24.9	34.2	26.9	1.8
Teaching career interrupted (34.1%)	7.9%	15.0	48.3	21.4	1.0

Source: Shimada, "Jokyōshi no enshoku to rōgo no mondai," p. 152.

less than five years, and another 21 percent of from six through ten years.

The total career length of women teachers seems to be unrelated to whether or not their career is interrupted, yet an interrupted career means the loss of a considerable amount in lump-sum retirement pay. In the same survey, when asked to state the reason for resigning, 25 percent replied that they had been asked to resign; 24 percent cited household circumstances; 12 percent gave reasons of health; 8 percent, childbirth; and 3.4 percent, marriage. Only 5 percent mentioned the official retirement age.[41] The percentages for childbirth (8 percent) and marriage (3.4 percent) are very low compared with the reasons given by women in the private business sector. This would seem to indicate that (1) teachers can generally continue teaching even while raising small children; (2) teachers are career-oriented in outlook; (3) working conditions in the public schools compare favorably with other occupations. Nonetheless, that 24 percent replied that "household circumstances" would not permit their continued employment suggests the stubbornness with which traditional values persist. Finally, although only 5 percent mentioned the official retirement age, more than one-fourth of the respondents retired with the retirement bonus. The principal may entice a teacher to retire early by offering her full retirement benefits and annuities even though she has not yet reached the official retirement age.[42]

PROMOTION TO ADMINISTRATIVE AND LEADERSHIP POSITIONS

A century has passed since a national system of public education was organized. During the early part of that century, a pattern was established for allocating teaching positions in the elementary and secondary schools. Women were appointed to the lower grades where it was thought their talents and "natural" abilities would be best utilized. Men were handed the responsibility for more rigorous education in the upper grades. This pattern remains entrenched today (see Table VIII). As suggested above, nursery schools or day-care centers (*hoikuen*) and kindergartens (*yōchien*) are staffed almost

Table VIII

A. Percentage of Women Teaching Each Grade in the Elementary Schools of "S" Prefecture

Grade	Elementary Schools										Middle Schools
	No class	1	2	3	4	5	6	7	8	9	No class
%	8	28	19	15	17	7	6	27	20	5	48

Source: Hashiguchi, "Jokyōshi e no Sabetsu no Genjo," p. 38.

B. Percentage of Women Teachers in Charge of Curricula in the Elementary Schools of "S" Prefecture

Subject	Home Economics	Music	Social Studies	Japanese	Arithmetic	Drawing	Penmanship
Percentage	50	27	8	6	3	3	3

Source: Hashiguchi, "Jokyōshi e no Sabetsu no Genjō," p. 71.

exclusively by women. At the elementary schools, women account for just over 50 percent of the teachers. Moreover, as Table VIII-A shows, the percentage of women teachers falls as the grade level increases. The same trend can be seen in middle schools and high schools where women account for less than thirty and twenty percent respectively of the teaching staff. The same pattern can be seen in the tendency to assign women to teach "easy" subjects.

Historical precedence and present opinion serve to perpetuate this imbalance. A school principal might approach a teacher in a quite fatherly manner, explaining that he has decided to give her a class of second-graders the following year as she now has a husband and baby to care for in addition to her responsibilities at school. He will perhaps point out to her how wonderful she is with the younger children and that the profession needs more teachers like her. As it is the principal who has the final word in this matter, and in the appointment of head teachers and new teachers, those in the position are quite influential. Yet, in 1972 women accounted for only 1.1 percent of all principals in the elementary schools, 0.2 percent (17 in all of Japan) in the middle schools, and 3.6 percent in the senior high schools. In addition, out of the 150 women principals in high schools, 146 were at private women's high schools.[43]

Thus, while women principals are more the rule than the exception in many Western countries, in Japan the woman principal is still the extreme exception. Although women can be appointed to administrative positions providing they pass a national examination, the results of a survey taken in 1973 of 8,000 women teachers throughout Japan, indicated that only 3 percent were at all interested in becoming school principals, while 70.8 percent replied that they had no interest. Among the latter, one-third stated that they did not feel they could carry such responsibility together with their household duties. Another third criticized administrative work as unmeaningful.[44] Thus, whether or not the percentage of women school administrators will increase appreciably in the coming years will no doubt depend upon (1) a change in attitude and consciousness and (2) more satisfactory household arrangements.

MATERNITY AND CHILD-CARE LEAVE

That women should devote their lives exclusively to the care of their families is an ideal that has been reiterated in literary and moral works down through the centuries. That they have in fact also been working outside the home at other pursuits, whether out of financial necessity or because of the desire to participate in the larger society, is also undeniable. Over the years there has been a gradual decrease in the number of women who subscribe to the ethic that "a woman's place is in the home."

Looking at society as a whole, teachers have been able to obtain more equitable working conditions than women in any other occupation in Japan. Yet, child care remains one of the areas which is still unsatisfactory. As urbanization has progressed, women teachers have become concentrated in the cities, and, it is precisely in the cities that the housing problem is most acute. Most families no longer live together with the grandparents, who in the past took care of the grandchildren while the mother taught school. Also, Japan has never adopted the "babysitter system" prevalent in the West. Consequently, there is a real need for public child care facilities so that women might continue working. Because salaries are based primarily upon a seniority-wage system, it has been important for women to continue working without taking any time off for child care, except as provided by law. Since the war, public daycare centers have been set up throughout the nation. Preference is given to working mothers, and when applicants outnumber spaces available, income also becomes a criterion for entrance. As the demand exceeds the supply, many parents are forced to put their children in private facilities which are often expensive, inadequate, and unlicensed. Cases of death due to improper care or lack of attendants at these private centers are occasionally reported by the mass media. Yet, as there is usually no other alternative for many women, these facilities are always filled to greater than capacity. The government, primarily for budgetary reasons, has been slow to create more and better public facilities. Under these circumstances, it is not surprising that half of the women teachers polled in a survey in 1973 said it was better for mothers to care for their own children until they are at least three years of age before putting them in nursery schools. Furthermore, nearly a quarter of the respondents replied that it was the responsibility of the mother, or someone who can qualify to take her place, to raise the children. In a 1965 survey taken by the Women's Bureau of the Japan Teacher's Union (Nikkyōso), it was found that 47 percent of all women teachers had family or relatives look after their children; 29 percent asked a neighbor or acquaintance to take care of them; 13 percent hired someone; 4 percent put them in daycare centers; and 7 percent found other means.[45]

Given the results of these surveys, it was surprising to find that the majority of teachers interviewed by this author felt that daycare centers were *ideally* better for children than the home environment. Most were quick to point out, however, that with the poor standards maintained at most nursery schools, they were reluctant at the present to send their own children to them. Nevertheless, it is interesting to note that almost half of the mothers of children in many public daycare centers are teachers, attesting to the growing importance of and demand for childcare facilities among women in teaching.

Regulations on maternity and child-care leave for teachers have been revised considerably over the years, due mainly to the efforts of the Women's Bureau of Nikkyōso. According to a directive issued by the Ministry of Education in 1922, teachers were allowed a maternity leave of two weeks before birth and up to six weeks after birth. In practice, however, the number who took off the full eight weeks was small, as substitute teachers often could not be found and public opinion looked unfavorably upon any type of "vacation" for teachers who already had such long Spring and Summer vacations.

In 1947, a twelve-week maternity leave was provided for all working women in the Labor Standards Law (Art. 34). In addition, women teachers were allowed an hour leave each day (which could be taken in two thirty-minute periods) for one year after childbirth, to be used for child care. As might have been expected, a survey conducted by Nikkyōso in 1955 on maternity and child-care leave revealed that serious problems existed in utilizing these provisions. Although a period of six weeks, both before and after birth, was provided for by law, 22 percent of the women polled took less than five weeks. Most continued to teach up until just before giving birth. Again, the shortage of teachers and unsympathetic public opinion were the main reasons. Working under such conditions, 57 percent of the teachers reported having had miscarriages. Sixty-eight percent had given birth prematurely, and 36 percent had experienced stillbirths.46

By the 1970s most prefectures had increased the maternity leave from the twelve weeks provided by law to fourteen weeks, with some having extended it up to sixteen weeks. In only seven prefectures are husbands entitled to paternity leave. The average allowance is a mere three days. Also the daily child-care leave during the first year after birth has been increased from sixty to ninety minutes or more in many prefectures. A survey taken by Nikkyōso in 1972 revealed, however, that more than 40 percent were unable to take this daily break at all (see Table IX). One might conclude, then, that

Table IX
Utilization of Daily Child-Care Leave (for the First Year after Childbirth)

| | Teaching location | | Teaching level | | | |
Leave	Urban Cities	Rural Towns & Villages	Elementary Schools	Junior High Schools	Senior High Schools	Total
Cannot take off at all	43.6	44.1	44.5	44.6	35.7	43.7
Take morning and afternoon in two parts	6.9	4.3	5.2	5.8	9.3	5.8
Take all at once	17.6	7.1	11.1	14.3	18.2	12.8
Take during the lunch break	1.6	1.8	1.9	1.4	1.5	1.7
Take at other times	11.6	11.5	10.2	13.2	15.2	11.6

Source: Okuyama Emiko, "Ikuji Jikan. Ikuji Kyukeisei e no Torikumi," [Time for Child Care: Toward a Systematic Approach], Kyōiku Hō (No. 9: Autumn, 1973), p. 130.

regulations have been liberalized over the years, while actual conditions have remained more-or-less unchanged from the situation of several decades ago. The reasons are only too obvious: lack of substitute teachers, the career-orientation of teachers who are conscientious about their teaching responsibilities, and, perhaps most importantly, public opinion. In this regard, one national newspaper reported a sharp increase in the vehemency with which the parents of schoolchildren are criticizing teachers who take off "more time than necessary" for childbirth. They complain that the use of substitute teachers is upsetting their children, resulting in their failure to study or otherwise settle down.[47] Less than two years later the paper reported the suicide of an elementary school teacher who could not stand up under the deluge of criticism from parents who denounced her selfishness for having taken the full sixteen weeks of leave as provided by law.[48] Such suicides are rare, but parental criticism remains sharp and frequent.

All in all, the system has not worked well. Nikkyōso had been lobbying for years to amend the law so as to conform with the standards set down by ILO. In July 1975, a new maternity and child-care leave law was passed and will go into effect in April 1976. It covers primary and secondary school teachers, nurses, and daycare center attendents in *public* institutions. It does not cover teachers in private schools who account for more than 20 percent of all women teachers. Nor does it cover teachers in higher education. Nevertheless, the law provides for a one-year leave of absence, without salary, beginning at the time of birth. During that time, for purposes of calculating salary and retirement benefits after she returns to work, the teacher will receive credit for half the time spent on leave. Although she receives no salary during her leave of absence, it is generally seen as the first step not only toward getting maternity leave with salary, but also toward obtaining paternity leave as well. While this law should be seen as a progressive step, not so much because it provides the "right" or the "only" solution, but rather because it provides an additional option, those who would like to stay at work fear that the new law will hinder the further development of public daycare centers. At the present, limited funds from the Ministry of Welfare mean that children under the age of one are not accepted at most daycare centers. Since the new law covers teachers, nurses, and daycare center workers, precisely those who utilize daycare facilities most, there is now concern that the Ministry of Welfare will use the new law as an excuse for not extending the facilities to the care of infants. In other words, there is the possibility that the step forward in providing teachers with new options will in fact be a step backward in that the result will be the channeling of teachers into one fixed pattern. For example, teachers who choose to work will no longer be able to receive a one-year daily leave for child care. This may very well force some to take the year's leave of absence. Finally, until some kind of paternity leave is established, the law may only serve to strengthen traditional mores that (1) women should care for infants and (2) husbands as household heads should continue to enjoy uninterrupted careers. In other words, the desire to imprint distinctively patterned sex roles is still very firmly implanted in the minds of most policy makers at the Ministry of Education.

THREE WOMEN TEACHERS

The three persons introduced in this section were selected from among more than thirty persons with whom I held in-depth interviews during the summer of 1975. All three are very different human beings in philosophical outlook, social awareness, family background, educational training, and present life-styles. It is hoped that the reader will gain some kind of understanding and appreciation for how they live and think. Above all, in this the age of the stereotyped Japanese, it is important that we realize how much values and attitudes vary from one person to another. This diversity is also reflected in the way in which the teachers presented here interpret women's real and ideal roles in society. There are, however, some generalizations which I feel can be made about these women.

First, teaching has always been a rather highly respected occupation in Japan. Those women who become teachers are often born into the homes of middle-class intellectuals, or they are singled out as children for their high ability, disciplined mind, and tenacious spirit, all of which are necessary for a woman to pursue a life-long career. Second, their level of awareness of sex discrimination and prejudice does not necessarily correlate with their age, though there seems to be some correlation with the type of school in which they teach. Teachers in private schools generally tend to be closest to the traditional stereotype of the Japanese woman. Their language is polite and especially respectful of the male sex. They believe that it is woman's natural role to care for the family while her husband earns a living. They somehow see themselves in their career roles as "exceptions" or "different." Teachers in kindergartens and elementary schools, whether they be public or private institutions, are also comparatively traditional in outlook. This is perhaps related to the stereotype which suggests that women are "naturally suited" to working with small children. The very high turnover of kindergarten and elementary school teachers supports the argument that teaching in the lower levels is still thought of as preparation for child care after marriage.

Women teachers, especially in the public high schools and to some extent also in the junior high schools, are more career-oriented and therefore more sensitive to the difficulties and discrimination to which women are subjected in Japanese society. Those whose husbands are also school teachers seem to have comparatively fewer problems with their household arrangement. Their husbands "help" with the housework much more than the average Japanese husband. Accustomed to working with women who are colleagues rather than assistants, tea servers, or errand runners, men teachers view their wives more as equals than do those husbands who work in most other occupations.

Momoyama *Sensei*[49] has been the director of a private daycare center in suburban Tokyo for more than twenty-five years. A slightly built, wisp of a woman with an unusually child-like face, she talked with me while I followed her about the nursery as she fixed a broken doll, mended an inflatable swimming pool, received a telephone call from a leftist newspaper which planned to do a feature on her, consulted with a *hobo san*[50] about an ill child, and served us tea. She apologized for not being able to give me her full attention, and explained that she was looking forward to having a good talk as things had been running rather smoothly that day.

Finally, we were able to sit down and begin talking. I had been gazing around the room while she had been on the phone. A copy of *Akahata* (the official newspaper of the Communist Party which, literally translated, means "The Red Flag") lay open across her desk. Children's books were neatly stacked on a table. There were some old favorites, like *Peach Boy,* but the ones on pollution and the horrors of atomic warfare caught my eye. I paged through them slowly and was moved by their sense of pathos. Momoyama Sensei has always taken an active interest in social problems and sought to make the children at her center, young as they are, socially aware. Before she set up this center, she spent the early postwar years as the director of another daycare center in one of Tokyo's war-torn districts. Parents of the children worked at any job they could get. Many were Koreans. Most lived in makeshift housing—under a train trestle or inside an old bus or chicken coop. She was then in her early twenties, and based upon that experience vowed that she would never marry, but would instead devote her life to daycare center work.

I asked about the *hobo san.* Do they all feel as strongly about their work as Momoyama Sensei does, I wondered.

> In the early postwar years those who became *hobo san* were often anti-war activists and thus attached ideological importance to this kind of work. The wages were low, and the hours were long. Today, however, it's just a job. Yes, they're better educated in child psychology and the like, but they're not as committed. They will probably work about four years, and then quit to marry. Only two out of the fifteen *hobo san* here are married. People just don't feel committed to the social and political significance of this kind of work anymore.

As she talked on, I was impressed by how simply and matter-of-factly she spoke.

After she graduated from junior high school, Momoyama went to work as an "OL"[51] in the late 1930s. In those days, like today, this kind of work was considered appropriate for a young woman. But Momoyama *san*[52] was soon bored with that life and entered a public junior college in order to obtain a license to become a *hobo san*. In the beginning her parents, who were proprietors of a small rice shop, protested; but eventually they reconciled themselves to the fact that she was bent upon such a career. Born the youngest of eight children, she had always been spoiled a bit, she said. She never dreamed she would not marry. Like most little girls, she often talked about becoming an *oyome san* (bride) when she grew up. Her dreams had never extended beyond that. But, with the war, all was changed.

Today, she lives together with her niece, who is a college student. Now fifty-four, she says she likes to sleep a little longer in the mornings, so she doesn't arrive at the center until about 8:30 a.m. By this time the children have already been there an hour, and are busy playing or finishing the packed breakfasts which their parents sent with them. I asked about the children. She said that about half of their mothers are teachers, many are shopkeepers or factory workers, and nearly a fourth are *hobo san*. She quickly added that it is a general policy for *hobo san* to put their children in a center different from the one where they are working. As she spoke, she picked up a little boy who was crying. Looking at him, I realized that I had seen no male *hobo san* at the center. Her smiling face became serious as she explained:

> Yes, there is one here. He's taking a nap with the two-year olds now. That's why you haven't seen him yet. He's very serious about this kind of work. But by law, men cannot obtain a license to work in public day-care centers. They can't even enter the training programs at the colleges. It's too bad, isn't it. The children need father figures here as well as at home.

> A few years ago a young fellow working on his doctoral thesis in psychology stayed with us for several months. He did everything we did, including toilet training. He was so good with the children. But when the mothers would come to pick up their children in the evening, you could always hear them sympathizing with him. "Poor Yamada sensei," they would say, "he even has to change diapers!" Traditional ideas about what is hard work for men and what is hard work for women die pretty slowly. Even among the four- and five-year olds, sex stereotypes are already formed. When asked what kind of a girl he likes, one little boy replied, "someone who's smart and can play baseball and run fast." But when asked what kind of a girl he wanted to marry, he responded, "someone who is cute and sweet."

Momoyama Sensei is a very liberated woman who is trying to give meaning to her ideas. Although she tries to socialize these children in as open and as free an environment as possible, she must in the end compete with traditionally minded parents, comic books and television.

She talked on about the children. There are now eighty children, between one and five years of age, with fifteen *hobo san* looking after them at this center. She explained that most private daycare centers are plagued with endless staff shortages and financial problems, especially in the rural areas. She attributes the relatively good facilities at both public and private centers in Tokyo to the present political leadership under Communist and Socialist-backed Independent Governor Minobe Ryōkichi.

I asked her what her plans were for the future. She replied quite simply, "As long as my legs will carry me the ten minutes walk from my apartment to this nursery, I'll come. This is my life; it gives me meaning and hopefully adds to the lives of others."

We met in an empty classroom at the public high school in Tokyo where Tomita Sensei has been teaching English for sixteen years. Like most public school buildings in Japan, it was a concrete structure that had been hastily built after the war. There was nothing pretty about it at all. I commented upon the somewhat grungy, stark atmosphere to her as we climbed the four flights of stairs. She shrugged. This is what students are used to. An old Japanese proverb relates that the mind functions best when physical comforts are few. I agreed that they were few indeed.

Over a cup of tea we began to talk. Born fifty years ago in the very wealthy Semba district of Osaka, Tomita Sensei was the daughter of a prosperous trading merchant. She explained that in the prewar days Semba was a stronghold of all the upper-class traditional values exemplified in *Onna Daigaku,* a book written about 1715 which exerted a great influence in teaching women in Japan that their role was subordinate to men. In Semba, women were pampered as children, groomed in the traditional arts of dance, flower arranging, tea ceremony, calligraphy, and sewing as teenagers. They were married off at an early age to another influential family in the same district, where as wives and mothers they would command a household of servants from morning until night. Amidst this atmosphere the head of the household would often have concubines living in the same house with his wife and children. Tomita Sensei quickly added with a laugh that no concubine ever lived in her home, however.

Families were large then. Out of ten children in her family, the first eight were girls, prompting her parents to keep making children until the *chōnan* (eldest son) and *jinan* (second son) were born. As such the boys were treated quite differently from their sisters.

The boys and my father always had the very best quality of food, and were always the first to get in the bath. This was etiquette that no one was supposed to question. I remember once when I asked why, and was told not' to be so impertinent. It seems I was always being told how difficult or argumentative I was.

In school I showed an interest in academic things and was allowed to study as I pleased. My other seven sisters were rather typical "proper ladies" of Semba, and were sent off to "proper" high schools (*jogakkō*) in preparation for marriage.

With the war came the bankruptcy of her father's trading firm. Still, she managed to get permission from her father to attend Tsuda College, then a leading women's college in Japan. With her parent's blessings she came up to Tokyo and stayed in a school dormitory until she graduated. By then her family's financial circumstances had worsened considerably. The war had ended and she wanted to go to work. "Perhaps teaching," she thought. At this point her father put his foot down. Proper young ladies do not go out to work. It would be indecent.

Discouraged but nonetheless obedient, she gave up career plans and entered a sewing school only to soon be bored with it. "I've never been interested in fashion anyway. It all seemed so silly to waste my time and my father's money," she went on. By that time most of her sisters had already married, but she was still at home dreaming that someday she would like to enter Tokyo University to study sociology. Until after the war, the imperial universities had been reserved exclusively for men. Also, they were extremely competitive. But Tomita san resolved to pass the entrance examination for Tokyo University, the most prestigious university in Japan. Without telling her father, she won her mother's approval, and went up to Tokyo. She successfully passed the exam, and even won a scholarship. Entering the prestigious university in sociology, she found a part-time job to cover lodging and other expenses. Her father was, of course, quite shaken when he learned of the fact. But he apparently was able to maintain his composure. "After all," Tomita Sensei laughed, "he had seven other daughters, each a model of feminine propriety and behavior!"

Tomita Sensei reminisced about her days at Tokyo University. "In the beginning there weren't any bathrooms for women in the class buildings. There was only a handful of us. I imagine we were regarded as curiosities." I asked about the attitudes of her professors. "Yes, some of them told us we were wasting the taxpayers' money. 'Women will only get married anyway,' they would say. At first the other students chose to ignore us, though some made fun of us. But it wasn't long before we had gained their respect as competent fellow students." Tomita Sensei was married while still a student at

Tokyo University, a very unusual thing for that time. It didn't work out, and after five years she filed for divorce. "I was too young, but you know the old saying: two can live more cheaply than one. It didn't last. He wanted someone to pick up his socks, make his meals, and give him children."

She did have a child by him. After separating from her husband, she worked for a while in the local community to set up both a daycare center and an after-school center for young children of working mothers. She, herself, had been working for a publishing firm which she quit after two years:

> I knew I would always be some man's assistant, and so decided I'd had enough. Next I took the civil service exam and worked at the Tokyo City Office. Within a year I realized that there, too, women would rarely pass beyond the lower ranks. Next I decided to teach. Here, I thought, one wouldn't have to put up with job discrimination. And, in addition, I would to some extent be my own boss.

I asked whether teaching has lived up to her expectations.

> For the most part, yes. Yet there is definitely a tendency for male principals to promote men to head teacherships. We need more women principals, but most women aren't interested. Most have family responsibilities. Others back off from leadership roles. I suppose there's a little of that in me too. But, to tell the truth, I truly enjoy teaching. I'm not interested in administrative work. Then there are the parents. Especially the mothers. They're absolutely disappointed when they find out that their son's English teacher or whatever is a woman. How can their son possibly pass the college entrance exams if a woman teaches? It's one of the most frustrating aspects of this work!

Tomita Sensei has remarried and now has two teenage children. Her husband teaches science in a public junior high school. I asked about housework, though I had already guessed her answer. "We pretty much divide everything, though he sometimes complains that he is doing more than I."

We talked on, this time about Japanese women teachers in general. She said she is generally optimistic that Japan is getting to be an easier society for women to live in, though she sometimes wonders about the attitudes of young women.

> Just after the war, teachers took great pains to teach democratic principles, particularly with regard to the equality of the sexes. But today the new teachers often seem only interested in flaunting their femininity. They wear heavy make-up, frilly clothes, and encourage suggestive remarks from the male students. I'm sure that not all young teachers are this way. But it is something that has concerned me in recent years.

Tomita Sensei herself is a very attractive woman, and she takes her work seriously. Japan could use many more women like her.

Suda Sensei was born into a family of teachers twenty-five years ago. She teaches third-graders at a public elementary school in Tokyo. Her mother graduated from a normal school and taught elementary school until a couple of years ago. Her father is a retired junior high school principal. Her older sister taught elementary school for seven years and then "retired" to marry a man whose three sisters also left teaching for marriage.

We were meeting in a coffee shop in the Ginza known for its classical record collection and superb pastries. Although it was humid, we were drinking hot tea. The air-conditioning system was working all too well.

"I've never wanted to become anything but a teacher. I'm sure you can understand why." Yes, I thought I could. "With the exception of your mother, all of them have quit teaching. Why is that?" I ventured. She explained, "They all wanted to have children soon after marrying."

"Do they plan to go back?"

"Yes, probably, but not until their children are older."

"About how much older?" I continued.

"Well, perhaps at least until they're in junior high school or older."

"Suda Sensei, what are your own plans?" I was almost afraid to ask.

"I'd like to work until marriage or maybe even until we have children. But then I think it's better for the children that the mother stay home until they've grown up."

As for daycare centers, she thought that they were a necessary evil, because some mothers, for financial reasons, are not in a position to be able to stay home with their children. Her main criticism was simple: daycare centers cannot provide the warmth and security which mothers can give their children.

Her own mother had taught continuously for nearly thirty-five years, taking time off only to give birth to four children. Often she had come home as late as nine or ten in the evening. "Teachers in those days had so much more work to do. Mother could spend very little time with us. She never had time for flower arranging or sewing, or other pleasant pastimes like many mothers." Grandmother had taken care of the children. "Grandma was really good to us. But as I look back on it now, I think it was too much for her physically to handle four kids. I wouldn't want to make my mother care for my children. It's not good for the children either."

I recalled another interview I had had a few days earlier. The grandparents had been taking care of their daughter-in-law's first child so that she could go back to teach. But within a year or so she began to worry that the grandparents were doting too much over their cute little grandson, Mako. Mako was never left alone even for fifteen minutes. His mother was certain that if this kept up the child would have serious problems later on. She decided that Mako should be put in a daycare center and discussed it with her husband several times, but each time he shrugged it off. When she brought it up to the grandparents, they were crestfallen and hurt. Not only that, they worried what the neighbors might think. The mother was persistent and before Mako was three he found himself enrolled in a daycare center. It took him an entire month to adjust. Every day he cried when taken away from home, and spent most of the day sulking alone by himself. He had never played with other children, and didn't know how. But with time and the patience of the *hobo san,* he learned to play with the other children and fully adjusted. Several years later the grandparents would occasionally look back on it and say, "You know, putting Mako in the daycare center was one of the best decisions *we* ever made."

I ordered another cup of hot tea as Suda Sensei told me about her childhood. "I had three older brothers and an older sister. As the youngest child I was allowed to do pretty much as I pleased. I climbed trees with my brothers and almost never wore skirts, except for school. My father didn't mind at all. He thought it was good for my sister and I to play hard—that it would make us strong." We both laughed, for Suda Sensei is barely five feet tall, and although she looks healthy enough, she is by no means the "tomboy" she professed once to be. Wearing a rather delicate, fine cotton dress, she looked more like a child dressed up for Sunday school.

"Everyone says I look young, but I'm really rather old, you know. Many of my friends are already married."

Right now she says that she is content to teach school for another couple of years. "I don't think my father wants to even think about it. My brothers and sisters all have married, leaving just the three of us in what was once a very lively house."

Suda Sensei spends most of her evenings at home, usually reading or talking with her parents. She is critical of television for its bad influence on children. "Some of the programs are quite good, to be sure. Right now they're showing 'Dog of Flanders' in a cartoon series. Last winter they ran one on 'Heidi.' But by far the majority of children's programs are violent and crude."

Sometimes her father discusses politics with her. They subscribe to three major national dailies, which he usually reads from cover to cover now that he is retired. Suda Sensei usually reads only the columns on education and household matters. She depends on her father to keep her informed about the front page and the editorials.

Generally speaking, she is little concerned with social problems and events which are not directly related to her role as an elementary school teacher, a role which she seems to define rather narrowly in comparison with Momoyama Sensei. For the past couple of years there have been heated debates in the Diet on the possible revision of the current liberal abortion law which Japan has had throughout the postwar period. Suda Sensei was almost totally unaware of this discussion. She admitted that she had never even thought about it. She imagines that someday she will marry, most likely through *omiai* (by which she enjoys a formal introduction to a prospective husband). She has never dated, even though she attended a four-year coeducational teachers' college.

"I knew many guys through the tennis club I belonged to, but was never close to any of them." Suda Sensei is not unusual in this respect by any means. Although dating has increased remarkably in the last several years, many women of her age still do not date until it is time to choose a husband. In the meantime she is putting all of her energy and enthusiasm into her work. She loves children. "They're so creative; their minds are so free from stereotypes and patterns, and their ideas are so fresh and alive." Her eyes were so bright and alive as she spoke. I wondered whether she would be able to keep her naive optimism after she married. Maybe she would. If she were lucky. Japan is changing rapidly and so too are the values of society.

NOTES

[1]Mombu Shō Daijin Kanbō Chōsa Tokei Ka [The Department of Statistical Research, Office of the Minister of Education], *Gakkō Kihon Chōsa Sokuhō: Shōwa 49 Nendo* [The Early Results of the Basic Survey on Education: 1974], pp. 4-5.

[2]For example, the labor force participation rate for women over age fifteen has fallen steadily from a high of 56.7 percent in 1955 to 46.6 percent in 1974. Sōrifu Tōkei Kyoku [Bureau of Statistics, Office of the Prime Minister], *Rōdōryoku Chōsa* [Labor Force Survey], monthly reports. These figures are given in Rōdō Shō, ed., *Rōdō Hakusho: Shōwa 50 Nenpan* [Labor White Paper: 1975], p. 232.

[3]On this point, see Fujii Harue, "Sengo Joshi Kyoiku Ron" [Arguments on Education for Women in Postwar Japan], in *Fujin Gakushū Kyōiku* [Education and Learning for Women], ed. by Hane Setsuko and Ogawa Toshio, *Gendai Fujin Mondai Kōza* [Reading on Modern Women], vol. V, pp. 332-333.

[4]NAFE 21 Seiki Kyōiku no Kai [The Japan Association for Education 2001 "NAFE"], *Sekai no Kyōiku no Genjō to Wagakuni Kyōiku no Shōrai* [Education in the World and the Future of Education in Japan], pamphlet prepared for Kokusai Kyōiku Ten [The International Educational Exhibition], August, 1973 p. 13.

[5]Hashiguchi Kazuko, "Jokyōshi e no Sabetsu no Genjō" [The Realities of Discriminatory Treatment Against Women Teachers], in *Jokyōshi no Fujin Mondai* [Issues Concerning Women as Teachers], ed. by Ichibangase Yasuko, Kigawa Tatsuji and Miyata Takeo, p. 63.

[6]Benjamin Rush, *Thoughts Upon Female Education* (1798), p. 76.

[7]Takamure Itsue, *Takamure Itsue Zenshū—Josei no Rekishi* [The Collected Works of Takamure Itsue: The History of Women], vol. 11, p. 553.

[8]Murakami Nobuhiko, *Meiji Josei Shi* [History of Women in the Meiji Period], vol. III, p. 199.

[9]Karasawa Tomitarō, "Kyōshi no Rekishi" [The History of Teachers], in *Chiba Ken Joshi Shihan Gakkō Matsu no Kasa* [The Pinetree Umbrella: Magazine of the Chiba Prefectural Women's Normal School]. Quoted from Ichibangase Yasuko, "Jokyōshi no Rekishi" [The History of Women Teachers], in *Jokyōshi no Fujin Mondai*, ed. by Ichibangase, *et al.*, p. 3. This same story is related by Murakami Mobuhiko, who goes on to add that the father had been indebted to the prefectural governor for other reasons, and had thus found it difficult to turn down the governor's request that his daughter enter the school. See his *Meiji Josei Shi* [History of Women in Meiji], vol. III, pp. 300-301.

[10]Ichibangase, "Jokyōshi no Rekishi," p. 3.

[11]Kido Wakao, *Fujin Kyōshi no Hyakunen* [One Hundred Years of Women in Teaching].

[12]Ishidoya Tetsuo, *Nihon Kyōin Shi Kenkyū* [Research on the History of Teachers in Japan], p. 255.

[13]Ichibangase, "Jokyōshi no Rekishi," p. 9.

[14]Fukaya Masashi and Fukaya Kazuko, *Jokyōshi no Mondai no Kenkyū* [Research on Women Teachers' Problems], p. 264.

[15]For further information, consult Imanaka Yasuko, "Taishōki Burujoa Fujin Undō to Fujin Kyoshi—S hin Fujin Kyōkai Hiroshima Shibu no Setchi o Megutte" [Bourgeois Women's Movements and Women Teachers During the Taishō Period: Regarding the Establishment of the Hiroshima Branch of the New Women's Association], *Rekishi Hyōron* (No. 217: September 1968).

[16]Takamure Itsue, *Jokyōin Kaihō Ron*, pp. 3-35.

[17]This problem is also taken up by Takamure. *Ibid.*, p. 5.

[18]Quoted from Ichibangase, "Jokyōshi no Rekishi," p. 8.

[19]Unfortunately, there are no statistics on the prevalence of maids. However, in my interviews with teachers in 1975, many cited as one important difference from the past the fact that teachers in the prewar period were able to afford maids whereas they cannot do so today.

[20]To Kyōso Fujin Bu 25 Nen Shi Henshū Iin Kai [The 25 Year History Committee of the Women's Bureau in the Metropolitan Teachers' Union], ed., *Hi no Yō ni* [Like fire], p. 12. Quoted in Ichibangase, "Jokyōshi no Rekishi," p. 8.

[21]Teikoku Kyōiku (August 1916), pp. 9-10. Quoted in Ichibangase, "Jokyōshi no Rekishi," p. 10.

[22]Quoted from Shibusawa Hisako, "An Education for Making Good Wives and Wise Mothers," *Education in Japan: A Journal for Overseas* (vol. VI: 1971), p. 53. Only the English translation of the title of Shimoda's book (*Japanese Women*) is given.

[23]Shoji Masako, "Women Educators Who Contributed to the Education of Women (I)," *Education in Japan: A Journal for Overseas* (vol. VI: 1971), pp. 70-71.

[24]Ichibangase, "Jokyōin no Rekishi," p. 14.

[25]Hashiguchi, "Jokyōshi e no Sabetsu no Genjō," p. 66.

[26]Juji Tsūshin Sha [Current Affairs Institute], "Jokyōshi Jidai o Irokoku Han'ei" [Clear Trend Shown Toward the Age of the Woman Teacher], *Naigai Kyōiku* (No. 2467: September 19, 1973), p. 5.

[27]Shinoda Tomie, "Jokyōshi no Nayami to Jokyōshi o Torimaku Henken" [Women Teachers: Anguish and Prejudice], in *Jokyōshi no Fujin Mondai*, ed. by Ichibangase, *et al.*, p. 46.

190

28In Japan joint filing is not recognized. Each earner must file his own tax return.

29On this point, see Hashiguchi, "Jokyōshi e no Sabetsu Genjō," p. 74.

30*Ibid.*

31This point came out very clearly in my interviews.

32Mochizuki Muneaki, *Nihon no Fujin Kyōshi* [Women Teachers in Japan], pp. 228-233.

33Such a system would tend to work to the disadvantage of (1) those ideologically pre-disposed to Nikkyōso and (2) women. When Nagai Michio became the new Minister of Education under the newly formed Miki Cabinet last December, a number of top-level meetings were held with Makieda Motofuni, the head of Nikkyōso. In an effort to normalize relations with the union, Nagai agreed that no such system would be introduced in the near future.

34Tsukamoto Shiuko, "Jokyōshi no Genjō," in *Jokyōshi no Fujin Mondai,* ed. by Ichibangase, *et al.,* p. 38.

35Yasue Tomoko, "Kōkō Kyōiku to Onna" [High School Education and Women], *AGORA* (No. 11: 1975), pp. 87-98.

36The case involved an employee of the Izu Cactus Park who was forced to retire at the age of forty-seven, ten years earlier than male employees. With the number of favorable rulings increasing, many companies are reconsidering their retirement policy.

37Nikkyōso Teikyō [An Introduction to the Japan Teachers' Union] (Tokyo: 1973). Quoted from Ichibangase Yasujo and Tsukamoto Shiuko, "Sankō Shiryō" (Reference Materials), in *Jokyōshi no Fujin Mondai* [Issues Concerning Women as Teachers], ed. by Ichibangase, *et al.,* pp. 200-203.

38*Asahi Shimbun,* March 25, 1975.

39While this is not the only source of the problem, it should be reiterated that this is a point which comes out time and again in all kinds of discussions on discrimination.

40Shimada Tomiko, "Jokyōshi no Enshoku to Rōgo no Mondai" [Problems of Women Teachers Related to Retirement and Old Age], in *Jokyōshi no Fujin Mondai,* ed. by Ichibangase, *et al.,* p. 150.

41Shimada, "Jokyōshi no Enshoku to Rōgo no Mondai," pp. 151-152.

42*Ibid.,* p. 153.

43Mombushō, *Gakkō Kihon Chōsa.*

44Tsukamoto, "Jokyōshi no Genjō," p. 41.

45Mochizuki, *Nihon no Fujin Kyōshi,* pp. 282-283.

46*Ibid.,* pp. 277-278.

47*Mainichi Shimbun,* October 19, 1973.

48*Ibid.,* April 3, 1975.

49*"Sensei"* literally means "teacher" and is used as a form of address for all educators including college professors and outside lecturers regardless of academic background.

50*"Hobo"* literally means "protective mother," but has also come to mean "nurse." Here it refers to an assistant at a daycare center.

51"OL" stands for "office lady." Their work includes simple routine desk work, serving tea, and so on, in Japan's business firms.

52*"San"* is the most commonly used title in Japan. It is used irrespective of sex, and may mean "Mr." or "Mrs." It represents the absence of one kind of rather subtle but nonetheless vexatious discrimination in the United States and many of the countries of Europe.

CHAPTER 9
WOMEN IN THE PROFESSIONS

In a country where the traditional image of the ideal woman is still strongly adhered to, it is perhaps surprising to find that a relatively large number of women are professionals. Yet this is the case. Approximately 10 percent of Japan's doctors are women; about 10 percent of the dentists are women; and about 13 percent of the teachers in junior colleges, colleges, and universities are women. Of 140,000 qualified lawyers in Japan, 299 are women; an additional 50 women are judges and 21 are public prosecutors.[1] Many of these women are married and raising families, thus being faced with the sometimes conflicting demands of multiple roles. And all of them are professional women in a society that still emphasizes and respects the marriage/mother role for its women and raises real questions about the desire of a woman to pursue her own career.

The fact that a professional career carries with it higher status than do most other types of employment perhaps eases the situation a little. One of my Japanese friends commented, while arrangements were being made for interviews: "Being a doctor or a college professor is a safer career choice for a woman than going into one of the newly opened fields [e.g., journalism] because these professions are high status and are already seen as all right for a woman." However, the fact remains that even this "safer" career choice involves a life style that is in many ways unlike the ideal image for the Japanese woman. And although today almost one out of every two adult women in Japan is engaged in some kind of work for pay,[2] the large majority of these women are working until marriage or to supplement family income; they are not involved in careers. Professional women, then, are a special category in modern Japan. They are women whose situation is, in many cases, equal to that of

191

men; whose employment, by the very definition of profession, demands independence of judgement and personal commitment to work; and whose career choices may put them into direct competition with men in a "man's world."

Japanese women began entering the professions in small numbers during the Meiji Period. It is interesting that the first field open to women was medicine, an arena that perhaps seemed then, as it does now to many Japanese, to be appropriate to the basically "nurturant" character of women. In 1884, women were allowed to take the national licensing examination in Medical Arts.[3] That year, one woman did take the examination and passed it; the next year she opened her office. In 1900, the first school for training doctors, now Tokyo Women's Medical College, was opened. Because at that time women were not admitted to the imperial universities or to other colleges and universities for men, the opening of special colleges for women was a necessary step toward their entering the professions. In that same year, two other "colleges" for women were opened.[4] One of them, now Tsuda College, had as a main purpose the training of women to be teachers of English. Tsuda College was finally recognized in 1948 as an institution of university status.

In the years following 1900, numerous colleges for women were opened in Japan, including several other medical colleges. Women doctors and women college teachers (in colleges specifically for women) were the first of Japan's professional women. In those early years, as is pretty much still the case, women doctors were trained as pediatricians and obstetricians, and women professors taught in colleges where young women were given the literature, language, humanities, and home economics courses considered appropriate for women.

In 1929 two universities (one in Tokyo, one in Hiroshima) allowed men and women to enter as equals. In 1927, the 1893 legislation that had specifically excluded women from the law profession was amended to allow women to enter, but only with their husbands' permission. Finally, in 1933, the law was revised to allow women to take the law examination; three women passed the examination in 1938. With the end of World War II, the new Japanese Constitution solidified the beginnings that had been made in the 1930s to assure women equal access with men to all public colleges and universities. Thus the permission for women to enter a variety of professions in the postwar years had become law. Women were no longer limited by separate and unequal educational systems. Their access is now based on performance on competitive examinations. Perhaps at least two barriers still exist, however, to women entering fully into the professions: (1) the remaining informal systems of patronage and discipleship in coeducational institutions that favor men and effectively exclude women; and (2) the strong cultural admonition to women, even if educated enough to attract an even more highly educated husband, to marry, stay home, and raise a family. Both of these we will explore as we consider the information gained through interviews with Japanese professional women.

The interviews which I conducted with eleven professional women (three doctors, two lawyers, one dentist, three university professors, and two junior college professors) focused on three major areas: (1) What were the reasons for the woman's choice of a professional career? (2) What problems, obstacles, or special treatment did she encounter in achieving her education, getting employment, and pursuing her professional career? (3) What are her attitudes and opinions regarding a variety of questions having to do with women's role in modern Japan? I also asked each respondent a number of questions about her family background, childhood, and present life style.

All but one of the respondents live and work in Tokyo; one practices in Nagoya. Three of them completed their education prior to World War II (two doctors, one college professor); four completed their education between 1945 and 1960 (two lawyers, one junior college professor, one university professor); and four completed their education after 1960 (one dentist, one doctor, one junior college professor, one college professor). Six of them are married, one separated, three single, one single and engaged. Five have children.

The backgrounds, experiences, and attitudes of these women were varied, and there seemed to be no correlation among age group, marital status, professional category, or presence or absence of children with attitudes. There did seem to be, however, two major patterns that emerged from all of the stories seen together (and from information gained from other conversations and resources in Japan). These I will call the "woman's track" and the "equal opportunity track." The woman's track represents ways of pursuing a professional career that use women's educational systems and/or involve working with women or in areas deemed appropriate for women. The equal opportunity track represents attempts by women to pursue professional careers through the normal paths taken by men, in areas heavily dominated by men, and to work in competition with men.

The following biographies are presented as typical stories of women following these two patterns.5

EQUAL OPPORTUNITY TRACK

Kumiko Yoshioka is attractive, soft-spoken, somewhat reserved and serious in demeanor. She is forty-seven years old, married, with two children. When we met in the small faculty lounge of the women's junior college where she teaches science as a full-time faculty member, she greeted me and my interpreter warmly and served us tea. She assured us that though she had limited time (she teaches a very full schedule of introductory courses), she would be happy to tell me whatever I wanted to know.

Kumiko was born in Tokyo, where her father, graduate of a normal school, was principal of a primary school. Her mother, also a normal school graduate, was a primary school teacher. Kumiko's father died shortly after she was born. Before that, her father's mother had taken care of Kumiko's four older sisters, while Kumiko's mother worked; they also had a maid. After her father's death, her mother stopped working and lived alone with the five children, raising them on a government pension.[6]

Kumiko said that she had decided very early that she wanted to be a scientist, that she feels her mother supported her in her plans.[7] She felt that perhaps her mother was willing to accept her decision because she had worked herself and had been widowed fairly young. At any rate, Kumiko did take the necessary competitive examinations and was admitted to undergraduate study in science at a prestigious national university. She did not know why she had not chosen to go to a women's college, except that she said she had felt it was quite an honor to have done so well on the competitive examinations. After completing her undergraduate work, Kumiko was admitted into the masters program at the same university, also on a competitive basis. She completed her masters degree in 1955 and immediately continued on into the Ph.D. program. At that same time, she was married, to a fellow graduate student.

Kumiko completed all the course work for her Ph.D. but she had to stop before completing the research for her dissertation because of the birth of her first son.[8] Kumiko said, somewhat wistfully: "I had always wanted to be a research scientist, and I enjoyed especially the part of my education that involved research—but, when the children began arriving, I had to stop that phase. My husband did complete his dissertation research, and he is now a researcher in a large company." She went on to tell me that when she was in the science department of the graduate school, there were only three other women out of 160 students.[9] Today only about 5 percent of the science students are women.

When I asked Kumiko what problems, if any, she saw with her education and career, she answered, quite calmly: "Even if boys and girls get the same education and the same degree, boys can stay at their college as faculty members or researchers; girls can't." She explained that in Japan, most colleges (including the women's colleges) hire their own graduates as faculty members. There is also a rigidly defined system of discipleship-patronage between students and professors. A male student at a top university like the one Kumiko attended has a brilliant career pretty well guaranteed if he is able to become one of the disciples to an important professor. Even if he is not quite so fortunate, a fine career is assured him. But this system applies only to men. As Kumiko explained it, favoring the men comes from the recognition that men have financial responsibilities for families. Since in Japan pay is not very high for university teaching and there are not abundant jobs, the feeling is that what jobs there are should go to men. She said she had been lucky to find her present position, which allows for no research and involves a heavy teaching schedule. She found it not through academic contacts, since those are reserved for men students, but through personal friends of her husband's family. When I asked Kumiko if she felt all this was unfair, she said: "If I can be happy where I am, it's not important that I do research. You have to make the best of what you have. And I think it is really necessary to improve education for the ordinary woman in Japan—so I am happy to be in a junior college." After a pause, she continued: "Had I been able to go on the faculty at my university, I could have improved my career, been in contact with researchers in foreign countries. . . but, maybe men can improve the top of higher education, and women can improve education for the ordinary woman in society."

Kumiko then talked more about her career and how she has been able to manage family responsibilities over the years. She began by saying: "The situation for women is difficult, especially if they marry. A woman's ability to continue working depends on her family situation. If there is a grandmother or a good nursery school available—fine. It is very difficult now to get servants, and there are not nearly enough good nursery schools to meet the needs of working mothers."[10] In Kumiko's case, she did have a servant for the first five years after her first child was born. Then she worked part-time for a while until both her children were in school. She is now working full-time, does all the housework at home, and has taken major care of her sons. Her husband does very little. She entertains their friends and colleagues at home, or both she and her husband go out together with old school friends. In general, she leads an extremely busy life and feels fortunate that somehow she has been able to continue working, even though it is not the career she dreamed of having. She is not openly bitter nor angry. And, at the end of our conversation, she laughed and told me: "My sons do their own laundry at my house. That is unusual for Japan!"

Kumiko's story is not atypical, although her career decisions, choosing to go to a national university and to take science as a major, are still not nearly as common for women as are the women's college, "women's field" choices. It is important to note that Kumiko took one track now legally open to women, the equal opportunity track, while the large majority of women still attend women's junior colleges, colleges, or universities, and most of those who attend coeducational colleges and universities major in "women's fields" like literature, humanities, teaching, or home economics.[11] For Kumiko and others like her, the fact that the law now requires that men and women in Japan have equal access to educational opportunities does not guarantee equal access to career possibilities through the academic patronage system.

I talked at length with a young woman in Tokyo who had chosen, as did Kumiko, a men's area of study and had achieved her masters degree at the elite national university of Japan. She told me that what she termed the "boss" system was all-important there, and not open to women. "The Japanese academic world is a male chauvinist world. If you have a boss and he says you are good, then that is more important to your career than whether or not you are competent. Occasionally a woman may become a disciple to a boss, but she is never number one." This woman, like Kumiko, received no help from her academic mentors when she looked for work. She did comment, however, that more and more women are entering graduate departments in men's fields, in coeducational colleges, and she hopes the system will be forced to change.

Another woman whom I interviewed had wanted to be a research physicist but had gone to a women's college where the science department was not strong enough to qualify her for the entrance examination into a masters program in physics.[12] She therefore took her masters in mathematics at a coeducational college, then returned to teach math at the women's college from which she graduated. (There are not very many women mathematics professors, even at women's schools.) She would still like to go on in theoretical physics, but she doubts that she will ever be able to do it. She will undoubtedly stay in the woman's track.

There are many other similar cases of women in Japan who seem clearly capable of entering "men's fields," but whose careers are stymied by separate men's and women's systems or by the patronage system. This system seems to have acted as a very real barrier to Kumiko in her desire to enter fully into the professional field of her choice. As a man I talked with said, when I asked him what was the elite course for a woman in Japan (paralleling the elite course for men wanting to enter the professions or government service): "There is no elite course for women. They marry."

Perhaps a few of Japan's new professional women have found a way into full participation in a man's world. There is now (since 1970) one woman faculty member at Japan's most elite national university, and there are a few at other coeducational universities. But even for them, the way is not easy and the competition is not balanced, it seems.

Kumiko's story illustrates a second barrier to professional women, one that is no more serious for those like her who have chosen the equal opportunity track than it is for those who choose the woman's track to professional participation. If a professional woman wishes to combine a career with having a family, rather than to make the choice which for centuries has been open to a few Japanese women who decided to enter the *mizu shōbai* or the solitary life of nun or scholar, she faces the strong cultural tradition that for a woman her home and family must come first and are *her* responsibility. In Kumiko's case, her education was ended with the birth of her first child, and her working life had to be tailored to the needs of two small children. In her case, and in the case of all the other married women I interviewed, the responsibilities of home and child care are hers and hers alone. Several of my respondents reported great conflict with parents and in-laws at the time they decided to continue working after children were born, although all but one reported support from their parents in their decision to seek professional training.13 All also said that the problems of finding a good nursery school, or household help, were great. All but one of my married respondents (whose mother-in-law had lived with her and done all the housework and child care since the birth of the first child) combined their career responsibilities with full home responsibilities, always with no help from husbands. And all expressed the strong opinion that this was as it should be, that women should be responsible for the home. As Kumiko said: "I think a woman should work after she is married. But it would be good for her to plan ahead twenty or thirty years so that she can do it." She also told me, as did other college faculty I interviewed, that most of the graduates of her junior college worked for a year or two, then married and stayed home.

In general, I found that all of my respondents, with the exception of one who was separated from her husband and had no children, echoed in their attitudes the cultural admonition that woman's first duty is to her family. Their way of reconciling this view with their desire to continue professional careers was to demand of themselves, and of other women who might want to pursue careers, almost superhuman strength, stamina, and dedication. One of the women, working full-time, mother of a four-year-old, said, almost proudly: "I never have a moment to myself. I get up at 6 a.m., get my daughter ready for the day, cook breakfast, work from 9 until 6, prepare supper, prepare my husband's bath, and stay home working while he goes out most evenings with his friends." (She and her husband have a dental practice together; they work the same hours.) When asked whether husbands should help working wives, this woman conceded that perhaps a husband might plug in the electric rice cooker or turn on the heater for the bath if he arrived home before his working wife. Otherwise, the home duties should be the woman's.

198

For women who enter the professions through the woman's track, this second barrier is fully as formidable as it is for Kumiko and her kind. Other things, however, are different, as the following biography will illustrate.

WOMAN'S TRACK

Akiko Matsui is a sixty-year-old physician, an ear, nose, and throat specialist. She is a beautiful and charming woman, very feminine in her mannerisms, yet outspoken and forthright, exhibiting a robust sense of humor. She is married to a doctor, with whom she shares a practice; they have two grown children.

Akiko was born in a city in southeastern Japan, the oldest of four girls. Her father and mother were both high school graduates. Her mother never worked; her father was the owner of a clothing store. Akiko said that as a child she had read and heard about women who had been nurses during the Russo-Japanese War of 1904-05 and was impressed by how much they had been able to help people. She did not realize there was a difference between nurses and doctors, and decided she wanted to be a doctor. A male family friend, who was a doctor, and her father encouraged her in this ambition, as did her mother, who had always wanted to be a midwife. Her father suggested that being a doctor would be better than being a nurse, because it would be a higher status occupation and would allow her to help people more. Akiko laughed and said: "When I graduated from medical school, the same family friend who had encouraged me to become a doctor congratulated me and then said, 'Now go home and get the milk started,' "—which she explained meant he thought it was time she stopped all this nonsense and had babies.

Akiko went to Tokyo in 1934 and entered a women's medical college there. She graduated in 1939. Since there were no internships as such at that time, she and her classmates used summer vacations to "visit hospitals and learn the real world." When I asked her if she had encountered any special problems as a woman in her education, she answered: "No. It was a women's college. Some of my parents' friends talked about my doing something a woman shouldn't. If you ignore that, there's no problem."

Following her graduation Akiko returned to her home city and worked in a medical center there as "a kind of intern." There she met her husband, through an *omiai,* had a few dates with him, and was married in 1941. She laughed a little about her arranged marriage, actually done through a professor who had taught both of them, but she said that in those days there were not many chances for men and women to meet.

Immediately after their marriage, Akiko's husband went off to war, and she went to a private ear, nose, and throat hospital near Tokyo. She was the only doctor there and was in charge of the hospital all during the war. She said: "As all women did in those days, I took over men's work. There were many diphtheria epidemics in those days, and many people died because of a shortage of vaccine. It was a bad time." Akiko and others I interviewed had many memories of the war years, when women were forced to take over "men's work" and handle it capably. One of the university professors remembered interrupting her Ph.D. studies to work in a barrage balloon factory in 1945. And all of them said that women who were trained were needed and had to work. Akiko said that all of the 100 Japanese members of her graduating class worked then and are still working.

When the war ended, Akiko's husband came home, they started a family, and she stopped working for ten years, except to occasionally assist her husband in surgery, his specialty. They had two children, a daughter and a son. Akiko said that she did not mind staying home during those years to care for the household and the children. She laughed and said that she really was "not efficient enough" to work and keep up with home responsibilities.

After Akiko returned to work eighteen years ago, sharing an office and practice with her husband, she continued to do all her own housework; her husband helped "a little." She is an ear, nose, and throat specialist (a fairly common specialty for women doctors in Japan). She does not feel that patients discriminate against her as a woman. She said that patients come to her when they need her services, and they judge her on the basis of her competence. When I asked her why she had chosen this specialty, she said that she had done so because she had experienced many ear and throat problems as a child. She did not feel that she had been routed into this specialty because of being a woman, although she did agree with the comments made by other women doctors I interviewed, that her specialty, along with obstetrics and pediatrics, were the most common and acceptable areas for women.

Akiko and her husband now live alone; both work very hard in their practice and as a result seldom entertain at home or go out. She said that she sees 100 patients a day and has very little time or energy for outside activities. She does stay in touch with other members of her medical college class, working with them on a variety of projects, and she keeps in contact by phone with high school friends in her home city.

The latest projects she and her classmates have done have been studies of the graduates of her medical college since 1940, and a recent study of women who are primary school teachers. She and a classmate of hers whom I also interviewed told me that their interest in doing these studies is primarily to find out how married women are managing to combine careers with children and home responsibilities. As Akiko's classmate explained it to me, they are increasingly concerned about the problems facing young professional women and anxious to find ways of encouraging them to continue their professional work along with marriage and childraising. She feels that one reason all of their classmates continued with their careers was that their work was desperately needed during the war years. Now, however, they feel that many young women may graduate from medical school, marry, have children fairly soon, and then stop working because of the demands of husbands and children.

Akiko's story reveals several things about the woman's track. For one thing, her choice of medicine as a career was supported by her parents, as a high status career deemed appropriate for women. The other women doctors with whom I talked reported similar parental support, as did the dentist. And as one of them pointed out, the high cost of attending medical or dental schools in Japan (most of the schools are private and require an entry "gift" of $30,000 to $50,000) makes it necessary that the student have parental support and financial help.

A second point that seems typical for women who enter women's colleges, whether medical schools or general colleges, is that they do not encounter any special barriers as women, since all of their fellow students and many of the faculty are women. At the medical college Akiko attended, about 50 percent of the faculty are women. At women's junior colleges and colleges, many faculty are women, especially in departments that are still most attractive to women, like literature and humanities.

A third point, not directly illustrated by Akiko's story but often important in the woman's track, is that once a woman has completed her professional education in a women's college, or if she received her undergraduate degree from one, her career in the woman's track is fairly well assured. She may return to the women's college as a faculty member, or, in the case of a graduate of the women's medical college, she may become a faculty member there and/or staff member at the hospital associated with the college. One recent graduate of Tokyo Women's Medical College with whom I talked was serving as a staff doctor at the Medical Center. She told me that she felt much more comfortable working there than she would at a hospital not associated with the women's college. She and her fiancé, with whom I also talked briefly, agreed that there were few women staff members at the other hospitals. As she put it: "It is more natural to work where there are many women doctors. If I go out to work in that system [regular hospitals], I would become smaller." She also said that she felt men doctors were more energetic than women and could do harder work, work longer hours than women; it is therefore difficult to compete with them. Almost half the graduates in her class went home to practice in their home towns (mostly as obstetricians or pediatricians); about half stayed in Tokyo, and many of them are in some way associated with the Tokyo Women's Medical Center.

Akiko took another path that is often open to women doctors; she married a doctor and eventually set up practice with him, after meeting her home responsibilities. A faculty member at Tokyo Women's Medical College told me this was fairly common. She saw it as a problem for women doctors, as she felt they should somehow find ways to continue their careers uninterrupted. The dentist with whom I talked said that she was the only woman member of her graduating class who was now working full-time as a dentist; she practices with her husband. She said that most of her classmates were not practicing because of family responsibilities. When I asked her if she thought most would return to practice when their children were older, she said she thought not, in many cases. She said many of the husbands do not approve of their wives working, and some of the women really do not want to practice.

One of the most interesting questions arising regarding the woman's track professional career pattern has to do with the limitations this track seems to impose on women in terms of the breadth of specialization open to them in their chosen fields. For doctors, as mentioned earlier, the specialties chosen by most women are obstetrics, pediatrics, or ear, nose, and throat specialty. In my discussions with women doctors, the women did not feel that they had been unfairly routed into these areas. They argued, rather, that these specialties were more appropriate for women because they took advantage of women's "natural" nurturant skills (dealing with women or children) or because they allowed women to keep on schedules not involving night calls. When I pursued the latter "excuse," as I saw it, suggesting that perhaps both obstetricians and pediatricians might need to be on call more than surgeons or persons in other specialties, I received no answers. It occurred to me that these "appropriate specialties for women" may be justified out of a culturally complex set of notions about what women can and should do, just as they seem to be in medicine in the United States. The women themselves are justifying patterns that may have little or no logical basis in terms of their "natural" abilities or skills or social needs, but they may have great relevance in terms of reserving the higher status specialties for men. It also appears likely that women doctors select these women's specialties as the result of a whole series of subtle influences, some beginning long before medical school, rather than because of obvious routing and blocking.

In a little different way, the woman's track in academia seems to encourage women to develop professional careers in "women's areas" and makes it relatively easy for them to pursue those careers in women's colleges and junior colleges. For example, I found that most women's colleges do not yet offer the Ph.D. degree. If they do offer that degree, as Tsuda College does in English Literature, following a 1965 decision by the Japanese Ministry of Education, it is likely to be in a "woman's field." Thus even in the women's colleges and junior colleges, the faculty is made up of large numbers of women in the "women's areas" but is dominated by men in areas such as science and mathematics. Another interesting note is that, according to my respondents, most women attending four-year colleges in Japan today are in women's colleges; if they are in coeducational colleges and universities, they tend to major in literature and the arts. And even in those areas in coeducational colleges, the faculty is predominantly male. Perhaps the most interesting aspect of all this is that, at least among my respondents, few questions are raised about the appropriateness of such patterns. One of my respondents, the mathematics professor at a women's college, did raise some questions, however. She felt that more women should be encouraged to enter the fields of mathematics and science, and she thought it was unfortunate that so many women in Japan major in literature in college. It was her strong opinion that "such women do not need to go to college; they can get knowledge in literature throughout their lives in other ways." She went on to say that most women majoring in literature and like fields do not pursue professional careers after marriage, whereas almost all of the women who choose to major in math or science do continue working "in spite of" marriage. Another woman with whom I talked at length, a university professor who had completed her graduate education abroad, commented that she felt it was essential that more Japanese women be encouraged to enter fields not traditionally reserved for women.

My interviews with the two women lawyers tended to confirm these opinions. Both of them felt that they were not discriminated against as women practicing law, although one did say that there were a few old judges who felt women should stay at home. But both of them pointed out that there are still very few women in this field: less than three-tenths of a percent. One of them also said that for a woman trained in law to choose to become a judge or prosecuting attorney (a choice which involves taking the government examination at the end of college) is still even more rare, and it is discouraged. Both of these career fields require that the person qualifying by examination move every three years, something seen as almost impossible for a woman, who should be married and therefore unable to move freely. Finally, one of the lawyers said that she felt the main reason there were not more women lawyers was the combination of women's reluctance to enter a "man's field" and lack of encouragement or downright discouragement, throughout the educational system, of this career choice for women.

To summarize, then, from these two biographies and the material discussed regarding them, it appears to me that Japanese professional women are faced with at least two major barriers to achieving full equality with their male counter parts. *First,* all professional women must overcome the general cultural admonition that women should really marry and stay at home to run households and raise "good" children. Having done that, if they choose to be "career women," it is up to them to make whatever career compromises and arrangements may be necessary to insure that if they choose to marry and become mothers, their husbands and children will not suffer from their aberrant behavior. It is fascinating to note that among my respondents, all agreed that the ideal life for a woman would be to combine a professional career with an equally successful career as wife and mother. They said such things as: "Women have an obligation to grow something—not only to care for and educate children, but also to help in developing all kinds of things for the society." "To have a very wonderful husband, and to be able to work at her career and pursue her own hobbies and interests." "To be supported by her husband, to be able to work or not as she wishes." "Getting married and both husband and wife working, and bringing up two children. Both husband and wife should contribute something to society." However, all but one agreed that career demands or desires should not get in the way of the primary obligation of women, to raise children. The one dissenter, who was separated from her husband and had no children, was the only one of my respondents who belonged to any women's activist groups. She felt that her major obligation as a woman was to improve social conditions for other women. All the others, while feeling to various degrees that a professional commitment was important, also seemed to accept the societal rule that such a commitment might have to take second place to family commitments—although several said quite vehemently that they would not marry a man who would not "let them" work, if all else were taken care of somehow. The surprising thing about these kinds of answers is not that the society assumes that women are to be responsible for home and family first. This, I think, is equally true in the United States. It is surprising, however, that there seemed to be considerable ambiguity among the women I interviewed regarding whether this is the way it *should* be. Only four, for example, said without reservations that they felt husbands of working wives should help with household and child-care duties. The others echoed in various ways the following comments of one young respondent: "Partly the husband has to help his wife. But if married women want to work, I think they have to work almost twice as much. When women decide to work after marriage, they are needed to work more and more in society and at home. If they don't like to work more, they should stop their outside work. It's a most important condition for a working woman after marriage to have a strong body. . . .In Japan, men cannot do housework; they have not been trained to do this." There seemed to be among the

respondents a strong feeling that perhaps housework and certainly
child care were more "naturally" woman's responsibility. Most were
concerned about the absence of good child-care facilities in Japan,
and most mentioned that household help was unfortunately unavailable. But none except the one dissenter was thinking clearly in terms
of a broad new division of responsibility between men and women.

Second, there appears to be a rather clear division between women's
areas and men's areas in the professions, a division strongly supported by the academic patronage system and the cultural assumptions,
held by many of these women, that certain kinds of work are more
appropriate or more "natural" for women. One of my respondents,
in answer to the question about whether men and women should do
the same kinds of work, said that she felt some jobs were not good
for women, others not good for men. Expanding on this, she said
that good jobs for women are college professor, teacher, and nurse;
that a business job, except as an assistant to a man, is too demanding for a woman, requires too many hours. "Businessmen are involved in a big, complicated system. There is a difference in talent
between men and women, and business is too big and complicated a
system for women's talents." Although most of the respondents did
not answer this particular question in quite this way—most said that
men and women should be allowed to do whatever work they wanted to do—most of them indicated during the interview a feeling that
while men are not better than women, men and women have "naturally different" talents. As long as these divisions remain, supported
by patronage and belief systems, it seems unlikely that many wom-
en will be able to achieve fully equal participation in the professions
with men. As one of the woman lawyers said, in a slightly different
context: "The heredity of the old family system remains, in spite
of changes in the law following World War II. Family law has completely changed, but tradition dies hard."

OPINIONS AND ATTITUDES

The opinions and attitudes of the women I interviewed varied considerably and did not seem to show a consistent pattern by age group,
profession, or even within the opinions of any one respondent as
contrasted to another respondent (i.e., no pattern of consistently
"liberal" vs. consistently "traditional"). Some of their answers do
warrant exposition, however, as representing issues to which professional women seem to have given some attention.

All of my respondents seemed to agree that boys and girls should be
trained in the home and educated in the same way. One gave as an
example of this the fact that when her daughter and son were children, she gave her son a doll to play with when her daughter received
a doll. All seemed to place great value on a college education for

women, although several seemed to see the value as much in terms
of general preparation for living as in terms of career preparation.
All of the respondents felt that women should be able to choose
their own husbands. And all of them felt that women should be involved in politics, although two pointed out that it would take an unusually strong and committed woman to be a politician. Most of
them felt that women should have the right to divorce, although two
felt divorce should be only as a last resort. One sixty-year-old respondent laughed heartily at this question and told me she felt women
often married men who were inferior to them. She said that since
there was no longer a temple in Kamakura (as there used to be in
the old days) especially reserved as a refuge for women whose husbands had been mistreating them, divorce was now a necessity.

I received an interesting variety of answers to the question about whether men are better than women. Only one respondent said flatly that
she thought men were indeed better than women—better in personality,
in inborn mental talent, and in their "different way of thinking about
their lives." But several, while saying that men and women were equally good and equally important to society, pointed out that men were
physically stronger and more energetic. Three of the women, two of
them doctors, told me that they felt women's menstrual problems made
them physically less able to work consistently than men and in that
sense that men might be better.[14] Only one of the respondents said
vehemently that she thought men and women were clearly equally
capable, that only society had made it impossible for women to contribute in the variety of ways that men can. The most common overall
answer to this question seemed to me to imply that while men are not
better than women—some men are better, some women better—there
are ways in which they are basically different.

When I asked the respondents to tell me what was a successful woman, I received a variety of answers. Most respondents first looked
puzzled, or asked me to tell them what I meant by success. Then
they would go on to comment, still obviously not sure what the
word meant, perhaps especially as applied to women. One said:
"Success implies something that a person has done in society that is
evaluated highly by society. This doesn't mean a thing for me. I
like a person who fulfills her own life, does what she wants to do,
regardless of what society says." Another said: "The woman who
fulfills her life, does what she wants do do, pursues her own interests—and at the same time brings up her children well. A motherly
type of woman. If possible, it's best for human beings, men and
women both, to get married and have children. Therefore a woman
should fulfill herself *and* raise children successfully." Several others
gave very similar answers. Finally, several respondents gave answers
like the following: "It depends on the situation. Success depends on
each person's desires. If a person wants to be a good wife and does
so, then she is successful. If she wants to be something else, then
she is still successful if she does it. . . . I think that for women, if

they really want to be independent, then marriage will interfere and they will not be successful in their own minds." There seemed to be agreement in all the answers that success for a woman is important and involves some kind of self-fulfillment. Beyond that, some respondents stressed that a truly successful woman would need to be married and have children as part of her success, while others felt that success was an individual matter, depending on what the woman —or man— wanted to accomplish in life. Incidentally, the married respondents were not necessarily the ones who saw marriage as a necessary part of success.

Other answers that were quite interesting were those having to do with whether girls should live away from home. The respondents were about equally divided on this, between those who felt strongly that girls should live away from home in order to develop their own personalities, and those who said quite vehemently that a girl might live away from home if it was necessary during college but then should return to live with her parents until marriage. Of the first group, one respondent said that she felt it was impossible for either boys or girls to develop their own opinions and find out "who they are" as long as they stay at home, where the influence of parents is strong and, in Japan, highly respected. Of the second group, one respondent quoted the old Japanese saying: "Keep the daughter in a box." She said she felt that this was still an important condition to marriage for a girl, to have been kept pure and protected from "bad men." She also said that she felt most girls would want to stay home and care for their parents as long as possible, since at marriage they would have to leave home "soon enough."

Finally, the answers I received regarding the major obligation of women and the most important contribution women could make to society seemed to fall into two fairly distinct groupings.[15] One group of respondents said that they felt there was not really one single obligation for women as women. "Obligations should be thought of as what human beings should do." They gave similar answers regarding women's contribution to society, although some of them pointed out that in present-day Japan, women were sometimes limited in the contribution they *could* make by their lower status and defined role. The other group, however, tended to emphasize women's obligation to raise children and saw this as the most important contribution women could make. As one respondent stated this position: "The major obligation of a woman is to have children and to raise them well. If a woman has a job, her obligations to her children are still the most important. And her contribution to society is the same; children are the basis of a better society."[16]

The professional women whom I interviewed, then, seemed to hold a broad spectrum of opinions on questions deemed by the interviewing team to be important to the eventual status of women in Japan.

Although these women were all articulate and had apparently well formulated opinions in the areas we explored, their answers do not seem to reflect any particular influence from their experience as professional women, whether married or single, young or relatively old. Some of the women expressed opinions that seemed to be rejecting traditional definitions of women and their role, but even among these women, there were in most cases occasional answers that showed some ties to traditional values.

CONCLUSION

It is my impression that the professional women whom I interviewed are, in one sense, a "new breed" of Japanese women. They are strong-willed, well educated, not apologetic about their possibly "unwomanly" interest in and commitment to careers for themselves and for other women. And most of them are seriously, thoughtfully searching for ways in which to make it more possible for other women in Japan to be professionals without sacrificing the human joys of home and family. It does not seem to have occurred to most of them, however, that they still share with other Japanese women certain socially structured limitations on their career potential, nor do they seem to be exploring the possibilities of eliminating these barriers. Only one of them verbalized clearly the belief that the status of all women in Japan must be raised, that roles of men and women must be restructured. For the rest, to varying degrees, it was their belief that any strides toward true equality between men and women can and must be made without disturbing the traditional notion that woman's natural responsibility and talent lies in raising children. They want help with this task, but in general they do not want to suggest that it could or should be shared equally with men or that men's position of power and perhaps too heavy responsibility in the outside world (many Japanese men work six days a week and meet demanding business and social obligations beyond the work day) might be changed. Such ideas, it seems to me, are much more in the thinking of professional women in the United States, although I do not see that much difference in the realistic situations confronting American professional women from those faced by their Japanese sisters. The major difference I see between the United States and Japan is not in the actual conditions faced by women seeking to have careers. It lies in the somewhat wider consciousness among American professional women that major social changes are needed. Perhaps this is because of the differing strength of traditional family patterns in the two cultures. Perhaps it reflects only a time lag in Japan, one which one of my respondents feels will be overcome as more and more women enter the equal opportunity track and challenge the inequities there as well as the status quo aspects of the woman's track. Whatever the reasons, only time, and the quiet dedication and sometimes superhuman efforts of women like my respondents, will tell the story.

NOTES

[1] Figures on the numbers of doctors, dentists, and lawyers come from interviews. Those on teaching are taken from: Ministry of Foreign Affairs, *Status of Women in Modern Japan: Report on Nationwide Survey*, p. 43.

[2] Etsuko Kaji, "The Invisible Proletariat: Working Women in Japan," *in* Task Force of the White Paper on Sexism—Japan, *Japanese Women Speak Out*, p. 27.

[3] This date and some of the historical information in this and the following two paragraphs were given to me by a member of a women's collective in Nagoya, Japan. Information about lawyers was given to me by Professor Yoriko Nojiri of Sophia University in Tokyo from her translation of Periodicals 12 (1971), 13 (1974), and 14 (1975) of the Japan Women's Bar Association.

[4] Although they are now called colleges, these institutions did not in their early years offer curricula equivalent to what is now offered in four-year colleges. They functioned as "finishing schools" and as training institutions for teachers.

[5] The names and some of the details in these two biographies have been changed to protect the anonymity of the respondents.

[6] Of the eleven respondents, three had mothers who were teachers, one's mother was a doctor, one's mother worked after her father died, and the other mothers were housewives. No consistent pattern emerged regarding father's education or occupation, nor regarding respondent's birth rank or sex of siblings.

[7] All but one of the respondents reported that they had been fully supported and even encouraged in their career plans by their parents. Most had fathers living, and frequently the father gave strong encouragement, with the mother's full agreement. The one who did not report full support said her parents did not oppose her plans.

[8] Even for men in Japan, it is frequently the case that graduate work ends with the issuance of a certificate at the completion of Ph.D. course work, rather than with completion of the Ph.D. dissertation.

[9] One of my other respondents was a graduate student at a coeducational university during World War II. At that time, there were only three women in the university, two in the law department and the respondent in Japanese Literature. There was a special room reserved for the women to use for study, eating lunch, and resting.

[10] For an excellent discussion of the problems of child care in Japan, see: Hidemi Azuma, "A Child's Death—The Beginning of Struggle for Day Care," *in* Task Force of the White Paper on Sexism—Japan, pp. 17-25. In all of my interviews, this issue was raised as a crucial one for professional women.

[11] For current information on women in higher education, see: Social Education Bureau, *Women and Education in Japan*.

[12] This respondent told me, and other people confirmed it, that although some women's colleges are better than some of the men's schools, in general the coeducational colleges and universities get more financial support, can therefore have better laboratory facilities and attract "top" faculty.

[13] It may be that the parental support given to professional women in their career plans was in some cases support not so much for a career as for attaining an education that would make the daughter more sure of making a "good" marriage.

[14] Most businesses and even the women's hospital I visited in Japan automatically give women two days menstrual leave per month.

[15] In the first group were three married respondents, one single, one single and engaged, and one separated. In the second group were two single women, along with three married respondents.

[16] For a report of a recent survey of Japanese women university graduates, including questions about their views on raising children, see: Japanese Association of University Women, *Japanese University Women: Issues and Views, Volumes One and Two*, 1974. In one part of the survey, reported on pp. 45-46 of Volume Two, 22 percent of the respondents said that it was better for the mother not to work if there were no nursery facilities. In addition, 15 percent of these women graduates said (reported on p. 30, Volume Two) that child rearing is an important contribution to the community.

CHAPTER
10
WOMEN IN MEDIA

Women journalists are not a new phenomenon in Japan: they once dominated the field. During the Heian period (794-1185), women excelled in observation, analysis, insight, and reporting. In *The Tale of Genji*, Murasaki Shikibu captured the sights and sound of aristocratic life as well as making an acute analysis of human nature. Sei Shonagon, in her *Pillow Book*, describes the lighter side of everyday life while commenting on the social and political foibles of her day. Women reported on the outside world in travel diaries and, in private diaries, revealed the inner experiences of loneliness and jealousy in their often isolated lives.

Two languages were in use in Heian Japan. Chinese was the language of government and religion, the tool of officialdom. Cumbersome but prestigious Chinese characters were precluded for women. A simple and practical syllabary, *hiragana*, was developed from abbreviated characters to represent the sounds of everyday Japanese speech. Closed off from the Chinese, women made of *hiragana* a sensitive and expressive instrument.

It has been generally assumed that Heian women were better writers than men because they used native Japanese while men wrote in Chinese. To make that assumption the sole reason for their literary supremacy, however, is to neglect another aspect of Heian women—their good self-image.

Lacking the independence of the later Kamakura women, aristocratic Heian ladies nevertheless had certain advantages. In the matrilocal residence system of the period, a husband sought social advancement through his father-in-law and took care not to offend his wife. Women understood their position as a link to power, not as the hostages and household servants they would later become. Self-respect underlay the skills which they were expected to develop in poetry, music, calligraphy, painting, and perfume-blending as well as the more domestic skills of silk-dyeing and sewing. They competed openly with men in many of these skills and sometimes even won.

Poetry and calligraphy—writing—were by far the most important accomplishments. Heian media was the written word. Communication was indirect; the content and appearance of the message were scrutinized and the writer judged accordingly. How a woman wrote was more important than how she looked—small wonder women developed the ability to express themselves.

Another factor which contributed to a good female self-image was the absence of a military cult to despise feminine qualities. Furthermore, in spite of the presence of Chinese culture, this was not a period of strong antifeminine Buddhist activity, nor was the Confucian family system operative.

Finally, while they were not immune to the pain and jealousy which accompany a polygamous society, neither were women expected to remain entirely faithful. A discreet woman could have any number of affairs, expecially in the aristocracy.

With talents well developed and self-respect intact, and permitted some latitude of experience, the Heian woman wrote well because she had something important to say and knew she could say it well. Japanese women of today have not lost the ability to express themselves—only the opportunity.

The media play a profound role in shaping and maintaining the image of Japanese women. The massive volume of printed and projected material plus Japan's small size and concentrated population create a nearly total media saturation. Yet women occupy only about 1 percent of the effective positions in media. Nearly everything which the Japanese woman sees or hears about herself has been filtered through the male consciousness. Female effectiveness is further hampered because nearly half of the women in media are employed in the traditionally feminine areas of cooking, child care, and housekeeping. No women work in the serious areas—politics, foreign affairs, or economics.

Media will be discussed in three categories—newspapers, magazines, and television broadcasting.

MEDIA HISTORY

Japan's literacy rate, approaching 99 percent, is reflected in a daily newspaper circulation exceeding one copy for every two people.[1] The earliest newspapers were one- to two-page lithographed news sheets which were read aloud by hawkers. *Yomiuri,* the name of one of the three largest national dailies, means "hawked about."[2] *Yomiuri* were sponsored by Ieyasu, founder of the Tokugawa regime, who distributed news of his victories to promote aid from feudal lords. When Japan was unified in 1600, a period of peace and prosperity followed. During the Genroku Era (1688-1703) ballads printed and sung by a pair of hawkers describing sensational incidents replaced the newsheets. The news of the forty-seven *rōnin* who carried out a forbidden vendetta for their dead lord was brought to the public in this manner. The government response was to forbid ballads, establishing a pattern of government censorship and suppression of newspapers which ended only after the American occupation.

The Meiji Restoration (1868) returned political power from the shogun to the emperor. It brought the promise of a Western-type constitution and the possibility of parliamentary rule and party politics. The first modern newspapers were party organs, published privately. Newspapers became an important force in the pro-parliamentary popular rights movement, and editorials grew increasingly antigovernment. The conservative government responded with the Press Laws of 1875 and 1877, which required registration of the owner, editor, and printer and held the publisher responsible for subversive or slanderous material. Pen names were prohibited. Political criticism was restricted. Fines, imprisonment, and suspension were provided for violators. The Press Laws were directed mainly against advocates of parliamentary rule. Arrests became so common the practice of hiring "jail editors" to serve the sentences developed. The long-awaited constitution did little to promote free public discussion. Two more examples further illustrate the press struggle with government censorship.

The increase in Japanese exports during World War I brought Japan from a recession in 1916 to inflation and a doubled price of rice by 1918. A demonstration by housewives in July 1918 against rising rice prices led to riots. By summer's end, 700,000 people had participated in riots throughout the country.[3] Believing the newspapers responsible for aggravating the riots, the Terauchi government attempted to impose curbs on the press—an action which increased public opposition to the government.

In the 1930s the government again resorted to press censorship to curb criticism of the government's increasingly militaristic attitude. Publications critical of the war effort were likely to find newsprint unavailable, a most effective means of bringing the press into line. By the end of 1939, 500 publishers had gone out of business. Those who remained accepted the official policy of brainwashing which helped turn Japan into a war-minded nation.[4]

Military censorship continued throughout World War II, to be replaced by the censorship of the United States occupation. During this time a policy of hiring women (who were "safer" politically than men) was established. With the end of the American occupation in 1952 the press was, for the first time in its history, legally free of censorship and responsible to the people as a whole. Unfortunately for women, however, many newspapers emulated the government's "reverse course" which revised some of the occupation-introduced reforms. For more than fifteen years, until 1974, women reporters were not hired by most publications. This policy created a very real problem for women in newspaper work—a generation gap between women hired just after the war and women hired only recently.

Magazines, like newspapers, have political origins. While the early newspapers were party organs, journals were issued by the many enlightenment and discussion societies of the Meiji period (1868-1912). Democratic forces reached a prewar pinnacle during the Taisho period (1912-1926). Labor and social reform movements, including a feminine rights movement, flourished. An increase in literacy and an atmosphere of intellectual freedom provided a growing press and a larger subscription base. Competition for subscriptions resulted in a new format for magazines which included entertainment and serialized novels. Seiji Noma, genius of popular journalism, developed a formula for producing "the most entertaining, the most beneficial, the cheapest, and the best selling magazine in Japan." His magazines contained samurai adventure, sentimental romance, melodrama, and didactic tales. He attributed his success to his policy of including articles which "were always a step behind the times." As leader of the popular magazine field from the 1920s until the end of World War II, he had a tremendous influence on popular culture.[5]

Now a world leader in volume of magazine output, Japan nearly equals the United Kingdom and ranks well ahead of the United States.[6] Publications range from the intellectual, political publications such as *Bungei Shunju* (Literary Annals), *Chūō Kōron* (Central Reviews) and *Sekai* (World) to the popular women's weeklies, called "gossips," which would be considered pornographic in the United States, and the lurid comic books which are favored by men.

Japan's postwar freedom of expression has resulted in a degree of "sensationalism and vulgarity" which many groups feel is "damaging to the nation's youth."[7] Legal restraints have been understandably opposed by newspapers. The weeklies are expected to exercise self-restraint. In the face of strong competition for sales and advertising, however, weeklies are noticeably lacking in self-restraint.

Broadcasting, both radio and television, functions in Japan under government supervision as well as through commercial stations. NHK, Nippon Hōsō Kyōkai (Japan Broadcasting Company), is a nonprofit, government-supervised organization sustained by fees from set owners. NHK began in 1925 with the establishment of radio stations in three cities—Tokyo, Osaka, and Nagoya.[8] The democratization of mass communication led to the establishment of commercial organizations after World War II. In 1953 both NHK and Japan Television Network Corporation, a commercial station, began television broadcasting in Tokyo. Program ratios for NHK and commercial stations show NHK devotes more time to news and culture while the commercial stations heavily favor entertainment.[9]

Television has also received public criticism—"too full of murder and violence and too short of restraint in matters of sex and morality."[10] Like magazines, television is expected to exercise self-restraint.

In the area of "decency and good taste" media does its own censoring. Aside from this area there is another more subtle form of censorship, the reporter's self-imposed restraint stemming from the system of close and lengthy association with a particular company or governmental agency. The resulting dependency on a particular official or agency for information prevents truly candid reporting.[11]

Another subtle form of censorship affects women in media who attempt innovation or image change. It operates through the "group consensus" decision-making practice. In the rare instances when a woman is employed she is almost always the sole female member of a group or "section" which usually numbers from six to ten. If she works alone rather than in a group she still needs the approval of her male chief. It seems clear that while the possibilities for the media effecting a change in the status and image of women are limitless, the prospect of the media doing so is limited so long as the number of women employed remains low and women are kept out of decision-making positions.

MEDIA REPRESENTATION

Twelve women were interviewed in Tokyo for the media categories representing a newspaper, a news service, an intellectual magazine, a woman's monthly, a gossip weekly, and a television broadcasting company. Data is altered to protect the identity of the women and the companies.

One newspaper woman was a reporter for nineteen years and has recently been promoted to editor. At middle management she is at the highest level ever reached by a woman at this newspaper. The second newspaper woman is a reporter, also with twenty years' service, on the woman's pages. Her chief is a man. The news service correspondent has been at her job for thirteen years. She is thirty-five.

The two women from the intellectual publication are twenty-two and twenty-seven, with four years of service apiece. They edit for the reader's pages. Of the three women from the woman's monthly two were relatively young reporters, thirty-three and thirty-four. The third, at forty-six, is a vice-editor, the highest-ranking woman on the magazine staff. The "gossip" reporter is twenty-six. Her work, in the fashion section, is actually of an editorial nature, associated with and coordinating all aspects of each particular project.

Three women represent television broadcasting. Two are directors, one in science, one in drama. The third is a news commentator. Their ages range from forty-three to fifty-one and they have worked in television for nineteen to twenty-eight years.

What do these female representatives of media have to say about media and the companies for which they work?

THE MEDIA

The newspaper for which the respondents work, one of the three largest national dailies, is nearly 100 years old. The first female employee was hired in 1915. In 1925 a special section for women was established—a response to the feminine rights movement. Journalists from the women's section became involved with problems of Tokyo prostitutes who were unprotected by law and caught up in the social movement which opposed legalized prostitution. The journalists investigated and reported on conditions in the prostitutes' quarters.

The women's section is still radical—the image which it presents of women is liberal. Speculating on reasons for this permissiveness, the newspaper women suggest that the women's section is not taken seriously by male editors. "It is small and lacks influence so it doesn't really matter what it says."

The newspaper as a whole, however, presents quite a different image. The women's movement is "put down—treated as a joke." In covering women, the sensational is played up: the unmarried woman who kills her baby or the wife who runs away. The news service correspondent agrees. The news service's function is to select from international and national news for local papers. Thus, a male correspondent in Tokyo decides what women all over Japan will read. Emphasis is put on the bad things women do. The wife who kills herself when her husband leaves her is blamed, not the husband who leaves. What women are allowed to read about other women perpetuates the "weak and emotional" self-image. Women are denied news about other women which would encourage a good self-image.

"If you get married, read *Shufu* [The Housewife]." The format of this monthly magazine for housewives has not changed in its nearly sixty years of publication, but its perspective has. Conceived by its founder as a family project, its specific purpose was to raise the status of women. It has always employed women. The term "shufu," which is today the most commonly used term for housewife, was then as radical as was "Ms." when it recently appeared.

The magazine "turned a corner for women" by making a wider view of life available to them. For the first time, for example, knitting instructions were offered. Women were no longer so dependent on their immediate families for means of creative expression. *Shufu* took an early (and unpopular) pro-birth control stand in an attempt to improve the health of women.

Shufu's radical aspect disappeared in the wake of postwar changes. It now quite frankly caters to the middle-class housewife between the ages of twenty-three and forty-five. In the service of the "professional housewife" the magazine offers a myriad of classes, maintains a library and even devotes space in a corporation-owned store for the sale of products by women readers. The image presented today is the modern industrial society ideal—a prosperous, attractive housewife ever busy creating and spending for the care and comfort of her family.

The magazine is big and beautiful—slick, tasteful, and high class. It sells for about $1.50. With the magazine the buyer receives several supplements. A recent copy included patterns for sewing a woman's blouse and a child's suit, needlework patterns, and a large wall poster. A quality publication, *Shufu* is nevertheless a highly effective device for promoting female consumption.

Young Miss is the product of a large and respected publishing house. Of the sixteen magazines published here, four are for women. They also publish "adult" comic books, children's magazines and intellectual magazines. The company has been publishing for sixty years. The first woman's magazine appeared fifty years ago—another response to the social reform movement.

Young Miss is one of the "gossip" weeklies. Designed to appeal to the young, unmarried woman, *Young Miss* has something for every taste. There is a good fashion section, a food section, and a feature section on women. There are also "how to" articles on sex, nude photographs of lovely young women, dreamy and misty-eyed, and even a comic strip story in which the woman is seduced and abandoned.

The image reflected by *Young Miss* is of a young unmarried working girl, passing the time until she marries, concerned with clothes, pleasing a man, and finding a husband.

The intellectual magazines rarely contain articles especially for or about women. There might be an article about nutrition, but not about cooking. A story entitled "There are No Bad Women" discussed the traditional qualities of women. If any image comes through, it is the traditional image.

There is also, however, a paucity of articles written *by* women. This lack could lead the reader to the conclusion that women cannot write. A negative image of women is presented by default.

Television provides the most effortless means, for the child especially, to fabricate a role model. What is available for building material? Mornings offer advice and household hints to the housewife, proving a woman's interests lie solely within the home. Afternoons provide game shows with teams of young girls and boys. The boys usually win. Music shows have the usual male lead and female back-up. The cartoons still have mommy in the kitchen and daddy at work.

Prime time for capturing housewives and working wives is 6 to 6:30 p.m. Both are likely to be fixing dinner and feeding the children. The husband will probably work late or stop for a bit of socializing on the way home. A 6 p.m. "educational" show has a Japanese woman, a Japanese man and a Brazilian woman discussing a film on grocery shopping in Rio de Janeiro. The women sit on either side of the man. He narrates and explains while the Japanese woman, in a delicate, pleasant voice, expresses surprise and delight. The Brazilian woman, whom one would expect to be the expert, agrees and expands on the man's statements. A pleasant, relaxed and informative program, but the man—the central figure—is very clearly the authority symbol.

The women who work in television have more serious complaints. "Men control television," says Mrs. W. "A man wants his own wife to be more modest and helpful in the home, so that is what they show." A woman's task, as depicted by television, is "strict behavior—obey, be a nice girl, and a good wife." Mrs. H. says the work of many women writers is produced on television but when men direct they change the writer's meaning. Men prefer to see a traditional woman in drama. She would like to see an independent woman. "But," says Mrs. H., "it's a man's world, and men are certain that is the way it should be."

Large companies in Japan are usually organized in sections. The section members are the base of a pyramid; the chief is the apex.

At *Young Miss'* publishing house there are sixteen magazines or sections. Each section has approximately thirty-six reporters at the base. Over the reporters are six subeditors and at the top is the editor-in-chief. There are no female editors-in-chief. Three of the ninety-six subeditors are women. This company employs an unusually high number of female reporters—nearly fifty out of six hundred.

The newspaper employs more than one thousand reporters—six are women. Four of the six are in the women's section. One woman has reached the class of editor which is third from the top. Total employment of women by newspapers in Japan (including office girls and telephone operators) decreased by one-third from 1957 to 1964, reflecting the policy of not hiring women.[12]

The news service has ten women correspondents out of nine hundred. Five of the ten are in the women's section or domestic matters. At the intellectual monthly there are twenty section chiefs; none are women. The woman's monthly had one female section chief in fifty-eight years. There are now two women who are vice-chiefs but no female section chiefs.

The broadcasting company is structured into two upper levels. The professional level is below the administrative level. Of sixty-five directors at the professional level, five are women. There are no women among the eighty administrators.

In 1947 the Labor Standards Law was established to protect women workers.[13] In media, women feel that some parts of the law work against them more often than for them. Other articles are ignored or manipulated by the employer.

Men and women are supposed to receive equal pay for work of equal value. For many jobs the pay starts at the same rate and promotions are used to differentiate rates of increase. At the newspaper women are paid thirty percent less than men. Reporters are classified at three pay levels—A, B, and C. "Men always get the A classifications." The news service gives special pay for dependents. A married woman with dependents would not be able to receive this pay even if her husband lost his job. It would be assumed that he was simply lazy because men can in no way be considered dependent. The intellectual magazine hires male graduates of four-year colleges and female graduates of two-year colleges and uses this to justify pay differences. Salaries start with a $30 per month difference that grows with each pay increase. Another method used to pay men more is a dual system of raises—an annual increment plus an increase based on ability. Men are, of course, considered more "able."

The work week for women is limited to six days, forty-eight hours per week. Overtime is limited to two hours a day, six hours a week, and one hundred fifty hours a year. Women (except in specified jobs such as air-stewardesses and telephone operators) are not to work between 10 p.m. and 5 a.m. These limitations are especially hard on women in media. In theory the law is used to limit hiring and promotion of women. "What good is a woman if the news happens at night?" In practice women usually work the same hours as men. If there is a deadline, everyone stays to meet it. The woman, however, will often not be paid for overtime since she is not "officially" working. Miss E. recently worked until 4 a.m. and was not paid. Companies which pay overtime for night work risk a fine. Most women in media are not interested in avoiding overtime or night work—they want to be permitted to do their jobs.

Eleven of the twelve women interviewed feel that promotion practices are not fair. Women must wait longer and work harder. Whenever a man and woman are equally qualified, the promotion goes to the man.

Employers are required to provide six weeks of maternity leave before and six weeks after childbirth. Many companies "pat the woman on the shoulder and tell her to stay home." Some companies even encourage women to quit when they marry. Miss E. said "married women are given harder jobs." Mrs. K., a fifteen-year employee, has two children, six and nine years old. She is grateful to have been able to continue working but feels maternity leave should be longer. She has a health problem she thinks is related to returning to work so soon after her children were born.

Women in media feel that the protective laws in most cases are ineffective. The laws offer no real protection for women in media but rather give employers an excuse to either not hire or not promote women. The only provision women are able to use to advantage is for maternity leave and that needs to be extended.

The image of women presented by the media will not be changed until many more women are not only employed in media but are promoted on the same basis as men. While the number of women employed in media actually regressed from 1955 to 1970, the recent return to the practice of hiring women is leading "little by little" to an improvement in the female image. "Once in awhile" an article expressing the woman's point of view is "permitted."

A foreseeable problem is the generation gap caused by the fifteen-year policy of not hiring women. Most women in effective positions (senior or administrative) are over forty years old and will reach retirement age, fifty-five, in from five to fifteen years. Some may be allowed to continue working in an unofficial capacity—a practice followed in Japan for retired executives. The younger women are not old enough to fill the authority positions as they become vacant. Perhaps the older women will serve as unofficial mentors until the younger generation is firmly established.

THE WOMEN

Though no attempt was made to be selective, the twelve women interviewed from media fall rather neatly into two age groups. The prewar group, born before 1932, are old enough to have experienced wartime deprivation. They have all been employed for at least twenty years. The postwar group, born after 1940, escaped adverse wartime experience. One has been employed twelve years; others have worked from three to six years. This inadvertent delineation very likely results from the widespread policy, discussed in the preceding section, of not hiring women.

Overall similarities among the women as well as differences between the two groups emerge from the interviews. With one exception, the women were born in Tokyo or were moved there as infants and reared there. Mrs. T., a newspaper woman, was born an hour's distance from Tokyo but was educated at Keiō University in Tokyo.

The fathers of the twelve were all educated beyond high school. Two attended vocational schools and ten received four-year university degrees. Fathers were business men (from shop owner to steel company president), public servants, a banker, a senator, and a judge. Mrs. K.'s brother is the eighth generation operating a continuous family business.

Nearly all the women consciously chose media, a nontraditional choice. Teaching and public service are "safe," conservative fields, traditionally preferred for women. Media, a relatively new field for women, is nontraditional and therefore "unsafe." Fathers of prewar women were much more likely to oppose a choice of any kind by their daughters. Mothers in both groups were, on the other hand, almost always supportive of their daughters' ambitions.

None of the twelve women received rigorous household training from their mothers—several, in fact, took cooking lessons after they were married. There were limitations placed on rough play and sometimes brothers were given more help. Femininity was taught by example. There was no recollection, by any of the women, of being forced into a traditional wife-role. "My mother taught us to be people."

Two of the prewar women lost their fathers during childhood. Required by circumstances to be self-supporting, they were encouraged by their mothers to seek professional training. "Be independent, get a good job" and "be earnest, stand by yourself—you must eat alone" was the advice offered by the widowed mothers who had personally experienced dependency on relatives and children. Both of the fatherless women rejected marriage. "I had two chances to get married. I liked them both. They said they wanted me to keep my job but I was afraid in the end I would have to give up my work so I didn't marry."

The other four women experienced all the traditional fatherly opposition to any alternative except marriage. The fathers first opposed education beyond high school. Faced with their daughters' determination to attend college, the fathers then favored a proper girls' school. These women, born from 1924 to 1932, reached college age from 1942 to 1950. Under the old system, colleges were segregated and those for women provided an inferior education. After the war, women were admitted to some male universities. For the first time women had an opportunity to get an education equal to that of men.

Mrs. W.'s father didn't want her to go to a university. He wanted her to get married. "I didn't want to get married and be someone's slave." She went to Tōdai (Tokyo University), Japan's most prestigious university.

Mrs. T. grew up expecting to go to Kyōdai (Kyoto University) as her brothers had done. Her father resisted a coeducational university but her mother helped overcome her father's resistance. She went to Keiō.

Some fathers gave up when their daughters entered a university, but one committed his daughter to a teaching job. She taught for three years and escaped by marrying and taking a job with a magazine.

Most of the mothers encouraged their daughters. They had experienced the excitement of the women's rights movement, its suppression, and the rise of repressive nationalism and militarism. Several had wanted to work. Mrs. T.'s mother had married young and "had a hard time." She thought women should be independent so she "helped me against my father. My mother was very traditional— she had a strong will. She said women could overcome, be flexible. That is what I learned from my mother."

World War II may have intensified, for the older media women, the importance of a skill or profession for survival. Postwar women either experienced less resistance or exhibited less determination. The oldest, born in 1940, was told by her father that junior college was enough for a woman. She worked to support herself at a national university for women, but she gave up her first choice, botany, for psychology, a major more suitable for a woman. The other two women, also over thirty, have four-year degrees in literature. They received support and encouragement from both parents.

The three youngest women, twenty-two to twenty-seven, have two-year degrees. Two were not accepted at a university. The intellectual monthly which employs them limits its hiring of women to those with two-year degrees. Miss M. would like to marry and find an easier job—perhaps teaching flower arranging or tea ceremony. Her mother went to high school and did not work. Miss E. wants to work until she retires. She chose publishing rather than the teaching, office work, or interpreting she was offered because she hoped it would be creative. She feels her education is inadequate and would like another chance. Her mother went to a four-year college and taught school for two years. She told her daughter to be financially independent and to be a person before a woman.

The third, Miss Y., went to a vocational school instead of an art school because her parents suggested it. Her father wanted her to marry but he now feels her job is good for her. When she was sixteen, he said she was old enough to be responsible for her own decisions. She is determined to make a career in media in spite of her educational limitations.

Women in media generally have been encouraged to adopt an independent role model. They have been strengthened by their mothers' support and some have been toughened by their father's opposition.

Attitudes of eleven of the twelve women in media are liberal. They feel women should be able to choose the kind of work they want and compete on an equal basis with men. They believe a woman should have the right to control her own body—to make decisions related to birth control and abortion. They think, though, that abortion is a last resort and that better birth control methods should be available. The man should be consulted but the decision belongs to the woman.

They agree that neither men nor women are better than the other or more important to society. They say the obligations and contributions of women to society do not differ from those of men; both are responsible to the next generation. That women bear children is acknowledged as a physical fact, not a determining factor in a woman's life.

One of the young women, Miss M., expressed more conventional attitudes. She thinks men are better than women, and boys should be educated differently. Women may be too emotional to do the same work as men. She thinks that since the magazine she is working for is "concerned with politics and economics," men should be the ones who work for it. She disapproves of abortion and "maybe" approves of divorce. A woman's obligation is to raise children. Miss M., who would quit her job if she married, fits the traditional image, but she is atypical of women in media.

Media, as it has been noted, was, in the late 1940s and early 1950s, an untried field. What drew these women to the untraditional, to an uncertain future? Miss M. worked first in radio.

"I went to work in a brewery when my father died because I had three younger brothers and sisters. I saw great discrimination against women there—women never became foremen, even after ten years. I believed women's qualifications should be recognized. In 1949 the radio broadcasting company opened its announcer's examination to women. There were some women announcers before the war but after the war they had to hire more because of the constitution. Two thousand people took the tests—six were hired. I wanted to be a director. I wanted to make radio programs for women about emancipation. I wanted to raise the status of women."

Mrs. T. was interested in publishing. "In 1954 it was getting harder for a woman to get a job. I wanted to work for a magazine but I failed the test so I took a newspaper job."

Mrs. A. wanted to be a newspaper reporter when she was in college. "My parents were against it so my father arranged for me to teach high school. I taught three years. The second year I married. When my husband was established I went to Tokyo to look for a job and found this one."

Mrs. H. wanted to be an actress. "I wasn't confident in myself as a performer. I decided to be a director for this TV company. Directing is my interest—not TV, but I got a degree because I knew this company required it."

The economy was good when Mrs. K. finished college. "I had several choices. There was trouble then between the people and the government over the security treaty. I wanted to understand, objectively, what was happening so I took this job with the news service."

Two reporters at the women's monthly were educated young mothers with time on their hands when *Shufu* advertised for housewives. *Shufu* was initiating a new policy of hiring housewives who reflected real lives. Since very few places hire mothers, these talented and energetic women are delighted to have an outlet for their experience and creativity.

Miss K. of *Young Miss* studied fashion and dressmaking in vocational school. "I wanted to use my skills and I wanted to be in management. Editing in fashions, I can do both."

The youngest woman in media, Miss H., wanted creative work. The junior college she attended has a placement service. "I could have been a teacher, a secretary or an interpreter. I wanted publishing or Japan Air Lines. I majored in English and I love to write."

Most of the women did not simply drift into their work. They had definite goals, some societal and some personal. Their sense of purpose perhaps accounts for their choice of the untried field. The choices these women made have shaped their lives. For some, work has become their life. Their work days are long. Many work mainly with men. They talk about life, their work, and men.

Miss K. said, "Of course I like my job. I enjoy getting a reaction from an audience. It is a joy to make programs and see others enjoy them. Also, I have an interest in this field and my work allows me to study. I want to work until I retire."

All the women enjoyed their work and nearly all planned to work until retirement. Many hoped to work beyond retirement. Fifty-five is very young to stop working. Mrs. K. planned to quit her job when the two children she has had since she began work become teenagers. "I want to be home when they are growing up. Others can raise them when they are young." Her mother cares for the children now. She will not stop working though. "I'm thinking of starting a children's library in my home. I want to teach children to enjoy books." She is collecting the children's books she receives through her work for her library.

Mrs. M. has only been working three years, but she plans to work until retirement. "I work because I enjoy it—not for the money. Many women are not really living. I can do something for them in my work."

Miss K. has been working for twenty-nine years. She is the highest ranking woman in her field. "I was lucky to get promoted early. Usually women must work two or three years longer than men." She lives with her mother so her household duties are minimal. She works late almost every night. She thinks women as a class are not treated fairly. "Men generalize about women. If one woman is foolish, they say all women are foolish." But she prefers talking with men. "They are more interesting, more logical. Women are more emotional because of the way they are brought up. But," she says, "sometimes women have an advantage. Men will say yes to a woman." That is a benefit of working with the opposite sex which she feels would also be true for men working with women.

While eleven of the women feel women are not treated fairly, they blame society as a whole, not the men with whom they work. Miss M. points out that a woman's salary in Japan is one-half that of a man, yet women are 40 percent of the work force. "I wonder what would happen if all the women stayed home?" She likes men as co-workers. "I get some arguments but they always treat me well. I don't like being considered an exception. When men tell me I am different it sounds as if other women aren't good."

Twenty-two-year-old Miss E. agrees that promotions are limited for women. "This is my first job. I was very disappointed in women's status at first. There is a ceiling on promotion for women. Vice-department-chief is the highest. Another problem here for women is the content—the importance of the work differs from men's. The second year I was here I had more important work because of my boss. He has hope for women. I had to work until eleven or twelve every night. I had much work—more than men. I got tired and asked for a transfer. I think he was very disappointed in me. The men in our office have an image of women. We are supposed to be less intelligent, silly, and cute. The men are generous. Some girls take advantage of such sweet treatment, but I try not to be indulged. I try to be serious." Some men are helpful she says. Some friends, men about thirty, married to career women, make suggestions about her work.

Mrs. M. and Mrs. A. say working conditions at the woman's monthly are good but "promotions are not fair. This place is better than most." Mrs. N. says, "This magazine is good to use women who are married and have children. Our bosses feel they need us so they trust us." She does not think it is necessary to have a woman as section chief. She thinks the magazine is fair even though "men are promoted after fewer years. This is a good company. If women are better than men, they can get better jobs." She says, "Women are more emotional than men—they can't deal with people." This is partly nature and partly environment. "Women are more pleasant to work with if their private lives are going well. Women take things differently from men than they do from women." Yet she says some men are emotionally unbalanced when they are troubled.

The appraisal of women as more emotional than men was given by nearly half the women interviewed. Yet when asked "Who helps you?" nearly every response named a woman. "My mother" and "my mother-in-law" because "She cared for my children when they were young." "All the women reporters help" and "the other women at work" were typical responses. One mentioned a famous woman commentator now in city government. At the woman's monthly the three young mothers support each other. They have tea break together and "talk, talk, talk."

Women's language is more polite than that of men. Recently, Fumiko Enchi said the use of women's language should be discontinued because it puts women at a psychological disadvantage.[14] The question,

"Do you use women's language?" was criticized by Japanese women as meaningless. "Women are brought up to speak a different language and it is natural for them." The question was nevertheless asked and most women did indeed respond with "Of course." The women who have been working with men for a long time are more aware of the difference. Miss M. says women's language is "good for negotiating with men—it flatters them. Sometimes I use men's words and they don't mind." Mrs. A. uses women's language with customers and the company president. Mrs. T. tends to use men's language—she is "surrounded by men." As a director, Mrs. F. gives orders to men. "Sometimes they don't work nicely, so I use women's language when I direct."

Some of the women in media are as successful as a woman can be in Japan. What is success? What is the ideal life? For many, success is a personal matter—"A successful woman lives the way she wants, makes her own way." "People who are independent, choose their own work and stay with it." "A woman is successful if she completes what she chooses. It doesn't have to be a job. A high position is nice but not necessary." "A man's success is judged by society. A man must achieve more than a woman to be considered successful." Women, they feel, can make their own evaluations. "Doing what she likes is success. It depends upon whether or not she is satisfied, even though others might not think she succeeded."

But for some, success involves all woman-kind; one woman achieves for all. "Women have a great task" to handle choice. "They don't need to become men. They can work and still be women." "There are lots of limits on a woman. If she fights back and does what she wants I would respect her. So long as she contributes something, that's the best thing she can do." "So many women are on a lower level. If one woman rises it doesn't mean all are better. When one woman rises it's still a problem because men don't have the same attitude. All women should achieve higher status together."

Even though many women maintain that a job is not essential to success, eleven indicated that for them the ideal life includes a job. It also includes children—work, marriage, and children. Of the twelve women, six are married, five are single, and one is divorced. Three of the six single women may yet marry and have children; the other three have passed child-bearing age (have decided irrevocably not to bear children). Of the six married women, one is childless and has passed the child-bearing age. The remaining five have eight children. None plan to have more. It seems clear that there have been deliberate limitations on motherhood. Yet motherhood is considered part of the ideal life. Even those without children say, "A woman misses something if she doesn't have children."

It is only recently that nursery schools have become available for working mothers. There are still too few, some are actually unsafe and most are too expensive for the average working woman.15
There has been, and still is, tremendous pressure on the Japanese woman to care for her own children. Women still do not leave their children in the evenings, even with their mother or mother-in-law. If women go out in the evening it is usually with the family, perhaps for dinner. Among the five mothers, two are prewar women whose mothers-in-law live with them and care for the children, now teen-agers.

The oldest of the three postwar women has a mother who lives with her and cares for her six- and nine-year-old children. This woman plans to stay home when the children reach their teens. The two youngest mothers (who began work after their children were born) keep their preschool children in private nursery schools.

One thing seems certain. Children complicate the work experience for women. It is not possible to say that working is easier for the younger woman who takes her child to nursery school than it is for the woman whose live-in mother or mother-in-law takes care of her children. The nursery school alternative merely makes it possible for more middle-class women to choose to work. So long as "good wife and wise mother" remains part of the ideal image, the woman who wants a career outside the home will have three jobs.

It takes determination (not to mention physical strength) to manage three jobs, to be, in a sense, three people. How do women in media organize their lives?

Mrs. K., a newspaper woman, works six days a week, never less than eight hours a day, more when she needs to. She commutes one and one-half hours daily, reading five to six books monthly on the train. She rises first and fixes breakfast for her family. Her mother, who lives with her, takes care of the two grade-school children and cooks dinner for them. Mrs. K. arrives home after the children have eaten but early enough to spend time with them before they go to bed. Her husband usually comes home later than she does. Sometimes she waits to eat with him, other times she eats alone. She never goes out in the evening with him. "It's the Japanese way," she says. Her friends come over after work sometimes, and once or twice a month her brother comes to visit their mother. On Sundays Mrs. K. cleans, does the laundry, and shops.

Mrs. F.'s mother-in-law lives with her. In this household the mother-in-law gets up first and fixes breakfast. Mrs. F. works later than her husband—so late she usually eats dinner at work. She sometimes goes to the theater in the evening as part of her job, and "once in a while" she goes out with her husband, leaving her teen-age son with her mother-in-law. Mrs. F. commutes six, sometimes seven days a week for one hour and fifteen minutes. On Sundays, if she does not go to work, she cleans and does laundry.

Mrs. T.'s mother-in-law also lives with her. She helps care for the two teenage boys. Mrs. T. says her husband is happy about her work but her mother-in-law is not. For that reason, she has a housekeeper come four mornings a week to clean and two afternoons to cook. The housekeeper also cooks extra meals to be eaten on other nights. When the children were babies, Mrs. T. had a full time housekeeper but she has never felt she could take out-of-town assignments. She commutes eighty minutes daily and works irregular hours. She eats at home, however, but seldom goes out with her husband. Sometimes the whole family goes out. Mrs. T. doesn't like television but she watches it with her children.

These three women have the security of knowing grandmother is there when the children come home from school, but they have not given over complete care of children or house. They still discipline the children (with their husbands) and make time to be with them. They still handle the finances, do most of the household organizational work, and a good part of the physical work. Their husbands help very little. As one woman said, "My husband's good point is that he doesn't complain." One very time-consuming chore they have largely escaped is meal planning and preparation. There may be an advantage for the Japanese working woman in having a husband who works late and eats out.

Mrs. M. and Mrs. N. both keep their young children in nursery school while they work from 9:30 to 5:30. Mrs. M. has a babysitter who takes her child home and stays with him until Mrs. M. gets home. Mr. N. picks up their two children. Both husbands are home nearly every night. Mr. M. bathes his son. They eat dinner at 8:30. Mr. N. does the laundry.

Mrs. N. does some cleaning on Sunday, but tries to spend as much time as possible with the children. Mrs. M. always fixes breakfast, Mrs. N. sometimes does. Both women handle the family budget. Neither go out in the evening as a couple, but both sometimes go out as a family.

Mrs. M. and Mrs. N., with no live-in help, both fix dinner every night. They also have their husbands at home to help give the constant attention that young children demand. The trend in Japan is to the nuclear family. In the right circumstances, however, the three-generation family could be a boon to the working mother.

Mrs. W., forty-seven, is the only childless married woman. She is the only one who did not include children in her version of the ideal life. Mr. and Mrs. W. go their separate ways during the week. They both eat breakfast out. He often plays mahjong and comes home late. She eats dinner with friends on the way home. "Once in a while" she goes to the theater by herself. "Once in ten years" they go out together in the evening. Sundays Mr. and Mrs. W. spend together. She cleans and does the laundry and he helps "quite a lot." They have dinner together.

Mrs. W. expends considerably less energy on domestic activity than do working mothers. Her energy expense is very similar to that of the older single women. Her life actually resembles that of the Japanese male executive except that she handles the household finances and does the bulk of the housework—and of course she does not go to the mahjong parlor!

Ten of the women express dissatisfaction with the media-shaped image of women. Some have idealistic hopes for changing media, others have pragmatic plans.

Miss K. thinks the image of women presented on television is far from reality. Program guests are too often wives of salary men or business men—the white collar wife, not the woman working at a man's job. The ideal Japanese woman, according to television, is the business man's wife. Miss K. would like to show farm wives and working women.

One of the reporters at the woman's monthly thinks the magazine's professional housewife image is justified—"that is who the magazine is for." Another would like to see something included for the 50 percent of the women who are working. The third would like to deal with women on a different level. Out of her research on the *Kyōiku Mama* (education mother), whose life revolves around pushing her child up the education ladder to the "right" school, has come a real concern for the many women dependent on their children for gratification. She would like to start an adult education school for housewives—a school with solid content—offerings such as economics, psychology, and history. She says, "Women are looking for something but they don't know what. If they knew more about the world they would be less dependent on their children." She feels a wider view for women would lead to a decrease in the female suicide and infanticide rates as well as in the *Kyōiku Mama* phenomenon.

At *Young Miss*, Miss Y. would like to substitute the image of "a woman who can live on her own" for the present image of a young woman looking for a husband. Mrs. W. hopes to improve the image by judicious selection of books for the paperback publishing department. Miss E. finds it impossible to present any image in the intellectual publications but hopes, by her personal behavior, to promote more respect for women among her colleagues.

The newspaper women cite the problem of too few women reporters. The woman reporter who uses her initiative to counteract the sensational image which newspapers maintain will not get the approval of her chief. "If there were more women reporters they would have more strength." They also emphasize the necessity of hiring women reporters on a continuing basis to assure contemporary representation. Censorship in numbers is really the overriding problem—each woman knows the futility of lone action. Almost none has seen even minimal change in the image or status of women.

In an effort to build numbers many of the women participate in women's organizations, the purposes of which range from problem discussion groups to retraining classes for women who want to get back into media after having children. They also maintain contact with other women in media throughout Japan. The older women are more likely to belong to groups—some are active in as many as six— perhaps because they have more freedom than the younger women who are involved in child rearing or dating.

The older women attach more importance to higher status within the company—a higher position is more effective, they maintain, for improving conditions for all women. The younger women claim disinterest in personal status. They also present the most pragmatic schemes—the school for housewives and the library for children.

One older woman expresses the fear that younger women are the victims of affluence. Older women often went to inferior schools and were not taught English (she learned English from television lessons). "I envy the young women—they are better prepared. They could be more successful, but they haven't strong wills. They are easily discouraged—they go back home. They choose the easier way to live."

Hopefully, Miss M.'s estimate of the younger generation is wrong. The only certainty is the need for more women in media—women to shape and maintain their own image.

A PROFILE

My name is Keiko. I am the first woman in Japan to be doing, officially, the work I am doing. This work is my life. I am forty-four. I have been working toward this goal for thirty years. How can that be? Maybe not this specific goal—I had many dreams as a child. But

I understood very early that to make my dreams come true, I would have to work hard—harder than my brother—harder than any man.

My father went to a very good university and is respected in his profession. Of course, he planned for my older brother to go to the same university, so a great deal of care had to be taken with my brother's education. My father loved me, I was well treated, but the big thing in our home was my brother's education. He had a tutor and everyone had to keep quiet while my brother studied with his tutor. My father bought a big western-style desk for my brother. I envied him that desk. I worked at the dining room table and I had to get my books out and put them away every time I studied. My brother could just leave everything right in his desk. I think that desk crystalized my dreams. I was determined to do as well as my brother. That desk was, and still is, a symbol of what women must overcome to succeed.

I was lucky in my mother. I can't honestly say how it would have been for me with a different mother. She went to college—the old style girl's college. She wanted to work but she was the oldest in her family, so she helped her mother care for the household until her marriage to my father was arranged. That was how she learned to keep house. My mother didn't teach me very much about housework. She let me study instead of making me help her. She really encouraged me—it wasn't that she told me to work hard, but rather, that she let me know she respected my purpose. She let me feel I could be what I wanted. She never pushed me into being womanly, into being a wife and a mother, but she was realistic about life for women. She said it was wiser, better for my purposes if I acted in a feminine way.

When I was very young I was naughty. I played roughly. Of course, I wanted to be a boy. But I couldn't be, could I? What my mother did for me was to help me accept what I couldn't be without giving up what I could be.

My first real struggle against my father happened when I wanted to go to Tokyo University. It is the best university in Japan. My father and brother went there and I knew it would be the key for the work I wanted. Tokyo University had only recently accepted women and it was hard for my father to think about his daughter at a male university—*his* university. He was well known. Because of his career my mother had given up her wish to work. Now, there was I, his small, quiet, stubborn daughter, knocking at male doors. But in the end, he was fair. I was a better student than my brother had been. If I could pass the exam, my father said, if they would take me, I could go.

I majored in fine arts. I liked drama but I didn't feel good about myself as a performer. I joined a performing group. I liked the group—it was a good experience—but I knew I couldn't make a career of acting. Our culture offers other ways to say what must be said—to express oneself—so I chose another route in media. My first job was for a women's program on television. I cut out newspaper articles.

It was over my job that I had my second struggle with my father. He wanted me to work in education or government. All my school friends are now teachers or governmental officials. My father had strong reasons on his side. I had many good job offers in those fields, but here I was, cutting out newspaper articles for a women's show. Besides, television in Japan was only three years old. Who could tell what would happen? I had to be very firm.

My father began speaking of marriage. I knew what I wanted to do—what I must do—with my life. Through working I would express what was in me—things I could say in no other way. I also knew I could not avoid marriage. A woman cannot be firm beyond a certain degree. If a branch is not flexible it breaks under the snow. I thought "If I accept my father's choice for my husband, he will accept my choice for my work." Some women marry so they won't have to work. I married so that I would be able to work.

When my family's friend was searching for the right husband for me, I set one condition—that my work must come first. I don't think that my husband was told about that condition even though sometimes I used my work as an excuse not to go out. But he accepts it now. It just seems natural to me to work and I don't ask him about it.

I think our marriage is a good one. I never question that either. My husband has a profession completely different from mine—I would never want to work with him.

We have one child—a son. My husband's mother lives with us—she really raises our son. I want him to be independent but she is too nice to him. If he were a girl she wouldn't be so lenient. If I had a daughter I would treat her just as I do my son, but I would make her understand what life is for women.

My work—my life—is good, but it seems too short. In only eleven years I will be fifty-five, the age for retiring. I hope I can keep working. I have done so little of what I planned. I hoped to help women to a higher place in society, but change is slow. I try to show the independent woman, something all women can strive for. Each woman has a different idea about life but there should be no limitation because she is a woman. The most important obligation a woman has is to ask for the right to do what she wants and do it.

232

NOTES

[1] UNESCO, *Statistical Yearbook,* pp. 676-679.

[2] Kisaburo Kawabe, *The Press and Politics in Japan,* p. 14.

[3] Mikiso Hane, *Japan, A Historical Survey,* p. 397.

[4] *Ibid.,* p. 499.

[5] *Ibid.,* p. 429.

[6] UNESCO, pp. 683-685.

[7] Nihon Shimbun Kyōkai, *The Japanese Press,* 1964, p. 15.

[8] Nihon Shimbun Kyōkai, 1954, p. 30.

[9] Nihon Shimbun Kyōkai, 1964, p. 76.

[10] *Ibid.,* p. 15.

[11] Frank Langdon, *Politics in Japan,* p. 248.

[12] Nihon Shimbun Kyōkai, 1957, p. 33, 1964, p. 53.

[13] Women's and Minors' Bureau, *Status of Women in Japan,* 1974, pp. 19-20.

[14] "Kitchen Cabinet," *Newsweek,* 23 June 1975, pp. 8-9.

[15] Hidemi Azuma, "A Child's Death—The Beginning of Struggle for Day Care" *in* Task Force of the White Paper on Sexism—Japan, *Japanese Women Speak Out,* 1975, pp. 17-25.

CHAPTER
11
WOMEN IN THE
POLITICAL SYSTEM

Although men have traditionally dominated the political system in
Japan, frequently women have held important political positions.
Prior to the eighth century, women could succeed to the throne and
rule as empresses. Chinese thought and custom influenced the adoption of the Taihō Code which undermined women's position in Japan.
Women's basic equality was replaced by the Chinese concept of wom-
en's inferiority and heavenly ordained subjugation to men. These
changes were slow in penetrating the Japanese social and political
systems. In the Kamakura period (1185-1333), women could no longer succeed to the throne, but they were still acknowledged as legal
persons. They retained their property rights and could avail themselves of divorce, although their access to power was not as great as
men's. During this period an exceptional woman, Masako Hōjō, took
power in the wake of the death of her husband, the Shogun Yoritomo.
She kept the loyalty of her late husband's retainers and manipulated
Court relationships in her efforts to consolidate her position and power. With the help of her father, she made her son the Shogun and
ruled as his regent. Later she had him murdered when he attempted
to rule himself and exiled her father when he opposed her. Masako
Hōjō later ruled through her brother as the regent of her late husband's two-year-old great grand nephew, the Shogun. Ruling through
sons, brothers and other relatives was not required because of her
sex, but it was rather a traditional means of exercising political power.

Political confusion and internal warfare characterized the period between 1336 and 1573, when the central government lost its control
over the local leaders. Military power became a prerequisite for political power. The social code of the newly dominant military class
assigned women to subordinate roles within the family and limited

their access to political roles. Without direct access to military power, women resorted to personal influence on the men in powerful positions. Marriage was a political device for the powerful families to create alliances, often using the women as hostages. Married women provided access to power through their husbands for their male relatives. During this period, women had no legitimate access to political positions. During the Tokugawa period (1600-1867), the rigid social and political system prevented women from taking active political roles; women's positions were limited to those in and around the home. What little political influence they could obtain was exercised through their personal and family relationships, a common means of exercising political power.

The Meiji Restoration and the consequent opening up of Japan to new ideas and schools of thought encouraged women to take a more active role in the political system. The women's movement was a part of the new intellectual and social movements. Literary organizations such as *Seitōsha* (Blue Stockings) discussed needed changes in society and the political system. The labor movement fostered the growth of labor unions which were supported by socialist intellectuals. The plight of women laborers was the focal point of many new women's groups. Women in the liberal and socialist movements expected to further the position of women in Japan. They anticipated radical social change after the Meiji Restoration. These hopes were quickly quashed. The Peace Police Law of 1900 attempted to contain the communist and socialist liberalism that was spreading through Japan. Article 5 of the Peace Police Law of 1900 prohibited women from joining political parties and attending political meetings. Legitimation of women's political participation was the first goal of the new women activists.

Women's organizations were created to press for reform of the above law. In 1920, Fusae Ichikawa began more than fifty years of political activity with the founding of the Shin Fujin Kyōkai (New Woman's Organization). Its general objective was to improve women's positions in the political, economic and social spheres. A more specific objective was the reform of the Peace Police Law of 1900. With their freedom of movement and association restricted, these women found it necessary to work through men politicians. When unable to obtain admittance to the Diet building, they went to members' homes to lobby for support. Through a letter writing campaign, they supported the candidates who favored women's issues.[1] This small group of dedicated women persevered in the face of police harassment, arrest, and personal insult; they were rewarded in 1922 when the reform bill was passed. Although women could now attend and hold political meetings, additional civil rights were much more difficult to come by.

With their new-found freedom of association, many women became more actively involved in politics. However, the difficulty in affecting the political process and in attaining additional civil rights discouraged many women. Some political parties tried to exploit the novelty of women speakers and associations; their naiveté and ineptness in public activities created a negative image of women in politics. Women's limited participation in politics did not result in great changes in the Japanese political system.

The birth control movement was intertwined with the movement for women's political rights. The women in these movements anticipated the freeing of women from the pressure of large families and the resulting poor economic conditions. Shizue Ishimoto (Katō) was a feminist primarily concerned with making contraception available to women, but she also worked very hard for women's suffrage through the Fusen Kakutoku Dōmei (Federation to Secure Women's Suffrage). Government censorship was light until 1934. Through lectures and publications, Ishimoto attempted to educate men and women on birth control. As military activity increased in Manchuria, the government began to stress the country's needs for workers and soldiers; the birth control movement was one threat to these new government policies. Activists in the birth control movement, the feminist movement and other liberal groups were quickly suppressed. The cooperation between feminists and birth control advocates was different from the early American and British experiences of the suffragettes' hostility and indifference toward birth control.[2]

Women's suffrage was still an important goal for many women. Fusae Ichikawa formed the Fusen Kakutoku Dōmei (FKD) with that goal in mind. The Universal Manhood Suffrage Act was passed in 1925, but it did not extend suffrage to women as hoped. It did encourage the growth of socialist and communist political parties. The women's movement fragmented as disagreements arose over priorities. Women's auxiliaries were formed supporting the various proletarian parties. Schisms between parties were reflected in the women's auxiliaries; women's suffrage was not always as important as other social reforms. The communists and socialists felt that supporting suffrage was tantamount to accepting a capitalist society. In 1930, women's groups mounted a new campaign for suffrage and full civil rights, and it seemed possible that the legislation would be passed. The Lower House passed a women's civil rights bill, but the Upper House voted it down. The government (Cabinet and upper level administrators) took a positive stand on the legislation specifying that the age for attaining full civil rights be raised to twenty-five (it was twenty for men) and that a husband's permission be required to stand for office or to take public office. Even this limited bill failed to pass the Upper House. The assassination of Prime Minister Inukai, who had promised to support women's issues, and the increasing power of the militarists brought an end to the possibilities for such legislation.[3] The ultranationalist and authoritarian political system forced women's organizations to take a low profile on these politically sensitive issues. Their activities focused on improvement of working conditions and legislation protecting mothers and children. Radical women like Shizue Ishimoto (Katō) were arrested and their organizations dissolved, ending the women's suffrage and birth control movements until after World War II.

After the war, many government officials still opposed the extension of suffrage and civil rights to women. Fusae Ichikawa did not find Prime Minister Higashikuni receptive to the idea, but Ichirō Hatoyama, president of *Jiyūtō* (Liberal Party), accepted the idea. After he promised to include it in the Liberal Party platform, directives were received from the Occupation Forces that women's suffrage would be required in the new political system.[4] The Diet passed a women's suffrage bill in 1946, and 67 percent of the women eligible to vote participated in the general election for the House of Representatives.[5] Thirty-nine women were elected to this lower house, as women exercised the rights they had long aspired to. The Councils that were set up to revise the Civil and Criminal Codes and to draft the Constitution included women Diet members. Shizue Ishimoto (Katō), as a member of the Diet and the latter Council, was able to work on women's legislation while Fusae Ichikawa was purged for activities during the war. In spite of popular appeals, she was depurged only in 1950; she stood for election to the House of Councilors and has been active ever since. She has worked for many issues including those important to women and those fighting political corruption.

According to a survey by the Prime Minister's office, women's general political interest is lower than men's. (Table I). However, the

Table I

Question: To what extent are you interested in politics?

	Percentage of Women	Percentage of Men
Very interested	3	11
Considerably interested	13	32
Somewhat interested	54	44
Almost no interest	28	12
Do not know	2	1

Source: *The Status of Women in Modern Japan,* Ministry of Foreign Affairs, Japan, 1975, p. 29.

percentage of women voting relative to the men voting has been increasing since 1946 when 10 percent more men than women voted. In 1974, 1.5 percent more women than men voted.[6] This increase in the women's percentage of the total vote has not contributed to an increase in the number of women elected to the more important House of Representatives. Although there were thirty-nine women originally elected to the House of Representatives, there were only fifteen women elected one year later. In 1972, only seven women were elected to the lower house. The House of Councilors indicates a different trend; in 1974, eighteen women were elected to this House, the second highest number of women so elected.[7] The House of Councilors' political power is less than that of the House of Representatives and its membership is drawn from less political sources, such as sports and entertainment personalities. In Japan, as in the United States, women do not vote as a bloc for women candidates. Political parties are very important in Japan, and party policy, the candidate's personality, and mass media appeal are important determinants of voting behavior. These are some of the factors which prevent women from emphasizing women's issues in their campaigns.

WOMEN'S POSITION IN CONTEMPORARY POLITICS

Twelve women were interviewed for this chapter. They included women Diet members, women in central and local administrative jobs, and women in the judiciary. Their descriptions of their jobs, their colleagues and their working conditions are contained in the following section. Their perspectives provide an understanding of the environment surrounding the statistical data on women in the political system.

Women candidates for national offices face a variety of disadvantages. Large amounts of money are required, much of which comes from business sources. These sources are unlikely to contribute to women because they are poor political risks. The parties themselves do not provide much financial support for their candidates, with the exception of the Japan Communist Party, which handles the financing for all of its candidates. The party factions have more access to funding and organization and are more viable political units. The responsibility for funding and organization lies with the candidate, who must seek party and faction support as well as constituent support. Election regulations work against a new candidate by restricting his/her activities while allowing the incumbent to stay in contact with her/his constituency as part of his/her responsibility. Political parties have encouraged well-known women to run, but party financial support from other than the Japanese Communist Party is limited. Public visibility is a vital asset for women since they generally do not have a strong organization backing them. The difficulties in running for office apply to both men and women candidates, but being a woman compounds the problems. The need for public visibility has led to "talent candidates" who have obtained political seats in the House of Councilors by virtue of being nationally known as television or sports personalities. The women "talent candidates" contribute to a politically naive image of women Diet members. Fusae Ichikawa is an exceptionally independent Diet member; she runs as an independent candidate and stays strictly within the election regulations. This is extremely unusual in Japan where election finance laws are generally circumvented and most independent candidates, if they do win, join the majority Liberal Democratic Party. These generalizations about women candidates do not apply to all women equally, but they illustrate some of the difficulties that face women running for public office.

Although women's representation in local government remains small, the activities of local government affect women more directly than the central government. According to some women interviewed, the Tokyo metropolitan government discriminates less against women than the central or other local governments. Local governments outside of Tokyo tend to pay special attention to promotions for women. A promotion for a woman must be discussed in special sessions, and she must be consulted as to whether or not she is interested in a promotion. A man is assumed to be interested, but a woman is not. According to a survey done by one woman, many women in local government are afraid of the increased responsibility that accompanies a promotion, and they lack the self-confidence to undertake the job. This woman feels that it is as important that women realize that they are capable of management-level work as it is necessary to provide them with opportunities to fill these positions.

Women have access to political influence through women's organizations and consumer groups. These associations tend to be oriented toward specific goals and loosely organized. *Shufuren*, a federation of local housewives' associations, coordinates national pressure tactics such as boycotts and demonstrations to attain their goals. *Chifuren*, another national organization of local associations, pressured the Ministry of International Trade and Industry and the Fair Trade Commission to exert more control over color television retail practices. These organizations wield a large bloc of voting power, and politicians are aware of this. The membership of these organizations is mainly housewives, since men and working women do not have the time to spend on such activities. These organizations have forced local governments to restrict amusement areas and to reassess priorities for providing social services. These organizations are oriented toward issues relevant to housewives, such as consumer problems and political corruption.

Women were appointed to the administrative positions during the Occupation, and the Women's and Minors' Bureau of the Labor Ministry was created to deal with the improvement of the status of women. Although most of the first women appointments were in this Bureau, several other women were appointed to other

ministries, including Miss Tsuroyo Kondo, who was appointed parliamentary secretary in the Foreign Office. Although the Constitution guarantees women equal employment opportunities, women
in the administration remain concentrated in the Women's and
Minors' Bureau. Opportunities to advance have been greater here
than in other ministries. A group of women in important ministry positions have asked Prime Minister Miki to see that more wom-
en are appointed to and promoted in the ministries. In the fall of
1975, a traditional time of appointments and promotions, they
were to meet with him again to emphasize the necessity of such
appointments in recognition of International Women's Year. Women
holding management-level civil servant positions dropped from 1.1
percent in 1960 to 1.0 percent in 1970 of the employees in such
positions. This is a small drop, but in a time when increased participation by women is a goal, such a drop indicates a resistance
to change.

After graduating from a university, it is necessary to pass a government examination to obtain employment in a ministry. There are
three levels of examinations, and each level determines what type
of work one will do and what the upper limits of employment
are. Passage of the highest examination is necessary to obtain a
management-level position. Women are now allowed to take these
examinations, but the women interviewed felt that the major problems occur before the examination is taken. Families frequently
do not encourage daughters to try for top-level positions; universities also are instrumental in discouraging women who are interested in such careers. A professional career is not considered con-
ducive to marriage, and marriage is expected to take priority. After the examination is passed, the applicant must apply to a ministry which will usually administer an oral interview or examination. According to the women interviewed, Tokyo University graduates have an advantage as do men. Once in a ministry, a woman
advances slower than her male counterpart; there are conspicuous
exceptions where women have acquired better promotions than
their male colleagues. According to a male colleague of a woman
interviewed, this proves that women in government receive special
privileges because of their sex instead of being discriminated against.
Neither women nor men change ministries, and a successful career
depends on moving up through the ministry that one has entered.
Unofficial discrimination includes poor promotion opportunities,
discrimination in hiring those who pass the examinations, and upon
retirement, assisting men, but not women, in obtaining consulting
or business management positions. Women are working to change
these inequities, but the general situation changes slowly.

The judiciary has a higher percentage of professional women than
the Diet or the administration. Of the 12,490 judges, prosecutors,
and lawyers, 300 are women (about 2.4 percent).[8] The system of

promotions and assignments is more regularized and less discriminatory according to the women in the judiciary who were interviewed.
A student must pass the National Law Examination and attend the
Legal Training and Research Institute before taking the final qualifying examination. Upon passing it, she/he may be appointed as
an assistant judge, and after ten years, as a full judge. Seniority is
important in all Japanese promotions, and the judiciary is no exception. Supreme Court judges are appointed by the Cabinet, and lower court judges are appointed by the Cabinet from a list drawn up
by the Supreme Court. Women have not been in the system long
enough to attain Supreme Court positions, but opportunities for
women are increasing.

The Japanese Court system (Figure 1) differs from the United
States system in its use of a family court system. Family Courts

Figure 1. Japanese Court system

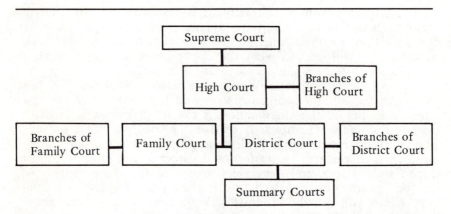

are responsible for family-related actions, including juvenile crime,
adoption, child abuse, divorce, and inheritance. Family Courts
operate differently from the other courts in Japan, in that they
emphasize conciliation of the two (or more) parties rather than a
decision for one of them. Mediators, who are not members of
the legal profession, research the cases and make recommendations
based on the particulars of the individual cases. The emphasis is
on what is best for the individuals, not on what law applies. Decisions are binding, although they can be appealed to the High
Court. According to some of the women interviewed, the Family
Courts represent a system apart from the ordinary civil and criminal system. Women are more often found in the Family Courts
both as judges and as mediators (35 percent of the family court
mediators are women).9 The Family Court decisions relate directly to women and their positions in the family as supported by law,
requiring women's opinions and understanding. It is analogous to
the Women's and Minors' Bureau of the Labor Ministry because

women's promotions and opportunities within the Family Court are better than in the main system. In spite of the difficulties in obtaining higher appointments, the women in the judiciary feel it is more merit-oriented than the bureaucracy.

It is difficult to describe adequately the situations that women face in political and government positions. The range of experiences is too wide and the number of women too small to claim any general validity for the above descriptions of the three branches of government service. A sample of twelve interviews and limited readings cannot provide statistical data; the value of the study is in its descriptions drawn from the experiences of specific women's lives. Until more research can be done and more works are published, this can serve as one indicator of the situation.

Women who are interested in political power and influence face a variety of obstacles, but, if their interest and desire is strong enough, there are some positions available for well-qualified women. An equally qualified man will have an easier time and better promotion possibilities. After the initial acceptance of a number of women into government positions, the novelty has worn off, and public pressure to improve opportunities for women is not as great. After a period of adopting foreign customs and ideas, Japan has traditionally adapted them to make such customs and ideas compatible with Japanese culture. The surge of women into new positions has been controlled by concentrating women in fields that are compatible with the traditional Japanese ideal of womanhood. Women's position will change as individual women work their way into high positions and use their power to help other women. Most women interviewed are very concerned with women's issues and in improving the conditions for women in general. As young women respond to these female role models, and men become more accustomed to working with women, there will be more opportunities available for them.

The women interviewed were finding satisfaction in their careers in the "establishment," and other women participate in the political system through consumers' groups and voting, but some women have chosen to challenge the conventional political system. Members of the *Sekigun* (Red Army) are dedicated to radical social and political change, one aspect of which is women's equality in all areas of life. Fusako Shigenobu, one such woman, was involved in the plotting of the Tel Aviv terrorist attack in May 1972. Hiroko Nagata, another member, confessed to murdering fourteen comrades in an intrafactional dispute. These women have been unwilling to work through the established political system to accomplish their goals. As women involved in politics outside of the political system, they give an added perspective to the women interviewed.

A BIOGRAPHY

This biography is a drawing together of experiences of the twelve women interviewed. The interviews were concentrated in the management-level government positions; women who had chosen political activity as a career. They included women judges, Diet members, women in several ministries, and women in political parties. The more significant elements were extracted from the interview notes and woven together to create the following biography. Kyoko Taneda is a fictional name of an imaginary person, but her experiences are taken from the women interviewed. She chose a career in the administration, a political position which is not at the whim of the voters and differs from the professional specialization of judicial positions.

I was born in 1925 in Yokohama. My family was well off and my childhood was very comfortable. My father was a university graduate in engineering and went into business. He traveled overseas on business and lived in the United States for several years. My mother accompanied him many times on trips and lived with him in the United States. She had a junior college *(jogakkō)* education which was the highest level that a woman could attain at that time. My mother spent some of her school years with an uncle who ran a small Christian school. There she was exposed to progressive ideas, and she developed a sense of independence and interest in western customs. My parents' marriage was arranged; my father took my mother's family name and moved in with her family in order to preserve her family name. After my father and mother were married, they proved too independent for my grandparents, so they moved to Yokohama to start a new family. They were quick to adopt liberal, western ways while living abroad. I never remember seeing my mother in a kimono even when we were in Japan.

My family was not very traditional so I never felt trapped by the Japanese family system. My older sister was born in the United States, and my brother and I were born in Japan. My mother returned to Japan without my father because she wanted to raise her children in Japan. We were exposed to many western visitors and as a child I enjoyed having many people in our house. My parents believed that a woman should be educated and independent. My father always told my sister and I that we must be independent when we grew up. He felt that a woman must be able to support herself so she would not need to depend on her husband. This was the most important advice given to me on marriage. My mother agreed with my father, but she did not hold as strong opinions as he did. She supported me in what I decided to do, but it was my father's encouragement that convinced me to pursue a career. My mother

disliked housework and preferred to entertain guests. She did not
enjoy the traditional women's arts of ikebana, *chanoyu,* and so on.
I received only minimal training in the necessary household arts of
sewing, cooking, and cleaning.

Although my older sister was also encouraged to develop a career, after graduating from Tsuda College with a degree in English, she married. She taught English for three years and then decided that she
wanted to stay at home and take care of her husband, child, and
house. She never really used her education. My sister's example was
a constant reminder to me that I must work hard to pursue a career.
I did not want to end up like her. I had a younger brother who was
not treated much differently from my sister and me. We were all expected to assist my mother around the house. My father emphasized
the importance of a career for all of us, not just my brother. I don't
know if my brother retained my parents' liberal ideas. He did marry
and has two children. I don't think he helps around the house very
much. I never learned flower arranging or tea ceremony, but I did
take piano lessons for a while. I know I grew up in an unusual
family; the Japanese family system broke down very early in my
family.

When I was in high school, I read about the first woman law graduate
of Meiji University. I was very impressed that a woman had entered
that university in such an important field. Her example inspired me
to pursue a career in government. I passed the examinations for
Tokyo University and graduated in law. My brother and I had very
similar educational experiences, so I didn't feel he was better than I.
I would have liked to do some graduate work in the United States,
but I do not think I will have the time. My parents supported my
decisions about my career, and they were very excited about my acceptance into Tokyo University.

I became involved in women's issues while I was at Tokyo University,
and I wrote several articles on women's rights under the new government. Some of the women who had been appointed to the Women's
and Minors' Bureau encouraged me to seek a position in the Bureau.
The system was more open during the Occupation and I joined the
ministry, then took the new examinations which would determine
what my prospects were. I passed the highest examination and could
look forward to a good career within the bureau. Women receive
many promotions within the bureau, but it is more difficult to be
appointed to a high position outside it. The activity of rebuilding
Japan immediately after the war dissolved many of the barriers for
educated women. Skilled, educated people were needed regardless
of sex. Women were seen as individuals capable of making contributions. The bureaucrats seemed less afraid of taking risks; it was an
active period of change. Now the bureaucracy seems very slow and
people are afraid to upset things; they are very security-minded. It

was an exciting time to begin work. I accepted the job because I had an opportunity to have a fulfilling personal life while contributing to the changes that were occurring in Japan. After experiencing Japan before the war, I wanted to improve the situation of women in Japan. I see my career as very meaningful and important for social change, not just personal fulfillment.

The higher ministry positions are very political. Government policy is frequently created within the bureaucracy. My job often requires the preparation and promotion of legislation created by the Women's and Minors' Bureau. I work with men and women in the Diet promoting passage of the legislation. It is difficult to draw the women of the Diet together to support some legislation on women's issues. A woman's position in the party is more precarious than a man's and party loyalty is expected. Party support of legislation is necessary before a woman Diet member will support the legislation. There is a caucus of women Diet members which contributes to communication on women's issues. They are very concerned with women's issues, but some of them feel that party policy must come first.

I enjoy my work very much and am satisfied with what I am doing. In addition to working for the ministry, I write books and articles about women. I am especially interested in women workers and have written several articles on them and the problems they face. Writing and ministry work keep me very busy, and I am satisfied with the level in government that I have reached. There is a need for more women in high ministry positions, but women receive promotions only if they demand them. The higher a woman climbs in a ministry, the easier it will be for those who come after her; it is important for society to become accustomed to women in high positions. For these reasons, I cannot talk as if I am satisfied; I must pressure my superiors for promotions and better positions. Older women in the government must set examples for the younger women in lower positions and those considering a government career. Although I chose an administrative career, I feel it is more important for women to learn skills which lead to professional careers rather than administrative careers. I receive both social and personal satisfaction from my job, and I hope to continue to rise in the ministry. I must retire in several years and will then devote my time to working on women's problems. I will probably write more and work more with women's organizations. I cannot imagine staying home and waiting for my grandchildren. I guess I will never really stop working and stay at home.

Since I work for the government, my working conditions are the same as a man's. We receive the same fringe benefits and work the same hours. I usually eat lunch with my colleagues, both men and women, and occasionally after work, we have dinner and drinks together. Both men and women in administrative positions must occasionally work through lunch and late into the night. There is unofficial discrimination toward women, but it is not as overt as in companies where women must pour tea and clean the men's desks. Discrimination in promotion policy is difficult to record objectively; promotions are based on many factors. Those employees from poorer schools do not receive promotions like those from Tokyo University. In the same way, women do not receive promotions like men. I think of this as a working condition that must be accepted. When a man retires, the ministry assists him in obtaining other employment as a consultant or in business. He may run for office on the basis of his experience in policy making. There is no assistance given retiring women who, at age 56, may still be very interested in working. One problem I personally faced was, while men colleagues worked well with me, they refused to accompany me outside the country to conferences and meetings. This was socially unacceptable to them, but it did not disturb me. It points up the adjustments that men must make when working with women.

I don't feel that I have been a victim of severe discrimination. I feel that being a woman has had both advantages and disadvantages. Some men treat me poorly because I am a woman, but I have received help from others because I was a woman and they were impressed with the work that I was doing. I see discrimination as something that women as a group face, more than something I have personally faced. The advantages and disadvantages of my being a woman have cancelled each other out. My colleagues accept me as an equal; they do not talk down to me. I am treated as one of them. One colleague characterized me as a neutral being, neither male nor female, which I took as a compliment because I was accepted as a person. I do not use men's language, but professional career women use a shorter, more direct language than that commonly used by housewives. Professional women's language uses fewer extra syllables and is less lyrical than housewives' language. I have never felt that using women's language was degrading; it would just be impolite to use men's language.

My husband and I met when we were students at Tokyo University; he is only one year older than I am. He is now a professor and teaches economics. I was attracted by his liberal ideas and his understanding of my pursuit of a career. My parents did not pressure me to marry, but, since he was willing to accept my career, we married. When we were first married, we had a maid and we did not need to worry about housework. We live alone now and do not have a maid. Since my husband did not like having live-in help, we decided to renovate our house to minimize the time and effort required by housework. We bought modern convenience appliances which reduced the amount of time required for housekeeping. Neither of us likes housework, so we divided the necessary chores and allocated certain ones to each of us. My husband is responsible for cleaning and decorating the house. I am responsible for cooking, laundry, and the dishwashing. We have a washer, dryer, dishwasher, and a modern stove with an oven. We share the responsibility for major financial decisions. Each of us takes care of our own daily expenses out of our own money. My husband was willing to take responsibility for part of the housekeeping because he thought my work was very important for society and for my own personal satisfaction. He understands the social importance of my work. Although my husband is very tolerant and helpful, I think he is more conservative than I am; there are times he resents the inconvenience of my career. He is a liberal thinker, but he is accustomed to a conservative life style.

We get up together in the mornings and leave for work at the same time. We both drive about an hour to work. Frequently one or both of us will meet with colleagues for dinner, arriving home late in the evening. I usually read until I go to bed. I have not had a real vacation in many years. Both my husband and I have traveled abroad, but we have never been able to travel together. When I have been abroad, he has had to remain in Japan, and when he studied abroad for a year, my work kept me here. We were able to meet only once for a few days in the United States. Since we are both very busy, we cannot take many vacations together. Occasionally, we go to the hot springs together to relax. We both have many friends among our colleagues, and since these social circles do not overlap, we frequently go out separately. We rarely socialize together, unless it is with relatives. Neither of us brings colleagues home. Our home is for our private lives; my husband likes to relax at home and visitors would be an intrusion. There are times when we do not see much of each other because our jobs are very demanding and time-consuming. We do not discuss politics together because if we argue, it becomes too personal and causes us much pain. My husband and son argue some together, but I do not take part. My husband speaks about his work sometimes, but not often. We have found that it is better for us not to discuss politics or work together. I think our marriage is a very good marriage.

We have two children, a boy and a girl. My mother-in-law lived with us and helped take care of the children when they were young. My husband took responsibility for disciplining them; he came from a very strict family and was therefore very strict with our children. We tried to raise them equally. We wanted both of them to get a good education, so we sent them to good private schools. I never helped them with their homework; I assumed that the school was responsible for teaching them. I tried to raise them to be self-sufficient. Both of them are able to cook, mend, clean house, and generally take care of themselves. I think it is important for men to learn these things, so they are less dependent on women to house and feed them. Men need to be independent in the home while women need

to be financially independent and free to have a career. My son is
married and has one child. My daughter has graduated from university and is now working as a teacher at a junior college. I hope that
she will continue to work after she marries. It will be difficult for
her to continue to work after she has children, and it is difficult and
expensive to put the children in nurseries or to hire someone to look
after them. She may have a mother-in-law to help her, but I know
that I will not be able to live with her because I have a career of my
own. Many women of my age had mothers or relatives to help them
with their children, but now couples live alone, making it more difficult for a woman to have a career. Japan needs more daycare facilities to allow women to work; women have much to contribute to
Japan. I think there is a need to change the traditional family roles.
A couple should rationally discuss what is the best way for them to
raise a family; society should not determine how they are to live.
The family is still very important to society and the raising of children is important to society, not just to the mothers and families.
Society should take some of the responsibility through daycare and
childbirth leave for mothers. Everyone, not just mothers, is responsible for Japan's children.

I do not have much spare time for hobbies or recreation activities.
I read the journals relevant to my field and an occasional detective
novel for fun. I try to keep in touch with the women's magazines
so I know what is being read by Japanese women. I look for articles on women's problems in these magazines. I do not belong to
many women's organizations, since I have so little free time. I do
participate in the Tokyo University Women's Alumnae organization
which is not limited to career women. Some are housewives who
have organized women in the P.T.A. and other organizations to increase their awareness of their roles as women. It is a group of very
active women. I keep in touch with other women's groups through
informal meetings with friends who do belong. My informal contacts with women are more important than formal membership in
any particular group. I am on the mailing list for several groups
and keep in contact with their activities through their publications.
I have very little time for my family after working and my "free
time" activities.

I would like to comment briefly on the family system in Japan. I
believe that boys and girls should be raised in the same way, and
that it should be made clear to them that men and women are equal,
men are not better than women. When children grow up, they want
to live away from the family, but it is very expensive. It isn't necessary for a young man or woman to live with their families, but it
is usually the only practical solution. Dating is a good way for
young men and women to get to know each other, but I do not
think that premarital sex is a good idea. There should be limits to
dating to prevent this. The *omiai* (traditional, formal introduction

of a man and a woman to see if they would be interested in marriage) is still a valuable way to find a marriage partner. It helps young people meet more possible spouses. Often young people go to work immediately after they finish school and they do not know many people outside their working place. This is why many people marry within the company they work for. It can be very difficult if a husband and wife work for the same company, so usually the wife has to quit. This discriminates against the woman, but her husband's job is normally more important than hers. I think a husband and wife should be able to work for the same company, but some arrangements should be made so that they do not work together very much.

Men should become more involved in their families. They should help around the house and take a larger role in the raising of children. It would help both men and women if the working hours were shorter; Japanese business requires too much from employees and does not allow them to have a good family life. With shorter hours, women would find it easier to have children and work outside the home. It would be better for men also to spend more time with their families. I understand that some American families want the husband to stay at home and the wife to work. I find this very hard to understand, perhaps because I would not want to stay at home. I do not see this happening in Japan.

I think the biological differences of men and women must be recognized. Women are the only ones to bear children and this function must be protected. However, women's contributions to society should not be limited to the bearing and raising of children. They have much to contribute with their skills in various jobs to society and the economy. A successful woman is one who makes a decision about what she wants to do and then does it to the best of her ability. This means that she can be a successful wife and mother, that she can be a successful professional woman, that she can be a successful hair stylist or secretary. It is important for her to have the choice; her success is measured by how well she does what she chooses to do. Unfortunately many young women do not make decisions, they just take the easiest path. Women should not have to marry, but I think they may be very lonely when they get old. I do not think there is any ideal life for a woman; no one life is good for all women.

If women's position in Japan is going to change, women must also change. Women must be raised differently. They must prepare themselves to make a decision about what they want, to work, to have a career, to have a family. Legislation cannot improve women's position if they are not prepared to take advantage of the new opportunities. Discouragement of women begins in the elementary school and in the family. Here is where much work is needed; some of the Tokyo University alumnae are working on textbook revision, trying to change the image of women in textbooks. Women must develop the necessary skills to take advantage of the opening job market. The companies and government also must recognize that women have valuable skills to contribute and they will lose if women do not work after marriage or childbirth. The government should help women who want to work and have a family. Legislation has been passed so that teachers, nurses, and government employees will have one year's leave after childbirth, and they are assured of their reinstatement at the level they were at before they took leave. This leave gives women a choice; it should not be considered mandatory. More daycare nurseries are needed to care for children from a very young age so that a woman does not have to miss the whole year, if she does not want to. The government should protect the social unit of the family without confining women to a family role. It is important that both men and women have choices in their family and personal lives as well as their economic lives. These ideas were based on giving women more choices, but as I think about it, I realize that many women now feel they must work for economic reasons, which is another reason why the government must provide daycare and legislation protecting women's jobs.

CONCLUSION

The women interviewed were over fifty with one exception; the young woman differed from the older ones in many respects, so she is treated separately. Marital status is very important in Japan, but it did not seem an important factor in the women interviewed. The young woman, who was twenty-two, and an older woman who was fifty-two, are the only single women interviewed. One woman has been divorced and remarried, and another has been a widow for twenty years. The eight remaining women are married and living with their husbands. An internal comparison of these women did not reveal any determining factors which would account for the differences between them. It is more valuable to compare them as a group with other Japanese women.

The young woman interviewed, Miss Satō (not her real name) works for a government agency and lives with her parents. She graduated from Sophia University and faces the problem that many Japanese young women face: she wants a career, but she also wants to marry. Miss Satō would like to stay at home with her children when they are young, which would make it difficult to pursue a career. She is more socially conservative than the older women. She feels it is natural for women to serve tea to men at work; she doesn't mind it because it breaks up her daily work routine. Miss Satō believes that women should have equal opportunities to work and should receive equal pay, but she is not a strong advocate of social change. She feels that men should help more around the house, but she doesn't think her husband will nor that there is much hope for Japanese men adopting this behavior pattern. She has not given much thought to women's issues. There is a vague sense of discrimination against women, but it is not focussed on specific problems, and they do not seem to relate to her personally. Like the older women, Miss Satō feels that contraception should be more available, and she personally would like to see abortions limited. She has little opportunity for promotion but she does not seem to blame the system for this nor see it as a result of her being a woman. The older women are concerned with this uninvolved attitude. The lack of willingness to press for women's rights and the inability to identify discrimination is one of the biggest obstacles that must be overcome, according to some of the older women interviewed.

Certain attributes are held in common by the older women. They generally dislike housework and they do not spend much time on it. Either their husbands help, they have maid service, or they have enough modern appliances to minimize the work required. They consider their careers more important than housework. For similar reasons, they are not especially interested in the traditional Japanese women's arts such as tea ceremony and flower arranging. Several of the women received training in these arts at school, but none of them are caught up in these "leisure time" activities. These women spend much time at their jobs; their families take up what little time they have left. Vacations and recreation are not a part of their lives. Several play golf, and one woman enjoys the hot mineral baths as a way of relaxing. However, they do not spend much time on these activities. All of them have traveled outside of Japan. Two women spent time studying in the United States. Most of their travel is done in connection with their jobs; it is not for recreation. Being married does not seem to inhibit their opportunities or their willingness to travel.

The family structure is still a strong part of their image of women. They feel it is important for women to combine roles as mother/wife/working woman. The working women's welfare law, passed in 1972, aimed at "furthering the welfare and improving the status of working women by taking appropriate actions to help them combine their dual responsibilities of work and home, and to enable them to develop and make best use of their abilities."[10] This typifies the attitude of the women interviewed, including the single women. The emphasis was on choice and, while marriage was not seen as necessary for the ideal woman, they expected it to be a part of most women's lives. The emphasis is on better daycare and working conditions to enable women to do both, as opposed to United States trends for some women to support their husbands and children, or for alternative life styles such as single parents or communal living. One woman did mention that socialization of housekeeping would make women's lives better, but it was difficult to understand the implications of such socialization. The family is still the center of these women's expectations, and they want to improve women's positions within the social structure that Japan has now.

These women who were taking an active part in the promoting of political and social change were concerned over the young women who will succeed them. Most of the women felt that the young women were not active enough nor demanding their rights from the government. Inability to make decisions and follow them through was cited as one problem. Others feel that young educated women want to take the easy way out and marry a man who will support them. They feel that few young women are willing to put in the time and effort required to pursue careers in the political system. One woman expressed a contrasting view. This older woman in the judiciary had been criticized by a young woman for not being radical enough or promoting enough change. She feels that she has worked very hard against many odds to attain her position and this included working hard for women. She feels that she does a service by providing a role model and breaking ground for other women. It would seem that the young social and political radicals are not working within the established political system and the women feel there are not enough women willing to work for change within the "establishment."

The married women seem to have understanding husbands, a prerequisite for a career woman. Some seem stronger proponents of change within the family structure than the others. The more conservative husbands support their wives' careers and change within the family system, but they have trouble living with that change. They might prefer that their wives stay home, but they would never force this issue. They prefer not to have guests at home because that is their private domain. These conservative husbands adapt to a nontraditional way of life for their wives, but they do not always see it as a new and better home life. The more radical of the husbands are enthusiastic about this change in family life and see it as a change that society should make.

The more politically radical women are in the minority parties, but they are neither more nor less radical in terms of social and family change. Everyone feels that men should help working wives with the household tasks: some said it would be nice if they helped, one woman insisted that her husband help, another woman feels that household chores should be determined by mutual discussion. Daycare is seen as a viable alternative to staying at home to raise children, and one woman pointed out that children might do better at a good daycare center than they would alone with their mother. Only the young woman feels that a mother might want to stop working to stay home with her children. An older woman with children of her own said that women should not stop work when they have children because they will not be able to pursue their work, and it is important for women to keep their skills polished and not let them deteriorate while raising children.

Availability of contraception is closely tied with their opinions of abortion and infanticide. The problem is considered a social problem by all but two women. Only these two women favor a liberal abortion policy which would provide women with a choice that is safe and inexpensive; they emphasize the individual nature of abortion rather than the social. The other women favor better contraception and less abortion because abortion is only a small step from infanticide. They feel that contraception is not an acceptable topic of conversation to many Japanese women and so these women remain ignorant about it. One woman pointed out that some of the vaginal deodorant spray advertisements hint that they have contraceptive value. All of the women feel that Japan is deficient in promoting contraceptive knowledge and availability. One woman explained that the government is liable for any drug it permits if the drug later causes bad side effects (like thalidomide); therefore the pill is not generally available. She also admitted that the government is concerned about the moral effect of pill availability. The consensus was that pills should be made available, but several women did express concern over the possible side effects. The women favoring limited abortions feel that it is not a good alternative. One woman said that it shows a lack of respect for life, and her politics are founded on respect for life. Abortion is a better alternative than infanticide. Four women specified infanticide as a problem resulting from the lack of contraceptive knowledge and alternatives. One woman who supported a more liberal abortion policy pointed out that the law is written as the Eugenic Protection Law, which is not concerned with the protection of mothers, but with the alleviation of population pressure and the number of handicapped children. She feels that the law should be rewritten with an emphasis on the availability of abortion for all women safely without reference to eugenic protection and population control. She feels abortion is a right that women should have. While abortion is not an overtly controversial topic, many of the women were conservative in their approach and qualified their approval of abortion, emphasizing the lack of contraceptive knowledge and practices.

Two factors which seemed relevant to these women's careers were their exposure to western influence in their family and their father's encouragement of their career. These women were exposed to western/foreign influence as children. Their family had adopted many western ideas and customs. One nontraditional custom was the encouragement these women received to educate themselves and become self-sufficient. The father's encouragement was important; he influenced the family more than the mother. One woman pointed out that her mother encouraged her school work so that she would get into a good high school, hoping that this would help her get a good husband. However, her father encouraged her to go on and get a good university education. Her father, and later her husband, constantly encouraged her career decisions, but her mother never understood why she was so interested in working instead of being a wife and mother. Some mothers were more understanding, but none of them played as important a role as the father did. The widow interviewed was forced to find work to support her mother and children after her father and husband died. Her father had encouraged her education, although not a working career, and she was able to find work with a local government and made it her career. The fathers of these women were strong figures while the mothers played a supportive role to his dominant one.

These women became motivated early to follow careers and those in the administration and judiciary have been working at this since they graduated from university. Several of the women in the Diet entered upon request by the political party they were involved with. Education policy was a motivating factor for two of them. They were not as actively trying to alter or improve the position of women; that seems to have come after they were elected. Women's issues were important to all of the women interviewed, but they were not of primary importance.

These women are conservative in their estimate of the discrimination they have personally faced. They see discrimination against women, but not against themselves. This may be why they do not seem bitter or angry toward men. Although admitting that they have faced problems, being a woman in a man's world, they play that aspect down and emphasize what they have accomplished for themselves and other women. It has probably been necessary for women in the government to come to terms with their personal ambitions and a system in which they could not succeed if they took a militant, radical stance.

NOTES

[1] Dee Ann Vavich, "The Japanese Woman's Movement," pp. 411-412.

[2] Margi Haas, "The First Birth Control Movement in Japan, 1902-1937."

[3] Emma Nyun-Han, "The Socio-Political Roles of Women in Japan and Burma," p. 438.

[4] *Ibid.*, p. 437.

[5] Women's and Minors' Bureau, *The Status of Women in Japan*, 1974, p. 2.

[6] Women's and Minors' Bureau, *The Status of Women in Japan*, 1974, pp. 2-3.

[7] *Ibid.*, pp. 2-3.

[8] Women's and Minors' Bureau, *Women Workers in Japan*, 1975, p. 13.

[9] *Japan Report*, Vol. 20, No. 16, August 16, 1974.

[10] Women's and Minors' Bureau, *About the Women's and Minors' Bureau*, 1973, p. 2.

CHAPTER 12
WOMEN IN SPORTS

The image of the Japanese woman that most Westerners, especially men, have is that of the childish, confiding, sweet girl—quiet, unobtrusive, ladylike, feminine, pleasing, all those adjectives that stereotype the Japanese female. There is a historical basis for this image. According to "The Greater Learning for Women" by the Japanese moralist Kaibara the only qualities that befit a woman are gentle obedience, chastity, mercy, and quietness. "The great life-long duty of a woman is obedience. In her dealings with her husband, both the expression of her countenance and the style of her address should be courteous, humble, and conciliatory," wrote the celebrated man. "Without her husband's permission, she must go nowhere." These attitudes about women's behavior stem from a strong Confucian tradition and influenced the activities of middle- and upper-class Japanese women until World War II.

Before World War II the purpose of a woman's education was to get her ready for marriage: mathematics in order to handle the family budget; reading and writing for composing elegant letters. Learnedness would only spoil a girl's modesty, was the opinion of the educators. Physical education would, of course, produce only tomboys, so, except in a few progressive schools, such education declined as girls reached high school. A section from Sumie Mishima's book on growing up in Japan describes her school training in physical conduct:

> We received the most rigorous discipline in the class for social etiquette. We had an elderly lady teacher who was a perfect model for all girls in movement and speech. For this class, we sat on the mat floor in a large Japanese drawing room. . . . We learned how to walk properly without ever stepping on the joints of the mats even while holding a flower vase

or ceremonial tray in both hands to the height of one's chin; which foot to step on first when entering a room and which way to turn when retiring from the presence of a superior person; how to take up and put down the chopsticks at each mouthful and in what order to eat from the numerous dishes served at a Japanese dinner, and approximately how many grains of rice to eat at a mouthful—no more than thirty grains at a time.[1]

The Confucian influence was only later (seventeenth century) a strong one. From very early times, the tenth century onward, women of the warrior families (*buke*) were expected to ride and use weapons, partly for physical exercise but mainly for defense of the home when the men were away. Early Japanese society was not one in which the individual counted, and each member of a group had to contribute to the group's solidarity, protecting lands, revenues, and so on. The martial disciplines (sixty different weapons systems) developed as a way of life that has not much to do with the present practice of martial sports. In life-and-death situations (as warring feudal Japanese society was) there was no time to get up and do calisthenics, a common prelude to today's *kendō, judō,* and so on. Spiritual discipline was involved. One woke up and was ready in an instant to draw one's weapon and kill. From that time come the martial arts still practiced today as exclusively women's disciplines, like *naginata.* The *naginata* was a long spear with a curved blade which samurai women were taught to use.

The present-day practice of the martial arts can be distinguished from the older style by the suffix *dō* that is added to the name of the art; for instance, *kendō, judō, aikidō.* The old disciplines are referred to with *jitsu,* such as *kenjitsu, jujitsu, naginatajitsu.* Some descendants of the early warrior families continue to maintain the traditional disciplines that were part of *buke* culture, and in these families the discipline will be handed down from parent to child, regardless of sex. Some of the old families hold matches among themselves, not publicized of course, for those families have pride in their old ways that has nothing to do with the postwar material culture of Japan. Needless to say, the practice of the martial disciplines in this way is dying out, and is being replaced with martial arts whose emphasis is on aesthetic physical form and not on preserving life. Another difference is in the weapons used. The early *naginata* was a very heavy instrument, meant to deal a fatal blow; in contrast, the modern one is very light.

Women of the court aristocracy indulged in very little physical exercise, and from that social stratum arose the image of the fine and fair Japanese lady. Farm women were little better off than animals, and it is certain that none of the ideals of the *buke* or of the *kuge* (court nobles) affected their lives.

Since World War II Japanese society has changed considerably, although how deeply is yet to be assessed. Under the 1946 constitution, the position of women was "equalized," a radical change from the Confucian belief of men's place first, and women's second.

One of the big benefits of the postwar reforms was that Japanese women were given for the first time equal opportunity in education with men. The subjects followed in school are the same for both (except for the one requirement of home economics for girls), and likewise girls and boys receive equal amounts of physical education. Ministry of Education guidelines specify the same amount of time for boys and girls in calisthenics, gymnastics, track and field, swimming, and sports theory. One prejudice in the sports allotment is that no time is provided for girls for combat sports (*kendō, judō,* etc.), in contrast to 10 to 20 percent for boys; also, boys get no dancing, although the time for girls is 15 to 20 percent. In the country there are only 565 *judō* clubs for girls (105,000 for boys) and 2,000 *kendō* clubs (107,000 for boys). Yet, the popularity of the martial arts (under which fall the combat sports) is increasing among women (no such clubs before the war).

Besides the big educational changes that have given women more opportunities, Japan since World War II has joined the other advanced industrial nations of the world, and the conveniences of modern life have increased women's physical activity, in sports, physical recreation, and serious athletic competition, although women's participation is still far behind men's. A Japan Amateur Athletic Association (J.A.A.A.) survey shows a 56 percent "ignorance level" (i.e., nonparticipation in physical activity) among women, as compared with 25 percent for men. Sports clubs that come under the J.A.A.A. are those with high-level participation and capabilities. Of the members of these clubs over 1,600,000 are men, but only 116,860 women. Most of the women's participation is limited to belonging to what in Japanese is called *dōkōkai* (literally, "they like it together"), groups in companies or schools. The *dōkōkai* do not belong to the J.A.A.A., but are strictly for recreation, improving physical fitness, and fun. A survey by the education department of the University of Tokyo of women high school graduates showed bowling, calisthenics, volleyball, and badminton at the top of the list of favorite sports: all sports that can be played with friends with little outlay of money, time, or space.

Volleyball is the sport in which there is the most participation, with over 5,000,000 women playing. There are probably 300,000 girls' volleyball clubs in the secondary schools. The real impetus to the popularity of volleyball can be traced to the 1964 Tokyo Olympics, when the Japanese women's volleyball team won the gold medal in the final match against very strong Soviet players. Besides being an emotional moment for the nation, the feat of the women's team represented to Japanese women that they too could achieve something. The members of the team were employees of Hitachi, a big electrical company. Some were married and had children. Volleyball popularity reached such a height that Prime Minister Satō acted as go-between in the marriage of the volleyball team's captain.

The J.A.A.A. has been trying to encourage adult participation in sports, and one of its notable successes in this area is what is popularly known as *mamasan* (mothers') volleyball. The Mamasan Volleyball Association acts as a promotion agency in disseminating information about getting involved in volleyball and improving women's physical condition. Presently there are over 500,000 housewives across the nation participating in the sport. *Mamasan* teams practice once or twice a week and take part in tournaments from the local to the national level. The national tournament is held every year in Tokyo, with teams from each prefecture participating. One-year goals of a *mamasan* group include achieving correct posture, increasing physical strength, learning and perfecting techniques, and learning strategy. Volleyball is, of course, a group sport, and although the group orientation is open to criticism in many respects, there are beneficial aspects to group activities. For instance, in connection with achieving the above-mentioned one-year goals, a Mamasan Volleyball Association publication lays stress on helping the other members of the team; if one woman's serve is not good, everyone pitches in with help and suggestions for her. Also, the participation in volleyball pinpoints another Japanese belief in sports: everyone should participate. Sports are not just for champions. This kind of low-key approach encourages many women who simply do not feel secure about their physical capabilities. Also, because of the social structure of male-female relationships in Japan, housewives are one of the most isolated groups. Besides the important physical benefits of volleyball, women receive a much-needed social opportunity to meet other women.

One negative aspect of *mamasan* volleyball is that the encouragement for participation is strictly from the top; it is not a grass-roots movement of women. Most of the coaches are male. Only housewives are allowed to join, and it is a somewhat conservative way of dealing with the frustrations that housewives in Japan are experiencing. The head of the Mamasan Volleyball Association (a man) told me that his private opinion was that getting women out and involved in such an activity made them "happy"; thus, the husband will be happy, the family will learn good health habits, and so on. Letters in the association newsletter from volleyball players read like testimonials: one 50-year-old woman describes how unhappy she was before she started playing volleyball and how she has gained self-confidence since participating. Her younger friends envy her. The Mamasan office has posters on the wall portraying women in sweatsuits playing volleyball, with children amusing themselves happily in the background, usually in fields of flowers.

One plus in Japanese attitudes, however, is the lack of prejudice toward women's participation in sports. Thirty-five years ago physical activity on the part of well-brought-up girls was frowned upon. Women were trained to sit for hours, in the most uncomfortable of clothes, without moving. Artificial gestures—for instance, the coy covering of the mouth when smiling—were regarded as the most natural, and spontaneous physical activity after childhood was an aberration. The U.S. prejudice, that a physical education major is not quite feminine, if not downright abnormal, does not exist in Japan. The Japanese have been said to be easily adaptable to new ideas, and this seems to be one area where that saying is true.

What about the development of serious competitive athletics in Japan, the training of female athletes who fare well in international competitions? Japan has, of course, had some big stars, besides the well-known volleyball players. At the 1972 Olympics in Munich, Mayuki Aoki placed first in the 100-meter butterfly. In the Asian Games, Japanese athletes usually nab most of the medals. The swimmer Toshimi Nishigawa took home five gold ones from the seventh Asian Games held in Teheran. But her 100-meter freestyle of 1.01.63 is not the fastest in the world.

For female and male athletes alike the biggest problem is the lack of professional coaches. The J.A.A.A. licenses about twenty thousand coaches, but stipulates that in most cases coaches of amateur sports cannot be professionals. Thus, the coaches do not have the experience and training of their Western counterparts, despite their devotion, and as might be expected the best coaching is reserved for male athletes. Even Olympic coaches are volunteers, although there are very important prestige and social rewards, which are often every bit as important to Japanese as monetary remuneration. Many coaches are shop owners or salaried people who go to a local gym twice weekly and teach a swimming class or coach a volleyball team. In my visits to community gyms I observed that most of the coaches are men. I met one woman table tennis coach. However, every year the J.A.A.A. sponsors leadership-training seminars for women's sports groups. A kind of mini-physical education program is held for four days, and about one hundred women take part. The training is divided into theoretical and practical aspects. In the former is taught the role of sports in modern society, the physiological basis of physical fitness and how to keep fit, how to organize groups and the role of leadership, and how to utilize public facilities. The practical part emphasizes calisthenics for women and the family, and sports and recreational games. Perhaps from these sessions will come female coaches, although at the moment, as in most things in Japan, men take the lead and women follow.

Quite a few coaches and sports teachers have themselves been athletes. After their sports careers, they join physical education colleges or start their own sports clubs. One such person is Ginko Chiba, who was on the six-member women's gymnastics team that took a bronze medal at the 1964 Olympics. Now a professor at the Japanese College of Physical Education in Tokyo, Chiba is putting into practice the inspiration she received as a young girl from a physical education teacher. As she relates her story, Chiba tells how as a child she liked being active. The typical "tomboy," all sports excited her. An elementary-school teacher encouraged her to take up dancing. At twelve she got involved in gymnastics. Because of her admiration for her teacher, Chiba decided to go into physical education in college and participated in most sports. It was not until her third year of college, after many national competitions, that she decided to aim for the Olympics. Her mentor at that time was the famous Japanese woman gymnast, Keiko Ikeda. Thus, Chiba began international competition at a time when most Western athletes are giving up their sports careers and going into other professions. Chiba said that one of the things that impressed her about other athletes she met at the Olympics was how many of them were teachers, doctors, business people, and so on, but not people involved in sports as a career. Even professional athletes start their professional life late. Kazuko Sawamatsu, Japan's top woman tennis player and recent winner in the Wimbledon women's doubles, turned professional in 1974 at the age of twenty-three. Billie Jean King had already won the Wimbledon singles at nineteen. The J.A.A.A. is now trying to develop sports clubs along Western lines, which will spot talent early and develop it, but, at the moment, most sports participation takes place in the school or place of work.

There are private sports clubs in Japan with more or less professional coaches, yet the costs of joining (some as high as ¥3,000,000 in addition to monthly dues) keep the average person from taking part. The abundance of even unstaffed tennis courts as in the U.S. is unheard of in Japan, where the population is large (one hundred million) and the country small (about the size of California). Yet, professional women athletes of high caliber are coming along. The golfer Hisako Higuchi is one. Coached early by Pete Nakamura, she is now playing all over the world, earning over $50,000 a year. I caught Higuchi in her manager's office, downing a bowl of Japanese noodles, symbolic of the Japanese quick lunch and Higuchi's busy schedule. Sun-tanned and wonderfully healthy-looking, she had just returned from a two-month golf circuit in the United States and was to be off in a few hours to a tournament in Osaka. So far, the high point of her career was winning the 1975 Australian Women's Open. But, as Higuchi stressed, although she never felt any prejudice against herself as a woman athlete, she had no models, only the encouragement of an older sister who liked to play golf. No Japanese Margaret Court for a Japanese Evonne Goolagong Cawley to idolize and strive to emulate. Higuchi is herself now a model for Japanese women golfers, although she got to the top on her own, without the professional companionship of other women.

The rise of athletes like Higuchi is accompanied by pressures that American athletes are not likely to face. General sports participation and competition within Japan are fairly low-key. People are involved for fun and physical benefits. However, when a really hot item, so to speak, comes along, an incredible amount of effort is put into developing the athlete as fast as possible. One woman bowler in the early days of bowling popularity in Japan tried to commit suicide because of pressures on her. Her promoters held her to a rigorous training schedule in order to make a top bowler out of her and, in addition, forced her into sponsoring numerous products on television. The idea seems to be that the excellent athlete is really only good for a few years and thus should be exploited as much and as fast as possible. This may also be related to the phenomenal rise in popularity of certain sports followed within a few years by an equally phenomenal decline. During the bowling boom alleys were built everywhere in Japan; now, many have been vacated due to lack of participation in bowling.

The same kind of exploitation has taken place in connection with the Hitachi volleyball team. The coach, Hirofumi Daimatsu, was famous for his cruel, tyrannical, and severe training of the players. For instance, a tosser had only one day's leave from the team when her father died. Another was commanded to continue practice after a fractured rib was bandaged. In Asia, Japanese athletes are usually the best in most sports, and so there is not great competition for them. Beating Westerners is often very emotional for Japanese, a reaction that is often rather nationalistic. A leading Japanese woman writer, Sawako Ariyoshi, wrote in a newspaper at the time of the women's volleyball victory at the Tokyo Olympics: "They have striven for so many years just for the sake of this moment. The immense obligation they must have felt that they owed to the whole nation and their equally strong will that they would by all means win through the matches. . . . Thank you, Mr. Daimatsu!" Likewise, when Sawamatsu won at Wimbledon, Tokyo newspapers described her victory as the fulfillment of *her father's* lifetime ambition. The father was a former tennis player who had developed Sawamatsu's talent with a "strenuous training regimen since her primary school days." From the *buke* culture, through volleyball and now to tennis, accomplishments are never for oneself. One can only be glad that women are participating and that, with the gradual growth of awareness, women too will come to feel that their accomplishments are individual, are for themselves, even in group sports. The golfer Higuchi, for instance, displays none of the doing-it-for-Japan mentality. Significant, perhaps, is that Higuchi prefers the life style of the West.

Despite the obstacles, Japanese women are starting to join their Western counterparts in sports excellence and in being recognized for it. A not-uncommon sight on Japanese television is the broadcasting of a baseball game between two women's teams or the finals of the women's national bowling tournament—perhaps on a Sunday afternoon, just when millions of Americans are sitting down to watch their favorite male baseball or football team. Japanese women have come a long way in sports since a young girl named Kinue Hitomi became, in 1928, the first Japanese woman to go to the Olympics. Just a school girl, she snared a silver medal in the 800-meter track. One important aspect of sports is body development and a moving-away from the traditional postures and gestures of the Japanese woman. In sports, a woman learns to know about her body and what she can do with it. Still a lingering sight in Japan is what might be called the kimono walk. Young women in Western clothes often move as if they were wearing a kimono, which allows about a six-inch gait. It is caused by a state of mind produced by long-established attitudes about how a woman should move. One can admire the sports achievements of Western women, but one sees also that they are still battling with the problems of being liberated women. Japanese women have had to take on a lot in a very short time. One must always keep in mind the strength and determination they have demonstrated.

The first woman to ski in Japan, back in the early part of the century, was a geisha, in Takaba City. She went down the snowy slopes on two skis, but used only one pole, the other hand holding up the edges of her unwieldy clothes. Going up snowy slopes in 1975 was a group of Japanese women, the first women's team ever to scale Mount Everest—a wonderful symbol, in International Women's Year, of how far Japanese women have come. The fifteen-member team (five of whom were housewives) had worked five years in preparation for the Mount Everest attempt. A previous feat was climbing Anantapur in India in 1970; that expedition was led by Mrs. Eiko Hisano, also the leader of the Mount Everest expedition. Among the preparations for the climb was the raising of ¥43,000,000. Each member was thus responsible for gathering over $5,000. Struck by an avalanche at the last base camp, Junko Tabei spent two days in an oxygen tent before making the final assault on Everest. Despite the fact that one of the Tokyo newspapers thought it necessary to mention that Mrs. Tabei's husband and child "had been taken care of" by her elder sister during her absence, it was a stunning achievement, not to be minimized by such comments about where women's place in Japan *really* is. After the climb Tabei was asked by reporters about the women's feat in comparison with men's achievements in mountain climbing. Her response: "Men are stronger, it's true. But we women have lots of endurance. It just takes us a little longer."

NOTES

[1]Sumie Seo Mishima, *My Narrow Isle: The Story of a Modern Woman in Japan* (New York: John Day Company, 1941), p. 38.

CHAPTER
13
WOMEN AND SUICIDE

Women everywhere face the conflict between the ascribed role in the family and the achieved role in society. This conflict is perhaps more acute in Japan because tradition so rigidly prescribes the family role as the ideal. Some women struggle to achieve for themselves, others for women or for society generally. How do these women resolve the conflict between the traditional role and the will to achieve? Some women live within the ascribed role, for their own advantage or for a broader social benefit. What is the fate of a woman who loses the only role she has, her place within the family? Japanese women in all walks of life are not only seeking to meet new challenges but at the same time to preserve the most cherished values of womanhood. It is concern for the importance of each woman's life which motivates this study.

WOMEN AT LIFE'S CROSSROADS

Among nations with the highest suicide rates for women from 1967 to 1971, Japan's rate fluctuated from fourth to sixth place. The overall rates for women were higher in Hungary, German Democratic Republic, Czechoslovakia, Austria, and Denmark (see Table I). However, for young women between the ages of fifteen and twenty-four, Japan has maintained the highest annual suicide rate between 1967 and 1971, preceding Hungary, German Democratic Republic, Czechoslovakia, Austria, Denmark, and Sweden. In addition, for women between sixty-five and seventy-four years of age, Japan records the second highest suicide rate after Hungary in the same period.[*] In international comparisons, therefore, it becomes evident that suicide

[*] Editor's note: Japan also has the highest female to male suicide ratio in the world.

263

Table I
Nations With Highest Suicide Rates for Women, 1967-1971

	1967	1968	1969	1970	1971
Hungary	18.4 (1)	19.3 (1)	18.9 (1)	19.8 (1)	21.0 (1)
GDR	13.9 (2)	------a	14.7 (3)	15.0 (3)	14.9 (3)
Czechoslovakia	13.5 (3)	------a	12.7 (5)	13.6 (5)	12.6 (6)
Austria	13.4 (4)	12.8 (3)	14.4 (4)	14.2 (4)	14.7 (4)
Japan	12.1 (5)	12.5 (4)	12.7 (5)	13.2 (6)	13.3 (5)
Denmark	11.6 (6)	14.6 (2)	15.2 (2)	15.7 (2)	18.1 (2)
Sweden	11.4 (7)	11.7 (5)	12.7 (5)	13.2 (6)	12.3 (7)

Rate: per 100,000 population
Source: *World Health Statistics Annual 1971*, Vol. 1
aNo statistics available

Table II
Age Group Comparison between Nations with Highest Suicide Rates for Women
1967-1971

	15-24 Years of Age					65-74 Years of Age				
	1967	1968	1969	1970	1971	1967	1968	1969	1970	1971
Japan	(1)	(1)	(1)	(1)	(1)	(2)	(2)	(2)	(2)	(2)
	11.7	10.6	10.8	11.9	12.2	36.3	39.4	30.4	40.5	40.1
Czechoslovakia	(2)		(2)	(2)	(2)	(3)		(4)	(4)	(5)
	10.8	--a	9.5	11.6	9.5	34.9	--a	28.0	27.5	27.2
Hungary	(3)	(2)	(4)	(3)	(3)	(1)	(1)	(1)	(1)	(1)
	10.7	9.0	8.2	9.6	9.3	38.7	47.1	39.6	46.2	47.9
Sweden	(4)	(3)	(3)	(4)	(5)	(7)	(5)	(7)	(7)	(7)
	7.4	7.6	8.3	7.9	7.0	14.4	16.8	14.3	15.6	17.1
GDR	(5)		(5)	(5)	(6)	(5)		(5)	(6)	(4)
	5.2	--a	6.9	6.9	6.9	24.4	--a	26.7	26.1	27.3
Austria	(6)	(4)	(6)	(6)	(4)	(4)	(3)	(3)	(3)	(3)
	5.1	5.4	6.3	5.7	7.4	26.2	25.0	28.1	27.6	29.4
Denmark	(7)	(4)	(7)	(6)	(7)	(6)	(4)	(6)	(5)	(6)
	4.3	5.4	4.6	5.7	5.8	20.9	22.4	23.4	26.7	26.0

Rate: per 100,000 population
Source: *World Health Statistics Annual 1971*, Vol. 1
aNo statistics available

among Japanese women continues to claim the lives of the very young and very old to a comparatively greater degree than those nations having a higher average rate of suicide among women generally (see Table II).

The suicide patterns for women in Japan from 1947 to 1973 indicate very definite trends in each age group. These figures and fluctuations become mute yet forceful indicators of the presence of particular stresses, conflicts or crises commonly experienced by women. Although such stressful situations might have been resolved in any number of ways, 8,129 women in 1973 chose suicide as their final means of ultimately resolving insurmountable difficulties in life.

Three significant patterns emerge from an overview of this period (see Figure 1). First, the lowest suicide rate recorded for women fluctuated

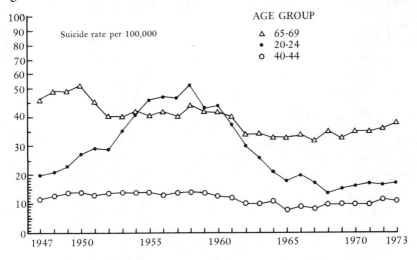

Figure 1.   1947 to 1973: Postwar Comparison of Suicide Rates for Women.

Source: Ministry of Health and Welfare, Statistics and Information Department, 1975.

between the thirty-five to thirty-nine and forty to forty-four age groups, with the latter age group maintaining the lowest average. From this observable trend, it would seem that Japanese women, in general, experience the least amount of unresolvable tension and conflict between the ages of thirty-five to forty-four, the childrearing years.

Secondly, women in the twenty to twenty-four age group revealed the most erratic and fluctuating suicide pattern during this same period. Even up to the present, the twenty to twenty-four age group continues to have a higher suicide rate than the forty to forty-four age group. In 1973, suicide remained the highest cause of death for women aged twenty to twenty-nine. This gives rise to a number of questions. Why does Japan's youngest adult women's group continue to demonstrate a higher suicide rate than middle-aged women? This pattern seems unusual in relation to international statistics for women. What are the factors or stresses which can dissolve the strong human instinct for survival in young adults socialized by society to assume active roles which assure the future of that society?

A third significant pattern is that women from sixty-five and over have maintained the highest suicide level from 1947 to the present.

What does this imply for women facing this particular phase of life? (See Figure 2.)

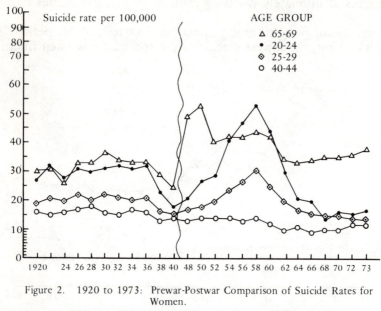

Figure 2. 1920 to 1973: Prewar-Postwar Comparison of Suicide Rates for Women.

Source: Ministry of Health and Welfare, Statistics and Information Department, 1975.

Reports on the marital status of women who had committed suicide became available in 1965 and are now published at every five-year interval. We see clearly in both 1965 and 1970 that in the extremely high suicide age group of twenty to twenty-four most were divorced or widowed (see Figures 3 and 4). The suicide rate of married women remained low between the ages of twenty to twenty-four, while the single women's rate was somewhat higher for this same age group. It is important to remember that the unmarried category also includes students. In both 1965 and 1970, for those fifteen to nineteen years of age, the suicide rate of widows exceeded that of single women, which would include students of high school and university level (1965: Single 5.9/Widowed 15.1; 1970: Single 6.8/Widowed 8.8). In the twenty to twenty-four age bracket, the gap as previously described is even greater, with the widowed and divorced far outdistancing the suicide rates of single women, which would include students at college or university level (1965: Single 21.2/ Widowed 96.6/ Divorced 105.5; 1970: Single 18.5/ Widowed 58.1/ Divorced 85.6). In addition, only the suicide patterns of divorced and widowed women produce the U-shaped curve pattern which is considered unique for Japan and Taiwan.[1]

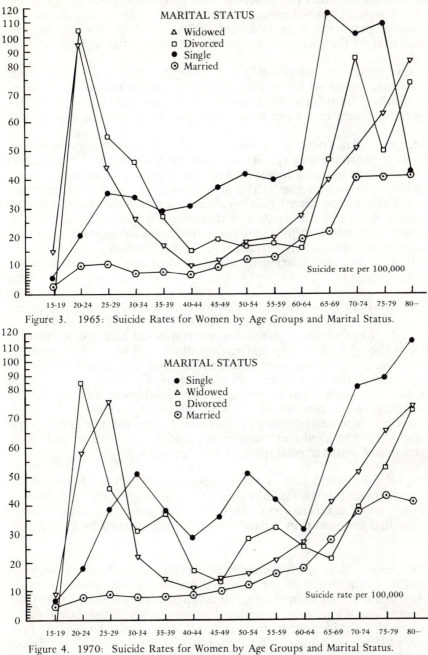

Figure 3. 1965: Suicide Rates for Women by Age Groups and Marital Status.

Figure 4. 1970: Suicide Rates for Women by Age Groups and Marital Status.
Source: Ministry of Health and Welfare, 1970.

Married women had the lowest suicide rate throughout all age groups, with a slow upward-climbing pattern. Single women had the most irregular pattern in both 1965 and 1970, but their rate rises higher than that of the divorced, widowed or married after the age of forty.

A very significant relationship now emerges between a woman's age, the continuation of her marital status, or disruption due to divorce or death. The roles women attempt to balance and integrate will be quite different, therefore, depending upon their age and marital status.

This study will focus exclusively upon the suicide among women in postwar Japanese society. We will suggest a sociological explanation of the varied patterns in age-differentiated groups of women, from 1947 to the present time. The analysis will pay particular attention to underlying, persistent religio-cultural factors which have influenced suicide in Japan. The analytical framework will consider the ideals, values, demands, conflicts and contradictions evolving during Japan's industrialization and modernization. Modernization called for a re-definition and readaptation of women's ideal and actual roles in postwar Japan.

This study addresses itself to questions arising from patterns evident in the suicide statistics for Japanese women from 1947 to 1973: (1) Why has the suicide rate been so erratic and high for women between the ages of twenty and twenty-nine? (2) Why have women sixty-five to sixty-nine, and older, maintained the highest suicide rate throughout the greater part of the period? In evolving a theory of suicide among Japanese women, three fundamental factors will be linked to the concept of role conflict among women in Japanese society. These underlying elements are (1) persistent religio-cultural factors, (2) the ideal and actual role paradigm for women and (3) prewar and postwar education. (See Figure 5A.)

The religio-cultural factors to be explored in depth are Japanese attitudes toward death (as influenced by folk religion, Shinto, Buddhism, and the Bushido code of ethics) and the relationship between individual and group in Japanese society, also shaped by traditional elements.

Four main characteristics emerge in the Japanese attitude toward death: (1) the spirits of the deceased remain in their own country after death rather than residing in a supra-world abode far off; (2) there is communication between the two worlds of the living and the dead (as evidenced in the yearly *Obon* festivals throughout Japan); (3) the dying wish of a person is taken seriously by his descendants as a duty to carry out, and (4) through the belief in reincarnation, the deceased can be reborn many times over in a recurring cycle, so as to complete a specific life work.[2]

Figure 5. **A**: Model of theory. **B**: High unresolved role conflict related to suicidal thoughts/acts.

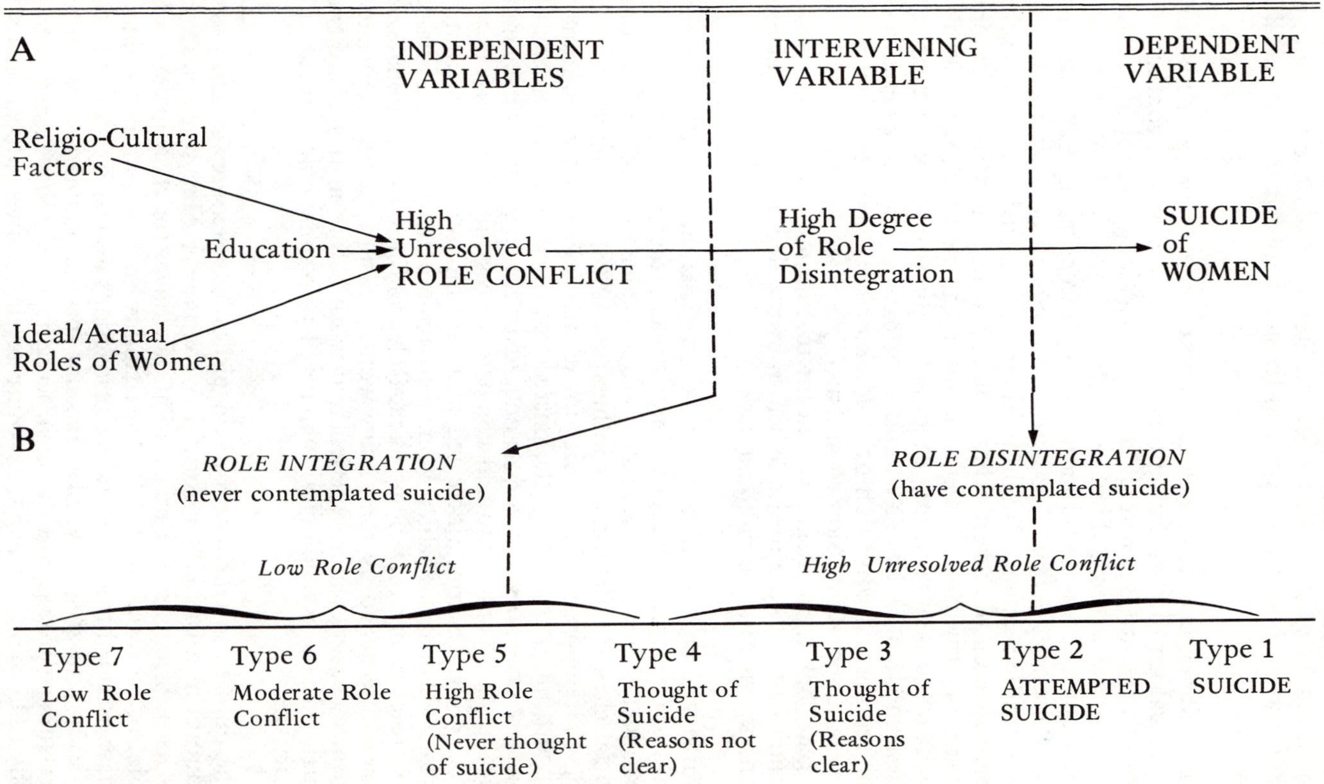

The second important religio-cultural factor is the basic relationship between the individual and the group in Japan, as well as the manner of resolving tensions arising from the conflicting interests of the two.[3] In *Anatomy of Dependence,* Takeo Doi describes the dynamics of *amae*[4] as an underlying factor in tension between the individual and the group.

The distinction between ideal and actual roles[5] for Japanese women is crucial for differentiating types and degrees of role conflict. Role conflict in turn is a pivotal factor in explaining the suicide patterns of Japanese women. Ideal here refers to traditional role expectations for women as wives and mothers which were legally enforced during the Tokugawa Period (1603 to 1868). Subsequent legislation aimed at extending samurai family patterns, crystallized during the Tokugawa regime, to all of society. For women, such ideal patterns required that they strive for obedient submission to husband, faithful fulfillment of household duties, devotion to the rearing and education of their children, and the assumption of passive roles in spheres outside the rearing and education of children or household financial management. Overt submission to husband, preceded by strict obedience to parents before marriage, was meant to continue throughout life. Aging mothers complied obediently to the decisions of the eldest son, grown children or son-in-law.

Wartime upheaval and postwar industrialization created severe and drastic cleavages between traditional ideal role expectations for women and the actual role demands which evolved in the wake of rapid social change. Three major influences must be considered in describing contemporary, actual roles for women. First, equal educational opportunities created by the postwar coeducational system enabled more women to go to college and achieve higher levels of technological skills to enter into and compete successfully with men in the work force. Second, increased postwar employment opportunities prior to marriage enabled women to achieve at least limited status and roles rather than being exclusively confined to traditional ascribed roles determined by their being women. Third, postwar educated women, having wider experience of work before marriage, are better qualified and psychologically prepared to resume employment after marriage.

The third essential concept distinguishes between prewar and postwar education in curriculum for girls. The prewar educational system had as its primary aim the preparation of women for their main ascribed roles of wife and mother.[6] The inability to function in fulfilling these ascribed roles, and severe restrictions against striving for achieved roles in prewar society, may account for the traumatic experiences of certain age groups and the high percentages of those resorting to suicide. On the other hand, exposure to the postwar educational system is significantly different in that it permits women to undertake similar studies to men and allows attainment of higher educational levels[7] for those girls who can compete successfully.

Since role conflict is another essential concept, a number of basic notions require clarification. A role is defined as a pattern of behavior associated with a distinctive social position, for example, wife, mother, teacher, or employee. To a large extent, society has predefined what is expected of individuals in social positions. The role prescribes the rights and duties belonging to a specific social position. Initially, through interaction with others, a woman learns what is expected of her as wife, mother, or employee, to whom she has obligations and upon whom she can make rightful claim. Actual role behavior needs to be differentiated as the actual responses made by the person in a social position as influenced by the setting and one's unique personality. Role conflict, therefore, may be defined as the strain or tension experienced by an individual in responding to role expectations of differing or even inconsistent kinds of behavior required of the same individual.[8]

More specifically, what are the actual components and underlying sources of role conflicts of Japanese women? These can be summarized as stemming from increased opportunities for achievement on the one hand and mounting difficulties in balancing such achievement with traditionally defined expectations for women. The resulting demands, pressures and conflicts cause contradictions in everyday life.

ROLE INTEGRATION OR ROLE DISINTEGRATION?

A survey questionnaire and interview schedule were designed to obtain information from approximately 1,300 women regarding the variables considered most significant for the study of suicide. Figure 5 illustrates the underlying theory, as well as the suspected relationship between progressive stages of unresolved role conflict, leading to a high role disintegration and suicidal thoughts and behavior.[9] Both the survey questionnaire and interview schedule contained three questions to elicit the suicidal thoughts and related experiences of respondents. These proved to be extraordinarily revealing and also significantly linked to role conflict and role disintegration.

Table III illustrates a number of assumptions regarding selected factors considered to promote high degrees of role disintegration. Basically, role disintegration is defined as an inability to satisfactorily integrate family-oriented roles with society-oriented roles. Such disintegration might also arise from absence of one or the other of these two different sets of roles, creating imbalance in a woman's life.

Table III
Indicators for Intervening Variable

Indicators for Intervening Variable	Low Degree of Role Disintegration	High Degree of Role Disintegration
Presence of family-oriented roles (wife, mother, daughter-in-law, mother-in-law, grandmother)	+	
Presence of society-oriented roles (employee, professional, student, volunteer worker, member of society-oriented organization)	+	
Presently employed or working (full-time or part-time)	+	
Presently not employed		+
Experience suicidal thoughts		+
Attempt suicidal act		+

Role integration thus encompasses two meanings. First, it implies a successful integration of one role with other roles a person may have. Second, it implies an ongoing unity between the roles enacted within the family and those achieved in society through utilization of talents, training, education or technical skills. The first meaning, any one role would be integrated into a person's life as part of a larger reality or entity. The actor would not concentrate on any single role as though totally confined to it, as though it were the entirety of life and the source of all meaning. The second meaning refers to those who would have a real need to interact with other individuals beyond the familial sphere, in broader society. The needs might be psychological, sociological, economic, political, or a combination of these.

Figure 6 presents a Parallel Role-Integration Scale[10] composed of ascribed and achieved roles for women, ranked according to high, medium and low fulfillment (also possibly high, medium and low satisfaction) experienced in each of the two distinct role sets. Ascriptive roles are defined according to personal participation in the socioeconomic political spheres beyond one's family, through gainful employment or volunteer service, ranked according to the individual's specific education or technical training.

SUICIDE AND JAPANESE WOMEN

Viewing suicide in Japan as a predominantly many-layered system of tension management[11] it is possible to trace values and influences

Figure 6
Parallel Role-Integration Scale

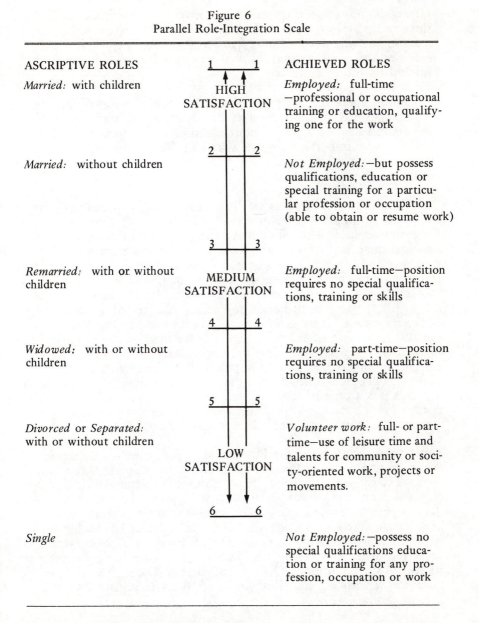

ASCRIPTIVE ROLES			ACHIEVED ROLES

ASCRIPTIVE ROLES   1   1   ACHIEVED ROLES

Married: with children   HIGH SATISFACTION   *Employed:* full-time —professional or occupational training or education, qualifying one for the work

2   2

Married: without children   *Not Employed:*—but possess qualifications, education or special training for a particular profession or occupation (able to obtain or resume work)

3   3

Remarried: with or without children   MEDIUM SATISFACTION   *Employed:* full-time—position requires no special qualifications, training or skills

4   4

Widowed: with or without children   *Employed:* part-time—position requires no special qualifications, training or skills

5   5

Divorced or *Separated:* with or without children   LOW SATISFACTION   *Volunteer work:* full- or part-time—use of leisure time and talents for community or society-oriented work, projects or movements.

6   6

Single   *Not Employed:*—possess no special qualifications education or training for any profession, occupation or work

in distinct layers and patterns. They help explain why suicide has been a positive, value-infused act throughout the course of Japanese history. "In Japanese society committing suicide has never been regarded as a sin, or a shame."[12] Only from this perspective can the many, yet unanswered questions regarding suicide in general and among Japanese women in particular, be approached with the hope of gaining greater human insight. This understanding may then lead to informed description and explanation of present day suicide.

Indigenous folk religion (primitive Shinto)[13] provided core beliefs,
values and practices which still influence the lives of contemporary
Japanese. At the deepest level was a common belief in a hierarchy
of deities and spirits (*kami*), as well as a popular belief in the human
soul and its future existence.

One of the important early functions of the religious medium, often
a woman,[14] was transmitting a deceased spirit's final wish, when
the person had died alone without communicating to others. This
was especially important for one who had died in the prime of life,
since any plans or hopes left unfulfilled were to be carried out by
family members or followers.

Buddhism influenced beliefs and practices regarding death and after-
life. A teaching of Buddhism was of a universal salvation based upon
the ultimate oneness of all beings. The influence of Buddhism on
Bushido came largely through adapting Zen to the training of the
warrior class. The ideal of Zen was inculcated so that a warrior, by
transcending either happiness or sadness, might live single-heartedly
in obedience to the inner voice of his spirit. From this code arose
norms for the suicide of honor, *seppuku*. Also the ideal of dying
isagi-yoki meant "leaving no regrets," "with a clear conscience,"
"in full possession of mind," "like a brave man." The samurai,
imbued with the spirit of Zen, became a model of strength and
courage, popularizing the philosophy and its values among the broad
masses of people. Among the various forms of *seppuku* during feudal times was a type of self-immolation used as a means of protest
against one's superior, known as *kanshi*. In such cases, suicide was
a means of protest and created impetus for social change.[15]

During the middle ages, the Bushido ideal for samurai was heroic
fortitude and courage; Buddhist priests had to maintain a continual
preference for purity, leaving life prematurely to demonstrate that preference. Examples of women[16] who had to prove they possessed similar courage were not lacking. Gracia Hosokawa met death by
gisei jisatsu (sacrifice suicide) in 1601 as Mitsumari Ishida, her husband's enemy, stormed Osaka Castle. Oichi, sister of Nobunaga Oda,
preferred death in 1583 by *gisei jisatsu* rather than joining the harem
of Hideyoshi Toyotomi. Chacha, daughter of Oichi, also died by
gisei jisatsu with her son Hideyori in 1616, as Tokugawa Ieyasu attacked Osaka Castle.

These religious, cultural, and historical factors are some of the significant layers of influence which have contributed toward a tradition
regarding death and suicide. Kishimoto has explained that the problem of facing death has developed in Japan as a peculiar pattern of
culture.

It makes the Japanese feel that they must meet death squarely, rather than avoid it. The cultural tradition encourages them to be prepared to accept death with courage and tranquility. So how one faces death has come to be regarded as an important feature of life. Death is not a mere end of life for the Japanese. It has been given a positive place in life. Facing death properly is one of the most important features of life. In that sense, it may well be said that for the Japanese death is within life.[17]

The Japanese *banzai* and *kamikaze* attacks during World War II, therefore did not mean the Japanese have emotionally less fear of death. Rather, owing to both conscious and unconscious factors within this cultural tradition, Japanese are trained from childhood to meet death in a courageous manner.[18]

Since current studies of suicide by Japanese scholars abound, it would be superfluous to discuss these works here. While many provided helpful insights on the suicide of Japanese women, a number stand out as particularly significant. Hidetoshi Katō asserts that *oyako shinjū* (parent-child suicide) as well as *ikka shinjū* (family suicide) are actually infanticide combined with adult suicide. He attributes this type of suicide to a long tradition in both the family and society whereby parents bear full responsibility for their children's lives and future. *Shinjū* (double love suicide) in postwar Japan developed a type which he terms "a love united in heaven." This type has been influenced by a kind of romanticism prevailing during the postwar decades. Utilizing newspaper reports and other sources, Katō presents a classification of the styles of suicide which became common from 1877 (Meiji 10) to 1959.[19]

Kenichi Chikazawa focuses upon high rates of suicide in the young as well as old and analyzes the act as one in which individuals vent emotions upon themselves rather than on others.[20] Tetsuo Kajiya dismisses over-simplified assumptions which correlate a declining suicide rate with effects of postwar westernization and modernization. There have been some beneficial results from the introduction and increase of psychiatric treatment and social welfare assistance. At the same time, increases in suicide are seen as being influenced by the very processes of postwar modernization and westernization. Underlying such superficial factors, Kajiya[21] points out, are three more basic influences which he feels are significant in most suicides today in Japan. These are (1) a Japanese view of life which is still being maintained through customs and traditions within both family and society, (2) the fundamental religious view that life is transient, and (3) a kind of personal dependency (*amae*) which seemingly cannot tolerate the severance of close relationships, especially involving parents, family members, or superiors. A significant factor in the suicide of women, he believes, is that many are psychologically and economically dependent upon men.

SUICIDAL THOUGHT SURVIVORS

From the perspective of Zen, Suzuki describes *myō*[22] in relation to death thoughts. "When we have erased the conscious desire for life, we imagine that we willingly embrace death. But in point of fact is it not possible that we are still consciously craving life?"[23] Here inference is made to an interplay of life and death within the human instincts of the Japanese. Suzuki seems to lend support to an approach which strives to encompass and fathom "death thought experiences" within life. Struggles and conflicts are involved as well as the human affirmation of life, and the conscious desire for life is represented in those who live through such experiences.

Suicidal thoughts, therefore, for the purposes of this study are regarded as a human reality in the lives of women when they consider the possibility of suicide as an alternate solution to their genuine human anguish and suffering. The fact that these thoughts are experienced in the zone of life and that suicidal thought survivors passed through the experience and chose life casts light upon a region of human awareness still beset by ambiguity and darkness. As is true of all human experience, much can be learned in the way of greater appreciation of the human capacity for survival against all odds. These lessons may also reveal what type of internal and external pressures and conflicts are identified by women as the causes of their suicidal thoughts.

Over twelve hundred women, twenty to eighty years of age, were asked "Have you ever felt that you wanted to commit suicide?" Respondents were also requested to explain the cause of their suicidal thoughts and the means by which such thoughts or feelings had been overcome. The results indicate that special attention must be given to factors related to role conflict for women of varied ages.

Forty-five percent of all women[24] (Total 551/ Single 460/ Married 91) admitted having experienced suicidal thoughts (see Figures 7 and 8). A high ratio of single women (over one half or 51 percent) had undergone such experiences while only 28 percent of those married indicated having had such thoughts at all.

From the explanations volunteered or omitted by these women, four broad categories emerged: (1) no reasons given for suicidal thoughts; (2) reasons originating from personal, internal crises; (3) causes related to the person in relation to others or external factors; and (4) vague, unspecified reasons. Over one third of the respondents (37 percent) did not indicate any cause or causes for their suicidal

Figure 7
Percentage of Women with Experience of Suicidal Thoughts*

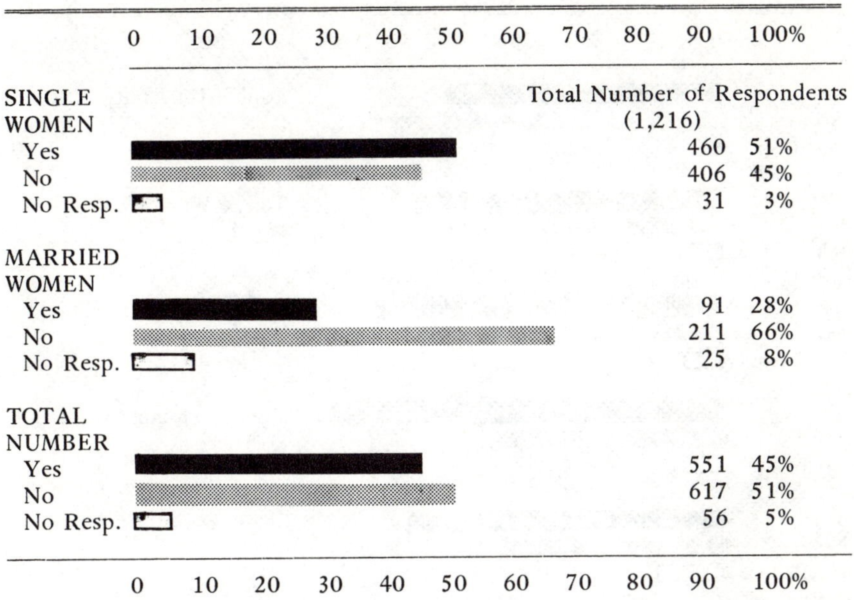

	0	10	20	30	40	50	60	70	80	90	100%		

SINGLE
WOMEN   Total Number of Respondents
                                                        (1,216)
Yes	460	51%
No	406	45%
No Resp.	31	3%

MARRIED
WOMEN
Yes	91	28%
No	211	66%
No Resp.	25	8%

TOTAL
NUMBER
Yes	551	45%
No	617	51%
No Resp.	56	5%

	0	10	20	30	40	50	60	70	80	90	100%

*Reply to question: "Anata wa jisatsu o shitai kimochi ni natta koto ga arimasu ka?" (Have you ever felt like you wanted to commit suicide?)

thoughts. Only a rare few among them explained the omission by "the matter now seems of minor significance," "I have forgotten what it was," or "I do not want to write it here." Causes related to internal, personal conflicts or crises constituted the largest majority, 38 percent. A variety of reasons related to "family," "human relationships or friendship," "disappointment in love," "illness," "society," "the husband-wife relationship" and "children" when all totaled amounted to 22 percent. Vague, unspecified causes comprised a very small 2 percent.

Interesting differences came to light when comparing reasons given by single and married women. While both groups were similar in combined percentages of "vague reasons" and "no reasons given" (Single, 39 percent/ Married, 43 percent), there was noticeable variation in reasons clearly stated. More single women tended to identify the cause of their suicidal thoughts as originating within themselves, 42 percent, while only 21 percent of the married women did so. University students were notably high in this regard (Sophia University, 43 percent/ Tokyo Women's College, 55 percent).

Students expressed their inner anguish in various ways. "I didn't know any longer why I was alive." "There didn't seem to be any meaning in the future. I felt all human beings were in the same

Figure 8
Percentage of Women with Experience of Suicidal Thoughts*

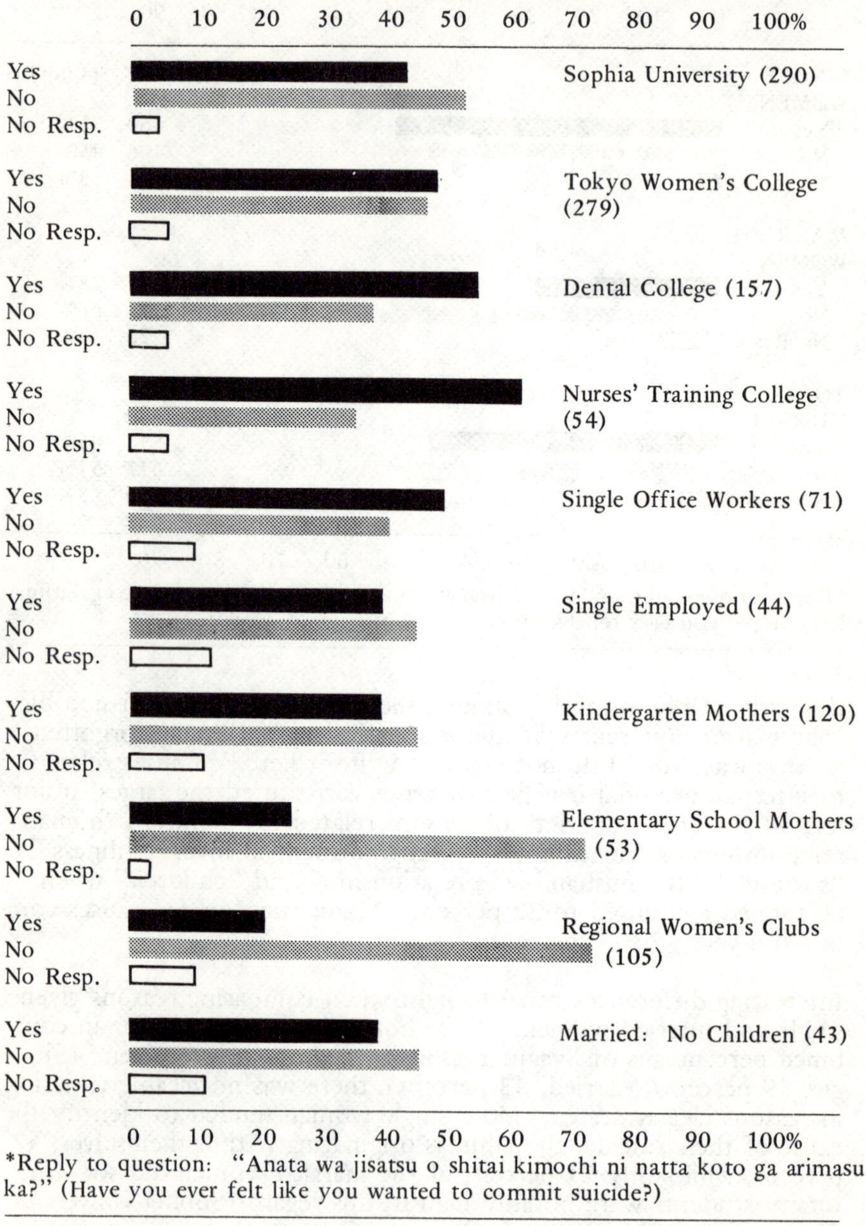

| | 0 | 10 | 20 | 30 | 40 | 50 | 60 | 70 | 80 | 90 | 100% |

Yes
No
No Resp.
Sophia University (290)

Yes
No
No Resp.
Tokyo Women's College (279)

Yes
No
No Resp.
Dental College (157)

Yes
No
No Resp.
Nurses' Training College (54)

Yes
No
No Resp.
Single Office Workers (71)

Yes
No
No Resp.
Single Employed (44)

Yes
No
No Resp.
Kindergarten Mothers (120)

Yes
No
No Resp.
Elementary School Mothers (53)

Yes
No
No Resp.
Regional Women's Clubs (105)

Yes
No
No Resp.
Married: No Children (43)

0   10   20   30   40   50   60   70   80   90   100%

*Reply to question: "Anata wa jisatsu o shitai kimochi ni natta koto ga arimasu ka?" (Have you ever felt like you wanted to commit suicide?)

helpless situation and could do nothing about it." "I felt there was no meaning in my own personal existence." "In the world, we are all actually alone. Even though we continue to live, we hurt other people and cause them worry and inconvenience. I felt there was no meaning in human life." "I was in anguish over the value of my own existence." "I have become weary of asking myself what the real purpose of my life is and not being able to find any real answer. I have not overcome my thoughts of suicide." "I could see no meaning in my own life. At two different times when I felt this strongly, I thought of committing suicide." "I had no reason for continuing to live, yet I had no reason to die." "I felt my existence had no value in this world." "Having no principle of belief or real purpose in life, I could not find any meaning in my personal existence." "Every day seemed void and empty. I could find no meaning in my life."

Reasons pertaining to relations to others were more frequently cited by married women (35 percent) than those single, 19 percent. "I was unable to act as I wanted because of the people around me." "I was misunderstood by many people." "I was betrayed by other people." "My work did not go successfully and I fell into despair. My family used violence against me. I had no income and was unable to make a living." "I did not want to continue married life any longer but felt I had no way to escape from it. I became melancholic." "While I was ill, my husband became sexually involved with another woman." Twelve married women had contemplated suicide when they had learned of their husband's sexual relations with another woman.

Among "personal reasons" as the cause of suicidal thoughts, the highest number of single women (67) had experienced anguish and resulting thoughts of suicide over the loss of meaning in their lives, a questioning of the meaning of human existence and the value of human life itself. The next highest number (51) experienced an "aversion toward self" or "self-hatred" *(jiko ken-o, jibun ga iya ni natta, jibun fishin ga kirai).* The third largest number within this category (43) explained that their suicidal thoughts had arisen from feelings of despair, weariness with life and sense of powerlessness, including a loss of self-confidence. All inclusive, "personal internal reasons" accounted for 42 percent (193) of the total 460 reasons reported by single women. Among the small number of married women who reported "personal reasons" (19), thirteen explained their suicidal thoughts as having come from despair, a sense of weariness and helplessness in life. Four referred to a loss of meaning in life; two mentioned "self-aversion" or "self-hatred."

Under varied reasons for suicidal thoughts, single women tended to give "family quarrels and discord" (18), "problems in human relationships" (18), "disappointment in love" (16) and "problems in society related to education, employment or other pressures" (13). Married women mentioned problems in the "husband-wife relationship" (12), "death of husband" (2), "illness or a physical impediment in children"

(2), "family problems, including mother-in-law trouble" (4), "human relations" (4), and "earlier crises during adolescence" (8). The remaining forty married women gave no reason at all for their suicidal thoughts.

Two hundred and ninety-five single and married women described how they had overcome the feeling of wanting to commit suicide. Regardless of the reasons presented as the root cause of their suffering, similarities emerged between single and married women in the means taken to overcome the wish to resort to suicide. The majority of single (52 percent) and married (32 percent) women made an effort to discover meaning and values in life by inner reflection, talking to trusted family members or friends, reading and other means of searching for meaning in life. The next highest number of women (Single, 22 percent/ Married, 29 percent) simply allowed the passing of time to heal their suffering and thoughts of death. As one married woman reflected, "Everything passes with time." The second group seemed to take a more passive approach to overcoming suicidal thoughts and perhaps reflected the intuitive reaction Suzuki referred to in explaining *myō*.

The third highest percentage (15 percent) gave "lack of courage to actually commit suicide" or "fear of death" as their reason for not carrying out the act. Lastly, only a small percentage of single (4 percent) and married (8 percent) women were deterred from suicide because "they did not wish to cause their parents suffering" or "cause others inconvenience." Nine percent of the women had been able to overcome suicidal thoughts by deliberately seeking distractions or becoming engrossed in studies, work, sports, hobbies, or amusement. An additional 9 percent had been helped by experiencing the discovery of personal religious faith. The one outstanding difference among married women was that 10 percent reported having been restrained from committing suicide because of their children, who were dependent upon them.

The foregoing personal accounts have revealed that suicidal thoughts are critical, that they indicate something fundamentally wrong with the situation of the person and that they mean something about the person herself. How is this data related to unresolved role conflict and subsequent role disintegration in single and married women of varied ages?

First of all, the crisis of inner growth experienced and reported by the majority of single women during adolescence, late teens and early twenties especially, can be viewed as one of the first major role conflicts for women. If this role conflict is not resolved successfully, there may be serious consequences later in life. The crisis in adolescence reported frequently as cause of suicidal thoughts, is generated by a breaking away from all values, norms, ideals, and roles ascribed to the individual during her socialization within family and society. All of it suddenly becomes meaningless and without value. The young woman no longer feels security or purpose in being "a part of" family or society. Everything is questioned from the ground up. There no longer appears to be any purpose at all in human existence, as many described it. Therefore, the values and roles ascribed through family influence and socialization seem to disintegrate entirely. The young person must now begin to achieve her own meaning and values and to define roles as a human being if she is to continue choosing life, while considering the possibility of ending it all in suicide.

Young women undergoing this crisis showed significant differences, as alluded to previously. While most attempted to find their own reason for living, or allowed themselves time for growth, the third largest number fell into "self-aversion" or "self-hatred." In these cases, there were negative feelings directed inward toward self. In the former cases, feelings of suffering, alienation, and distress became the impetus for a positive search in quest of life itself. An important question arises here: how do those with feelings of hatred directed toward self during such crises develop positive appreciation of their human worth and the meaning of their lives? If young women at this stage do not begin discovering their own human values but simply conform with norms and roles expected of them by family or others, this may well contribute toward increasing role disintegration for women.

This critical period for young women and their ability to resolve the conflict seems critical for two important reasons. First of all, if women at this stage in life fail to achieve their own answers to human life, they may be incapable of resolving or balancing subsequent conflicts which arise in their multiple roles in society. Without a supporting base for such roles within themselves or any inner integrating force there may be too great an identification with any one role. They may tend to equate failure in any one role with total failure in life itself. If the role fails, they may feel they, too, have failed. Later, as wives and mothers, women who have failed to fully discover appreciation for the value of their own human lives may become incapable of recognizing the value of human life in their own infants. Some may then dispose of them as unwanted, useless possessions.

Second, in tensions experienced between traditional, ideal roles for women and the actual role demands for women in modern society, much conflict seems concentrated around the role of woman-person. The conservative power in Japanese society retains ideals for women today which continue to place the main burden upon her as woman, that is, on her capacity for childbearing, childrearing, perpetuating culture, venerating of ancestors. The modern sectors of society, on the contrary, place greater stress upon woman as person, as a center of life and meaning, possessing uniqueness, creativity, responsibility, inner strength and purpose, spiritual as well as material needs. The burden rests upon her capacity to integrate multiple roles, demands, conflicts, and contradictory expectations from a personalized base. It is deeper and stronger than any one role or set of roles, either within the sphere of the family or in society. From her inner resourcefulness and vitality she is called upon to solve problems and to change situations, rather than being swept along by her environment. Therefore, women from adolescence onward are compelled to discover and deepen their role as woman-person in modern society to grow toward personal integration.

If each successive crisis in life, whether originating from within or from human relations, can be overcome with a deepening of personal meaning in life, it is more likely that such women would be capable of integrating multiple roles in family and society. They would be less apt to identify completely with any one role or become so enclosed in one small sphere that they lose sight of what is happening in the rest of society and the world. Ultimately, the strength of woman's connecting link between family and social roles may be tested and measured by her consciousness of the value of her own life. Here is found a woman's self-respect, self-confidence, and attitude toward dependence upon others.

Within women's social milieu, it is evident that general factors, experienced by all, and particular factors, dependent upon personal choices and decisions, are significantly correlated with role conflict. There is a relationship between high, unresolved role conflict and increasing role disintegration, which if not contained or resolved can lead to suicidal thoughts or attempted or realized suicide. In addition, the eruption of personal problems or crises and the alternatives either open or closed to them are significant in determining the final choices women make in their lives.

The general factors most influential for women have been the ideal and actual role demands, the postwar educational system and religio-cultural factors. The most fundamental role the majority of women described was that of woman-person. Within women's social milieu, most tensions and conflicts concentrate around this most basic of all roles in life. The ideal for women, still supported by strong traditional influences, emphasizes her ascribed roles within the family through marriage and motherhood. She bears the main burden as woman, as childbearer, childrearer, bearer-transmitter of family and cultural traditions, and ancestor worshipper. The religio-cultural influences to which she is exposed throughout life also emphasize the womanly aspects of her woman-person role.

On the other hand, the postwar educational system with its attendant opportunities for women through coeducation and higher education places greater emphasis upon her as person. Here she has unique ability, talent, creativity, an almost limitless capacity for intellectual, psychological, spiritual, and physical development and achievement. Thus, from early education onward the growing girl is made keenly aware of the demands and roles placed upon her in the outer modern spheres of society, beyond the family.

The particular factors in each woman's social environment are largely determined by a woman's own choices and decisions throughout life, and the extent to which her ascribed and/or achieved roles are integrated over the span of her lifetime. The particular conflicts women described were closely related to underlying tension in integration or disintegration of their family and social roles. More specifically, how did single, married, widowed and aging women experience their own particular types of role conflict? How did they describe the tensions experienced between ascribed and achieved roles, family-oriented roles and those enacted within society?

Single women pursuing higher education, professional, or technical training and using their skills in employment tended to describe experiences pertaining to development of the person aspect of their woman-person role. However, the longer they pursued achievement-oriented roles, the more they seemed to encounter strong counter-currents around them, reminding them in myriad ways of their "failure" to marry. In a sense, it can be said that these women are "swimming upstream" prior to marriage, and the longer they do so, the greater the determination and perseverance required to pursue such direction. They go in the face of ideals upheld for all women even in the most modern of settings. Numerous examples could be cited from interviews with young and middle-aged single women.

Suicide rates for women according to marital status support a view that strong role conflicts and counter-currents in society are experienced by single women after the age of thirty. In 1965, the highest suicide rate recorded in every category after thirty-four years of age was for single women. The second highest rate for all ages after thirty-four was among either divorced or widowed women. In 1970, from the age of thirty onward, the highest suicide ratio was reported for single women consistently, with divorced or widowed following as the second highest rate. A high degree of role disintegration for single women would arise from the lack of compensating alternatives for the ascribed roles of wife and mother.

For young women who seem more interested in marriage and motherhood as their prime aim in life, with a college degree as a means toward this end, the way is considerably easier. They concentrate on finding a suitable husband and learning practical skills in homemaking after high school or college graduation until marriage. This is all very much in conformity with the traditional ideal for women. In fact, it is not rare for wealthy, high-status families to forbid their daughters to take on any kind of outside employment. Working reflects badly upon the family and is generally regarded as below their status. However, in itself, early and almost complete identification with ascribed roles for women seems very natural.

In the entire life span of women in modern Japanese society many unanswered questions arise. What happens when, at an early stage of adulthood, women follow strong traditional currents both within the family and society? Without sufficiently developing the personal base of their role as woman-person, what may result when they are prematurely catapulted from the family sphere and forced to confront the strong counter-current of modern society for which they are little prepared?

Middle-aged and older single women interviewed expressed positive regard for marriage and motherhood. Middle-aged single women acknowledged their willingness to marry should they meet the right man. However, none felt an urgent necessity to do so simply for the sake of marrying. In varied ways, these women explained the meaning of fulfillment they had discovered and enjoyed through alternative life styles and roles. A forty-five-year-old single bank employee expressed no regrets over having relinquished her chances for marriage in order to care for her aging parents until their recent death. A sixty-six-year-old Red Cross nurse, now residing in a home for the aged, had served during World War II and later had cared for wounded United Nations Forces during the Korean War. She explained her reasons for not having married. "The Japanese have a strong family consciousness. They tend to judge everything according to whether or not it is good for their family or good for their children. I think it is more important to look beyond one's own children and family, to see the needs of other people in the world. Perhaps I would have had a much more ordinary life had I married, and I did have many proposals. But I do not regret the path I have chosen in life." Aged, single women who had been school teachers or teachers of tea ceremony, flower arrangement, or the arts, explained the satisfaction they derived therefrom. They had strong ties with their former pupils who looked after them "as though they were their own children."

The conflict older single women experience may be most keenly felt because of having to fall back on the ideal woman aspect of their woman-person role.

The societal mirror seems to reflect the uncompromising ideal image of woman, marriage, and motherhood. Thus these women may be tempted to regard themselves as "deviant" or "failures" in later life, when they no longer experience the daily rewards of active service and collaboration with others in society. However, women who have lived out their ideals against the counter-currents of society do not seem to be lacking as persons or in inner resourcefulness.

Though the societal mirror in old age continues to reflect back to every woman the unbending traditional ideal, a dedicated single woman who aided many beyond her own family may actually have experienced the values of motherhood in Japanese society to a greater degree than those married women who spent themselves entirely on their children and family. Yet single women especially from middle age onward, who do not have a meaningful human nexus, a substitute family group or persons with whom they can associate, become increasingly vulnerable to exploitation in Japanese society in general, and to self-seeking individuals, in particular.

Beneath every woman's decision either to continue working or not at the time of marriage or the birth of her first child is a more fundamental role conflict described by mothers of all ages. This became apparent from interviews with seventy-five women who answered the question "Can a woman be satisfied with only her roles as wife and mother?" Fifty-nine percent replied "no," 31 percent answered "yes." Women were also asked to explain why they had either answered in the affirmative or negative. The reasons given by women who had replied "no" brought out sharply the conflicts they had or were experiencing in these two roles.

Let us now turn to relationship between high unresolved role conflict and role disintegration, utilizing the indicators shown in Figure 4: "suicidal thoughts," "attempted suicide," and "completed suicide." It seems important to emphasize that it is within this general social milieu that their personal crises or problems erupt. Therefore, whatever pressures may be felt by a woman from outside become compounded by internal pressures, especially when it seems to her impossible to change the situation. Suicidal thoughts and acts do not occur in a vacuum. They arise within the concrete life style of a particular woman. Her own social milieu is the culmination of her decisions, the fulfillment or neglect of her human potential both within the family and society. Moreover, the immediate personal crisis becomes a double burden for the woman who is unequipped to implement her own solutions in the face of life's difficulties.

Fifty-five percent of the women responding to the survey questionnaire had never thought of committing suicide. Among these 665 women, 435 were single, and 230 were married. Forty-eight percent of the women interviewed had never contemplated suicide in seeking solutions to their problems. According to the theory being proposed, these 700 women would be regarded as having experienced "low role conflict" (Type 7), "moderate role conflict" (Type 6) or "high role conflict," without having contemplated suicide (Type 5).

They were examples of women who had anguished through role conflict in their lives, who had persevered in trying to integrate family-oriented and society-oriented roles, or who had to discover substitutes or alternatives in the absence of either of these role sets.

Women who had experienced high role conflict and yet had not contemplated suicide had some important characteristics in common. First, each woman's basic attitude toward herself revealed a sense of meaning, purpose and appreciation for her own human life. Second, there was evidence of a mature independence, a self-reliance in decision and action to overcome the personal or family problem. Third, and stemming from the previous two, they manifested the self-confidence necessary to confront the conflict, decide and act without being overcome by doubts regarding their ability to persevere.

Forty percent of the women who had experienced suicidal thoughts were unable to specify or remember the cause, or else were unwilling to state their reasons for contemplating suicide. There were two hundred twenty women (Single 181/ Married 39) in this category of "high role conflict" (Type 4) with unspecified reasons for suicidal thoughts.

The majority of women, 60 percent, were able to express and explain quite clearly what had been the underlying cause for considering suicide as a possible solution to their difficulties. This group constituting Type 3 amounted to 331; 279 were single women, 52 married. The reasons given have already been discussed. Here it suffices to relate the data to the general theory being proposed, showing how it is integrated into the broader scheme.

Although none of the survey respondents reported any suicidal attempts (one woman had begun writing her suicide note when she reconsidered), two of the women among those randomly selected for interviews from the original sample volunteered information regarding their reasons for attempted suicide. One had been single and twenty-three years of age at the time; the other was married, twenty-eight years of age and the mother of a four-year-old son at the time of her suicide attempt. Out of a total of seventy-five women interviewed, thirty-nine had contemplated suicide and two from among these women had carried their thoughts into suicidal acts. A third woman was the trusted confidante of a thirty-three-year-old married woman who had committed suicide with her two children and husband (*ikka shinjū*). The interviewee had known of her friend's problem, conflict, and suffering, frequently offering help and assistance to aid her through the crisis. But these efforts proved of no avail in the end.

In both of the attempted suicides reported, there was a strong "element of protest" in carrying out the suicidal act. Mrs. O. was caught in an impossible situation, identifying with her ascribed role as daughter while she suffered ill effects to health and mind as a person. Although seemingly "trapped" between conflicting demands, her suicide attempt became a clear protest, as well as a cry for help, which enabled her to break loose and begin pursuing her own meaning in life, apart from her mother.

Mrs. N. demonstrated sufficient courage, self-reliance and self-confidence to ask her husband for a divorce rather than submit to an intolerable situation which betrayed her values as a person, as well as wife and mother. Nevertheless, she was unable to change the situation or work out a satisfactory settlement with her husband. Her "protest" seems clear in the choice of a prolonged method for terminating her life. Her determination to fight until the bitter end proved effective in rallying the support of her mother-in-law, which pressed her husband toward a reconsideration of his unreasonable demands. The fact that Mrs. N. is now preparing to become a qualified *koto* teacher as a result of her experience casts light upon another area of conflict where she may have felt particularly vulnerable and defenseless.

THE DEATH OF A FAMILY

"It can never be said that Kyoko Oba was a weak woman. Although a quiet person and mild in manner, I realized how strong she had been only after it was all over," confided Mrs. M., her close friend and confidante over the past few years. Their children had attended the same kindergarten. During that time, both mothers were elected officers of the P.T.A. necessitating their working together closely. From that beginning, their friendship deepened and continued, even though their children had gone to different elementary schools. Mrs. M.[25] shared what she had learned from Kyoko Oba during the last months of her life.

Kyoko Oba and her two children, Mitsuru and Akira, often stayed with us at our summer home. We would spend several days at a time there, sharing everything we did together. It was only two days after her last stay at the vacation house that I began noticing strange things happening. Even during her last stay with us, I am sure she already knew that her husband had killed Kyoko Seki, the woman then pregnant with his child. If Kyoko Oba had been a weak woman, she would surely have broken down in front of us or shown her distressed feelings in some way. Long before, I recall Kyoko saying that if her children ever had to go through life bearing some kind of social stigma or the burden of a crime against society, she would never permit them to live. After the family suicide, I remembered this and understood why she had said such a thing.

This is why I think she was basically a strong woman, despite her mild appearance and manner. Ordinarily, a woman with such anguish in her heart would not even want to face the other women she would have to meet at the kindergarten each day, where she brought her youngest daughter and came to get her. But she never once showed her real feelings in any way. She must have had some other idea in mind even then. After the tragic incident, I felt she had been a courageous woman. If it had been myself in such a situation, *I think* I would have found some other escape than dying with my children in my arms.

The Oba marriage had not been a happy one at all for years, even though it had been a "love" marriage. Mr. Oba rarely came home. He would stay away for long periods at a time, returning home only long enough to replenish his supply of clean clothing. I myself once asked Kyoko if she had ever considered divorcing him, especially after she had learned of his relations with Seki. I had even gone twice with Kyoko to talk to Kyoko Seki, but the younger woman was much stronger and more aggressive. Seki challenged Kyoko, "You get out of our way because I am going to become Oba's wife now!" Seki clashed fiercely with Kyoko and threatened her continually. I was there and heard it all. This happened at both of the meetings at which I was present. I told them to stop fighting. However, my impression was that Kyoko Oba did not have enough confidence in herself to really want to go on living. For one thing, she had no occupation or work to fall back on. I can say this for sure. Because she had no work, she did not know what to do on her own in the future. She herself once confided to me, "I don't have the confidence to go out into society and make a living for my two children and myself."

On another occasion Kyoko Oba remarked that if she were able to put up with all that had happened between her husband and herself, surely something good would come of it in the future. Oba was due to become a full professor soon at Rikkyō University. He was on his way to higher success, having even become assistant professor sooner than usual. His seniors at the university had been very good to him. "So even though it is very disagreeable for me to swallow this now" Kyoko told me, "the other woman's relationship with my husband is nothing more than sex as a business. Even though he did this in the shadows, I am able to forgive him. But if it were not for the fact that there is something better ahead, I would not be able to put up with it all."

The second time I went to see Kyoko Seki with Mr. and Mrs. Oba and the two children, Mr. Oba ended up by siding with Seki, adding to his wife's suffering and torment. When I saw and heard this, I tried to encourage Kyoko Oba later on to think of going her own way with the children. I said, "If you press for your own demands and really have the will to follow through on going your own way, something could be done to find a solution." I volunteered to take care of her two children for as long as was necessary for her to get started in her new life. The children had stayed with me and my children many times before. "If you are going to separate, hurry up and do it now," I advised.

But by this time, I felt that any love she had had for her husband had now turned to hatred. She was thinking of the future. If her husband became professor, she would have the status of professor's wife. There was vanity in her motivation. And she was determined not to give up her position as wife to Seki or let her have the final victory.

Five months before the family suicide, she once mentioned committing suicide herself. She said if that would ever happen she would never leave her children behind for others to take care of, even though her mother-in-law could have done so. "I will not allow the Oba line to live," she once told me.

WHY?

In order to understand the full significance of Kyoko Oba's final course of decision and action, it is essential to analyze the general framework of her own experienced society before the crisis reached its peak. In her ascriptive roles as wife and mother, Kyoko Oba had reached the pinnacle of fulfillment, until the serious problem intruded into her life through the role of wife. Awareness of this rupture between her husband and herself preceded the family suicide by years, according to a close friend. Yet, despite this, no adjustments were made by Kyoko Oba as a precaution for future self-reliance in outer society. She had never worked nor did she possess qualifications for any type of employment. From the first, she had been totally dependent financially upon well-to-do parents; after marriage, she had been totally dependent upon husband. There were no achievement-oriented roles in her life, other than her brief experience as an auxiliary officer in the kindergarten P.T.A. Yet she had a strong unfulfilled desire and capacity for achievement as was manifest in her willingness to endure the bitter betrayal of her husband, forgiving him for the sake of sharing in his prestige as a professor's wife in the proximate future. Only vicariously through her husband was it possible for her to achieve, and she was willing to pay the full price for such achievement.

Delving more deeply into the particular factors militating against
Kyoko Oba in her constricted social universe, it is important to recognize why she did not divorce her husband while there was time
to act, to change her situation and resolve the crisis in some way.
Kyoko Oba's complete dependence upon parents, then husband, had
prevented her from launching out into society, even for a short time.
There was no way to discover herself as human person beyond the
family sphere, to face the counter-currents of modern society while
she was still able to develop herself through social roles. Instead,
society remained an unknown, unexperienced world beyond. Her
dependency had resulted in a neglect to utilize talents and abilities
to equip her to participate in that society. These particular factors
are the basic cause of her vulnerability when the actual crisis erupted
in her life. She herself recognized this when she admitted she did
not have the confidence to go out into society and make a living
for her two children and herself.

Therefore, even in the early stages of her marital difficulties, Kyoko
Oba was already "frozen" in her limited sphere of the family. There
was no other course nor direction left for her but further entrench-
ment into that last fortress, her family. With Kyoko Seki challenging and threatening to usurp that central position within the family,
the position Kyoko Oba had sacrificed everything in life to maintain,
it is not at all surprising that it became a bitter fight to death. Kyoko
Oba, being the strong person she was, with no other possible avenue
outward for achieving a solution, would achieve in the only possible
way left, through her final victory. Even if her husband had not
killed Kyoko Seki, placing the social stigma upon the two children,
but had married the other woman instead, it would not have been
surprising if Kyoko Oba would still have exercised the last power
she had in deciding the death of her two daughters and herself as a
last protest and victory. In this light, Kyoko Oba indeed had her
victory. Hiroyoshi Oba joined his wife and two children in death
when in life his indifference and abandonment of them had been a
basic cause of their final suffering and path toward death.

There could be no clearer example of where one-sided dedication and
complete identification of the whole self with any one ascribed role
within the family sphere can lead for a woman who is trapped, who
has no possible alternate course of action. With no other avenue for
survival, death becomes a welcomed friend indeed. How many infanti-
cides and suicides of mothers in Japan's long history have been the
final protest and victory of women with no other alternative but
death?

The woman who has identified intensely with her ascribed roles of
wife and mother, made even more stationary by gravitational forces
in society today, will experience those narrow walls of pressure moving in mercilessly upon her and her children. The time for a woman

to pioneer her own way, to achieve her own position as human being, to develop the strength to endure on her own feet is long before any personal or family crisis erupts. If she waits until then before seriously considering such realities, she may find herself without strength, inner resources, values, confidence, any preparation, or qualifications to confront the strong counter-currents of a man-made, man-directed society.

SUICIDE AS PROTEST AND RECONCILIATION

In the attempt to better understand suicidal phenomena among Japanese women, attention has been directed repeatedly to the strong forces and influences converging upon women from two different spheres, those from modern Japanese society and those from the sphere of tradition and custom preserved through the family.

Modern Japanese society blends these varied layers of influence, both traditional and modern. Yet there are also times when the differing demands of these separate spheres clash sharply rather than harmonize. While the modern sphere provides most of the opportunities for woman's increased development and utilization of personal talents and qualifications to pursue life on her own when necessary, the traditional sphere as the family and ascriptive roles through marriage preserves the closest, most intimate human relationships and ties with family ancestors. Findings from surveys on the Japanese national character over the past twenty years have uncovered little or no change. "We could say . . . that the Japanese national character consists essentially in personal relations because the least changeable things are regarded of greatest value. Needless to say, these personal relations form the foundation of all social problems."[26]

Through family ties, therefore, the most essential, fundamental, and valued elements of Japanese culture are transmitted and preserved from generation to generation. And women, as explained previously, are the chief bearer-transmitters of that culture. This also helps to explain the unique demands made on Japanese women within their unique society, which only they have experienced and are capable of describing.

We have observed that the highest annual suicide rates over the past fifty years escalate in early adulthood (20-24/25-29), and again in advancing years, especially after sixty. Sufficient evidence has been presented by women who are fortunately still alive and able to share past crisis experiences. Hundreds described the trauma of adolescence and the early twenties, experiencing a loss of all meaning in human life, living while feeling dead within. The media, education, literature, many other influences from the modern sectors stimulated this questioning of values and traditions, of discovering their own meaning and answers in life. This period of traumatic struggle for growth and inner development would have been far more acute for the first wave of postwar coeducated young women who after high school or college sought to integrate themselves into a rebuilding society yet unaccustomed to extreme deviations from prewar traditional norms for women. The high rate of suicide among divorced and widowed women from twenty to twenty-nine years of age was evident during the peak years for this age group, 1954 to 1960, just as these factors have been shown to be highly significant in the suicide of women this age in 1965 and 1970.

During this stage in life and later, when young women launch out into society through employment, they experience pressures from traditional expectations of them even within the most modern work settings. Women experience tension and conflicts arising from these two spheres, the modern sector and the underlying tradition, due to contradictory demands on women in the same work place. The outer socioeconomic sphere requires from her proficiency, intelligence, responsibility, competency, creativity, initiative, and rational thought and behavior. Only if she is capable of meeting a certain standard in these demands, can she function at all in this modern sector, especially after her twenties. In the same work environment, however, traditional ascriptive ideals for her as woman require docility, obedience and submission to men, dependence and modesty, refraining from overt expression of creative thinking.

The conflicting demands of these distinct spheres of society create the basic conflicts women experience in their most fundamental role as woman-person. Here also is the source of the strong counter-currents women encounter through employment and participation in the modern institutions of society. Yet, for young women prior to marriage, "swimming upstream" against counter-currents and traditional pressures can serve as a kind of "life insurance" should a crisis arise. Withstanding pressures to marry and begin a family mechanically at a certain age can become life preserving in the end. Young women pursuing professions and employment seem to be discovering important values and gaining the necessary experience to integrate family and social roles throughout their lifetime. Such women do not seem to feel they have accomplished their life's purpose merely by finding a husband, giving birth to children and safeguarding their own families. Evidently, these women have been enlivened at another level, at the core of their being. Only continual deepening of their central values in life will satisfy them or enable them to respond through other contingent roles, whatever they may be.

Examples of such women were numerous and especially evident among student nurses interviewed. Their final decision to enter a nursing career was made in full awareness of unfavorable working conditions, poor wages and the low regard for this occupation in Japanese society today. Yet they finally decided upon nursing not for the sake of material values but because they would be able to pursue a nursing career throughout life, whether single or married. They had been first attracted to nursing out of human values, and these remained the first priority in the final decision. Not even protesting parents could force a change in this decision. One bitterly disappointed mother told her daughter, about to depart for Tokyo to enter nurses' training, "Don't ever come to us if you have any difficulties. From now on you are on your own."

Women divorced or widowed between twenty to twenty-nine years of age seem to be particularly vulnerable in their inability to resist the counter-currents of society when catapulted from within the family. Unfortunately, insufficient data from divorced and widowed women in their twenties was obtained from the survey and interviews. Nevertheless, it is possible to understand the conflicts they are required to endure and overcome. It is also apparent how easily suicide can become the final course of action for those ill prepared in crisis to cope in confidence and self-reliance for their own or their children's sake.

Death rates by age-specific groups in 1970, indicating whether employed or not employed at time of death, reveal that unemployed women between twenty to twenty-nine have suicide as the highest cause of death. Among unemployed women twenty to twenty-four years of age, the death ratio was 2.4 to 1, higher than for employed women (Employed Death Rate, 45.4/ Not Employed at Death, 111.1). Similarly, women unemployed between the ages of twenty-five and twenty-nine revealed a death ratio of 1.4 to 1 over employed women (Employed Death Rate, 67.4/ Not Employed at Death, 91.1). This may imply some type of relationship, since the high suicide rate for women between twenty and twenty-nine is largely attributed to divorced and widowed women this age (see Figures 3 and 4). It seems evident that there is some kind of correlation between the suicide rate for the twenty to twenty-nine age group, divorced or widowed status at this age, and the absence of employment at the time of death.

A difficult period in the life of single women arises in advancing years due to conflicting demands from the modern and traditional spheres of society. Single women with a profession or employment in society fulfilled high standards of achievement. At the same time, they may or may not have attempted to satisfy traditional expectations by finding alternatives for family-oriented ascriptive roles. However, retirement from active work in society forces the single women to fall back upon the traditional sphere of the family, sometimes completely. If alternate human relationships have not been formed and maintained throughout life, this can prove to be a crushing and discouraging experience. Since such a woman is no longer functioning for society, her long service and achievement may well be forgotten in the impersonalism and anonymity of modern society. Who will care for her in advancing old age? When she dies, who will remember and venerate her spirit? Perhaps these questions loom larger as women approach the sunset of life.

The two women who had attempted suicide had one important characteristic in common. Neither had entered into achievement-oriented roles beyond the family up to the time of their attempted suicide. Both were protesting in a hopeless situation, after attempts at solving the problem had failed. Fortunately, both women lived through the painful experience. The subsequent courses each pursued further emphasized the vulnerability keenly felt at the time of their suicide attempts. Both subsequently began preparing themselves for involvement in society and economic self-reliance through a specialized work or artistic skill.

Looking at events leading up to the family suicide reported, a new dimension in family relationships comes to light. The function of death in the Oba family suicide seems to be twofold: as protest and reconciliation. The protest of Kyoko Oba has been discussed at length, as well as the events pressing her to this last stand. No one else would ever usurp her rightfully-gained position within the Oba family. In defending this position, she exercised her one prerogative left in life. By the act of suicide and infanticide she took her two daughters with her back to their place of origin, where all family ancestors abide. Her husband most likely followed her and the children, since society would have vindicated his crime in other ways.

Death by suicide became a means of reconciling both the living and dead members of the family. The living were reconciled through the act because bonds between those who die together become secure forever. These same human bonds which had been hopelessly ruptured and severed in life became forged together in death, then fused eternally among the ancestral spirits. "Everything passes with time." The passage of time slowly but surely wipes away all memory of the crime and guilt against society. In the end, it is the family which preserves the ultimate relationship, the link between the living and deceased members of the family. Ultimately, the family does reward in its own way, long after society has forgotten, by preserving the bond with its members living on in spirit. They still abide close by, able to perceive gestures of affection from descendants and respond to their needs in a two-way relationship that has persisted throughout the ages. And it will continue.

In this final and ultimate reconciliation provided by death, the Japanese seem to maintain their preference for harmony at the deepest level of their character, culture, and society. This level lies far beneath the outer modern strata of society most apparent to the world, far below the discordant noises, pushing crowds, the hustle and hurry of everyday life and work in twentieth century Japan. Only by viewing this society through the life experiences of its women can one ever begin to comprehend the meaning of some of its truly gallant women.

NOTES

[1] Masaaki Kato, "Self-Destruction in Japan: A Cross-Cultural Epidemiological Analysis of Suicide," pp. 360-382.

[2] Throughout his works, Kunio Yanagida cites numerous examples of the Japanese attitude toward death, ancestral spirits and annual rituals which celebrate their beliefs. Kunio Yanagida, *Our Ancestors*, pp. 145-146.

[3] Nakamura Hajime has explained this principle in relation to contemporary Japan: "The people to whom a human nexus is important place great moral emphasis upon complete and willing dedication of the self to others in a specific human collective. This attitude, though it may be a 'basic moral requirement in all peoples, occupies a dominant position in Japanese social life. Self-dedication to a specific human nexus has been one of the most powerful factors in Japanese history." Nakamura Hajime, *Ways of Thinking of Eastern Peoples*, pp. 414-415.

[4] A comprehensive theory of *amae* is developed by Takeo Doi in *The Anatomy of Dependence;* see Doi's reference to individual-group tension, pp. 132-141.

[5] The necessity of making clear distinctions between ideal and actual roles is set forth by Marion Levy in *Modernization and the Structure of Societies,* Vol. 1 and 2.

[6] For discussions of prewar and postwar educational curricula for girls see: *Developments in Japanese Education: 1945-1952,* and *Education in 1962.*

[7] *Gendai Nihon Joshi Gakusei* [On Present-day Japanese Women Students], and Azumi Koya, *Higher Education and Business Recruitment in Japan.*

[8] William Goode outlines his theory of "role strain" as a key concept for investigating and understanding social structures. "A Theory of Role Strain," *American Sociological Review,* XXIV (1960) pp. 483-496.

[9] The present approach receives support from the fact that psychological autopsies are now being conducted routinely after suicides in some parts of the world. The Death Investigation Team of a California Suicide Prevention Center, which includes a psychologist, psychiatrist, social worker and sometimes a graphologist, "proceeds with careful non-leading interviews of the victim's friends and relations, investigating the period that preceded death, the biography and *life style,* the past history and possibility of death or *suicidal thoughts* [emphasis added], contemporary of or anterior to the fatal suicide." J. Doubrier, "Legal Aspects on Suicide and Attempted Suicide," *Suicide and Attempted Suicide* (Skandia International Symposia), pp. 148-159.

[10] Professor Kazuko Tsurumi's insights and valuable comments provided additional guidance in devising a parallel role scale which would aid in determining higher or lower degrees of fulfillment in ascribed roles, achieved roles or an integration of both family-oriented and society-oriented roles, assuming that experienced satisfaction is higher for women at the top of the scale.

[11] Kazuko Tsurumi develops the many-layered system of tension management theory in *Social Change and the Individual.* With regard to suicide, Professor Tsurumi proposes that suicide in Japan operates as a many-layered system of tension management in which are found distinct substrata of values, patterns and relationships pertaining to suicidal acts which have been accumulated and separately retained by folk religion, Shinto, Buddhism, Bushido, Confucianism, and the modern superstrata of exogenous ideologies, philosophies and religions.

[12] Hideo Kishimoto, "Some Japanese Cultural Traits and Religions," C.A. Moore (ed.), *The Japanese Mind,* p. 119.

[13]Ichiro Hori, *Folk Religion in Japan*, pp. 30-31; 206., Masaharu Anesaki, *History of Japanese Religion*, pp. 6-7; 11; 39-40., Hisako Kamata, "Daughters of the Gods: Shaman Priestesses in Japan and Okinawa," *Folk Cultures of Japan and East Asia*, pp. 56-73.

[14]As pointed out by Hori and Yanagida: Kunio Yanagida, *About our Ancestors*, pp. 166-168.

[15]Inazo Nitobe, *Bushido: The Soul of Japan*, pp. 11-12.

[16]Chiyoko Higuchi, *Her Place in the Sun: Women Who Shaped Japan*, pp. 27-69.

[17]Hideo Kishimoto, "Some Japanese Cultural Traits and Religions," C.A. Moore (ed.), *The Japanese Mind*, p. 119.

[18]*Ibid.*, pp. 119-120.

[19]Hidetoshi Katō, "Jisatsu Style no Hensen" [Changes in the Styles of Suicide], Ohara Kenjirō (ed.), *Jisatsu*, pp. 226-235.

[20]Keiichi Chikazawa, *Jisatsu no Kenkyū*.

[21]Tetsuo Kajiya, *Nihonjin no Jisatsu*, pp. 22-29.

[22]Suzuki describes *myō* as follows: "When one is resolved to die, that is when the thought of death is wiped off the field of consciousness, there arises something in it, or rather, apparently from the outside, the presence of which one has never been aware of, and when the strange presence begins to direct one's activities in an instinctual manner wonders are achieved. These wonders are called *myō*. *Myō* is thus in some way related to instinct. When life is not intellectually and therefore consciously conditioned but left to the inner working of the Unconscious, it takes care of itself in an almost reflex automatic fashion, as in the case of the physiological functioning of an organic body." Daisetz Suzuki, *Zen and Japanese Culture*, p. 197.

[23]*Ibid.*, p. 197.

[24]Among the 75 women interviewed, 52 percent acknowledged having contemplated suicide as a solution to their problems, a slightly higher ratio than the 45 percent reported by survey respondents. Inquiring further into the specific age at which they had experienced suicidal thoughts, 33 percent reported it had been between twenty and twenty-four years of age; 28 percent between the ages of fifteen and nineteen; 10 percent between ten and fourteen years of age; 10 percent between twenty-five and twenty-nine. Smaller percentages were distributed throughout the thirties, forties, and fifties. Reasons given by interviewees closely resembled those reported by survey respondents by specific age groups.

[25]Mrs. M. was among the persons requested by police to identify the recovered bodies of Kyoko Oba, Mitsuru, Akira, and Hiroyoshi Oba after they had taken a death leap into the sea from a cliff on the southern tip of Izu Peninsula on September 6, 1973. From April to June of the same year, the writer had taught Mitsuru as one of the pupils in her first grade class at Toshima Saturday School.

[26]Yosiyuki Sakamoto, "A Study of the Japanese National Character," Chikio Hayashi *et al.*, *An Analysis of the Institute of Statistical Mathematics*, p. 43. Sigeki Nisihira, also a member of the Committee on the Study of Japanese National Character, discusses these unchanged aspects in Japanese human relations in "Changed and Unchanged Characteristics of the Japanese " (translated from *Jiyū*), *Japan Echo*, Vol. 1, No. 2, 1974.

CHAPTER
14
CONCLUSIONS

There is no gainsaying that Japan has changed significantly in the postwar period, its women along with its men. Women are exercising their new legal rights to vote and hold office, to own and transmit property, and to divorce. More women sit in the Japanese Diet than in the United States Congress. Women have contributed too in significant ways to Japan's "miraculous" economic growth and power.

What we have traced here is how these external, objective changes have altered the lives and values of individual Japanese women. To what extent urbanization, the nuclear family residence pattern, increased participation in the work force, and new political rights have changed the life styles and aspirations of women has been the focus of this study. Despite numerous and impressive external changes in patterns of living, there is much of the fabric of the feminine tradition in Japan which has resisted change. Despite the growth in economic strength of individual women, they have been slow to incorporate their new financial independence into individual value structures. For most women the traditional domestic role identity remains a comfortable one.

The majority of women in Japan, whether married or single, cling to the traditional definition of woman as "good wife and wise mother." There has been no fundamental questioning of this traditional ideal. Many thousands of women are able to live fulfilling lives within this traditional role. There are indications, nonetheless, that many thousands of other women are exploring a two-role life style, fundamentally committed to the domestic role but also gainfully employed outside the home. There are indicators that it is

297

not always dire financial necessity that draws women out of the home but also a desire to work within a broader framework, to widen their horizons. The dual-role life style is increasingly important in the lives of Japanese women, who report considerable job satisfaction.

Women who adhere to the single-role life style are subject to tensions within that domestic role. Many women gain emotional satisfaction primarily through their relationships with their children, since companionship is not part of the traditional husband-wife relationship. Others, who find their identity threatened when their one role is dissolved through death or divorce are faced with an existential crisis. Some are unable to resolve the crisis and turn to the ultimate way out, suicide, as Sister Cecchini's authoritative study attests. Loss of a sole role is more threatening to women at the ends of the life span than to those in the middle years who can continue to find satisfaction in raising children or in jobs.

Housewives provide most of the volunteers for the consumers' groups, citizens' groups, and environmental protection groups that have burgeoned in the last ten years. Through working in these groups housewives have gained in confidence and in awareness of the effectiveness of their impact when they act collectively. Such volunteer work has also helped to alleviate the social isolation of the housewife.

Farm women are feeling acutely the effects of the progressive depopulation of the rural areas. Decline in the status of older women, greater independence of younger and middle-aged women, and multiple roles for those women left on the farms are all part of the transition from country to city. Among over-worked rural women who live out the roles of housewife, mother, farmer, and outside wage-earner, there is a wish for a day off, a rainy day at home, and an awareness that there will not be many more generations after them on the farm, as Bernstein indicates.

Japanese women have a longer history of working in factories than in nearly any other occupation except farming. Sheila Matsumoto vividly described the inhuman working and dormitory conditions endured by girls indentured by impoverished parents to silk-reeling factories in the early stages of the industrial revolution. Today over half the female factory workers are married, they are "protected" in part by postwar labor legislation, and they have more leisure time. Yet they do not question their lower salaries or the traditional feminine role.

For women working outside the home the dual-peak employment pattern is prevalent. Young women work until the age of twenty-four or twenty-five, the age when marriage withdraws them from the work force. During the childrearing years they remain at home in greater numbers. The second age peak in the work force occurs when they reach their mid-forties, when their children are in high school or older. This dual-age employment pattern is a matter of government policy as well as widespread employment practice. The dual-age-peak work force has wide-ranging economic and social ramifications. It means that women are generally employed in low-paying, menial jobs, often defined as "part-time" when in fact they may be more than full time. It means also that they are deprived of the usual fringe benefits enjoyed by male employees: pensions, insurance, medical care, vacations, and bonuses for seniority. Despite the legal provisions for equal pay, employers do not comply in practice. One of the reasons for nonobservance of the law is that the courts do not have a clear record as yet for enforcing legislation. Labor legislation in fact is often used not to protect women but to justify discriminatory practices. Women are thus effectively shut out from management positions in any large institution, whether government or private.

All these disadvantages are especially apparent in the largest category of working women, office girls, who comprise thirty percent of the female work force. These are girls who often come from the countryside, who with high school and even college education enter offices for two or three years before marriage, thus reinforcing the low expectations of managers of large firms. "Office ladies" and factory women, together nearly 60 percent of all working women, live dual-role lives for a few years but seldom abandon the single-role ideology. By and large they endure without questioning the possibilities beyond the traditional ideal.

As both students and teachers, women have been much slower than men to benefit from the educational advances of the past century. Coeducation began at the universities after World War II, yet women students form less than one-fifth the student body at four-year colleges but more than ninety percent at tradition-oriented two-year colleges. Women teachers outnumber men only at the primary school level, which has been considered their "natural" place as teachers. Before the war powerful sanctions in social attitudes and employment practices relegated women teachers to a minority position in schools at all levels. Today they still suffer discrimination in salary, retirement, medical benefits and promotion, especially to administration. Yet working conditions in public schools compare favorably with other occupations, as Mouer explains. Despite many drawbacks, women teachers are working with genuine dedication, and many do not accept the single-role ideology. As their ideas are transmitted to students, social attitudes toward the traditional ideal will gradually change.

Another traditional occupation for women is working in small family businesses. While women have been completely shut out from the managerial level of large corporations, women as accountants or managers of family businesses play a significant role in the small-scale domestic sector of the economy. Family businesses have a tradition stretching back at least as far as the Tokugawa period, when wives of merchants often acted as accountants in family enterprises. It was this small-scale domestic sector of the economy which Professor Lockwood believes in the Meiji industrial revolution provided the greatest impetus to real growth in the economy, by contrast with the "modern growth" of large corporations.[1] This sphere of the economy is a place where women are making a significant impact today. In a family business a woman with entrepreneurial skill is seen as an asset to the whole family, rather than as someone who has gone her own way, as Maxson points out. It is significant that a woman in the family business often functions as bookkeeper, a counterpart of her role within the family as manager of the family purse. In various other ways too the structure of the family business articulates with the structure of the family.

Women in the service industries, single or married, know from experience that they have earning power and can be financially self-sustaining, but they have difficulty verbalizing their independence. One reason may be that serving others is in accord with the traditional feminine ideal. Even when they have demonstrated considerable skill and acumen in business they have not repudiated some of the strictures of the old definition of woman's role. Yet the service industries are in many ways a symbolic category, and the women are proud of skills which distinguish them from women in the *mizu shōbai.*

Bar hostesses, contemporary counterparts of earlier geisha, enter the occupation not so much because of poverty as because of lack of vocational skills, and the expectation of making a large salary and meeting interesting people. These expectations attract thousands of young women to an occupation which has no real counterpart in the West. They are drawn to the hostess profession despite the social opprobrium which accompanies it. The bar and hostesses are part of an institution which is supported in large part by giant corporations and their expense-account executives. There are two million hostesses in Japan today.[2]

To make a subservient job psychologically palatable it appears necessary to demean oneself or one's sex verbally or intellectually. "Office ladies," stewardesses, factory workers, and bar hostesses tend to accept without question the tradition of male superiority. A host of proverbs about the nature of women perpetuates and popularizes the tradition of feminine inferiority. Such maxims as "a woman's thinking is shallow;" "women are thoughtless;" and "women are as changeable as the autumn sky" engender in women a belief in the male perspective. It is a perspective that women have not yet repudiated ideologically.

Of course there are exceptions, women of outstanding ability and drive who, often with an international connection, have propelled themselves to the top. But they remain an extremely small élite, and in some cases their concerns are élitist rather than for the majority of women. Success and achievement orientation have almost no place in the traditional aspirations of Japanese women. What Matina Horner speaks of as the "fear of success" among American women is a syndrome that has not developed in Japan, except perhaps as a fear of the unknown. The prescription that a woman does not achieve for herself outside the family has been inculcated for so long that when a woman does develop a will to achieve it is against such formidable societal barriers that she aspires without subtle psychological second thoughts.

Encouragement within the family of daughters who go into élite occupations differs significantly from the socialization of women who become housewives or enter the more traditional occupations. Seventy-five percent of parents in a recent nationwide survey hoped their sons would grow up to be "manly" and their daughters to be "womanly." While nearly 50 percent of mothers polled hoped their sons would go to universities, only 14 percent hoped their daughters would follow the same course.[3]

Women in the small élite occupations have achieved through early family support, and their motivation has been nurtured in the home environment. Where women in more usual occupations have not been given encouragement or the opportunity for higher education, women in the élite have been encouraged within the family, often from an early age, to believe that they can achieve anything to which they aspire. Women in the more traditional professions were often encouraged by both parents. Women in the media were frequently encouraged by mothers in the face of opposition from fathers, as Paulson related. Women in politics, on the other hand, were often encouraged by Westernized fathers, as Carlberg points out. They have become part of the political establishment and appear less committed to change than women in the media, who encountered obstacles at home from male authority and developed mechanisms for dealing with the opposition of the "establishment."

Social institutions have not-so-subtle tactics for dealing with women who seek to compete on equal terms with men. A woman who succeeds in obtaining a Ph.D. from a prestigious university, for example, is not likely to receive assistance in finding a job or in facilitating her career. One exceptionally able young woman who had completed all requirements for her degree, including her dissertation, was told she would not be able to get her Ph.D. for another ten years because she was "too young." This is not to say that men with degrees from the same university always have an easy time professionally. The academic scene in Japan is as ridden with cliquism as the American, if not more so. Yet if two candidates have equal qualifications a position will automatically go to the male candidate, not the female candidate. A woman who takes the safer, more traditional route— through the women's colleges and universities—will have an easier time in advancing her career than a woman who has attempted to compete in coeducational institutions. The more prestigious the institution the more likely a woman is to be shut out professionally, as Dilatush's findings attest.

Women who achieve in sports attain a kind of freedom and besides bring prestige and honor to Japan. They are part of a very small group of women who are entering a variety of new professions in Japan. One such was Junko Tabei, first woman ever to climb Mount Everest, yet her name is little known outside Japan. A much larger number of women are participating in amateur sports, especially *"mamasan* volleyball," drawing on the tradition of calisthenics practiced in all Japanese schools and many companies. Women in sports do not incur the opprobrium they are often accorded in the West, where professional sportswomen tend to be regarded as masculine.

Women who deviate so far from the feminine norm that societal prescriptions do not apply achieve a certain freedom. This is the freedom foreign women often experience in Japan. Society has not determined how to judge them. An early example of a woman who achieved this kind of freedom was Sayō Kitamura, the "dancing goddess," founder of one of the new religions. Harking back to the ancient shamanistic tradition, several women in the nineteenth and early twentieth centuries founded chiliastic new religions out of a combination of elements of Shinto, Buddhism, and the folk and shamanistic traditions. In the case of Sayō Kitamura, during World War II she referred to the emperor as the "maggot emperor," and railed so against political institutions that she was jailed briefly. Yet being so far beyond the pale lent her a kind of immunity.

How does a thinking woman protest against the relegation to inferiority? The degree to which a woman complies and works within the establishment or protests of course varies with the individual. It is up to each woman to determine how she can make her protest most effectively, or whether she will protest at all. Articulate protest is available primarily to the highly educated woman. Women working in the media are in perhaps the best position to effect change in the image of women, and many of these women do have proposals for producing change through the media. They also have the advantage of the media's traditional role as social critic. Yet most influential image-makers are still men, who perpetuate the traditional female image. Women in politics, by contrast, must necessarily work within the framework of their party structures, and they are relative newcomers. Women in education can exert their influence through their impact on the thinking of the next generation.

Some women despair of effecting change through the establishment. This is not a phenomenon unique to Japan. What recourse do women have in Japan once they have repudiated the notion of working within the establishment? We have the example of actions taken by some. One woman recently ran against Mayor Minobe in the mayoralty election in Tokyo. She did not have the support of a major party; her platform was a rejection of capitalism and imperialism. She worked on the fringes of the establishment and sought to attract its attention. Other young women have turned to violence. Hiroko Nagata was a member of the Red Army group implicated in the murders of fourteen students a few years ago. She was imprisoned along with the male members of the group. It was she, however, who was singled out for daily vilification by the press, which explained her aberrations as due to a "thyroid problem," but noted daily that she was "showing signs of weakening." The press was unwilling to credit her with convictions of any political or ideological significance. More recently Fusako Shigenobu, another leader of the Red Army, has gained international notoriety by her alleged master-minding of the violence at the airports in Tel Aviv and Kuala Lumpur. Political and economic reporting in the press remains strictly within the male purview, and news is accordingly reported from a male viewpoint.

The radical feminist movement in Japan is similarly a small underground phenomenon, shunning any publicity or activity in the mainstream of Japanese society. These are women who have completely repudiated the traditional role definition of wife and mother, who seek a kind of liberation not condoned within the social structure. This does not mean that they have necessarily turned to lesbianism, even though homosexuality has been tolerated for centuries in the male samurai society of feudal Japan, as well as in modern Japan. Their deviation is not sexual but rather social; they choose to pursue the development of their own individual potential, whatever it may be.

It is too early yet to determine whether Japanese women will return in a heightened consciousness to their nation's own mythic feminine cosmogenesis. If that should happen we might see a revival in modern form of an ancient tradition which differs sharply from Japan's patriarchally-written history. This remains, however, a very hypothetical prospect. If change is not generated from within the media and the image projected *by* the media, or by the power of economic independence that some women have achieved, it is difficult to project a paradigm for change in the Japanese feminine role.

What shows through in the profiles of many individual women presented in categories here is tremendous strength. Beyond the passive strength of endurance which most Japanese women have, many women display the courage to choose their own path and to follow it. In Japanese society this is often a feat of heroic proportions. These are women who, despite a rigidly submissive, self-sacrificing feminine tradition describe themselves as stubborn, independent, and choosing their own way. They are a moving testament to the human spirit.

NOTES

[1]William L. Lockwood, *The Economic Development of Japan: Growth and Structural Change*, p. 575.

[2]Ōba Ayako, *Fujin Rōdō* [Female Labor], p. 305. According to Ms. Jackson the government is unable to confirm this figure due to lack of data on hostesses.

[3]Ministry of Foreign Affairs, *Status of Women in Modern Japan: Report on a Nationwide Survey*, 1975, p. 22.

CHAPTER 1

Ackroyd, Joyce. "Women in Feudal Japan." *Transactions of Asiatic Society,*
7 (November 1959), 31-68.

Aston, W. G., ed. and tr. *Nihongi.* Rutland, Vermont, and Tokyo: Charles E.
Tuttle Company, Inc., 1972.

Bacon, Alice Mabel. *Japanese Girls and Women.* Boston and New York:
Houghton Mifflin and Company, 1902.

Beard, Mary R. *The Force of Women in Japanese History.* Washington, D.C.:
Public Affairs Press, 1953.

Burton, Margaret E. *Women Workers of the Orient.* West Medford, Mass.:
The Central Committee on the United Study of Foreign Missions, 1918.

Cranmer-Byng, L., and Dr. S. A. Kapadia, eds. *Women and Wisdom of Japan.*
London: John Murray, 1914.

Dore, R. P. *Education in Tokugawa Japan.* Berkeley: University of California
Press, 1965.

Haas, Margi. "The First Birth Control Movement in Japan." Unpublished
paper. Cambridge: Harvard University, 1975.

Hall, Robert King. *Education for a New Japan.* New Haven: Yale University
Press, 1949.

Hane, Mikiso. *Japan: A Historical Survey.* New York: Charles Scribner's
Sons, 1972.

Ishimoto, Shidzue. *Facing Two Ways: The Story of My Life.* New York:
Farrar & Rinehart, Inc., 1935.

Kaigo, Tokiomi. *Japanese Education—Its Past and Present.* Tokyo: Japan
Cultural Society, 1968.

Keene, Donald, ed. *Anthology of Japanese Literature.* Evergreen Edition.
New York: Grove Press, 1960.

Lebra, Joyce C. "The Feminine Ideal With Reference to Japanese Law." Unpublished paper. Cambridge: Harvard University, 1954.

Matsuoka, Yoko. *Daughter of the Pacific.* New York: Harper & Brothers, 1952.

McCullough, William H. "Japanese Marriage Institutions in the Heian Period." *Harvard Journal of Asiatic Studies,* 27 (1967), 103-167.

Mishima, Sumie Seo. *The Broader Way.* New York: The John Day Company, 1953.

Morris, Ivan. "Marriage in the World of Genji." *Asia,* 11 (Spring, 1968), 54-75.

Murasaki, Lady. *The Tale of Genji.* Trans. Arthur Waley. The Modern Library Edition. New York: Random House, 1960.

Nakane, Chie. *Human Relations in Japan.* Japan: Ministry of Foreign Affairs, 1972.

Nyun-Han, Emma. "The Socio-Political Roles of Women in Japan and Burma." Ph.D. dissertation, University of Colorado, Boulder, 1972.

Okamura, Masu. *Women's Status: Changing Japan.* Tokyo: The International Society for Educational Information, Inc., 1973.

Ōkuma, Count Shigenobu, ed. *Fifty Years of New Japan.* Vol. II. London: Smith, Elder & Co., 1910.

Passin, Herbert. *Society and Education in Japan.* New York: Teachers College, Columbia University, 1965.

Philippi, Donald L., ed. and tr. *Kojiki.* Tokyo: University of Tokyo Press, 1968.

Sansom, G. B. *A History of Japan to 1334.* Stanford, California: Stanford University Press, 1974.

——————. *Japan: A Short Cultural History.* New York: Appleton-Century-Crofts, 1962.

Sugimoto, Etsu Inagaki. *A Daughter of the Samurai.* Garden City, New York: Doubleday Doran and Co., Inc., 1934.

Totten, G. O. *The Social Democratic Movement in Prewar Japan.* New Haven: Yale University Press, 1966.

Vavich, Dee Ann. "The Japanese Woman's Movement: Ichikawa Fusae—A Pioneer in Woman's Suffrage." *Monumenta Nipponica,* 22, nos. 3-4 (1967), 401-436.

Women's and Minors' Bureau. *The Status of Women in Japan.* Japan: Ministry of Labor, 1973, 1974.

Yoshida, K. and T. Kaigo. *Japanese Education.* Japan: Board of Tourist Industry, Japanese Government Railways, 1937.

CHAPTER 2

Ehime-ken nen sekai nōringyō sensasu [Ehime Prefecture Annual World Farm and Forestry Census] 1971.

Fujin ni kansuru Shomondai Chōsa Kaigi [Conference for Investigating Various Problems Concerning Women], ed. *Gendai Nihon Josei to Kōdō* [Contemporary Japanese Women's Attitudes and Behavior]. Tokyo: Ōkurashō [Ministry of Finance], 1974.

Kazuo, Akasaka. "The Changing Farm Scene," *The East,* vol. VIII, no. 9 (Oct., 1972), 14-17.

Maruoka, Hideko, and Ōshima, Kiyoshi. *Nōson Fujin* [Rural Women]. Tokyo: Aki shobō, 1971.

Matsushita Kei'ichi, ed. *Gendai Fujin Mondai Nyūmon* [Introduction to the Problems of Modern Women]. Tokyo: Nihon Hyōronsha, 1970.

Minori (Harvest). no. 3 (1970), magazine of the Uwa township Women's Guild of the Farmers Cooperative Association.

Nōka Fujin no Rōdō Seikatsu ni kansuru Ishiki Chōsa [Survey of Farm Families' Attitudes Towards their Working Lives]. Tokyo: Rōdōshō Fujin-shōnenkyoku, 1968.

Nōkyō fujinbu techō [Handbook of the Women's Guild of the Farmers Cooperative Association], 1974.

Okamura, Masu. *Women's Status: Changing Japan.* Tokyo: International Society for Educational Information, Inc., 1973.

Rōdōshō Fujin-shōnenkyoku, ed. *Fujin no genjō* [The Status of Women]. Japan: Fujin-Shōnen Kyōkai [Women's and Minors' Bureau, Ministry of Labor], 1971.

Women's and Minors' Bureau. *The Status of Women in Japan.* Japan: Ministry of Labor, 1974.

Yamada, Keiko. *Nōson ni Ikiru Shufutachi* [Housewives Who Live in Farming Villages]. Tokyo: Nōsangyoson Bunka Kaigi, 1973.

CHAPTER 3
SOURCES IN WESTERN LANGUAGES

Abegglen, James. *Management and Worker, the Japanese Solution.* Tokyo: Kodansha International Ltd. and Sophia University, 1973.

Allinson, Gary D. *Japanese Urbanism: Industry and Politics in Kariya, 1872-1972.* Berkeley, Los Angeles, and London: University of California Press, 1975.

Ayusawa, Iwao F. *A History of Labor in Modern Japan.* Honolulu: East-West Center Press, 1966.

——————. *Organized Labor in Japan Part I: Postwar Developments in Organized Labor, 1945-1952.* Tokyo: The Foreign Affairs Association of Japan.

Bacon, A. *Japanese Girls and Women.* Boston and New York: Houghton Mifflin and Co., 1902.

Ballon, Robert J. *The Japanese Employee.* Tokyo: Sophia University, 1969.

Barbour, Katherine H. *Women of Japan.* New York: The Women's Press, 1936.

Beard, Mary R. *The Force of Women in Japanese History.* Washington, D.C.: Public Affairs Press, 1953.

Beardsley, Richard K. with John W. Hall and Robert E. Ward. *Village Japan.* Chicago: University of Chicago Press, 1959.

Benedict, Ruth. *The Chrysanthemum and the Sword.* Boston: Houghton, Mifflin and Co., 1946.

Cole, Robert E. *Japanese Blue Collar: The Changing Tradition.* Berkeley and Los Angeles: University of California Press, 1971.

Darbois, Dominique. *Noriko, Girl of Japan.* Chicago: Follett Publishing Co., 1954.

Dempster, Pru. *Japan Advances, a Geographical Study.* London: Methuen and Co. Ltd., 1969.

308

Dore, Ronald. *Aspects of Social Change in Modern Japan.* Princeton: Princeton University Press, 1967.

_____. *British Factory—Japanese Factory.* London: George Allen and Unwin, Ltd., 1973.

_____. *City Life in Japan.* Berkeley: University of California Press, 1963.

Dufource, Elisabeth. *Les Femmes Japonaises.* Paris: Denoëls, 1969.

Faust, Allen K. *The New Japanese Womanhood.* George H. Doran Co., 1926.

Fukutake, Tadashi. *Japanese Rural Society.* (Translated by R. P. Dore). Ithaca, N.Y.: Cornell University Press, 1972.

Gulick, Sidney L. *Working Women of Japan.* New York: Missionary Education Movement of the United States and Canada, 1915.

Harada, Siuchi. *Labor Conditions in Japan.* New York: AMS Press, Inc., 1928.

Hata, Riotaro. *Uber Die Frauen.* Wien: A. Hartleben's Verlag, 1896.

The Japanese Woman's Commission. *Japanese Women.* Chicago: World Columbian Exposition, 1893.

Katayama, Tetsu (Foreign Affairs Association of Japan). *Women's Movement in Japan.* Tokyo: Kenkyusha, 1938.

Kawai, Michi. *Japanese Women Speak.* Boston: Central Committee on the United Study of Foreign Missions, 1934.

Kirk, Ruth. *Sigemi: A Japanese Village Girl.* New York: Harcourt Brace Jovanovich, Inc., 1965.

Lal, Chaman. *Behind the Guns.* Bombay: New Book Co., 1940.

Lu, David John. *Sources of Japanese History.* New York: McGraw-Hill Book Company, 1974.

Mishima, Sumie. *The Broader Way.* Westport, Connecticut: Greenwood. Prepr. of 1953 ed.

Morley, James. *Japan and Korea—America's Allies in the Pacific.* New York: Walker and Company, 1965.

Nakane, Chie. *Japanese Society.* Berkeley and Los Angeles: University of California Press, 1972.

Nehru, S. S. *Money, Men, and Women in Japan.* Tokyo: International Publishing and Printing Company, 1936.

Norbeck, Edward. *Changing Japan.* New York: Holt, Rinehart, and Winston, 1965.

Okamura, Masu. *Women's Status: Changing Japan.* Tokyo: International Society for Educational Information, Inc., 1973.

Plath, David W. *The After Hours: Modern Japan and the Search for Enjoyment.* Berkeley: University of California Press, 1969.

Reischauer, E. O. *Japan: The Story of a Nation.* New York: Alfred A. Knopf, 1970.

_____ with J. K. Fairbank and A. M. Craig. *East Asia: The Modern Transformation.* Boston: Houghton Mifflin and Co., 1965.

Straelen, H., S.V.D. *The Japanese Woman Looking Forward.* Tokyo: Kyobunkuan, 1940.

Sugimoto, Etsu, Inagaki. *A Daughter of the Samurai.* Rutland, Vermont, and Tokyo: Charles E. Tuttle Co., 1966. Repr. of 1927 ed.

Taira, Koji. *Economic Development and the Labor Market in Japan.* New York: Columbia University Press, 1970.

Task Force of the White Paper on Sexism—Japan. *Japanese Women Speak Out.* Tokyo: "White Paper on Sexism—Japan" Task Force, c/o PARC, P. O. Box 5250, Tokyo International, Japan, June, 1975.

Tokyo Higher Normal School for Women. *Life of the Japanese Woman Today.* Tokyo: Kenkyusha, 1937.

Vogel, Ezra F. *Japan's New Middle Class: The Salary Man and his Family in a Tokyo Suburb.* Berkeley, San Francisco, and London: University of California Press, 1971.

Yamada, Waka. *The Social Status of Japanese Women.* Tokyo, 1935.

JAPANESE GOVERNMENT PUBLICATIONS IN ENGLISH

Japan Institute of National Affairs, *White Papers of Japan, 1970-71.*

Ministry of Education. *Women and Education in Japan.* 1972.

Ministry of Labor. *Labour, Administration in Japan.* 1973.

———————. *Women Workers in Japan.* 1975.

Office of the Prime Minister. *The Government of Japan,* 1974. Appendix 3, "The Constitution of Japan."

———————————. Bureau of Statistics. *Statistical Handbook of Japan.* 1974.

Women's and Minors' Bureau. *The Status of Women in Japan.* Japan: Ministry of Labor, 1974.

SOURCES IN JAPANESE

Aichi-ken Kinrō Kaikan, Fujin Rōdōshitsu. *Fujin Rōdō nikansuru Ishiki Chōsa* [Survey of Attitudes About Working Women]. 1973.

Aichi-ken Kinrō Kaikan, Nōryoku Kaibu. *Fujin Rōdōshitsu no Madoguchi Kara* [From the Window of the Working Women's Room]. Nagoya: Gōmei Gaisha, 1975.

Aichi-ken Rōdōbu Rōdō Keizai Chōsashitsu. *Fujin Shūgyō no Jittai* [Women and Employment]. 1974.

Hosoi, Wakizō. *Jokō Aishi* [The Pathetic History of Female Factory Workers]. Tokyo: Iwanami Bunko, 1954. Reprint, 1925.

Ichibangase, Yasuko. *Sengo Fujin Mondaishi* [The Postwar History of Women]. Tokyo: Domesu, 1971.

Itō, Yasuko. *Sengo Nihon Joseishi* [The Postwar History of Japanese Women]. Tokyo: Ōtsuki Shoten, 1974.

Kanaji, Nobuko. *Tomobataraki no Kurashi to Ishiki* [The Life and Attitudes of Working Wives]. Tokyo: Chōbunsha, 1972.

Kanda, Michiko, and Matsuhara, Jirō. *Gendai no Esupuri* [The Contemporary Spirit]. No. 56. Tokyo: March, 1973.

Kubota, Hideki. *Tango Onna* [The Women of Tango]. Tokyo: Sōjusha, 1973.

Mitsui, Reiko, ed. *Gendai Fujin Undō Shinenpyō* [A Chronology of the Women's Movement]. Tokyo: Sanichi Shobō, 1963.

Morosawa, Yoko. *Onna no Sengoshi* [The Postwar History of Women]. Tokyo: Miraisha, 1974.

Morosawa, Yoko. *Shina no Onna* [The Women of Shina] Vol. II. Tokyo: Miraisha, 1974.

Murakami, Nobuhiko. *Meiji Joseishi* [History of Women in the Meiji Period]. Tokyo: Rironsha, 1974.

Nagoya Joseishi Kenkyūkai, ed. *Haha no Jidai: Aichi no Joseishi* [Mother's Era: A History of Women in Aichi Prefecture]. Nagoya: Fūbōsha, 1969.

Nagoya Kyōiku Iinkai. *Hataraku Fujin no Ishiki* [The Attitudes of Working Women]. Nagoya: March, 1972.

Nagoyashi Shiminkyoku. *Hatarakitsuzukeru Fujintachi* [Women Who Continue Working]. Nagoya: Shōwa Purinto, 1973.

Nakahara, Seiichi. *Josei to Kempō Mondai* [Women and the Constitution]. Tokyo: Hyōronsha, 1969.

Nishi, Kiyoko. *Onna ga Hataraku Toiukoto* [On Women Working]. Tokyo: Seikatsu Kagaku Chōsa Kai, 1974.

Ōba, Arako. *Kawariyuku Fujin Rōdō* [Changing Women Workers]. Tokyo: Tōyō Keizai Shinpōsha, 1973.

_____, and Ujiwara, Shōjirō, eds. *Fujin Rōdō* [Women Workers]. Tokyo: Aki Shobō, 1974.

Ōkōchi, Kazuo. *Reimeiki no Nihon Rōdō Undō* [The Dawn of the Labor Movement in Japan]. Tokyo: Iwanami Shoten, 1952.

Ōtani, Kōichi. *Onna no Kindaishi* [Modern History of Japanese Women]. Tokyo: Kodansha, 1972.

Saitō, Ichi, ed. *Fujin Rōdō* [Women's Labor]. Rōdō Kagaku Kenkyūjo, 1954.

Sakayori, Toshio, and Takagi, Yoshio, eds. *Gendai Nihon no Rōdōsha* [The Contemporary Japanese Worker]. Tokyo: Nihon Hyōronsha, 1975.

Shibata, Etsuko, ed. *Fujin no Hataraku Kenri to Minshu Shugi* [Women's Right to Work and Democracy]. Tokyo: Chōbunsha, 1974.

Shimazu, Chitosei, ed. *Gōrika to Fujin Rōdōsha* [Rationalization and Women Employees]. Tokyo: Rōdōjunpōsha, 1970.

Shiosawa, Miyoko. *Kekkon Taishokugo Watakushitachi* [After Retiring for Marriage]. Tokyo: Iwanami Shinsho, 1971.

Takamura, Itsue. *Josei no Rekishi* [The History of Women] Vol. II. Tokyo: Genrōsha, 1974.

Tama no Onna no Tsuzurukai. *Tama no Onna* [The Women of Tama]. Tokyo: Sansaidō, 1973.

Tatewaki, Sadayo. *Nihon no Fujin* [The Japanese Woman]. Tokyo: Iwanami Shinsho, 1961.

Tōkyoto Rōdōkyoku. *Paato Taimaa—Shokushūbetsu Chingin oyobi Shokugyō Shōkai Jōkyō* [The Part-time Worker: Wages and Routes to Employment by Occupation]. Tokyo: 1973.

Uchiyama, Tadanobu. *Hataraku Fujin Rōdōho* [The Labor Laws of Working Women]. Tokyo: Sanshin Tosho, 1972.

Wada, Eiko. *Tomioka Nikki, Tomioka Goki* [The Tomioka Diary and Postscript]. Tokyo: Kokinshoin, 1931.

Wakamori, Tarō, and Yamamoto, Fujie. *Nihon no Joseishi* [The History of Japanese Women]. Tokyo: Shūeisha, 1975.

Yamamoto, Makiko. *Hataraku Fujin no Keizaiteki Shakaiteki Kenri no Byōdō o Mezashite* [Social and Economic Rights for Working Women]. Tokyo: Heiwa Press, 1972.

Yamamoto, Shigemi. *A, A, Nomugi Tōge* [Nomugi Mountain Pass] . Tokyo: Asahi Shinbunsha, 1969.

Yamashiro, Tomoe. *Niguruma no Uta* [Song of the Handcart] . Tokyo: Kadokawa Shoten Bunko, 1955.

Yokoyama, Gennosuke. *Nihon no Kasō Shakai* [Japan's Lower Social Stratum] . Tokyo: Iwanami Bunko, 1949.

Yokozaki, Shinhachirō. *Nihon Joshi Rōmu Kanrishi* [History of Personnel Management of Japanese Women] . Tokyo: Keibundō, 1968.

Yoneda, Sayoko. *Kindai Nihon Joseishi* [History of the Modern Japanese Woman] Vol. II. Tokyo: Shinnihon Shinsho, 1972.

JAPANESE GOVERNMENT PUBLICATIONS

Fujin ni kansuru Shomondai Chōsa Kaigi. [Conference for Investigating Various Problems Concerning Women] *Gendai Nihon Josei no Ishiki to Kōdō* [Contemporary Japanese Women's Attitudes and Behavior] . Tokyo: Ōkurashō [Ministry of Finance] , 1974.

Ministry of Agriculture. *Nōson Chōsa Kekka Hōkokusho* [The Results of an Agricultural Investigation] . 1973.

Ministry of Labor. *Chingin Kōzō Kihontōkei Chōsa Hōkoku* [Survey of Wage Structure] . 1973.

_____. *Chingin Rōdō Jikan Seido Sōdō Chōsa* [General Survey on Wages and Working Hours] . 1974.

_____. *Rōdō Hakusho* [White Paper on Labor] . Annual.

_____. *Rōdō Tōkei Chōsa Geppō* [Monthly Labor Statistics and Research Bulletin] . Vol. 27, No. 3: March 1975.

_____. Women's and Minors' Bureau. *Fujin nikansuru Shinenpyō* [A Chronological Table of the History of Women, 1868-1968] . Publication No. 64.

_____. *Fujin no Chii nikansuru Jittai Chōsa* [Survey on the Status of Women] . Publication No. 61, 1973.

_____. *Fujin Rōdō no Jitsujō* [The Condition of Women Workers] . Annual.

_____. *Joshi Hogo no Gaikyō* [Introduction to Protective Measures for Female Employees] . Publication No. 71, 1975.

_____. *Oyamoto o Hanarete Hataraku Seinen no Seikatsu to Ishiki nikansuru Chōsa Kekka* [Survey of the Life and Attitudes of Working Youths Who Live Away From Home] . Publication No. 62, August, 1973.

_____. *Seizōgyō Seisan Kōtei niokeru Joshi no Shūgyō Jōkyō nikansuru Chōsa* [The Condition of Women Employed in Manufacturing] . Publication No. 76, March, 1975.

_____. *Sen'i Kōgyō niokeru Fujin Rōdō Jittai Chōsa* [Survey of Women Workers in the Textile Industry] . Publication No. 73, 1975.

Office of the Prime Minister, Bureau of Statistics. *Shōwa 45 nen Kokusei Chōsa* [The 1970 National Census] .

_____. *Shūgyō Kōzō Kihon Chōsa Hōkoku—1974* [1974 Employment Status Survey—All Japan] .

CHAPTER 4

Asahi Evening News. . March 19, 1971.

Hirota, Hisako. *Hataraku Haha-oya to Hoikujō Zukuri no Undō* [Working Mothers and the Nursery School Movement]. Fujin Mondai Konwakai Kaiho Dai-nijuni-go. Tokyo: Women's Problems Discussion Club, No. 22, 1974.

Kaji, Etsuko. "The Invisible Proletariat: Working Women in Japan," *in* Task Force for the White Paper on Sexism—Japan. *Japanese Women Speak Out.* Tokyo: "White Paper on Sexism—Japan" Task Force, c/o PARC, P. O. Box 5250, Tokyo International, Japan, June, 1975, pp. 26-39.

Koyama, Takashi. *The Changing Social Position of Women in Japan.* Paris: Unesco, 1961.

Okamura, Masu. *Women's Status: Changing Japan.* Tokyo: International Society for Educational Information, Inc., 1973.

Task Force for the White Paper on Sexism—Japan. "The 'Woman Power' Fraud. C. Itoh and Co.: A Case in Point," *in* Task Force for the White Paper on Sexism—Japan. *Japanese Women Speak Out.* Tokyo: "White Paper on Sexism—Japan" Task Force, c/o PARC, P. O. Box 5250, Tokyo International, Japan, June, 1975, pp. 11-13.

Women's and Minors' Bureau. *The Status of Women in Japan.* Japan: Ministry of Labor, 1974.

——————————————. *Women Workers in Japan.* Japan: Ministry of Labor, 1975.

CHAPTER 5

Beardsley, Richard K., John W. Hall and Robert E. Ward. *Village Japan.* Chicago: The University of Chicago Press, 1959.

Befu, Harumi. *Japan: An Anthropological Introduction.* San Francisco: Chandler Publishing Company, 1971.

Dempster, Prue. *Japan Advances: A Geographical Study.* London: Methuen and Co., Ltd., 1967.

Keene, Donald. *Four Major Plays of Chikamatsu.* New York: Columbia University Press, 1961.

Ministry of Foreign Affairs. *Status of Women in Modern Japan—Report on Nationwide Survey.* Japan: 1975.

Nakane, Chie. *Japanese Society.* Berkeley: University of California Press, 1970.

Office of the Prime Minister. *Statistical Handbook of Japan.* Japan: Bureau of Statistics, 1972.

Okamura, Masu. *Women's Status: Changing Japan.* Tokyo: International Society for Educational Information, Inc., 1973.

Orchard, John E., with the collaboration of Dorothy Johnson Orchard. *Japan's Economic Position.* New York: McGraw-Hill Book Co., Inc., 1930. (Gives an interesting insight into the status of women workers before World War II.)

Saikaku, Ihara. *Five Women Who Loved Love.* Rutland, Vermont: Charles E. Tuttle Co., 1956.

Tanizaki, Junichiro. *The Makioka Sisters.* New York: The Universal Library, 1966.

Vogel, Ezra F. *Japan's New Middle Class.* Berkeley: University of California Press, 1971.

Women's and Minors' Bureau. *The Status of Women in Japan.* Japan: Ministry of Labor, 1974.

Yoshino, M. Y. *Japan's Managerial System, Tradition and Innovation.* Cambridge: The MIT Press, 1968.

CHAPTER 6

Fujin ni kansuru Shomondai Chōsa Kaigi [Conference for Investigating various Problems Concerning Women], ed. *Gendai Nihon Josei to Kōdō* [Contemporary Women's Attitudes and Behavior]. Tokyo: Ōkurashō [Ministry of Finance], 1974.

Ministry of Foreign Affiars. *Status of Women in Modern Japan, Report on Nationwide Survey.* Tokyo: 1975.

Okamura, Masu. *Women's Status: Changing Japan.* International Society for Educational Information, Tokyo, 1973.

Shiozawa Miyoko and Shimada Tomiko. *Hitori Kurashi no Sengōshi—senchū sedai no fujintachi* [Postwar history of living alone—women of the wartime generation], Tokyo: Iwanami Shinsho, 1975.

Social Education Bureau, Ministry of Education. *Women and Education in Japan,* Tokyo, 1973.

Women's and Minors' Bureau. *The Status of Women in Japan.* Japan: Ministry of Labor, 1973.

———————————. *The Status of Women in Japan.* Japan: Ministry of Labor, 1974.

Yamamoto, Cora Jean Emiko. "The Dual Work Families: The *Tomobataraki* Mother in Japan: An Emerging Pattern," B.A. honors thesis, Harvard University, 1975.

CHAPTER 7

De Becker, J. E. *The Nightless City.* Rutland, Vermont, and Tokyo: Charles E. Tuttle Co., 1971.

Fujimoto, T. *The Story of the Geisha Girl.* London: T. Warner Laurie, Ltd., n.d.

Fujin ni kansuru Shomondai Chōsa Kaigi [Conference for Investigating various Problems Concerning Women], ed. *Gendai Nihon Josei to Kōdō* [Contemporary Women's Attitudes and Behavior]. Tokyo: Ōkurashō [Ministry of Finance], 1974.

Gonda, Yasunosuke. *Goraku Gyōsha no Mure* [A Group of the Entertainment Trade] (Minshū Gorakuron). Tokyo: Bunwashobō, 1974.

Kanzaki, Kiyoshi. *Baishun* [Prostitution]. Tokyo: Gendaishi Shuppankai, 1974.

Kishii, Yoshie. *Onna Geisha no Jidai* [The Age of Women Geisha]. Tokyo: Seikei Sensho, 1974.

Masuda, Saiyo. *Geisha Kutō no Hanseigai* [A Geisha's Half-Life of Struggles].
Tokyo: Heibonsha, 1973.

Nakane, Chie. *Japanese Society.* Berkeley and Los Angeles: University of
California Press, 1970.

Nishi, Kiyoko. *Shokugyō Fujin no Gojūnen* [Fifty Years' History of Working
Women]. Tokyo: Nihon Hyōron Shinsha, 1955.

Ōba, Ayako and Ujihara, Shōjirō. *Fujin Rōdō* [Female Labor]. Tokyo: Aki
Shobō, 1974.

CHAPTER 8

SOURCES IN ENGLISH

Directorate for Scientific Affairs, Organization for Economic Co-operation and
Development. *Educational Policy and Planning: Japan.* Paris: OECD,
1973.

Duke, Benjamin C. *Japan's Militant Teachers: A History of the Left-wing
Teacher's Movement.* Honolulu: University of Hawaii Press, 1973.

Education in Japan: Journal for Overseas. Hiroshima: The International Edu-
cational Research Institute, Hiroshima University, Vols. I -VI. 1966-1971.
Vol. I. 1966. Development of Educational Thought in Japan.
Vol. II. 1967. Educational System in Japan.
Vol. III. 1968. Curriculum Development in Elementary Education.
Vol. IV. 1969. Curriculum Development in Secondary Education.
Vol. V. 1970. Social Education.
Vol. VI. 1971. Education for Women.

Japan Teacher's Union. *Japan Teacher's Union: Its Organization and Movement.* Tokyo: Japan Teacher's Union, 1966.

Kaigo, Tokiomi. *Japanese Education: Its Past and Present.* Tokyo: Kokusai
Bunka Shinkōkai [Japan Cultural Society], 1968.

Katayama, Tetsu. (Foreign Affairs Association of Japan). *Women's Movement
in Japan.* Tokyo: Kenkyūsha, 1938.

Kikuchi, Baron Dairoku. *Japanese Education.* London: John Murray, 1909.

Iijima, Aiko, *et al.,* ed. *Japanese Women Speak Out.* Tokyo: Task Force,
White Paper on Sexism—Japan, c/o PARC, P.O. Box 5250, Tokyo International, 1975.

Matsuoka, Yōko. *Daughter of the Pacific.* New York: Harper, 1953.

Mishima, Sumie Seo. *My Narrow Isle.* New York: John Day, 1941.

Nagai, Michio. *Higher Education in Japan.* Tokyo: University of Tokyo
Press, 1971.

Organization for Economic Co-operation and Development. *Reviews of National Policies for Education:* Japan. Paris: OECD, 1971.

Passin, Herbert. *Society and Education in Japan.* New York: Teacher's College Press, Columbia University, 1965.

Singleton, John. *Nitchū: A Japanese School.* New York: Holt, Rinehart,
and Winston, 1967.

Thurston, Donald R. *Teachers and Politics in Japan.* Princeton: Princeton
University Press, 1973.

Tokyo Higher Normal School for Women. *Life of the Japanese Woman Today.* Tokyo: Kenkyūsha, 1937.

JAPANESE GOVERNMENT PUBLICATIONS IN ENGLISH

Blewett, John E., ed. and trans. *Higher Education in Postwar Japan—The Ministry of Education's 1964 White Paper.* Tokyo: Sophia University Press, 1965.
Ministry of Education. *Basic Guidelines for the Reform of Education: Report of the Central Council for Education.* 1972.
——————. *Women and Education in Japan.* 1972.
——————. *Educational Standards in Japan.* 1970

SOURCES IN JAPANESE

Arıchi, Tōru. *Fujin no Chiito Gendai Shakai* [The Status of Women and Modern Society]. Tokyo: Hōritsu Bunka Sha, 1971.
Asahi Shimbun Gakugeibu [Literary Section, Asahi Newspaper], ed. *Otoko to Onna* [Men and Women]. Tokyo: Asahi Shimbun Sha, 1974.
Egawa, Hisako. "Joshi Daigakusei no Jittai Chōsa (I): Seikaku ni tsuite" [Survey of Actual Conditions of Students at Women's Universities (I): On Personal Character]. *Jissenjoshi Daigaku Kasei Gakubu Kiyo,* No. 7. (Dec., 1969), 141-148.
Enzawa, Miyoko and Shimada, Tomiko. *Hitorigurashi no Sengo Shi—Senchū Sedai no Fujin Tachi* [Living Alone in Postwar Japan: Young Women After the War]. Tokyo: Iwanami Shinsho, 1975.
Fukaya, Shoji. *Ryōsai Kembo Shugi no Kyōiku* [Education for the Making of "Good Wives and Wise Mothers"]. Nagoya: Reimei Shobō, 1966.
Fujii, Harue; Uchida, Sono; Satō, Reiko; Tamaro, Reiko;; and Hatsukawa, Misao. *Nihon no Joshi Kōtō Kyōiku* [Higher Education and Women in Japan]. Tokyo: Domesu Shuppan, 1973.
"Fujin Kyōshi no Rōdō Jōken" [Working Conditions of Women Teachers], a special feature including three articles, in *Kyōiku Hō* [Educational Law Review], No. 9 (Autumn, 1973), 114-134.
Fujin ni Kansuru Sho Mondai Chōsa Kaigi [Committee to Survey Issues Relating to Women]. *Gendai Nihon Josei no Ishiki to Kōdō* [The Consciousness and Behavior of Women in Contemporary Japan]. Tokyo: Ōkura Shō Insatsu Kyoku, 1974.
Fukaya, Masashi and Fukaya, Kazuko. *Jokyōshi no Mondai no Kankyū* [Research on Issues Regarding Women Teachers]. Tokyo: Reimei Shobō, 1971.
Fukuda, Toru. "Joshi Kōtō Kyōiku—Sono Tenkai Katei to Genjō no Kisoteki Rikai no tame ni" [Women's "Higher Education"—Toward a Basic Understanding of the Process of its Development and the Present State]. *Gekkan Shakaitō,* No. 150 (Sept., 1969), 52-62.
Gendai Fujin Mondai Kōza [Readings on Modern Women], Vol. V: Hane, Setsuko and Ogawa, Toshio, ed. *Fujin Gakushū Kyōiku* [Education and Learning for Women]. Tokyo: Aki Shobō, 1970.

"Gendai Jokyōshi o Kataru" [A Round-table Discussion by Women Teachers].
Kyōiku Aichi, Vol. 20, No. 10 (Jan., 1973), 19-29.

Hidaka, Yoshio. "Kyōshi no Sedaisa, Seisa o dō Kangae, Kaiketsu suru ka"
[How to Correct Age and Sex Differentials in Education among Teachers].
Chiba Kyōiku, No. 195 (Jan., 1973), 24-29.

Honma, Hisao. *Gendai no Fujin Mondai* [Contemporary Issues Concerning Wom-
en]. Tokyo: Tenyū Sha, 1919.

Ichibangase, Yasuko, ed. *Sengo Fujin Mondai Shi* [Issues Concerning Women
in the Postwar Period]. Tokyo: Domesu Shuppan, 1971.

——————, Kigawa, Tatsuji, and Miyata, Takeo, eds. *Jokyōshi no
Fujin Mondai* [Issues Concerning Women as Teachers]. Tokyo: Daiichi
Hōki Shuppan Sha, 1974.

Ikeda, Satoshi. *Joshi Daigaku* [Women's Universities]. Tokyo: Nihon Keizai
Shimbun Sha, 1966.

Imanaka, Yasuko. "Taishōki Burujoa Fujin Undō to Fujin Kyōshi–Shin Fujin
Kyōkai Hiroshima Shibu no Setchi o Megutte" [Bourgeois Women's Move-
ments and Women Teachers During the Taishō Period: Regarding the
Establishment of the Hiroshima Branch of the Shin Fujin Kyōkai (New
Women's Association)]. *Rekishi Hyōron*, No. 217 (Sept., 1968).

Inoue, Kiyoshi. *Gendai Nihon Josei Shi* [A History of Women in Contemporary
Japan]. Tokyo: San'ichi Shobō, 1971.

Ishidoya, Tetsuo. *Nihon Kyōin Shi Kenkyū* [Research on the History of
Teachers in Japan]. Tokyo: Kodansha, 1967.

Jiji Tsūshin Sha [Current Affairs Institute], "Jokyōshi Jidai o Irokoku Han'ei"
[Clear Trend Shown Toward the Age of the Women Teacher]. *Naigai
Kyōiku,* No. 2467 (Sept. 19, 1973), 2-10.

Karasawa, Tomitarō. *Kyōshi no Rekishi* [History of Teachers]. Tokyo: Sōbun
Sha, 1956.

Kawai, Akira and Arai, Yoshiko. "Nihon no Fujin Kyōshi" [Women Teachers
in Japan]. *Kokumin Kyōiku*, Winter Issue (Nov., 1971), 15-35.

Kido, Wakao. *Fujin Kyōshi no Haykunen* [One Hundred Years of Women in
Teaching]. Tokyo: Meiji Tosho, 1968.

Kuroda, Nubujuki and Tanaka, Michiko, *et al. Joshi Gakusei: Onna ni Totte
Daigaku wa Nani ka* [Women Students: What do the universities mean
to women?]. Tokyo: San'ichi Shobō, 1971.

Matsuda, Michio. *Haha Oya no Tame no Jinsei Ron* [Meaningful Lives for
Mothers]. Tokyo: Iwanami Shinsho, 1974.

Miyashiro, Eishō, *et al.,* ed. *Nihon Josei Shi* [A History of Japanese Women].
Tokyo: Yoshikawa Kōbunkan, 1970.

Mochizuki, Muneaki. *Nihon no Fujin Kyōshi* [Women Teachers in Japan].
Tokyo: Rōdō Junpō Sha, 1975.

Murai, Minoru and Maruoka, Hideko. *Otto mo Kyōshi Tsuma mo Kyōshi* [Hus-
band a Teacher, Wife a Teacher]. Tokyo: Meiji Tosho, 1962.

——————, Muro, Shunji and Higuchi, Keiko, eds. *Ningen no Tame no
Kyōiku (4): Josei* [Education for Humankind (4): Women]. Tokyo:
Nihon Hōsō Shuppan Kyōkai, 1973.

Murakami, Nobuhiko. *Meiji Josei Shi* [History of Women in the Meiji Period].
Vol. III. Tokyo: Riron Sha, 1974.

Muro, Shunji. *Ryōsai Kembō Hihan* [A Criticism of the "Good-Wife-and-Wise-Mother" Philosophy]. Tokyo: Mainichi Newspaper Pub. Co., 1969.

Nikkyōso [Japan Teacher's Union]. *Kumiaiin Ishiki: Chōsa no Matome* [Attitudes of Members in the Japan Teacher's Union: Survey Results]. Tokyo Nikkyōso, August, 1969.

_____. *Nikkyōso Nijūnen-shi* [Twenty-year History of the Japan Teacher's Union]. Tokyo: Nikkyōso, 1968.

Obi, Torao and Endo, Goro. *Jokyōshi no Sugao* [A True Picture of Women Teachers]. Tokyo: Kyoiku Shuppan Sha, 1975.

"Onna to Kyoiku" [Women and Education], special issue of *Agora* (Quarterly journal on contemporary issues concerning women), No. 11 (June, 1975).

Sakamoto, Fukuko. *Fujin no Kenri* [The Rights of Women]. Tokyo: Hōritsu Bunka Sha, 1973.

Shibukawa, Hisako. *Kindai Nihon Josei Shi (I)—Kyōiku* [History of Women in Contemporary Japan (I): Education]. Tokyo: Kajima Kenkyū Shuppan Kai, 1970.

Shinohara, Shinobu and Yanai, Michiko, "Joshi Gakusei no Seikatsu Ishiki to Shakai Taido no Kansuru Kenkyū" [Study on Women Student's Life-consciousness and Attitudes toward Society]. *Kōsei Hodō*, No. 20 (Jan., 1968), 54-64.

Sugita, Ayako. *Jokyōshi Bōkoku Ron* [Women Teachers and the Decline of the Nation]. Tokyo: Nisshin Hōdō, 1972.

Suzuki, Bunjirō. *Fujin Mondai no Hanashi* [Issues Concerning Women]. Tokyo: Asahi Shimbun Sha, 1931.

Takamure, Itsue. *Jokyōin Kaihō Ron* [The Liberation of Women Teachers]. Tokyo: Jiyū Sha, 1931.

_____. *Takamure Itsue Zenshū—Josei no Rekishi* [The Collected Works of Takamure Itsue: The History of Women]. Vol. II. Tokyo: Riron Sha, 1966.

Tatewaki, Sadayo. *Josei no Ikikata* [A Way for Women to Live]. Tokyo: Shin Nihon Shuppan Sha, 1973.

_____. *Nihon no Fujin* [Japanese Women] Tokyo: Iwanami Shinsho, 1961.

Uchiyama, Tadanobu. *Hataraku Fujin Rōdōhō* [Labor Laws Concerning Working Women]. Tokyo: Sanshin Tosho, 1972.

Wakamori, Tarō and Yamamoto, Fujie. *Nihon no Josei Shi* [History of Women in Japan]. Vol. IV. Tokyo: Shūei Sha, 1971

Yamaguchi, Makoto and Shibuyama, Mikiko. *Fujin Mondai Hōrei Handobukku* [Handbook on Laws Applying to Women]. Tokyo: Gyōsei, 1975.

Yamamoto, Hiroshi. *Joshi Kōkō Sei* [High School Women]. Tokyo: San'ichi Shobō, 1973.

Yoneda, Sayoko. *Kindai Nihon no Josei Shi—Jō* [History of Women in Contemporary Japan]. Vol. I. Tokyo: Shin Nihon Shuppan Sha, 1972.

JAPANESE GOVERNMENT PUBLICATIONS

Mombu Shō [Ministry of Education]. *Gakkō Kihon Chōsa Hōkoku Sho—1973* [Basic School Survey: 1973]. Tokyo: Ōkura Shō, Insatsu Kyoku, 1975.

Rōdō Shō [Ministry of Labor]. *Fujin no Chii ni Kansuru Jittai Chōsa* [An Investigation of the Status of Women]. Publication No. 61. Tokyo: Ōkura Shō, Insatsu Kyoku, 1973.

——————————————, Fujin Shonen Kyoku Hen [Women's and Minors' Bureau], ed. *Fujin Kankei Nempyō—1868-1968* [A Chronological Table of the History of Women, 1868-1968]. Tokyo: Ōkura Shō Insatsu Kyoku, 1968.

——————————————, Fujin Shonen Kyoku Hen [Women's and Minors' Bureau], ed. *Fujin Rōdō no Jitsujō* [The Actual Conditions of Women in the Labor Force]. Annual. Tokyo: Ōkura Shō Insatsu Kyoku, 1975.

Sōrifu Tōkei Kyoku [Office of the Prime Minister, Bureau of Statistics]. *Showa 45-nen Kokusai Chōsa* [National Census, 1970].

CHAPTER 9

Azuma, Hidemi. "A Child's Death—The Beginning of Struggle for Daycare." *in* Task Force of the White Paper on Sexism—Japan. *Japanese Women Speak Out.* Tokyo: Task Force, White Paper on Sexism—Japan, c/o PARC, P.O. Box 5250, Tokyo International, Japan, June, 1975, pp. 17-25.

Japanese Association of University Women. *Japanese University Women: Issues and Views, Volumes One and Two.* Tokyo: Kenkyusha Printing Company, 1974.

Kaji, Etsuko. "The Invisible Proletariat: Working Women in Japan." *in* Task Force of the White Paper on Sexism—Japan. *Japanese Women Speak Out.* Tokyo: Task Force, White Paper on Sexism—Japan, c/o PARC, P.O. Box 5250, Tokyo International, Japan, June, 1975, pp. 26-39.

Ministry of Foreign Affairs. *Status of Women in Modern Japan: Report on Nationwide Survey.* Japan: 1975.

Social Education Bureau. *Women and Education in Japan.* Japan: Ministry of Education, 1974.

Task Force of the White Paper on Sexism—Japan. *Japanese Women Speak Out.* Tokyo: "White Paper on Sexism—Japan" Task Force, c/o PARC, P.O. Box 5250, Tokyo International, Japan, June, 1975.

CHAPTER 10

Azuma, Hidemi. "A Child's Death—The Beginning of the Struggle for Daycare." *in* Task Force of the White Paper on Sexism—Japan. *Japanese Women Speak Out.* Tokyo: Task Force, White Paper on Sexism—Japan, c/o PARC, P.O. Box 5250, Tokyo International, Japan, 1975, pp. 17-25.

Hane, Mikiso. *Japan: A Historical Survey.* New York: Charles Scribner's Sons, 1972.

Kawabe, Kisaburo. *The Press and Politics in Japan.* Dissertation. Chicago: University of Chicago Press, 1921.

Langdon, Frank. *Politics in Japan.* Boston: Little, Brown and Co., 1967.

Murasaki, Lady. *The Tale of Genji.* Trans. Arthur Waley. The Modern Library Edition. New York: Random House, 1960.

Nihon Shimbun Kyōkai [The Japan Publishers and Editors Association]. *The Japanese Press.* Tokyo: 1954, 1957, 1964.

Unesco. *Statistical Yearbook.* Paris: Unesco, 1973.

Women's and Minors' Bureau. *The Status of Women in Japan.* Japan: Ministry of Labor, 1974.

CHAPTER 11

Haas, Margi. "The First Birth Control Movement in Japan." Unpublished paper. Cambridge: Harvard University, 1975.

Koyama, Takashi, Hachiro Nakamura, Masako Huramatsu, "Japan," in Patai, Raphael, *Women in the Modern World.* New York: Free Press, 1967.

Nyun-Han, Emma. "The Socio-Political Roles of Women in Japan and Burma." Ph.D. dissertation, University of Colorado, Boulder, 1972.

Pharr, Susan J. "Women in Japan," *Current History.* LXVIII, No. 404, April, 1975.

Vavich, Dee Ann. "The Japanese Woman's Movement: Ichikawa Fusae—A Pioneer in Woman's Suffrage." *Monumenta Nipponica,* XXII, Nos. 3-4, 1967.

Women's and Minors' Bureau. *About the Women's and Minors' Bureau.* Ministry of Labor, Japan, 1973.

_____. *The Status of Women in Japan.* Japan: Ministry of Labor, 1974.

_____. *Women Workers in Japan.* Japan: Ministry of Labor, 1975.

CHAPTER 12

Mishima, Sumie Seo. *My Narrow Isle: The Story of a Modern Woman in Japan.* New York: John Day Company, 1941.

CHAPTER 13

BOOKS

Anesaki, Masaharu. *History of Japanese Religion.* Tokyo: Charles E. Tuttle Co., 1971.

Armstrong, Robert. *Light from the East.* Canada: University of Toronto, 1914.

Aston, W. G. *Nihongi: Chronicles of Japan.* Tokyo: Charles E. Tuttle Co., 1972.

Barber, Bernard and Inkeles, Alex (eds.). *Stability and Social Change.* Boston: Little, Brown and Company, 1971.

Bernard, Jessie. *Women and the Public Interest.* Chicago: Aldine-Atherton, Inc., 1971.

320

Bruns, J. Edgar. *God as Woman, Woman as God.* New York: Paulist Press, 1973.

Cavan, Ruth. *Suicide.* Chicago: University of Chicago Press, 1928.

Chikazawa, Keiichi. *Jisatsu no Kenkyō* [Study of Suicide]. Tokyo: Kuriato Publishing Company, 1972.

Coale, Ansley J. *et al. Aspects of the Analysis of Family Structure.* New Jersey, Princeton University Press, 1965.

de Beauvoir, Simone. *The Second Sex.* New York: Alfred A. Knopf, Inc., 1952.

De Vos, George A. *Socialization for Achievement.* Berkeley: University of California, 1973.

Doi, Takeo. *The Anatomy of Dependence.* Tokyo: Kodansha International Ltd., 1973.

Dore, R. P. (ed.). *Aspects of Social Change in Modern Japan.* New Jersey: Princeton University Press, 1971.

Douglas, Jack. *The Social Meanings of Suicide.* New Jersey: Princeton University Press, 1967.

Durkheim, Emile. *Suicide.* London: Routledge and Kegan Paul, Ltd., 1952.

Eisenstadt, Shmuel Noah. *Modernization: Protest and Change.* New Jersey: Prentice-Hall, Inc., 1966.

Fukutake, Tadashi. *Japanese Society Today.* Tokyo: University of Tokyo Press, 1974.

Geiger, H. Kent (ed.). *Comparative Perspectives on Marriage and the Family.* Boston: Little, Brown and Company, 1968.

General Headquarters. *Developments in Japanese Education: 1945-1952.* Tokyo: General Headquarters Allied Command, 1953.

Goode, William J. (ed.). *Readings on the Family and Society.* New Jersey: Prentice-Hall, Inc., 1964.

——————. *The Family.* New Jersey: Prentice-Hall, Inc., 1964.

——————. *World Revolution and Family Patterns.* New York: The Free Press, 1970.

Gordon, Michael (ed.). *The Nuclear in Crisis: The Search for an Alternative.* New York: Harper & Row, Publishers, 1972.

Higuchi, Chiyoko. *Her Place in the Sun: Women Who Shaped Japan.* Tokyo: The East Publications, Inc., 1973.

Hori, Ichiro. *Folk Religion in Japan.* Chicago: University of Chicago Press, 1968.

Huber, Joan (ed.). *Changing Women in a Changing Society.* Chicago: The University of Chicago Press, 1973.

Itoo, Yasuko. *Sengo Nihon Joseishi* [Postwar History of Japanese Women]. Tokyo: Ootsuki Shoten, 1974.

Kajiya, Tetsuo. *Nihonjin no Jisatsu* [Japanese Suicide] Tokyo: Tetsudoo Byoin, 1973.

Koya, Azumi. *Higher Education and Business Recruitment in Japan.* New York: Columbia University Teachers College Press, 1969.

Levy Jr., Marion J. *Modernization and the Structure of Societies.* Vols. 1 & 2. New Jersey: Princeton University Press, 1966.

McClelland, David C. *The Achieving Society.* New York: The Free Press, 1961.

Ministry of Education. *Japan's Growth and Education.* Tokyo: 1963.

——————— *Education in 1962.* 1964.

Moore, Wilbert E. *Social Change.* New Jersey: Prentice-Hall, Inc., 1973.

Morosawa, Yooko. *Onna no Rekishi* [The History of Women]. Tokyo: Miraisha Publishing House, 1972.

_____. *Onna no Sengo Shi* [Postwar History of Women]. Tokyo: Miraisha Publishing House, 1971.

Nakamura, Hajime. *Ways of Thinking of Eastern Peoples.* Hawaii: East-West Center, 1964.

Nakane, Chie. *Japanese Society.* Berkeley and Los Angeles: University of California Press, 1972.

Nitobe, Inazo. *Bushido: The Soul of Japan.* Tokyo: Charles E. Tuttle Company, 1969.

Okamura, Masu. *Women's Status: Changing Japan.* Tokyo: The International Society for Educational Information, Inc., 1973.

Parsons, Talcott. *Essays in Sociological Theory.* New York: The Free Press, 1964.

Parsons, Talcott and Bales, Robert F. *Family, Socialization and Interaction Process.* New York: The Free Press, 1966.

Rowbotham, Sheila. *Women's Consciousness, Man's World.* Middlesex: Penguin Books Ltd., 1973.

Sakamoto, Yosiyuki. *A Study of the Japanese National Character.* (Fifth Nationwide Survey). Tokyo: Research Committee on the Study of the Japanese National Character, 1974.

Seishin Joshi Daigaku Ron. *Gendai Nihon Joshi Gakusei* [Modern Japanese Women Students]. Tokyo: Risosha, 1966.

Stengel, Erwin. *Suicide and Attempted Suicide.* Baltimore: Penguin Books, Inc., 1967.

Study Council on Problems Concerning Women. *Gendai Nihon Josei no Isshiki to Kōdo* [Modern Japanese Women's Consciousness and Behavior]. Tokyo: Minister's Secretariat Printer, 1974.

Suzuki, Daisetz. *Zen and Japanese Culture.* New Jersey: Princeton University Press, 1970.

Tamura, Kenji *et al. Tokyo to 23ku ni okeru jisatsusha no jittai* [A study of suicides in the 23 wards of Tokyo]. Toyo Daigaku Shakaigakubu, 1971.

Tsurumi, Kazuko. *Social Change and the Individual.* New Jersey: Princeton University Press, 1970.

Waldenstrom, Jan *et al. Suicide and Attempted Suicide.* Stockholm: Nordiska Bokhandelns Forlag, 1971.

Wallace, Samuel. *After Suicide.* New York: John Wiley & Sons, 1973.

ARTICLES

Bolander, Anne-Marie. "Nordic Suicide Statistics." Waldenstrom *et al. Suicide and Attempted Suicide.* Stockholm, Nordiska Bokhandelns Forlag, 1972.

Carter, Aiko. "On Being a Woman in Japan." *Japan Christian Activity News.* No. 449, March 8, 1974.

Cecchini, Rose Marie. "Dialogue with a Buddhist Nun on Life after Death." *The Japan Missionary Bulletin.* February 1970.

_____. "Modern Society and Japanese Women." *The Japan Missionary Bulletin.* May 1975.

De Vos, George. "Role Narcissism and the Etiology of Japanese Suicide." De Vos, George. *Socialization for Achievement.* Berkeley: University of California, 1973.

Doi, Takeo. "Giri-Ninjō: An Interpretation." Dore, R. P. (ed.), *Aspects of Social Change in Modern Japan.* New Jersey: Princeton University Press, 1971.

Gibbs, Jack. "Suicide." Merton, R. and Nisbet, R. (eds.). *Contemporary Social Problems.* New York: Harcourt Brace Jovanovich, Inc., 1971.

Goode, William. "A Theory of Role Strain," *American Sociological Review.* August 1960.

Isomura, Eiichi. "Shinjū kō." [Thoughts on Double Suicide] Oohara (ed.). *Jisatsu.* [Suicide] Tokyo: Shibundō, 1971.

Kamata, Hisako. "Daughters of the Gods: Shaman Priestesses in Japan and Okinawa," *Folk Cultures of Japan and East Asia.* Tokyo: Sophia University Press, 1966.

Kato, Hidetoshi. "Jisatsu style no hensen." [Changes in the Styles of Suicide]. Oohara, Kenjiro (ed.). *Jisatsu.* Tokyo: Shibundō, 1971.

Kato, Masaaki. "Self-Destruction in Japan: A Cross-cultural Epidemiological Analysis of Suicide." Lebra and Lebra (eds.). *Japanese Culture and Behavior.* Honolulu: The University Press of Hawaii, 1974.

Kishimoto, Ichiro. "Some Japanese Cultural Traits and Religions." Moore, Charles A. (ed.). *The Japanese Mind.* Honolulu: The University of Hawaii Press, 1967.

Nisihira, Sigeki. "Changed and Unchanged Characteristics of the Japanese." (translated from *Jiyū,* August 1974). *Japan Echo.* Vol. 1, No. 2, 1974.

Powell, Elwin H. "Occupation, Status and Suicide: Toward a Redefinition of Anomie," *American Sociological Review.* Vol. 23, April 1958.

Sourbrier, Jean-Pierre. "Legal Aspects on Suicide and Attempted Suicide." *Suicide and Attempted Suicide.* Stockholm: Nordiska Bokhandelns Forlag, 1972.

CHAPTER 14

Lockwood, William. *The Economic Development of Japan: Growth and Structural Change.* London: Oxford University Press, 1955.

Ministry of Foreign Affairs. *Status of Women in Modern Japan: Report on a Nationwide Survey.* Japan: 1975.

Ōba, Ayako, and Ujihara, Shōjiro. *Fujin Rōdō* [Female Labor]. Tokyo: Aki Shobō, 1974.